WE'RE NOT HERE
TO ENTERTAIN

WE'RE NOT HERE
TO ENTERTAIN

PUNK ROCK, RONALD REAGAN, AND THE REAL CULTURE WAR OF 1980S AMERICA

KEVIN MATTSON

OXFORD
UNIVERSITY PRESS

OXFORD
UNIVERSITY PRESS

Oxford University Press is a department of the University of Oxford. It furthers
the University's objective of excellence in research, scholarship, and education
by publishing worldwide. Oxford is a registered trade mark of Oxford University
Press in the UK and certain other countries.

Published in the United States of America by Oxford University Press
198 Madison Avenue, New York, NY 10016, United States of America.

Library of Congress Cataloging-in-Publication Data
Names: Mattson, Kevin, 1966– author.
Title: We're not here to entertain : punk rock, Ronald Reagan, and the real
culture war of 1980s America / Kevin Mattson.
Identifiers: LCCN 2019044699 (print) | LCCN 2019044700 (ebook) |
ISBN 9780190908232 (hardback) | ISBN 9780190908256 (epub)
Subjects: LCSH: Punk rock music—United States—1981–1990—History and
criticism. | Rock music—United States—1981–1990—History and
criticism. | United States. President (1981–1989 : Reagan)
Classification: LCC ML3534.3 .M385 2020 (print) |
LCC ML3534.3 (ebook) | DDC 306.4/84260973—dc23
LC record available at https://lccn.loc.gov/2019044699
LC ebook record available at https://lccn.loc.gov/2019044700

1 3 5 7 9 8 6 4 2

Printed by LSC Communications, United States of America

For Jay, so he can understand why his father seems so unglued at times

CONTENTS

PREFACE

FROM MEMORY . . . TO HISTORY

A person's life purpose is nothing more than to rediscover, through the detours of art, or love, or passionate work, those one or two images in the presence of which his heart first opened.

—Albert Camus[1]

After the blast, Kurt Cobain's body slumped. Next to his corpse lay a piece of paper with his last words. At the time the bullet seared his head, Cobain was a rock star, his grizzled face graced the covers of slick music industry magazines, his songs received mainstream radio play, his band Nirvana performed in huge arenas. But he had been thinking an awful lot about what he called the "punk rock world" that saved his life during his teen years and that he had subsequently abandoned for stardom.

He first encountered this world in the summer of 1983, at a free show the Melvins held in a Thriftway parking lot. After hearing the guttural sounds and watching kids dance by slamming against one another, he ran home and wrote in his journal: "This was what I was looking for," underlined twice. As he dove into this world, he recognized its blistering music played in odd venues, but also a wider array of creativity, like self-made zines, poetry, fiction, movies, artwork on flyers and record jackets, and even politics. This too: how all of these things opened up spaces for ideas and arguments. Now, in his suicide note, he reflected on his "punk rock 101 courses," where he learned "ethics involved with independence and the embracement of your community."[2]

There are people who can recount where they were when Cobain's suicide became news. I was in Ithaca, New York, finishing up my dissertation . . . but my mind was immediately hurled backward to growing up in Washington, D.C.'s "metropolitan area" (euphemism for suburban sprawl). I started to remember the first time I entered this "punk rock world." Around a year or two before Cobain went to the Thriftway parking lot, I opened the doors of the Chancery, a small club in Washington, D.C., and saw a tiny little stage, maybe a foot and a half off the ground. Suddenly, a small kid about my age (fifteen), his hair bleached into a shade of white that glowed in the lights, jumped up. I remember it being brighter than expected (unlike my earlier, wee-boy experiences in darkened, cavernous arenas where bands like Kiss or Cheap Trick would play to me and thousands of stoned audience members). This kid with the blond hair might have said something, I don't remember, what I recall is that his band broke into the fastest, most vicious-sounding music I had ever heard. Suddenly bodies started flying through the air, young men (mostly) propelling themselves off the ground into the space between one another, flailing their arms, skin smacking skin. Control was lost, for when a body moved in one direction, another body collided into its path. When someone fell over, another would pick him up. The bodies got pushed onto the stage, making it hard to differentiate performer from audience member. At one moment it appeared the singer had been tackled by a clump of kids, and he seemed to smile. Sometimes, I could even make out what the fifteen-year-old was shouting, especially, "I'm going to make their society bleed!" Overwhelmed, I rushed outside to clear my head.

There I found some kid hawking a fanzine for pocket change. Xeroxed images ran alongside typewritten commentary or handwritten prose, replete with scratching-outs. My visual senses came unglued, the way my aural senses had inside. It looked nothing like *Newsweek*, the slick magazine my mom subscribed to. This zine-meister explained to me that he was an anarchist who believed in producing his own culture and means of communication. I thought to myself: I could do that, and soon I would, with friends who were trying to make sense of this world opening up.

Other kids from inside the club spilled out onto the sidewalk. Conversations ensued. Most of these raggedy-looking kids came from what were called "broken homes," a byproduct of the skyrocketing divorce rate that defined the 1970s "me decade" and that played its course out during the 1980s. I noted ambivalence about parents, matched with a hatred of high school life, especially boring teachers and stupid bullies. Sometimes they'd talk about a zine they had read or a book outside of school assignments they perused, something by Kurt Vonnegut or George Orwell or Aldous Huxley. They'd talk about how the stoners and beer guzzlers at their schools were so bombed out that they became automatons. One kid bragged about how he had spray-painted "Too Stupid for Drugs" close to where the stoners hung out at his school. All of them came off as, well, pretty smart, but also funny, not dour or overly serious. They dissed the trendy "new wave" and "new romanticist" music that entertainment corporations pushed. Instead of listening to that, they'd go into their basements to rehearse for shows at places like the Chancery, or maybe share their music on a cassette tape, or maybe even press their own record. Pretty soon, I had my own band that did this. Our first show was held in the basement of a suburban house. It felt like we were creating our own culture.[3]

* * *

"Punk rock faggot!" I remember the shout and how it made my body tense up. That scream reminds me of the way it felt—after I had jumped into the "punk rock world"—to be a threat. It first happened when I came to high school with my hair cut into a spikey mess and then, over the course of a few weeks, changing my hair color from orange to blonde, red, and black. I remember wearing the ugliest shirt I could find in a thrift store; it was light blue with different drawings of Sylvester the Cat and Tweety Bird standing in front of Roman ruins (inexplicable and surreal). My hair and shirt didn't get the sort of reception they would today: Oh, OK, here we have a kid adopting a punk "style" and exhibiting a subculture's symbols. Instead, they garnered rage and reaction. I remember one kid in my chemistry class screaming, "You can't do that!" every time I came in with a different color in my hair. Kids much bigger than me would shove me into the lockers that lined our hallways. My homeroom teacher asked me in front of other students if I were a "fag." I remember how amused I was that bullies and jocks somehow felt threatened by my presence, that I could provoke such violence normally submerged underneath the quaint façade of my suburban high school.

This too I remember: the way the sooty print would rub off on my hands as I read *MAXIMUMROCKNROLL* (*MRR*) when it started to appear in 1982. I learned from this publication that this thing I had hitched myself to had taken off—there were now punk kids who had organized "scenes" in places like Oklahoma, Kansas, Oregon, Idaho, Michigan . . . nearly everywhere. It gave me a sense of hope, and certainly a feeling that this thing was spreading. It wasn't just New York City or Los Angeles, where you'd expect it. It was more democratic than that, and I sensed back then even more pervasive than the 1960s counterculture (which I knew about mostly from working at a used bookstore where I picked up copies of works like Theodore Roszak's *The Making of a Counterculture* [1969]). I'd roll my eyes when "sixties people" (that's what we'd call them) sung the glory days of the hippie counterculture. Producing and distributing our own music on our own terms felt much more like a counterculture (emphasis here on *counter*) than kids getting stoned on the streets of Haight-Ashbury back in the day. We wanted to change things rather than "drop out," in the words of the 1960s acid guru Timothy Leary.

And this reminds me that I not only learned how to play my own music and create my own zine, but also tried to alter the messages and advertisements that were everywhere in 1980s America, especially beaming off billboards. I remember learning how to spray-paint messages onto advertisements, one time sitting on the shoulders of my band's bass player to deface an armed forces recruiting ad. I remember talking my way out of arrest by a subway (Metro) police guard who caught me writing "Cancer is Macho" on an advertisement for Marlboro cigarettes that depicted a rugged-looking cowboy lighting up. Though feeble, these small acts confirmed my sense of being a threat, albeit a minor one.

The desire to alter billboards came in part from my shock at the way the mass media treated the spread of suburban punk at the time. The television and Hollywood studios loved to pump out sensationalist fare about the "punk rock world." On shows like *Quincy* and movies like *The Class of 1984* (both released in 1982), punks appeared as raging nihilists who raped and killed everything in sight. Phil Donahue had a penchant for getting adults on his television show to scream at punk kids for being wacked on drugs. Few of these adults knew that many of the kids in funky attire rejected drugs, as much as they rejected any notion of the prattle about the glorious 1960s. All of it seemed fake.

I forget when precisely, but I had an epiphany. One day, I started to think: If all these lies on movie and television screens were propagated by my elders, as I knew they were, maybe there were other lies. . . . And there were.

Many of them came from the White House. During the early 1980s, before Reagan discovered his supposed inner dove and negotiated with the new Russian leader Mikhail Gorbachev, there seemed a dark cloud hovering above the White House. Though Reagan had campaigned against Jimmy Carter's reinstitution of Selective Service registration, he then flip-flopped and endorsed the policy, cracking down harshly on nonregistrants (my mother nervously opened letters telling me that I should be ready to go to court for my unwillingness to register). Reagan heated up the Cold War not just with the Soviet Union, but also in the hotspots like El Salvador and especially Nicaragua. Plenty of my friends (well, only the males really) talked about being ready to face conscription in order to fight a land war somewhere in Central America or Afghanistan. At any dissent against his grandiose military buildup, Reagan turned rigid and almost divine in his reason. He claimed the nuclear freeze movement—a movement that numerous friends and I drifted into—was chock full of communists taking orders from Moscow, all the while calling the MX missile a "peacekeeper" and installing first-strike weapons in Europe. He talked about Armageddon while considering a "winnable" nuclear war with civil defense programs that seemed preposterous in their assumption that we could survive such a disaster. While rolling all this out, Reagan appeared like a performance artist; he winked and nodded while selling the American people his dreams. That only upped the anxiety. For a young man in the 1980s, including myself, Reagan seemed scary, more a source of fear, his bully pulpit channeling war-thumping movies like *Red Dawn* and *Rambo* and the chants of "USA! USA!" heard during the summer Olympics of 1984.

All of which explains my final act as a punk kid, circa 1984–1985. I helped form an organization to combat the hopelessness so many young people felt growing up in the Reagan years. We called ourselves Positive Force (PF), named after another group in Nevada (another sign of how this stuff was spreading). We dedicated ourselves to political discussion and seeking ways to protest and alleviate social problems like homelessness and hunger. The group saw connections between the music being produced and the growing political awareness about a president who lived in a bubble of entertainment, who referenced Hollywood films to justify his policies. PF became a place of collective self-education; it was the first place I encountered the avant-garde group of intellectuals known as the Situationist International and thinkers like George Orwell. I remember the thrill of learning outside of the classroom. And it felt like we were at least trying to do concrete things (i.e., feeding the homeless) while having pie in the sky discussions about anarchism and self-governance, the principles standing behind the desire to create our "own culture" that I first witnessed at the Chancery.

* * *

Turn from memory to history and draw back. . . . I no longer inhabit whatever is left of the "punk rock world." Today, I occupy quiet archives, perusing ephemera about matters I did not know when I was young and in that world. I can now see the spread of the movement more clearly in zines collected from places like Tulsa, Oklahoma, and Lawrence, Kansas, warehoused now in university libraries. There are sufficient ephemera and fragments that can be reassembled to reconstruct the "punk rock world," as best we can (though fragmented, as it has to be). Obviously, individual memories wouldn't suffice to recreate it, and we need to place the movement within its wider historical and political context to understand what it was about.

As time has passed since I occupied the punk rock world, the eighties have become the "age of Reagan." An entire decade and a grand sweep of things all placed under the umbrella of one man's existence and power. Indeed, one contemporary historian goes so far as to say that Reagan "invented" the eighties. He did so, Gil Troy argues, based on his "first-class temperament, . . . light touch, . . . affable manner, the sparkle in his eyes." In the words of John Patrick Diggins, Reagan was an Emersonian romanticist who transformed the country by being a "thoughtful, determined man of character and vision." For conservative activists, Reagan is nearly a saint, a man who united the nation against the "malaise" that Jimmy Carter had dragged the country through for four short years. And who could deny that

Reagan triumphed, as he did, and moved American politics to the right in ways we still live with today? Still, there seems something ludicrous about a single man's legacy defining an entire decade.[4]

With a few exceptions, any historical mention of young people growing up in the "Age of Reagan" becomes circumspect. We might remember nostalgically the "brat pack" movies of John Hughes, with their cheery portraits of kids from different cliques and backgrounds managing to find love and happiness in their suburban high schools (1985's *Breakfast Club* comes to mind, a movie loved by many today). Or perhaps there'll be mention of "preppy" culture, the sort that received heightened attention during the confirmation hearings of Supreme Court Judge Brett Kavanaugh: keg parties, elite prep schools, drinking, and often unwanted sex (what one punk labeled "chalk on your bedpost, as a scorecard" fucking). Or maybe mention of designer jeans and the uniform look of feathered hair. Or kids listening to electro-pop on their Walkmans while hanging around the mall, confirming their identity as consumers, the way they do in movies like *Fast Times at Ridgemont High* (1982). Or young "yuppies" dancing their minds out at clubs like Danceteria or the Palladium in Manhattan, coked up for thumping electro-pop music (the sort that dominated the 1980s). Or, worse yet, the moniker of the "MTV generation," whittling down young people's experience to watching videos provided by a corporation that advertised the wares of the entertainment industry. All this only confirms the idea that during the 1980s *everything* turned conservative, culture and politics both, helped by the power of a president who had sparkling eyes that looked down on the world he made, wearing a big grin.[5]

What's not included, of course, is the punk rock world that I and so many other kids inhabited. When discussed, it's siloed into band histories, insular and set apart from what else is happening during the eighties—or what are now *Reagan's* eighties. And yet, the punk rock world and its multifaceted creativity—found in zines, movies, fiction, poetry, flyers, graffiti—didn't just create things, it unleashed a culture war from below, one that aimed its sites on the entertainment industry—corporate record labels, FM radio, "blockbuster" movies, eventually MTV (all tying into one another through what corporate marketers liked to call "synergy"). Understanding this culture war bubbling up from below requires putting the punk rock world into the wider history of a fledgling music industry, which had hit the skids starting in 1979. It requires special attention to the way Reagan—best understood as the "entertainer-in-chief"—hinged his presidency to the industry's celebrity heroes like Michael Jackson, Bruce Springsteen, and Sylvester Stallone, among others who make cameos here. Punk's radicalism grew from its opposition to the power of the entertainment industry and its willingness to sell just about anything to kids. This is a history of a segment of young people making connections between politics and music, through conversations and local trade, and becoming "producers" instead of consumers during a moment when the music industry flailed in its desire to move product that wasn't moving. I will tell a history of creativity coming from the "punk rock world"—avoiding the standard story of one band biography after another—but also document its anger at a bloated entertainment industry and a president who equated governing with entertaining. This is not intended as a comprehensive treatment of Reagan's presidency. Instead, a history of punk becomes, in part, a punk (or punk'd) history of the president.

PRELUDE (1979–1980): WHEN PUNK BROKE . . . AND OPENED

And another lot of young people will appear, and consider us completely outdated, and they will write ballads to express their loathing of us, and there is no reason this should ever end.

—Alfred Jarry[1]

The year 1979 felt like a closing, or at least the end of a chapter in punk's longer history. There were the obituaries. That year Sid Vicious overdosed on heroin, having tried to build—after the demise of the Sex Pistols—a "solo" career out of wasted performances at a club in Manhattan known as Max's Kansas City. He could barely stand up or hold his trademark sneer during performances. . . . The Dead Boys—a band started in a lively punk scene in Cleveland, Ohio, who then became the "house" band of CBGB in New York City—flamed out. . . . That year Patti Smith (approaching her mid-thirties) released a single off her recent album *Wave*, "So You Want to be a Rock Star" (a cover of a Byrds' song), and then called the whole thing quits to become a wife and mother in the Detroit area . . . .[2]

Two publications died in 1979, both having self-identified as places where "punk" could be explained. The San Francisco–based *Search and*

Destroy, started in 1977, an intelligent publication edited by V. Vale, explored ideas like Dadaism or the surrealist fiction of J. G. Ballard and then set them alongside the new music being performed at Mabuhay Gardens by bands like the Dils and the Avengers (both of whom called it quits around the time *Search and Destroy* folded). In its one issue of 1979, V. Vale explained in enigmatic terms consistent with his publication's style: "Notice: S&D as a magazine now self-destructs. Reason: Objective accomplished." Whatever that meant precisely, who knows, but it certainly suggested that a chapter in the history of punk was closing.[3]

Search and Destroy's suicide was followed by the crash of New York's *Punk* magazine, which had started up in 1976 to champion music erupting from CBGB, the small club that hosted bands like the Ramones, Television, and the Patti Smith Group. Not as intellectual as *Search and Destroy*—more *Mad* magazine than *Paris Review*—*Punk* resembled a comic book. Interviews with bands often appeared as cartoon strips, with characters whose eyes bugged out. The magazine's coverage of the Sex Pistols tour in the United States from 1977 to 1978—itself something of a comic book scenario—was some of the most in-depth available. Nonetheless, the magazine had a hard time staying afloat financially, especially after its sugar daddy, Tom Forcade, a middle-aged radical and drug dealer, blew his brains out. *Punk* couldn't even publish its final issue, which focused on the release of the Ramones' silly movie *Rock and Roll High School*. Its editor, John Holmstrom, called it quits and would announce a year later that he was voting for Ronald Reagan.[4]

* * *

The success story of 1970s New York punk also suggested death of a certain kind. As the artist Diego Cortez wrote to John Holmstrom, "I was listening to a lot of radio this week. Blondie, Blondie, Blondie." That was the band who had graduated from the ranks of CBGB and was everywhere in 1979 and— unlike many others—kept it together into the dawn of the 1980s. Ironically, it was via "disco"—a genre of music dominant throughout the 1970s and loathed by *Punk* magazine—that Blondie seized its moment. In April 1979, Blondie struck gold as their single "Heart of Glass" charted to number one. It became one of the last successes of a broader "disco-crossover," wherein bands like the Rolling Stones and the Grateful Dead used the thump, thump beat of electronic dance music and the programed pulsations of synthesizers to rejuvenate their geriatric existence. Blondie's members called "Heart of Glass" their "disco song." Perfectly timed, seeing as the window of high disco-sales was about to close. Disco was no longer the music of a subculture of African American, gay men at Manhattan house parties (as it was in the early 1970s). It was now mass, blockbuster culture, and white and straight as could be. The *Los Angeles Times* noted when Blondie's song was at the top of the charts: "Disco has given birth to an $8 billion a year industry . . . of disco roller rinks, clothing, nightclubs, nonalcoholic kiddie discos, TV shows, films, Broadway musicals." Blondie rode the crest, and now billed itself "new wave" rather than the uglier term "punk."[5]

Soon after the band broke big, the rock journalist Lester Bangs—one of the first to deploy the term "punk" in his early 1970s writings for *Creem* magazine—blew his stack in his hastily written book *Blondie* (1980). For Bangs, Blondie's success exemplified "the shattered promise of 75–76," that explosion of bands at CBGB that *Punk* magazine documented. He'd once had good things to say about Blondie and the band's sense of humor, calling them at one point a relief from the "snotty" and "pretentious" Patti Smith. Now, it wasn't just the band's opportunism that irked him, it was the message they projected. "Heart of Glass," Bangs pointed out, exhumed an icy feeling, as it characterized love affairs as fleeting and passing and, in the original form of the song's lyrics, "a pain in the ass" (the band took out that line, at the request of music industry reps who sought radio play for a single version). Bangs chortled, "I used to think a lot of Blondie's more recent songs were about emotional ambivalence—now I know that's investing them with far too much tragic weight." The band's lead singer, Debbie Harry, was a knock-off of Marilyn Monroe, and Bangs explained in his typical spilling prose that "the hottest market-valued commodity you can give em now is an undifferentiated screen, a field upon which they can project themselves, whatever it is they want to see or think they do see when they don't because there's nothing there." The song and the band's attitude projected a war against *feeling*, a surrender to detachment, the distancing philosophy of Blondie's idol, the aged pop artist Andy Warhol (who once hosted a Studio 54 celebration for Debbie Harry, and had earlier explained that "love affairs get too involved," and that "fantasy love is much better than reality love"). Blondie, according to Bangs, projected a "WALL" and became "emotionally attenuated." If punk had been an expression of anger and angst, Bangs asked, "Who among our celebrity/folk-heroes is redolent of danger anymore? They're all a bunch of bland-outs."[6]

Blondie was stung by Bangs's attack, but that didn't stop them from seeking further commercial success. They knew how to play the game and followed in the footsteps of Elvis Presley by moving on to Hollywood. After a goofy appearance in the movie *Roadie*, the band hooked up with the director Paul Schrader, most famous for his screenplay for the neo-noir film *Taxi Driver*. Schrader was working on *American Gigolo*, a movie about a high-paid male escort who dressed in designer clothes and hired himself out to wealthy women. When the main character wasn't in bed with a client, he was exercising and chiseling his body or surveying his wardrobe. Schrader believed the movie depicted "a man who is quite articulate and who can move around extremely well within various social boundaries but has absolutely no contact with his inner life," a near perfect narcissist. The character explains at one moment, "I can't be possessed." Played by Richard Gere, who perfects a look of self-absorption (the *Los Angeles Weekly* claimed Gere "leaves a blank space in every movie he's ever been in"), the character lived in a culture of mirrors, coolness, and emotional distance.[7]

Debbie Harry loved Schrader's film for its "muted tones and hi-tech look" (a marked difference from Schrader's earlier neo-noir movies that were dark and gritty). She always claimed that visuals mattered to the band's style as much as the music, so writing a song for a movie came easy. "Call Me" was less disco-sounding but its content was remarkably similar to "Heart of Glass" in its assessment of postmodern love. Harry rolled out lines about cuddling in "designer sheets" and saying she'll "never get enough," only resentful that "emotions come" that try to "cover up love's alibi." The song had a lilt to it that made it synch well with a movie of emptiness and muted pastels; its sound was synth pop that would dominate the decade to come. Just as importantly, the song and film worked together with the single (some copies of which had Richard Gere on their cover) released at the same time as the movie, in hopes of building "synergy" across the industry. Long after Lester Bangs's *Blondie* moved to the remainder tables in bookstores, the band seized a good six weeks at number one in the charts.[8]

It didn't end there. All the popularity won Debbie Harry a designer-jeans commercial, for Murjani. Though it wouldn't go down into history with as much splash as the contemporaneous commercial done by Brooke Shields, who at age fifteen would say that nothing came between her and her Calvin Klein jeans, it certainly fused together "new wave" culture and one of the most iconic symbols of 1980s fashion. Tight, tapered, and expensive jeans—versus the bell bottoms of the sixties and seventies—became "the look of the eighties," according to *Time* magazine. Harry's advertisement was all postmodern image, with scenes of her walking foggy streets, passing a poster with her own visage on it (wearing wrap-around glasses). The voice-over offered empty advertising gibberish about shape shifting: "When you know where you're going, you know what to wear." Chris Stein, Harry's lover and the guitar player in Blondie, described it this way: "It's like a non-commercial. There's no mention of jeans in it. It's just like Debbie walking down the street and her outfits change but that's about it." But it *was* a commercial, and it brought in cash, making Harry $200,000 richer. And it consolidated and made more omnipresent Harry's bleached blonde hair and heavily mascara-ed face. The "Deborah Harry Look," designer jeans, and "new wave" music became nightclub chic, all thanks to a band who had been a part of "punk" in the mid-1970s.[9]

Which suggested that, in the words of the British critic George Melly, punk had repeated a historical process, moving from revolt into style. The "look" could be purchased, and punk's sensibility of anger flipped to hip coolness and televised surface, replaced by this thing called "new wave"—a sort of sanitized "punk"—and its electro-pop soundtrack that would dominate the 1980s.[10]

* * *

Blondie's blockbuster success could not cover up a sense of crisis in America's music industry. The disco sales crash of 1979—which Blondie just missed—symbolized something deeper. The *New York Times* would report in August about a "popular music business . . . slump, both in record sales and concert attendance." The historian Graham Thompson pointed out that the "U.S. phonographic industry entered its first recession for more than thirty years [in 1979]. Sales of vinyl records dropped 11 percent." A well-oiled machine had fallen apart—one where acts were found, acts were signed, acts were promoted, and consumers gobbled up the records by those acts. Some leaders in the industry blamed cassette taping, others the rise of home video games (Atari) that ate into the entertainment market. Some cursed how the cost of oil kept skyrocketing, making the production of albums increasingly expensive, with the costs passed onto consumers. Inflation was killing everything, most would agree, including the music business. But some leaders, who paid attention, grew aghast at how independent labels were doing better than the majors. Maybe, just maybe, it was the industry's fault itself—maybe the industry sucked?[11]

This crisis followed on the heels of a massive conglomeration of the music industry throughout the 1970s. In 1979, *New York* magazine would report, "It is estimated that a half dozen entertainment conglomerates— CBS, Warner Communications, Polygram, RCA, MCA, and Capitol-EMI— account for 85 percent of the records that are sold in the United States. And within a small strip of midtown Manhattan you can find the offices of four of these companies—CBS, Warner, Polygram, and RCA—which together control nearly 70 percent." The term "oligopoly" was being heard a lot now. These culture industry giants needed assured blockbusters, not risks, but the blockbuster strategy was failing them, even as their business units grew in size and proportion. The word on the street for "oligopoly capitalism" had become *corporate rock.*[12]

One thing for sure, mainstream, commercial radio could do nothing about the problem. During the 1970s, radio became an appendage of the record industry, blaring out the same titles over and over, taking marching orders from the major labels. Radio was, quite simply, a giant advertisement for the music industry's offerings. The end of the seventies witnessed the culminating sweep of "Top-40" radio replacing any lingering remnants of "progressive" or "free form" airplay, where disc jockeys called the shots (that was shunted over to down-the-dial college radio—safely marginalized). The "Top-40" format bulldozed disc jockeys who were told what to do, often given a crate full of records that they were to play in exact order. The DJ might still have some sort of persona to cultivate (like Doug Tracht, "the greaseman," or Howard Stern), but his central task had been proletarianized, stolen by upper management. A sign of how the music industry broke everything it touched.[13]

* * *

Even live performance of music was dehumanized. During the late 1960s, rock was a music of urban clubs like the Fillmore (in both San Francisco and New York City). It was also a music of festivals—most notoriously Woodstock and Altamont. Over the course of the 1970s, large festivals morphed into "arena rock," huge concerts usually at sports coliseums that appeared the most cost-effective way of delivering blockbuster acts to an increasingly suburban audience.

At the end of 1979, tragedy struck the world of arena rock. It occurred just a few days short of the ten-year anniversary of the infamous Altamont Concert (1969), where the Rolling Stones played a free gig for around 300,000 attendees that descended into mayhem and murder (what radical hippies known as Diggers called the "Charlie Manson Memorial Hippie Love Death Cult Festival"). Now, in place of the Rolling Stones, stood the Who, whose members, in their mid-thirties, found themselves whisked away to the Riverfront Coliseum in Cincinnati, Ohio, a large arena typical for blockbuster rock acts. Band members were delivered to the show in "five chauffeur-driven limousines," stocked with champagne, beer, and cognac. They had demanded a "specialist in internal medicine" on 24-hour call (their drummer Keith Moon had overdosed and died in the past year). The Who would gross $100,000 for the evening's performance. The band arrived late for soundcheck, blasé about just another show and bored with going through the motions (like the guitarist Pete Townshend's "windmill" style of swinging his arm around to bang his guitar strings).[14]

The show had been oversold and featured "festival" seating, meaning kids would rush into the stadium to get as close to the stage as possible. Which they did, starting early in the day, congregating outside the Coliseum. As evening dawned, there was a crush of bodies, and fans were screaming "Push!" as a small number of doors opened. Soon kids trampled over one another. Fans could feel as their feet raised off the ground, perhaps standing on a body or pressed up against someone else, literally squeezed upward. Outside the stadium, one survivor remembered being cold and yet sweating at the same time, and "everyone had their heads tilted straight back, their noses up to try to get some air," looking up at the steam "rising off the crowd in the moonlight." He remembered that he "couldn't breathe" at moments. Nor could others. Eleven Who fans died; twenty-six suffered serious injuries. The doctor who saw the bodies of the deceased noted "evidence of footprint-like injuries." Most died from suffocation and broken bones.[15]

And still, the Who, without knowing of the deaths, played their formulaic set, including "Baba O'Riley" with its line, "It's only teenage wasteland." When the story was fully reported, some critics suggested the band should cancel future tour dates. Townshend mulled over the idea but then confessed his middle-aged paralysis: "I just don't care, really I really don't care what happens anymore." The Who's lead singer, Roger Daltrey, concurred: "Initially, we felt stunned and empty. We felt we couldn't go on. But you gotta. There's no point in stopping." To which the aggrieved might ask, *Really?* Six months later, Townshend slammed his verdict down, without an ounce of ethical concern: "We're not going to let a *little thing* like that stop us." Townshend's sputtering statement represented the callousness of rock culture at the time, how bloated and distant performers became within the dehumanized world of arena rock.[16]

* * *

At the time the Who played their death mass, American political life was swinging fiercely to the right. President Jimmy Carter was flipping out at a political double whammy: the Iranian hostage crisis (November 1979) and the USSR's invasion of Afghanistan (December 1979). Like previous Democratic presidents (such as Harry Truman and Lyndon Baines Johnson), Carter feared his right flank and started to think in military rather than diplomatic terms, trying to look tough. He *had been* the president who wanted human rights to guide American foreign policy, and who projected a sense of humility about the failures of Vietnam. With pride, he would refrain that he had avoided war during his tenure in the White House. He wanted to tamp down the tensions of the Cold War, in order to overcome what he once called the country's "inordinate fear of communism which once led us to embrace any dictator who joined us in that fear." He had followed Nixon's policy of détente and had even pardoned Vietnam War draft dodgers. But in late 1979, he went bellicose, halted arms talks with the Soviet Union, canceled American participation in the upcoming Summer Olympics, and considered installing what appeared to be first-strike nuclear weapons in Europe.[17]

Which set a new mood in politics—from the "malaise" marking his early years as president (when Americans learned how to tune out his speeches) to a sense of impending war (what some would label "Cold War 2"). It could be heard in his newly proclaimed "Carter Doctrine." Its language was frank, bellicose, and frightening: "Let our position be absolutely clear: An attempt by any outside force to gain control of the Persian Gulf region will be regarded as an assault on the vital interests of the United States of America, and such an assault will be repelled by any means necessary, including military force." Simultaneously, Carter reinstituted registration with the Selective Service System just four years after Gerald Ford had ended the draft that provided troops for Vietnam. He hoped to look like a president moving onto a war footing. Still, his reputation as a wimp, the man who dared wear cardigans on television, propelled a growing cynicism about his march rightward and his embrace of toughness. *Rolling Stone* would lecture Carter: "This wasn't a real draft or mobilization for a real war. It was a cheap way to bluster at the Russians and show them America is at the ready." It was easy for the magazine's baby-boomer editors to downplay what the mood felt like for young people in their teens. For many, it felt like a tour of duty in Iran or Afghanistan was around the corner.[18]

* * *

So . . . as punk died or became a high-priced commodity, and as the music industry hit the skids with little understanding of what was going on, and as arena rock produced a blood bath, and as the sounds of war started to bellow from the White House, there were some who saw an opportunity in what, at first, looked bleak. These would be the pioneers of the "punk rock world" built in the 1980s. What better time than now to build a counterculture, something kids could call their "own." Something that rejected the dullness of MOR (middle-of-the-road) radio and the boredom of listening to oldster bands like Blondie chugging on fumes. It seemed time to go into a basement of a suburban home and rejuvenate the punk ethic of Do-It-Yourself (DIY). Starting some time in and around 1980, *punk went young*, sometimes taking inspiration from what Bangs called the promise of "75–76" (sometimes not), or what might best be called baby boomer punk of the 1970s. Young people would become pioneers of a new chapter of punk as boomer punk careened toward immolation. In death there were new beginnings.

1

TEENY PUNKS: PIONEER YOUR OWN CULTURE! (1980–1981)

From the moment that the rebel finds his voice—even though he says nothing but "no"—he begins to desire and to judge.

—Albert Camus[1]

XXX

Slamming into Something New That's Yours

My body's in wild convulsions . . .

—TSOL, "Dance with Me"

In June 1980, the *Los Angeles Times* reported on "the slam," short for slamdancing, which the paper called "a new 'dance' craze." To the reporter Patrick Goldstein, the slam looked like "dozens of fans hurtling across the dance floor like kamikaze pilots," a swarm of bodies bouncing off one another. Slamdancing was "new" not just because of how young the participants were (the first interviewee in the story was just ten), but also because "unlike previous dances, the Slam is neither elegant nor erotic. You don't twirl, twist or bump your partner."[2]

Precisely because you didn't have a single "partner." Or better, your partner was the collectivity of other audience members. The dance moved horizontally rather than up and down, accentuating the collective over the individual. Slamdancing opened up contingency; it was not a preplanned or scripted set of "dance steps" set out in books, for no one knew what would happen after any collision of bodies flung people in different directions.

The slam rejected other popular forms of dance at the time. In late 1970s "disco," dancing served as the art of seeing yourself (mirrors were ever present in the most famous disco club, Studio 54) while watching others grind and hump one another to songs like "Le Freak" (the upper section of Studio 54 had rubber floors, so maintenance workers could hose off all the semen that accrued each night). In contrast, there was the pogo, imported into America from the British punk scene, circa 1976, where each person on the dance floor jumped up and down in his or her own siloed world, reflecting, in many ways, Blondie's detached perspective on matters of love. The pogo, once pioneered by scruffy punks in England for fun, was now part of a "new wave" culture growing in America.

Slamdancing was not individual in expression like new wave, nor was it prefigurative sex. It was collective, spontaneous, and utterly amateur. It left kids feeling *physically spent*, as exhausted as the performers on the stage. Here was Los Angeles's Zizi "Carrot Woman" Howell, who wrote a year after the *Los Angeles Times* story (she would have been around nineteen at the time):

> The slam pit. The spit and the sweat. Bodies pressed against me. I like the feeling. Heat from the bodies matches the heat from the rage. The hurt is sudden and frequent. . . . No love. The mass is a temporary release.

Not seduction but a declaration of rage found only in physical contact with others, physical contact in an otherwise dehumanized culture.[3]

What the *Los Angeles Times* didn't know when it printed the story was that outsiders were busy studying slamdancing and thus turning it into a nationwide phenomenon. A group of young punks in Washington, D.C., had come with their band the Teen Idles to play a show in L.A. soon after the story ran. When they returned home, these "teeny punks," as their critics called them, were bubbling with ideas about slamdancing. For Henry Garfield (later known as Henry Rollins), who had roadied for the Teen Idles, the slam was "high energy," but also held to an ethic of equality and mutuality. "If someone bumps you, you don't go running around the floor, chasing him so you can get him back. You just go," Garfield explained. He saw this ethic every time a person picked up another who had fallen. Garfield's friend, Ian MacKaye, who played bass in the Teen Idles, remembered the communalism of slamdancing: "Slamming was orchestrated chaos—it looked like fighting, but it was actually people working among each other." The art critic and performance artist Dan Graham, a rare baby boomer who warmed to new developments in punk during the 1980s, stretched the historical perspective, close to the point of snapping, when he argued that slamdancing mimicked eighteenth-century Shakers, with their chaotic and circling religious rapture, where all souls were equal and all movement communal.[4]

One thing for certain: slamdancing combatted the icy, dehumanized feel of arena rock. There was a consciousness to it. A part of slamdancing included participants ascending whatever stage there was, dancing on it briefly (sometimes knocking into a performer), and then leaping back into the audience. "Stage diving" erased the line between performer and audience member. As slamdancing spread across the nation, a zine editor in Seattle, Washington, explained that when a "singer . . . took the stage, we knew at once that he was one of us. It wasn't Him the Singer and Us the Audience. We were united." There was hunger for "physical contact" between performer and audience that resisted depersonalized, prestaged arena rock, where the masses in an audience were washed over by the command and control of performers. Where, in the words of the punk poet Dennis Cooper, performers faced "warm eyes gazing up at them in audience, lives blown like a wheatfield by their beauty, our wild applause—their jackpot." Mike Watt, bass player for the band the Minutemen, went so far as to compare arena rock to Nuremberg rallies, where, as Hannah Arendt famously put it, "atomized, isolated individuals" turned into a "mass." Watt often pointed out that his band's name had multiple meanings, but one was the experience of arena rock where performers appeared to audience members as "minute" men, small and distant. Slamdancing intended to kill that dynamic. John Stabb of the D.C.-based band Government Issue (formed in 1980–1981) said punk shows allowed him to "avoid arena concerts." This felt like *his* "culture," not the culture of mega-rock promoters or celebrities, but rather the culture of kids standing or dancing next to him.[5]

XXX

The Art of Provocation

> Truly speaking, it is not instruction, but provocation, that I can receive from another soul.
>
> —Ralph Waldo Emerson[6]

As the *Los Angeles Times* announced the rise of slamdancing, the San Francisco band Dead Kennedys were putting final touches on their first album, *Fresh Fruit for Rotting Vegetables* (from now on *Fresh Fruit*). The album offered no love songs among its fourteen tracks. Instead, most were "protest" songs, often aimed at the dark clouds hovering over the Carter White House, with its bellicose talk about protecting the Persian Gulf at all cost, while jacking up the nuclear arms race and reinstituting the Selective Service System.

In "When Ya Get Drafted," a song under two minutes, Jello Biafra warned that when the "economy is looking bad . . . another war" appeals to those in power. The defense industry saw "easy money, easy jobs" in the growing war fever, and after all, "what Big Business wants . . . Big Business gets" (these lines sounded almost percussive in the song, as the vocals synched with the band's playing). Since the kids of today were sucking down six-packs of beer (too stoned to care), they'd just "sit on their ass" rather than protest. The song served up *noir* protest, pessimistic, hardboiled, and anxiety-ridden. It lacked the confidence of earlier protest songs like Woody Guthrie's "Dust Bowl Ballads" about building solidarity among the displaced poor (the move from "I" to "We," as John Steinbeck had put it). It certainly lacked the optimism of early sixties folk protest songs like Bob Dylan's "The Times They Are a Changing."[7]

Indeed, Biafra recognized that he offered as much irony and confusion in his songs as sure-footed critique. He could provide no solutions, just provocation. "Our lyrics are intricate enough that it takes a fair amount of intelligence to figure out where we're coming from," he'd explain later. Biafra often contrasted the Dead Kennedys to the Dils, one of the first-generation punk bands in San Francisco who had crashed in 1980. The Dils wrote songs like "I Hate the Rich" and "Class War" (the latter proclaiming, "I wanna war between the rich and poor!"). They were declarative and obvious. Biafra's own political sensibility was more open-ended. "The Dils" stood for "this is our opinion. Follow and believe it," Biafra explained. He contrasted that with the Dead Kennedys' attitude: "This is our opinion and now go out and find your own." He saw himself "ungluing peoples' minds" rather than sowing dogma.[8]

So a song like "Kill the Poor," clearly antiwar, wound up joking around with how the "Neutron bomb" was "nice and quick and clean and gets things done" (Biafra would often sing these lines in an ironically chirpy way). Since it killed people but preserved the "value" of "property," it might be used at home by the rich. Which sounds an awful lot like the dark humor pioneered by the seventeenth- to eighteenth-century writer Jonathan Swift, whose infamous essay "A Modest Proposal" called for eating kids who were dying of starvation (the great surrealist Andre Breton would open his edited book on black humor with Swift's essay). The essay shocked its readers by being explicit about something that was, figuratively, already happening (kids were dying of starvation), with a cunning logic pushed to an extreme. This aim was at the heart of Biafra's politics of provocation.[9]

You could hear it in his band's name—which continued to provoke the accusation of bad taste—as well as the name he chose for himself. Born Eric Reed Boucher, he turned himself into a juxtaposition, the first name signifying the bloated sugar diet of "First World" America, the second the underdeveloped world famine of Biafra. His black humor reverberated during his run for mayor of San Francisco a few months before recording *Fresh Fruit*. He had campaigned to make "downtown businessmen . . . wear clown suits" while making serious demands like the right of homeless people to squat in abandoned buildings. It was heard when he interrupted his band's performance at the 1980 Bay Area Music Awards (the Bammies) to provide a monologue about the sorry state of rock music, sung over the sounds of the (new wave) Knack song "My Sharona" (refurbished as "My Payola"). Biafra derided "cock rock" by asking a question to those gathered at the Bammies, most of them from the music industry: "Is my cock big enough, is my brain small enough, for you to make me a star?" To interrupt what people expected and to ask disturbing questions became Biafra's modus operandi, pushing further and further.[10]

His case for biting provocation grew from situating himself in contemporary American history (he was a college dropout and thus self-taught, having read a great deal on his own about the recent past). During the sixties, Biafra explained, there were "a lot of people just rebelling." But at some point things changed: "Gradually about '72 or '73 (different time for different people)," Biafra expounded, "the bubble seems to have burst, both for the hippies and others from that era, who had just gotten to the point of 'Where do I go from here?'" A massive depoliticization followed, as numerous one-time radicals turned to self-recovery programs like Erhard Seminars Training (EST) and transcendental meditation (Jerry Rubin being the most famous case). Biafra had grown up in Boulder, Colorado, which gave him privileged insight into what he called "an Organic Disneyland" of gray-haired ponytail types wasting away in a land of hippie kitsch (like hanging plants and smoke-stained copies of *High Times*). Biafra's friend and collage artist Winston Smith (who would design much of the art for the Dead Kennedys) explained the change best, having his own experience of leaving "the country in 1968" to study in Italy, returning around 1975: "When I left it was people fighting in the streets, wanting to burn everything down. When I returned everyone was frumped out on earth shoes [and] health food," Smith recalled. "The language changed—words appeared that didn't even exist before, like 'lifestyle.'" Biafra agreed, honing in on the popular expression, "mellow out, man." That attitude dominated popular rock music of the 1970s, exemplified in Olivia Newton John's "Have You Never Been Mellow?" (1975) and the Eagles' "Take It Easy" (1977). In "California Uber Alles," included on *Fresh Fruit*, Biafra warned, "Mellow out or you will pay," an ironic read of how the washed-up hippie feel of "take-it-easy" became its own form of conservatism in 1980.[11]

One thing enthused Biafra, and that was watching a growing number of kids coming from the suburbs of the Bay Area into San Francisco to attend shows in 1980. There were also those young punks from D.C. who had traveled from L.A. up to San Francisco to play their second West Coast show during the summer. Having taken notes on slamming in L.A., they observed the large stamps on young peoples' hands as they entered Mabuhay Gardens—a central venue for San Francisco punk. Those X'ed hands allowed underage kids to attend shows but prevented illegal underage drinking. Biafra too celebrated the spirit behind "all ages" shows and saw hope in punk growing in size and turning young (unlike some other oldsters in the punk scene who recoiled at the upstarts and condemned their high-energy dancing). All of this set out the battle lines for a culture war.[12]

XXX

No More Love Songs . . .

> Some of the wild boys do not talk at all. Others have developed cries, songs, words as weapons. Words that cut like buzz saws.
> —William Burroughs, *The Wild Boys*[13]

That sentiment spread into the suburbs surrounding San Francisco and then moved its way back down to Los Angeles. Protest songs of the Dead Kennedys' type became omnipresent as the 1980s dawned. For instance, the Circle Jerks offered "Paid Vacation" (1980). It was hard to ignore the song's reference to the reinstitution of the Selective Service and Carter's promise to defend American interests in the Persian Gulf. The future fight was "not Vietnam" but rather "another oil company scam . . . It's Afghanistan!!!" So, listeners were told, get some suntan lotion "cause you'll be fighting in the desert." The song ended on a vision of the future where "bodies burn and people die." The message was also in the sound of the song—with singer Keith Morris singing punchy lines in synch with a smack on the snare drum (that sounded like a gun blast) and his voice going up into a scream when he yelled about "Afghanistan."[14]

The loudest echo of the Dead Kennedys' spirit came from Mike Watt's band, the Minutemen, whose song "Paranoid Chant" (1980) fused existential grief with dark humor (written by Watt, sung by D. Boon). Facing the prospects of nuclear confrontation, the band's guitarist and singer D. Boon shouted, "I try to talk to girls and I keep thinkin' of World War III." He got a tone of panic as he yelled these lines (helped out by a scratchy guitar sound and bass line that moved high up the neck). Boon explained how he was prepping for political activism by learning all the "stats" about the number of "warheads" across the globe. But knowledge nurtured paralysis as much as activism. He felt "paranoid, stuck on overdrive" and looking at "so many goddamned scared faces." Put into a larger context, these lyrics articulated the demands of the growing nuclear freeze movement whose only chance of success required a "public awareness about the hideous reality of nuclear war," as two nuclear freeze supporters put it. Which led to, in the words of "Paranoid Chant," being "scared shitless," anxious and angry both at once. Psychologists at the time were starting to research the impact of nuclear war on young psyches. They would witness two reactions: "hopelessness" and "paralysis." The 1980s, some polling concluded, would become a decade in which "40% of young people claimed awareness of nuclear war's destruction by age 12" and when "47 percent of Americans thought that it was fairly likely that the United States would soon be in a nuclear war." When Jimmy Carter debated Ronald Reagan in October 1980, he admitted that his own thirteen-year-old daughter Amy was freaked out about the prospects of nuclear war. The Minutemen gave panicked voice—helped out by their rattling music—to the growing dread of nuclear war.[15]

Before the Minutemen were the Minutemen, the band had a more explicitly political name, the Reactionaries, which expressed their sense that the country was about to "swing to the right," a feeling that seemed to become reality from 1979 to 1980. In 1980, they adopted their new name, which like so much else of the band had a multiplicity to it. Not only did it reference the appearance of rock stars in arena settings, but it also alluded to the original minutemen, who were young fighters during the American Revolution, and to a mocking of the small reactionary and vigilante group that populated certain areas of Orange County, California (whose members had tried to "kill hippies" and once threatened to bomb the actress Jane Fonda). That group linked up with "national fascist organizations such as the John Birch Society, . . . Ku Klux Klan, Patriotic Party, and the Christian Anti-Communist Crusade," according to the punk historian Jeff Bale.[16]

The band always felt out of step with the Hollywood punk scene that had erupted by 1977. After all, they weren't from Hollywood but rather San Pedro. Every time they trucked up to Hollywood, they caught an ugly vibe. "The Hollywood In-Crowd," meaning punks who were "very in-bred and cliquish," were often called the "Hollywood 50." Many lived at the Canterbury Apartments, which was close to the central club, the Masque (shut down in the late 1970s). And this in-crowd perceived the Minutemen (and others) as outsiders, as working-class scruffy "kids" and, in the band's own words, "fucking corn dogs." As the Minutemen explained in an interview, "Hollywood people were just really bent on appearance."

The band would "go up there with our six packs and stuff and just watch bands. We always tried to get gigs but we were from the suburbs."[17]

Which helped explain the band's early alliance with Black Flag. Though Black Flag's roots went back to the Los Angeles scene of 1977, their location in Hermosa Beach made them outsiders to the first generation of punk in Los Angeles and the "Hollywood clique." As the band explained to *Ripper* (a zine published in the suburbs of San Jose), there was an "influx of suburban kids" in the L.A. scene who grew hostile to older punks who "have normal jobs now" and were "getting married." As bands like the Bags and Germs went belly up and the Go-Gos went commercial (following the lead of Blondie), a door flew open for younger suburban kids to create their own culture. Black Flag's bassist, Chuck Dukowski (his adopted last name a reference to the writer Charles Bukowski), explained, "We were from the suburbs and that wasn't 'cool.'" The older punks "tried to kick us out all the time, tried to get rid of us." Editors at the L.A. zine *Flipside*, a publication that started up in the 1970s and managed to survive into the 1980s, praised the Black Flag–Minutemen alliance as symbolic of the suburbanization of punk. The editors of *Flipside* saw this as a generational change of sorts (one not neatly correlated with age necessarily) and a shift in identity: "No more art damage for awhile and it's about time."[18]

Both bands rejected the "fashion" many associated with the Hollywood clique and with Malcolm McLaren, the manager of the Sex Pistols and owner of a punk fashion shop in London. Neither Black Flag nor the Minutemen "dressed up" for shows; what they donned during the day they donned in the evening. They never shopped at those "new wave" boutiques that started to dot Melrose Avenue in Los Angeles; they never sought the "Debbie Harry" look promoted in her 1980 designer jeans commercial. Their antifashion was nearly instinctual, a rejection of society's wastefulness, its throw-away culture, its mindless trendiness. And especially its emphasis on surface and appearance. "We're trying to always make a statement," Greg Ginn explained, "that it doesn't matter what you're wearing. It's how you feel and how you think." For the Minutemen—who sported flannel shirts—it reflected the band's working-class background and their sense of humility.[19]

Instinctual antifashion was part of the Minutemen's revolt, but so too were ideas and thinking. "We like reading books," the band explained to a zine, "which a lot of working class guys don't. There's this idea in America that you have to be stupid to be working class, which we don't believe." D. Boon had been an art major in college (and was also a painter), but his self-education about contemporary politics came from having "read a lot of history," as he put it. His interest in history mixed nicely with Mike Watt's in literature. The band's bassist had a love for James Joyce and also cited Anthony Burgess's *A Clockwork Orange*. The latter was a dystopian novel that told a story of a behavioral control system that eradicated human freedom, raising all sorts of ethical questions (both Joyce and Burgess invented their own language in their play with words, something that also rubbed off on Watt). This explains why the music journalist Mikal Gilmore (brother to the convicted murderer Gary) called the Minutemen, with confidence, "the thinking listener's and thinking musician's hardcore band."[20]

Fortunately, a relic of Black Flag and the Minutemen's 1980 alliance exists. It is the EP *Cracks in the Sidewalk*. Recorded from July to November of 1980 and released on the Minutemen's own independent label, New Alliance, the EP featured the Minutemen and Black Flag, plus Saccharine Trust, a band who came out of Wilmington, California, which was close to San Pedro and was described as "lower middle class and suburban." The sounds here were raw, angular, and abrasive. Another part of the product mattered in terms of expressing anxiety: the art chosen for the EP's cover. Here there was an image of a man and a woman, both who appear to have marks on their forehead (suggesting the sign of Charlie Manson devotees). The man and woman hold small knives and look through a large living room window at a couple on a couch who are watching a nuclear explosion on their television set. It was signed, "Raymond Pettibone."[21]

XXX

Drawing Punk

> Punk music—unlike its New Wave counterpart—is something that makes you wake up and think, something intellectual, something that redefines the meaning of "fun" like you've never known before.
> —Mickey Creep, zine editor, 1980[22]

Next to D. Boon, Mike Watt's biggest intellectual debt was to the creator of the artwork that donned *Cracks in the Sidewalk* and the Minutemen's own *Paranoid Chant* EP (both 1980). Raymond Pettibon (the e was dropped), who was the younger brother of Greg Ginn, spent a great deal of time discussing with Watt everything from the linguistic philosophy of Ludwig Wittgenstein to the explosion of modernist revolts in art throughout the twentieth century ("futurists, Dadaists, surrealists, and situationists," Watt recalled). They also talked about politics—Pettibon's anarchism clashing against Watt's growing sympathy for democratic socialism.[23]

By 1980, Pettibon had settled on his trademark form of expression: A black and white single-frame drawing, mixed with words—often just a single sentence. The form resembled traditional advertising (large image, some words). But while advertisements unified the two to promote sales, Pettibon troubled the relationship to prompt disassociation and open thought on the part of the viewer. The philosopher Michel Foucault would call this a surrealist practice (especially evident in René Magritte's famous "This Is Not a Pipe" painting). Foucault called it an "unraveled calligram," where "image and text" don't "coincide . . . but push against each other, thus creating tension and unforeseen meaning." Foucault—in his usual anarchist spirit—praised the infusion of "disorder" into the normal process of visual, narrative communication. As Pettibon would later explain to *Forced Exposure* zine, a single image and text could prompt viewers to question their own logic. Viewers were supposed to fill out their own meaning. "There's not any reason I can see to fill it out. Because it's implicit in the drawing. Looking at the drawing, you're supposed to fill all that in yourself." Pettibon admitted to getting his ideas from reading, not listening to music or looking at visuals. He inhabited "used bookstores" and "library sales," where he found his tools for inspiration. And though he tried his hand at it a few years back, he had rejected comic book narration (the sort that *Punk* magazine used), seeing it as too safe and formulaic.[24]

Pettibon rejected, simultaneously, two inheritances from the wider history of American art: the romanticist and expressive tradition of the 1950s Beats and the flatness, image-oriented pop art of Andy Warhol that dominated the 1960s. Pettibon found the effusive, expansive poetry of Allen Ginsberg, a Beat poet, absurd in the face of the violence and destruction of the late 1960s as well as the dominant materialism of a consumer culture. Pettibon even rewrote Ginsberg's famous "Howl" (1956), mixing in the realities of the Altamont tragedy of 1969 (when the Hell's Angels pummeled people in the audience with pool sticks and then stabbed to death a young African American, Meredith Hunter). He wrote about hipsters "who saw

Blake in the Safeway, but lost him in the fruit section . . . who waved a fist and lost a genital to a Hell's Angel." But as much as he rejected the romanticism of the Beats, he never embraced the surface images deployed by pop artists. There was depth to Pettibon's work. The viewer was supposed to find something beyond the image—unlike the soup cans Warhol redrew with no other purpose than to show off their reproducibility (Warhol began as a commercial artist and drawer for fashion magazines, eventually fueling, in the words of J. Hoberman, a "more detached and anti-expressive avant-garde"). Since Pettibon's "ideas came out of reading," he didn't want to make art that allowed people to rest their eyes on surface (the way Susan Sontag insisted Warhol and others had done by emphasizing "the sensuous surface of art without mucking about in it"). Pettibon explained, "I place myself in this state of consciousness where I'm receptive to associations and stuff."[25]

Pettibon's art rejected a growing movement toward "expressionism" in late 1970s, early 1980s art. His work contrasted with Johanna Went's punk performance art, which consisted of her "dancing and writhing on stage," using baby dolls and skinned animal heads, mixed with "worldless screams and gurgles." She employed huge constructions (made out of found items) onstage—including a "ritual sacrifice of a six-two tall papier mâché "goose." She flung garbage into the audience, the found items she used projecting an image of a "bewildered Alice in Produceland . . . struggling to burrow her way out of the surplus of the 20th century." Violence and destruction were exhibited, not intuited by the viewer looking at an inert image on paper. Went herself once explained that "words" were "worthless in a world of communication breakdown."[26]

Pettibon's rejection of such expressionism (his need for words, for instance) ran alongside his growing animosity toward 1960s hippie culture. Indeed, images of hippies started to dominate Pettibon's work by 1980. Pettibon's brother, Greg, once explained in an interview, "We're living with a lot of the results of the hippie nightmare. . . . Hippies have got control over the culture now." Like his brother, Pettibon hated all nostalgia for the sixties that would come to dominate 1980s culture—from the rise of "classic rock" to movies like 1981's *My Dinner with Andre*, in which one character says, "It seems to me quite possible that the 1960s represented the last burst of the human being before he was extinguished." Pettibon believed baby boomers overemphasized the themes of liberation and freedom while ignoring the self-destruction and deluded political visions of the 1960s.[27]

His chief target was Charles Manson, who Pettibon depicted in numerous drawings from 1980 to 1981, including one of Manson nailed to a cross (the cult leader had delusions of being Christ). Manson was the perfect symbol of hippie love gone rancid. He was the substitute father figure—his followers were named "the Family"—who was just as abusive as the fathers the young women escaped to join his cult. Manson "mindfucked" his followers, in the evocative term used by David Felton. Most members of "the Family" came from the suburbs, very often young women who flocked to Haight-Ashbury during the Summer of Love (1967) with "flowers in their hair"—only to find a counterculture populated by pimps, Hells Angels on the prowl, and hard drugs. On a flyer for a Black Flag show at the Mabuhay Gardens, Pettibon depicted a man on a scaffolding, his back turned to the viewer but with the shock of black hair he used to signify Manson. Then the words: "Turn on, tune in, drop out" (Timothy Leary's acid-fueled mantra). Just above the man is a long-haired hippie female replete with body-paint jumping from a window, looking wacked on acid. Dropping out looked like dropping dead. Indeed, Pettibon explained he was depicting the sick and twisted element of the counterculture, but also its apolitical side— the side that would live on past the 1960s into Jello Biafra's moment of "mellow out." "Most of my stuff on hippies," Pettibon explained, "is about apolitical hippies who . . . let's say it's '69 and '70 when the hippies were totally out of the political thing because nothing happened. . . . They hated authority figures who were knocking themselves on the head—cops and stuff of course—still, but they didn't really care about Vietnam bombing and abstract politics." Hippies had failed and punks inherited that failure within the great "mellow out."[28]

XXX

Writing Punk

Sometimes, reading Shirley, I can hear the guitars.

—William Gibson[29]

The summer of 1980 witnessed the release of *City Come A-Walkin'*, a novel by John Shirley, a writer who had inhabited a late 1970s punk "scene" in Portland, Oregon, that helped develop his ideas about writing. Most of his childhood was spent near the city, where he was kicked out of high school, in part, for his role in locking a teacher in a closet and publishing an underground student newspaper. He earned a GED and then did two years at Portland State University. He used some of his money set aside for college to attend the Clarion Writers' Workshop in Seattle, where he received instruction from Ursula K. Le Guin, Harlan Ellison, and Frank Herbert, all top-notch writers of science fiction as a type of intellectually rigorous political commentary. Shirley learned from the masters, so to speak. Still, punk was just as important.[30]

Portland punk erupted by 1977–1978 running alongside the growth of the San Francisco scene that buttressed the Dead Kennedys (a chief pioneer in Portland was the band the Wipers, who started up in 1977). Shirley formed his own band Sado-Nation with Mark Sten and Dave Corboy (the band survived into the 1980s, in altered form, after Shirley left for New York City). *How* the scene grew and flourished from 1978 into 1980 played a central role in Shirley's *bildungsroman*. Sten's influence on Shirley was crucial. By 1978, Sten had organized the Alternative Arts Association (AAA). The AAA hosted not-for-profit, communally run shows. Sten described how the AAA "runs along anarcho-syndicalist lines, as opposed to capitalist or authoritarian ones. We are a business, and we deal with money and real-life business problems, but our internal affairs are determined on a more progressive basis" than a for-profit club would be. By 1980, Sten had successfully organized Clockwork Joe's, a building that housed different band rooms and a central performance space, as well as a "Friction Art Gallery." Construction of Clockwork Joe's was done collectively, and some people wound up living there. The zine *Subterranean Pop* (eventually *Sub Pop*), published in Olympia, Washington, proclaimed that the radical localism and self-management on Sten's behalf had promised to defeat what it called, in 1980, "CORPORATE MANIPULATION OF OUR CULTURE." No surprise that Jello Biafra was thrilled any time that the Dead Kennedys performed there.[31]

This anarcho-syndicalist and anticorporate feel had a big impact on Shirley. So too did seeing the Sex Pistols' final performance on January 14, 1978, at the Winterland venue in San Francisco. Though he enjoyed the Pistols' performance, he hated the overall experience of what some called a "Punk Woodstock," especially once the media showed up. Suddenly, a contingent of fans started to shout at gathering news reporters. Shirley witnessed "posers" pretending to do "the cool thing" by being "strange-and-violent. . . . There was a lot of that surface let's-play-punks horseshit, carefully arranged safety pins, strategically ripped shirts." This was punk degenerating into fashion and simple fare for the mass media to sensationalize. For Shirley, redemption came in the form of Richard Meltzer, the gonzo rock journalist who emceed the show (before Bill Graham, owner of Winterland, booted him from the stage). Meltzer, Shirley remembered, started making fun of the posers in the crowd, barking out lines like, "Hey you with the stupid passé green hair, fuck you—all right?" Shirley worried about punk turning "pure pose." He feared revolt could turn into style and empty gestures, which made the democratic communalism of Portland that much more important to him.[32]

All the while he sang and wrote lyrics for Sado-Nation and helped organize shows, Shirley dreamed of becoming a serious writer. He once explained to John Holmstrom of *Punk* magazine that he wanted to write a "science fiction story entirely (or almost entirely) about rocknroll." The story would deal with "violence" and would be "told from the viewpoint of a paranoic." And by 1979, he had already published two novels— *Transmaniacon* (a title that tipped its hat to a Blue Oyster Cult song about Altamont, "Transmaniacon MC") and *Dracula in Love*—both written earlier in his youth and both feeling immature to him.[33]

City Come A-Walkin', his first "mature" book, so to speak, told the tale of Catz Wailen, a singer in a punk band who rants against "disco" as "all computer made" and "a tool of repression, a soothing social sedative that helped reaffirm things-as-they-are." Shirley set the novel in San Francisco. There were references to actual San Francisco punk institutions like the Deaf Club venue (a hangout for deaf people that sponsored punk shows and that shut down in 1979) and punk bands ("the Odds" in the novel sound an awful lot like the Offs, an actual San Francisco punk band who had moved to New York City in 1980).[34]

The novel's central character is an antiheroic, noir figure named Stu Cole. He owned a small venue and bar called Club Anesthesia that the city government tried to shut down (making him something of a radicalized petty proprietor, somewhat like Dirk Dirksen, manager of San Francisco's Mabuhay Gardens who found himself in constant battle against the police and city government). Cole lived in the Mission District (an area seeing an influx of punks at the time) and was approaching middle age, with a paunch. He was well-read and intelligent—a guy who could "vacillate between street talk and the speeching [sic] of an educated man" (perhaps a bit like Raymond Chandler's Philip Marlowe). Cole embarked on a Faustian pact with "City," a collective unconscious that, when it materialized, wore "mirror sunglasses" that reflected away its evil intent. City seeks Cole's help in taking on a Mafia-type of organization.[35]

The story portrays Stu Cole falling in love with Catz Wailen. But the novel doesn't read like a love story so much as a debate about ethics and politics. One conversation goes like this: Cole announces to Wailen that he's become City's "vehicle" and that he's "fulfilling the frustrated desires of all the people in the city. In spite of the conditioning that makes them want to consciously accept [the system], unconsciously they want to fight back." Which sounded an awful lot like a sort of Leninist politics and vanguardism, or perhaps the anarchist concept of a "propaganda of the deed" where acts of terror intend to propel the masses into action, a philosophy at the heart of Joseph Conrad's *The Secret Agent*—another key and noted influence on Shirley. Cole even denies his own guilt at one point by blurting out that he was "not a fucking secret agent."[36]

Catz—the antihero hero of sorts—opposes Cole's alliance with City and his vanguardist justification for violence. She distrusts the commands set by City and their implied arguments against free will. She argues that City is better conceived as "the subconscious of hundreds of thousands of very fallible people." When Cole reasons to her that "I have to go through with it. I was chosen," Catz explodes with vitriol: "You make me sick. 'Chosen.' That's been the excuse of terrorists and dictators and religious fanatics—always an excuse for living some hidden hate." City senses Catz's disloyalty and drives a wedge between her and Cole. Catz eventually abandons Cole to the fate of continuing his work for City. Cole engages on a bombing mission and contacts a journalist to do an exposé of corrupt credit systems (which winds up getting the journalist killed), and then City literally steals Cole's physical body, leaving him to inhabit a mysterious, transcendental condition. Cole is left with an ambivalent, almost tragic, conclusion about his role in fighting City's war. "He reflected that he didn't resent the pirating of his body. It had been inevitable; he'd played into City's hands." Meaning for Cole that "City wasn't respon-sible, particularly. No more than anyone else in San Francisco. He was simply a physical manifestation of the unconscious frustrations forming and deforming in the collective unconscious." At this point, the book reads like a combination of Conrad, Carl Jung (the idea of a "collective unconscious"), and Jean Paul Sartre (on the "stupor and semi-sleep" of most people's existence and bad faith).[37]

In the final scene of the novel, Catz is in a recording studio and hears Cole's disembodied voice. Cole announces his return to San Francisco with hopes to "help [Catz's] career," a freighted term. Catz retorts, "Don't do me any favors." That line captured Shirley's punk ethics and the rebellious "no" of Camus. Shirley had gleaned it in Portland's music scene (the anarcho-syndicalism of Mark Sten) and developed it further in his reading of Jung and Conrad (among others). Its message: Never compromise, don't "sell out," and resist becoming what you hate.[38]

XXX

Showing the Actors to Themselves and What They Own

> It's funny how the colors of the like real world only seem really real when you viddy them on the screen.
> —Anthony Burgess, *A Clockwork Orange*[39]

A month after *City* was published, a group of people huddled in the Museum of Art's Theater in downtown Pittsburgh. They were there to watch the debut of a low-budget, self-produced movie, *Debt Begins at Twenty*. Many expected they'd have a cameo or their friends might. Stephanie Beroes, a recent graduate of the San Francisco Art Institute (an art school that helped birth many a punk band in the late 1970s), had moved back to her hometown of Pittsburgh, where she shot the film. She received a grant from the Pennsylvania Council on the Arts and borrowed equipment from a nonprofit organization called Pittsburgh Filmmakers. She used 16 mm black and white film, making it as cheaply as possible. Friends of hers introduced her to the local punk scene, es-pecially Bill Bored, who played in a band and edited a zine called *New Magazine*.

To a certain extent, *Debt Begins at Twenty* resembled the first punk film produced in America, Amos Poe's *The Blank Generation* (1976). Poe's movie showcased performances from the CBGB wave of American punk, like Patti Smith, Blondie, Television, Talking Heads, the Ramones. The sound wasn't synched for the film, making it almost purposefully disassociational. But with a strong focus on the performers, Poe's film inevitably elevated them above the audience. In contrast, Beroes captured bands performing—including the Cardboards, Hans Brinker and the Dykes, and the Shakes—but took the camera off the bands to show the audience and the democratic and communal feel that the scene had for her. Knowing art history, much like Pettibon and Mike Watt, she thought of the Pittsburgh scene as akin to Dadaism and the experimental theater performed at the Cabaret Voltaire, both radically individualistic and yet communal at the same time. The scene was "more in the spirit of poetry and social criticism" than the drugged out scene of New York City. She included shots of Pittsburgh to accentuate the fact that this was, well, Pittsburgh, not New York City. A line recurs throughout the movie, taken from the song lyrics of Hans Brinker and the Dykes: "I want to improve things for everyone, I want Pittsburgh to be fun. . . . Because I'm bored."[40]

Beroes invented a fictional story that intertwined with the filmed performances. It was often difficult, watching *Debt Begins at Twenty*, to discern documentary from fiction (a technique already found in the 1969 classic *Medium Cool*). Beroes filmed Bill Bored in his disheveled, graffiti-ridden apartment. She told him to do what he normally would if there wasn't a hulking camera present. So we watch the banality of everyday life as Bored eats a can of food, writes in his notebook, lies down in bed, and turns on the television (there are hints of Andy Warhol's mid-1960s films about the mundane here, especially *Eat*). Bored receives a phone call about an upcoming show, and he provides details to the caller. He comes off as the furthest thing from a rock star; he's simply one member of a wider community, someone who appears happiest sitting behind a drum kit rather than occupying the spotlight. As he explained his "punk philosophy"—which is announced by words flashed on the screen (the way Jean Luc Godard had done earlier in his films)—he downplays the importance of technical ability, providing sly commentary on his own "acting" in the movie.

In the end, the movie revealed the community to itself. The final scene shows one of the bands breaking down its equipment after a show. People on the floor are milling about, coming onto the very small stage (a foot off the floor at most, it looks). One person hands a flyer to another person. People talk with one another. Usually when the performances in rock movies end, the camera stops. Not here. This communal interaction is the flare of energy that punk held for Beroes, much like the sort Shirley had witnessed in Portland and that Biafra saw growing in San Francisco.

* * *

Debt's thoughtfulness contrasts with another film released on its heels. Entitled *Times Square*, it was the brainchild of an Australian-born "music magnate," Robert Stigwood, who had great financial success with films built around prominent soundtracks—such as *Saturday Night Fever* and *Grease* (soundtrack albums were a prime example of corporate "synergy" or tie-in). The sound-track for *Times Square* was taken from the first wave of punk in America—with songs by Patti Smith (who wasn't performing any longer), the Talking Heads, and the Ramones. The movie's story was romantic and unfathomable. It focused on a tough street girl, Nicky, who liberates Pamela from a psych ward. Pamela's father is an environmental commissioner with loads of cash, gunning to gentrify the Times Square area of Manhattan, the same neighborhood the two girls escape to. They occupy an abandoned building and form their own punk-ish band called the Sleez Sisters. A DJ broadcasts one of their songs on the radio (truly an impossible task by 1980). The movie crescendos with a performance of the Sleez Sisters in Times Square, after which Nicky darts into the night, escaping the police, and Pamela reunites with her father.[41]

The film epitomized Hollywood rebellion with its stylized ease and happy ending. The girls, no matter their circumstances on the streets, manage to wear punk costumes that appear clean and sparkly throughout. For the *L.A. Reader*, the film was "a misguided attempt to cash in on 'punk' or 'new wave' or anything else that appears to be happening at the moment." The rise to fame of the Sleez Sisters flew in the face of contemporary reality, as did the heroic DJ who did what he wanted. The *L.A. Reader* concluded that the movie was "based on callous, commercial consideration without a moment's thought to the message." [42]

While *Debt* provided the nuts and bolts of how to create a Do-It-Yourself scene, *Times Square* offered romantic fantasy. Viewers could see themselves playing the role that Bill Bored played. That it was Pittsburgh, not New York, hammered that home. *Times Square*, on the other hand, was *just a movie*, with all the put-down pejoratives those words carry.

XXX

Meet Your Future Entertainer-in-Chief!

That which appears is good, that which is good appears.

—Guy Debord[43]

On October 28, 1980, the Minutemen watched as their prediction that America would "swing to the right" came true. That evening President Jimmy Carter and Ronald Reagan debated for a national television audience (their only debate). At one point, Reagan chuckled as Jimmy Carter provided a list of things he had enacted to edge toward a national healthcare system. "There you go again," Reagan snickered, all that bantering about the good government could do. It sounded like a line from a movie, as if Reagan had practiced it with hopes of laughing Jimmy Carter offstage with a quip. During their debate, Reagan had successfully smiled his way past the pinched and gaunt face of Jimmy Carter (who had dropped his trademark grin from the past). He almost looked younger than Carter.

Many of his handlers thought Reagan had already won the election long ago, or perhaps that Jimmy Carter lost the election, way back on July 15, 1979, when the president went on television to give what became known as his "malaise" speech (which was really titled "The Crisis of Confidence" speech). Reagan hated the mood of that speech—with its gloomy pronouncements about the country's energy crisis. Carter's chief political sin was "blaming" Americans for the state of the country, as Reagan and his pollsters saw it (in his diaries, Reagan derided Carter for "losing faith" in the American people). What must have really driven Reagan nuts—considering his background—was that Carter had called America's consumer culture into question during the speech. Sounding like a somber social critic, a bit like the German social theorist Herbert Marcuse, Carter complained that "too many of us now tend to worship self-indulgence and consumption.

Human identity is no longer defined by what one does, but by what one owns." The statement flustered Ronald Reagan; after all, he was a man whose very presence on the debate stage relied on a consumer and entertainment industry—having been a radio announcer, a Hollywood actor, a host of the TV show *General Electric Theater* (where by 1958 he was considered "one of the highest-paid stars on television"), and a man who, when elected governor of California back in 1966, explained, "Politics is just like show business." Where Carter used the language of sacrifice and conservation, Reagan beamed "consumption without guilt," as the journalist Sidney Blumenthal put it. Reagan and the entertainment industry were one.[44]

An optimist with faith in the dream factory of Hollywood, Reagan didn't always appear to be a classical conservative. For sure, he consistently condemned government and praised free enterprise. But he never had any feel for the petty-bourgeois elements in society—that is, any virtues in smallness or close association between a producer of an item and its consumer. He loved the bigness of corporations and monopoly capitalism, those stable companies that could eat their losses but still produce "blockbusters," a term invented back in his studio days that was being heard more and more in the 1980s. Anti-trust sentiment was lost on Reagan. He had become a good "organization man" while working within the vast bureaucracy of General Electric in the 1950s (a corporation charged with price-fixing—a classic monopolistic move—when Reagan represented the company on television). Reagan and his handlers recruited corporate leaders—with brand names like Bloomingdale and Coors—into their circle of advisors. Two consultants, John Sears and Lyn Nofziger, tried, "without success," to get Reagan to "say something unkind about big business." No surprise he defended Hollywood's big studios against critics who saw them as monopolies stifling creativity. If anything, he didn't even like how the big Hollywood studios weren't allowed to dictate to theaters across the country what they should show on their screens (due to legislation dating to the 1940s). He thought that only large companies could provide the sort of "brand proliferation," like different movie titles or a model of a car or a breakfast cereal product, that ensured "choice" and "variety" along with stability. Business gave people what they wanted, Reagan assumed, and so democracy was confirmed in the act of a purchase, or better yet many purchases of the same thing. Carter failed to understand this.[45]

Reagan also believed that America would reject Carter's pessimism about the country's role in the world. At the time of Carter's malaise speech, Reagan talked up the legacy of his recently deceased war hero, John Wayne, who in the roles he played on the screen asserted a sense of American triumphalism. Reagan loved Wayne's swagger (his famous "walk"), the frontier persona of macho toughness. Such confidence could move the country beyond the Vietnam syndrome. Reagan refused to see Vietnam as a foreign policy blunder but as a "noble cause." He figured, like his predecessor Richard Nixon, that if the country hadn't lost its confidence it would have won the war. Now it was necessary to summon that courage to ramp up the Cold War, to rearm the nation in its battle against communism, the way it had before Vietnam. And he knew full well that a build-up relied on the large corporate arms manufacturers—giants like Lockheed and Martin Marietta—who would build the weapons that secured the "peace" Reagan believed came through "strength." Reagan had promised, in the words of Ronnie Dugger, the "largest peacetime increase in military spending in U.S. history."[46]

Ronald Reagan's enamor for big corporations providing entertainment and bombs made it easy for some young punks to hate the man. So too that "there you go again" quip. He sold everything with a smiles-a-lot, aw-shucks style that gave him a massive appeal. Reagan hoped to become a blockbuster in politics—sort of like the summer movie of 1980, *The Empire Strikes Back*, with its simplistic good versus evil theme. To offer optimism and cheer, all to foil the dark and dour Carter. And thus his campaign slogan: "Let's Make America Great Again." It was a conservative look back to a time in the past, plus a look forward to a renewal of America's bounty in the future, once Carter was gone. Just a week after his only debate with Carter, Reagan coasted to victory, armed with a smile that got the job done.

XXX

"Do You Feel Insulted When They Pull Out the Dope?"[47]

> We all know the three mighty slogans of the ascetic ideal: poverty, humility, chastity, and when we examine the lives of the great productive spirits closely, we are bound to find all three present in some degree.
>
> —Friedrich Nietzsche[48]

A month before Reagan's inauguration, the nation's capital witnessed the "Unheard Music Festival." The organizers of the show, Mark Halpern and Howard Wuelfing, were in their twenties. They had noticed recently that there was a swarm of punk kids in their teens coming to shows, having learned what they knew from their experience visiting Los Angeles and San Francisco last summer. Halpern and Wuelfing saw energy and possibility here that could supplement their own band, the Nurses, and Wuelfing's own zine, *Discords*. The line-up included Henry Garfield fronting SOA (State of Alert) and Alec MacKaye singing for the Untouchables. But in the wider scheme of things, the band that mattered the most that evening was Ian MacKaye's Minor Threat. Especially the group's stand-out song, "Straight Edge." It offered an anthem for a counterculture gelling in the nation's capital, about to spread across the country.[49]

The song "Straight Edge" started out with a rollicking and slightly brutish two-chord pattern, with MacKaye intoning over top, "I'm a person just like you . . . " before breaking into screamed vocals. Being a sober, aware, and angry young man, MacKaye claimed to have an "edge" over all the drunks and stoners who surrounded him, those who seemed to be "lost in space" (the title of an SOA antidrug song). If ever there was a clear line drawn between countercultures of the past and the counterculture bubbling up in Washington, D.C., now, it was certainly here: a complete disassociation of the time-worn "sex, drugs, and rock 'n' roll." Drugs were no longer seen as liberating but rather as oppressive and controlling, creating a slave mentality (like Pettibon's depiction of self-destructive hippies). A command for young people to stay aware in order to reject "turning on and dropping out." Instead, straight edge offered an ethics built around self-awareness—to sharpen your consciousness and scrutinize the way you live.

Soon after "Straight Edge" was performed, First Lady Nancy Reagan started to conceive her own "Just Say No" campaign against kids using drugs (which would eventually become one element in a wider "war on drugs" carried out by her husband). So perhaps there was a creeping conservatism in D.C.'s youth culture? Though MacKaye's song didn't really have any political message (just personal), the sentiment of "Straight Edge" echoed a long-standing critique of alcohol and drug abuse among predominantly leftist authors.

The tradition is discernable in Upton Sinclair's socialist protest novel *The Jungle* (1906) and Jack London's memoir *John Barleycorn* (1913). Both described how alcohol was a dangerous compensation for those down the rungs of the American class system—an opiate of the masses, to put it crudely. A deadening of the senses and awareness kept the working class mired in a capitalist hell. Aldous Huxley, in *Brave New World*, (1932) imagined how totalitarian control could come via pleasure, and described a "soma holiday" that lulled citizens into a state of placidity. Drugs as controlling mechanisms showed up later in the writing of the Beat and junkie author William S. Burroughs, especially in *Naked Lunch* (1959), where he wrote that "control can never be a means to any practical end. . . . It can never be a means to anything but more control. . . . Like junk." And in the post-hippie 1970s, Philip K. Dick, who had his own problems with drugs, wrote *A Scanner Darkly* (1977), a novel that centered around a bunch of wasted stoners leading burnt-out lives and a central character addicted to Substance D, which induced "brain death." The stoner kids in Dick's novel scrounge for themselves, walled off from the wealthy, who live in "fortified huge apartment complexes" policed by private "guards." There seems just one ethic growing among the drug-induced young: self-interest, looking for any chance to score and shut off reality. Dick explained the political message of his novel: "There is no moral in this novel; it is not bourgeois; it does not say they were wrong to play when they should have toiled; it just tells what the consequences were." As the San Francisco zine *Creep* saw it, drug use was just "the extreme way in which passive consumerism is institutionalized in this culture. The goal of life is felt to be the satisfaction or desires by consuming something." Later, Kim Gordon, bass player for Sonic Youth, would explain that straight edge opposed drugs and drinking "not so much out of puritanism as from a desire to be in control, and to avoid being manipulated by the consumerist system," more like Jack London than Nancy Reagan.[50]

There had been bands from the 1977 wave of punk who rejected drugs as part of the stupidity of rock celebrity: the Dils in California called themselves an "anti-drug band" as early as 1977, and Wire, a British band whose songs Minor Threat would cover, associated drugs with "the kind of 60s idea of the continuous party." Minor Threat simply updated these ideas for the 1980s—finding a contemporary rationale for sober angst.[51]

In fact, a book was rising on the bestseller list at the time that helped explain MacKaye's thinking. *The Official Preppy Handbook* was becoming the grand hurrah for Reagan supporters. If preppy stood for anything, it was a fetish of wealth and style—the culture of prep schools and Ivy League colleges, plus the look of "Izod Lacoste shirts," "corduroy pants," and "feathered hair." MacKaye would have seen it proliferating in the D.C. neighborhood of Georgetown, where he worked his day jobs at a movie theater and an ice cream store. Central to preppy culture was consuming alcohol (in high schools this became the infamous "keg party"). *The Official Preppy Handbook* counseled, "Failure to master the skill of consuming large amounts of alcohol will result in a lifetime of denied invitations. The cocktail's ubiquitous presence proves that pleasure is life's main concern." Indeed, sex for the preppy took place usually "when both are drunk, after a big party." It was this social-cultural imperative to drink that MacKaye rejected. The preppy of 1980 didn't drink to liberate himself from society's restrictions, he drank to conform, enacting a social imperative.[52]

The straight edge ethic set off controversy from the beginning, including among those who identified with the Washington, D.C., punk scene and who derided what they labeled "teeny punks." One of D.C.'s early zines, *Capitol Crisis*, recoiled at the sober upstarts often coming from D.C.'s burgeoning suburbs. The zine, edited by Xyra Harper, was surprisingly conservative in much of its orientation. The same year that the editor of *Punk* magazine (now defunct) and Johnny Ramone announced their vote for Ronald Reagan, the editors of *Capitol Crisis* expressed hope in his dawning presidency, praised Vietnam War veterans, and explained that "the momentum building towards unity, in this country, is a positive step," which sounded like a page out of Ronald Reagan's playbook. Certainly, new kids playing at the Unheard Music Festival didn't broach politics (some of them were openly apolitical). Still, Harper played out the *what's-up-with-kids-nowadays* logic to the hilt. She expressed nostalgia for the British "punk mood (become manifest) '76–'77" that "never caught on here," except among her small group. Harper explained that "many of us old folks (over 20) were involved in the original Punk scene (some of us) and ya had to be a little daring to do it, in Washington, in '77–'78." She wanted respect for the pioneering bands in D.C. like the Slickee Boys, the Insect Surfers, and Black Market Baby. Her complaints sounded an awful lot like the Hollywood punks in Los Angeles who recoiled at kids coming into their scene, and her term "teeny punk" sounded condescending to those who hated nostalgia and wanted to move ahead and make their own culture.[53]

Ian MacKaye crouched with ferocity when facing a critic. To call him argumentative is an understatement. He came from a family of writers, and though he didn't do well in high school, he loved to read and debate (becoming, like Jello Biafra, an autodidact who didn't want to go to college). He shot back at *Capitol Crisis*: "Forget what's happening in England and forget what's trying to happen in NY, the biggest established punk scene left is in California." MacKaye here referenced his direct observations made the previous summer. And he referenced a growth in D.C. of young people committed to making their own culture—via live music, the slam, and the insistence on "all ages" shows (something that the 9:30 Club would begrudgingly accept by 1981).[54]

What Harper and the oldsters couldn't understand, MacKaye explained, was that "what is happening, in Washington, now, is different than what happened in London 77 and NY 78. We are not running up and down the streets screaming 'Anarchy.'" That was likely a reference to the Sex Pistols, who were treated as history in two movies released in 1980, *The Great Rock and Roll Swindle* and *DOA*. This for sure: MacKaye realized his own background as white collar and middle class didn't really synch with the Sex Pistols' working-class identity. Calvin Johnson, a writer for Washington state's *Sub Pop* and *Op*, described the kids flocking to the D.C. scene as "insular, white, upper middle-class teenagers from Wilson," a public high school near the D.C.-Maryland border. Later, Henry Rollins described the new young punks in D.C. as "kooks, intellectuals: people who thought, people who wanted to write, people who were poets." Which came out in MacKaye's diatribe, when he claimed, "We are not complaining about how poor and misfortunate we are, and we are not doing it (what we do) because it is such a neat fad. We are using music as a vent of frustration, anger and energy." He faced the reality: the scene was populated in large part by white suburban males alienated from preppies and the lingering drug culture.[55]

Energy was what he was after—the sort that alcohol and drugs numbed and sapped. This idea reverberated in Black Flag's "Six Pack" (1981), with its line, "I know it'll be OK, when I get a six pack in me alright." There was also the band's "TV Party" (1981) that mocked kids drinking beer and watching television ("we've got nothing better to do than sit around and have a couple of brews"). It crystallized in the Dead Kennedys' "Drug Me" and "Too Drunk to Fuck," songs that took on the twin pillars of macho sensibility—drinking and hunting for sex. Around the same time as these songs emerged, a zine called *Straight Edge* started publishing from Long Island, New York, and a scene in Boston modeled itself largely on straight edge principles.[56]

MacKaye was surprised his idea caught on. After all, "sex, drugs, and rock 'n' roll" seemed a permanent association, and straight edge felt like a personal ethic more than anything. And yet, the idea resonated because it skewered the hedonistic conservatism of preppy culture as well as the decadent sensibilities of rock stars gorging on groupie sex, cocaine, and booze. By December 1980, punk witnessed another dead rock star, when Darby Crash, lead singer of the Los Angles punk band the Germs, followed in the footsteps of Sid Vicious and overdosed on dope. Around the same time, Don Henley of the California "mellow out" hit-machine, the Eagles, was arrested after he called paramedics to his house in order to resuscitate a sixteen-year-old prostitute (cocaine, ludes, and pot were found). Straight edge, for MacKaye, helped open up a new culture war—one that pitted straight angry kids against decadent rock star excess, passive consumerism, and the great American mellow out.[57]

XXX

"Reagan's In"

The era of self-doubt is over. . . . We have every right to dream heroic dreams.

—Ronald Reagan, Inaugural Address, January 20, 1981[58]

One month after the "Unheard Festival," the nation's capital rang for the Reagans. The decadence that "straight edge" inveighed against was every-where on display. Nancy Reagan's inaugural wardrobe alone cost $25,000, and Ronald Reagan's became the "costliest, most opulent inauguration in American history." Eight million dollars spent over the course of four days. Some of that went toward entertainment—that is, if you found Frank Sinatra's crooning performances entertaining.[59]

Before the evening balls and the rush of rented limousines, Ronald Reagan's inaugural speech had managed to strike the conservative hard line that government was no longer the solution but "the problem." And yet, at one point, he seemed to suggest that he was—like his predecessors Jimmy Carter and JFK—prepared to call for national sacrifice. During his address, he cited an unknown soldier, Martin Treptow, who had fought and died in World War I and whose diary Reagan found an inspiration. The lost soldier wrote, "I will sacrifice. I will endure." Reagan pretended that Treptow was buried in Arlington Cemetery (not too far from his inaugural speech), even though he knew the man had been buried near his home town in Wisconsin (a reference to Arlington would stir-up the imagined visual drama for Reagan). The president also concluded that, fortunately, "sacrifice" didn't have to take the form of Treptow's. "The crisis we are facing today does not require of us the kind of sacrifice that Martin Treptow and so many thousands of others were called upon to make." This was to be an easy patriotism, one that could erase the memories Jimmy Carter had of Vietnam and other American failures.[60]

One of the more surprising attendees at Reagan's inauguration was Andy Warhol, the 1960s pop artist who had painted Campbell soup cans and used his studio, "The Factory," as a hangout for drug-addled drag queens. As Mary Harron, who wrote for *Punk* magazine during the 1970s, stated around the time of Reagan's inauguration: "Warhol and the Factory stood as a symbol for everything that was urban and cynical and decadent." And also for everything Reagan would oppose with his talk about family values and religious faith. But the 1960s Warhol was not the 1980s Warhol. The Warhol of the 1980s was a friend of Debbie Harry and the editor of *Interview* magazine, which mimicked *People* magazine's cult of celebrity. He was a man who fawned over wealth and loved to shop. One of the leading and most intelligent punk zines out of Ohio, *The Offense*, described Warhol close to the time of the inauguration as "running with jet-set socialites and assorted ruling class piggies, painting portraits of royalty at six figures a crack, publishing his 'end of the capitalist rainbow' magazine *Interview*." Warhol's presence at the wealthiest inauguration in American history (and his decision to put Nancy Reagan's visage on the cover of *Interview* later that year) exemplified the transformation of bohemian into haute bourgeois, from the 1960s to the 1980s. Warhol could lock arms with a president by ignoring all that antidrug talk, while emphasizing their shared love for celebrity and wealth (the sort Blondie now projected, having learned from the master).[61]

* * *

As Reagan stepped onto the presidential stage, a keg ignited throughout the suburbs of Los Angeles and San Francisco. It built on Black Flag's angry sounds, the Minutemen's hyperkinetic anxiety, and the Dead Kennedys' merger of politics and dark humor. One band called Wasted Youth (a name with multiple meanings), out of Culver City, California, explained their anthemic song, "Reagan's In" to the editors of *Outcry*, a zine published in Pasadena. The lead singer, Danny, had just graduated from high school—now getting heat to sign up with the Selective Service, as many teens were (an issue that seemed to stoke only the hearts of young men, perhaps hinting at why 1980s punk was made up mostly of young men). In this context, Danny had no trouble explaining the significance of a song he had written with the title "Reagan's In." "We're saying things," he explained, "like . . . we're going for good; we'll fight and kill the best we could; no one cares if we die, reinstate the draft and tell us lies." The lyrics came at listeners fast, pulsating forward, as the song created a sound of speed. The L.A. band Bad Religion echoed Wasted Youth (though they played a bit slower) when they released an EP on which every title seemed a protest song—from "World War III" to "Slaves," the latter warning of conscription, turning kids into "slaves . . . to troop commanders."[62]

The band who best captured the anxiety of being a young male in 1981 and watching Reagan's ascent was True Sounds of Liberty (TSOL) out of Long Beach. Ron Emory, the band's guitarist, recalled the anger he shared with fellow band members about Selective Service: "We were all mad about it. We always thought World War III was coming and we're going to be the crop for the front lines." In their song "World War III" (same title as Bad Religion's), they'd sing: "If I don't register I have to pay, I refuse to go there's no fucking way. I won't go!" And then there was even a chant sound to the song as the singer repeated, "I won't go, I won't go, I won't go" (it was easy to imagine listeners repeating that mantra to themselves when the band performed live, sort of an invitation to the audience that it could contribute to the performance). Intense, oppositional ethics like this contrasted with the band's humor. Their name came from a "late night evangelical TV show" that offered a Christian band whose "musical tribute to God was the Sound of Liberty Band." As they explained to a zine out of Kansas a little later, they simply made "Sons of Liberty Choir" into "True Sounds of Liberty," mocking, in the process, the growing power of the religious right. Their radicalism could be found on almost all the songs on their first EP. In "Property Is Theft," TSOL channeled what one zine called "a statement originally made by a French Anarchist 141 years ago," namely Joseph Proudhon, who attacked "non-working proprietors" as leeches and therefore helped the band develop its belief that "money runs the world." In "Peace through Power"—which mimicked Reagan's slogan of "Peace through Strength"—they bemoaned a "foreboding gloom upon us, of death ribbons and bows." It confronted "twisted minds" that had made "Peace Through Power . . . their motto" and had made "Power through peace . . . their crime."[63]

The band's lead singer, Jack Grisham, projected an aura of charismatic chaos, which helped explain the band's rise to popularity. He wore dresses and make-up just to provoke his military father into a rage (likely freaking out a few teenage boys confused about their own sexuality). He slipped identity by changing his name on every record the band released. He declared his faith in anarchism in songs like "Abolish Government" but would then check his seriousness by singing songs about being jilted by high school girls and going to the cemetery to eke out his frustration and "fuck the dead." His mix of politics and humor explains why Jello Biafra recruited the band to join his label Alternative Tentacles.

True Sounds of Liberty was part of a suburban explosion of punk in Los Angeles during 1981—much of it fueled by young male anxieties about Reagan's victory. Fellow bands—the numbers kept growing—like the Adolescents sang about hormonal problems and loneliness (having to jerk "white tears," as the song "Creatures" explained). The band Agent Orange, out of Placentia, sang about melancholy and the break-up of friendships in "Like a Cry for Help in a World Gone Mad." The Descendents, out of Manhattan Beach, sang "I'm not a Loser" and mocked those who wanted to live in a "suburban home" like their parents did (as with Agent Orange, the band managed to sound fast-paced and yet with an infusion of pop and melody). Social Distortion, out of Fullerton, sang "Telling Them" about rejecting their parents' values, all the while singing a melodic chorus. The typical state of male adolescence—anxiety-ridden and confused—fueled these songs. Reagan's victory simply upped the ante on anxiety. It was like the feeling captured in a Raymond Pettibon drawing of a field of crosses—clearly a military cemetery (perhaps Arlington, where Reagan wanted Martin Treptow to be buried). Above the crosses rang the words, "YOU ARE NECESSARY." Necessary meaning expendable, what some suburban punk males certainly felt.[64]

Young male anxiety spread through the suburbs of Los Angeles, often with a political tinge. All of these bands were drawing larger crowds at the few venues that remained open. The zine *Noise*, out of Dayton, Ohio, received reports of 4,000 kids attending a TSOL, Adolescents, and Wasted Youth show in the San Fernando Valley. As the rock journalist Charles Shaar Murray had said about the explosion of punk in the performances of Patti Smith in 1975 and the swelling energy of CBGB and bands like Television: "Something's happening."[65]

XXX

The Politics of Angst

> Unhappy is he to whom the memories of childhood bring only fear and sadness. . . . Such a lot the gods gave to me—the dazed, the disappointed, the barren, the broken.
>
> —H. P. Lovecraft[66]

North of Los Angeles in San Jose, on a tree-lined suburban street called Teresita Drive, there was the office of the zine *Ripper*. It was fast becoming the hotbed of antidraft and World War III anxiety shouted by the likes of TSOL (whose first EP the zine praised), and it noted that its own scene in San Jose was burgeoning with young punks who were restive about life under the new president.

The origin story of *Ripper* is telling. Like many zines of the time, it came out of conversations among those interested in local music and broader ideas. Its editor, Tim Tanooka, was "a high school dropout" and an autodidact who wanted to create a forum for discussing music and politics, and who hooked up with Verna Wilson and her sister (who became coeditors). One conversation, in which the zine got off the ground, took place at the Upstart Crow Coffee Shop in the Pruneyard Shopping Center slightly south of San Jose. In 1980, the same year *Ripper* started, the Pruneyard Shopping Center had tried to challenge the right of high school students to distribute petitions calling for the United Nations to vote on the resolution that "Zionism is racism." The Pruneyard case went all the way to the Supreme Court, which ruled in favor of the State Court's argument that students had rights to free speech no matter the private management of the mall. The case symbolized the growing uneasiness about the privatization and commercialization of public space in suburbia, an environment that not only locked people into the privacy of their cars but often made the simple act of walking through ribbons of roads with no sidewalks impossible. *Ripper's* editors carved out a conversation in an unlikely location.[67]

The zine noted its nearby San Francisco predecessors, *Creep* and *Damage*, both of which synched discussion of new music with politics, and both collapsing at the time *Ripper* emerged. *Damage* would publish stories about graffiti and the alteration of urban billboards, the power of film noir of the 1940s, the assemblage art of Bruce Conner (who worked both in sculpture and film), the influence of Sam Shepard, the performance art of Johanna Went, the legacy of Dadaism, and, toward the end of its existence, the proliferation of punk in suburban settings, with a special focus on Los Angeles. When it came to political topics—an area that *Creep* explored more consistently—*Damage* highlighted the issue of registration for Selective Service. "If nothing else, draft registration, 1980, is a symbolic watershed," the editors wrote. The reinstitution of Selective Service was not just about making "symbolic gestures," to project an image of strength to Russians (the way *Rolling Stone* had reported it). *Damage's* editors argued that registration reflected a growing bellicosity, especially in the Republican Party. They noted, for instance, that Barry Goldwater had bellowed at the recent Republican convention: "Weakness leads to war!" They could also have cited a book Reagan possessed, Norman Podhoretz's *The Present Danger* (1980), which argued that Vietnam had turned America into a nation of effeminate sissies. Whatever evidence was chosen, *Damage's* anxiety about the Selective Service System carried over into the pages of *Ripper*.[68]

Ripper's editors knew plenty of teenage kids who faced the prospect of registration. For instance, there were the members of the band Social Unrest, from Hayward, California, a suburb of San Francisco. At the time *Ripper* interviewed the band in 1980, the youngest member was sixteen, the oldest twenty—thus directly affected by the Selective Service Act. The band members saw themselves as young and distinct from the "old days" when urban bands like the Avengers, Crime, and the Nuns dominated. Their anxiety was suburban in nature. They sang songs like "Sick and Tired of the Suburbs," which lamented "house after house, lawn after lawn." They talked about hating the Army recruitment advertisements posted at their school. And after all this angst, they slipped in their final point: "Oh yeah, we all hate the draft."[69]

From 1980 onward, *Ripper* attacked the Selective Service Act, which became almost a first principle of punk protest. They praised bands like No Alternative, who played an "anti-draft show for the San Jose Peace Center" and then, with (Impatient) Youth, organized another "anti-draft benefit at a church downtown" on February 6, 1981 ((Impatient) Youth had developed their own and rather catchy version of "Praise the Lord and Pass the Ammunition," originally a prowar song by Kay Kyser). And the editors grew heartened by an open resistance of a handful of young men who refused to register and announced their dissent. There was Paul Jacob, who went underground during the summer of 1981 after declaring he would not register. There were Ben Sasway, Ed Hasbrouck, David Wayte, and Russ Ford, who openly resisted and accepted their fate to be put behind bars. Though they chafed at the idea of prison time, the editors of *Ripper* praised these activists' courage and justified their rationale. For them, the Selective Service Act "has made us a generation of outlaws." Playing up the anarchist politics resonating in the lyrics of Bad Religion and TSOL, the editors of *Ripper* called the potential for a draft a form of "slavery." They set out a difficult ethics of resistance. "By requiring registration the government is saying, 'Your life is not your own. You belong to US. You are government property. We will tell you what to do.'" The threat of the draft demeaned the autonomy of all young men. *Ripper* also took a page from *Damage*: kids shouldn't be fooled into disassociating the draft from the larger calls to war coming from the right. As they saw it, quiet acceptance and "apathy" translated into de facto "support" for the war machine America was becoming. Later in 1982, they'd conclude: "Registering is active and effective support for a draft, the government, and its wars." This was a tough ethic for any young man to face, especially since nonregistration carried with it the prospect of five years in prison and a $10,000 fine.[70]

Ripper played its role in a small but growing movement against Reagan's bellicosity. Indeed, the federal government, as the *L.A. Reader* would report, had declared draft resistance a "large problem." Just how large was difficult to assess, but the biggest organization working on Selective Service, Draft Action, declared that the numbers of resisters rose during 1981, with about 700,000 nonregistrants; that number would climb to one million by 1982. *Ripper* tried to take what might be seen as youthful apathy or simple forgetfulness to register and interpreted it as semiconscious resistance to Reagan's triumphalism and militarization of society.[71]

* * *

The energy spread from San Francisco's suburbs to the Seattle area, which by 1981 had developed a burgeoning scene. The band that seemed to get the most attention was the F@rtz, who sounded a lot like Wasted Youth, except a bit more humorous. Like TSOL, they were self-proclaimed anarchists, their political philosophy a peculiar blend of personal experience and reading about the American past. The bass player, Steve, had served in the American military and grew fed up with hierarchy and rigidity; the drummer, Loud, got his anarchism from reading the Yippie activist Abbie Hoffman (who had also inspired Jello Biafra). The band was, in the words of *Noise* zine (Dayton, Ohio), "very political," meaning "anti-War, anti-government, etc." The F@rtz welcomed "kids who come from the suburbs" and preserved a sense of democratic humility. As *The Attack* explained, "There's still room for humor (even a bit of self-parody which Blaine [the band's rambunctious lead singer] practically embodied)." The band took up Jello Biafra's art of provocation, hoping to avoid imposing their own views. "We're just offering an option that you have a choice to think for yourself." "We're not trying to brainwash people," explained Steve. One of the band's trademark songs was titled "You Got a Brain (Use It)" (which clocked in below a minute long). No wonder Biafra signed the band up with his independent label Alternative Tentacles, the way he had TSOL.[72]

The band's anti-authoritarianism made them staunch opponents of the growing religious right, but also of the totalitarian left. For instance, they hated the Revolutionary Communist Party (RCP), which was busy trying to recruit angst-ridden punk kids at shows. The RCP was a tiny faction that had split off from the disintegration of Students for a Democratic Society (SDS) in the late 1960s; it was now headed by Bob Avakian, who lived in exile in France while still overseeing the organization's newspaper, *The Revolutionary Worker* (the Teen Idles had a song that went, "Before you pillage, rape and rob, who in the hell is this guy named Bob?"). Not surprisingly, it was Steve who attacked the RCP, seeing similarities between military duty and following the ideology of a political party. "They get all their information straight out of a book or what was drilled into their head." Slaves to ideology, RCP members were "not thinking for themselves, they're thinking for Bob Avakian, for his gains." Inherently suspicious of those seeking power, Steve argued that Avakian "just wants to be a Hitler. He's gonna control the United States when the R.C.P. supposedly takes over in their revolution." Thus, anti-authoritarianism had enemies on both right and left. As the Southern California zine *Night Voices* argued in 1981, the RCP envisioned "another system . . . just as oppressive, if not more than the previous one." The F@rtz would have agreed.[73]

The F@rtz's drew much of their energy from their predecessors in a burgeoning Seattle scene that had grown out of the late 1970s. There were bands like the Refuzors, the Blackouts, the Fastbacks, and Solger (a group from whom the F@rtz literally drew from when the band's guitarist—Paul Dana (aka Paul Solger)—eventually left to play with the F@rtz). Energy also grew from bands forming close in time to the F@rtz—The Rejectors (who emerged a bit later and proclaimed their motivation, in part, was concern with "the draft, since we are all draft age") and the Accused. This growing energy wasn't just about bands but about zines forming at the time as well. Perhaps one of the most interesting pieces of evidence that energy was growing in Seattle was the zine, *Punk Lust*, edited by one of the more interesting characters in the history of early 1980s punk, Wilum Frogmarsh Pugmyr (aka W.H. Pugmire).[74]

Pugmire was no young, teeny punk. By the time he was editing *Punk Lust*, he was in his early thirties. He had a rough childhood, being raised a Mormon and becoming, in his own words, "a wimpy wee fag in high school" who got beaten up a lot. He took salvation in watching the *Twilight Zone* television show, with its weird, creepy sci-fi stories and signature hypnotic music. He turned bookish and created his own fanzines fifteen years before the Seattle punk scene erupted (the zines were predominantly sci-fi and horror oriented). The drawings he did for his zine were gothic and grotesque, unlike Pettibon's art in form, but still hoping to provoke associations and memories. When he first heard the F@rtz perform, he realized the way they *sounded* was "thrilling." For Pugmire, the band's music "never touched the realms where music usually dwelled, as entertainment, diversion, danceability at all, passing them at the speed of a thought. This sound was a . . . war." A war that ignited both anger and intelligence. "Punk has shown me," Pugmire explained, "that I should be angry, and that I can express my anger in the way I look, as well as the way I think."[75]

Pugmire's biggest literary debt was to "supernatural horror" as a form of social criticism. His favorite author was H. P. Lovecraft (John Shirley was turning to Lovecraft for inspiration at the time as well). Lovecraft's stories—his method descended from Edgar Allen Poe—criticized the idea of progress, the belief that the past could be forgotten as humankind charted its future (following Henry Ford's dictum, "History is bunk."). In Lovecraft's stories, the past haunts the present, as in "The Rats in the Wall" or "The Shunned House," in which buildings hide secrets that return to haunt present-day inhabitants. Lovecraft condemned "callous rationalism" that eschewed the supernatural and phantasm (much like the surrealists). He wrote largely about dreamlike states, where the unconscious erupted in grotesque visions and when things once thought inanimate turned alive, as Sigmund Freud once described "the uncanny." Lovecraft's dreams testified to humankind's limits, to inabilities to repress the past or control the present. His embrace of the gothic was heavily intellectual, unlike the fashionable "gothic" look of the East Coast band the Misfits (whose staged approach, replete with dark make-up and costumes, reminded Ian MacKaye of the "shtick" arena band Kiss). For Pugmire, gothic was not a look or a style but an idea that cut against the naive American faith that the past was absolutely past (the way Reagan tried to change Americans' memories of Vietnam). As the zine *Sub Pop* put it, Pugmire was "sincere, gothic, [and] totally original."[76]

Pugmire's zine invited letters, and one person who wrote him consistently was a young punk entering the scene at the time, Mark Arm (born Mark Thomas McLaughlin). Arm had grown up mostly in the suburb of Bellevue, where his parents sent him to a Christian school. Bellevue was a conservative suburb, very Republican, and Arm sweated out his teen years and suburban existence, trying to find some alternative to the arena rock of Kiss, Ted Nugent, REO Speedwagon, and Foreigner, whose records were sold at the Totem Lake Mall. And then he discovered punk, especially the British anarchist band Crass and the Minutemen. After finishing high school, he left the Seattle area for Linfield College in Oregon, but chafed at the provincialism there, returning to the Seattle area, where he took philosophy courses at the University of Washington. He was inspired by *Punk Lust* and the F@rtz, and went on to form his own band with his school friend Smitty, Mr. Epp and the Calculations (the band was named after one of their teachers). They became known for songs like "Mohawk Man," a humorous send-up that mocked the "trendy assholes of the punk scene," those reducing everything to style (the song also moved much slower than most of the band's contemporaries and cinched together beating drums with feedback and weird reverb). Arm also expressed himself in the zine he formed with Smitty, *The Attack*.[77]

The synergy between Mr. Epp and *The Attack*—the merger of band and zine, music and ideas, providing expression in sound and the printed word at once—was also visible in another experimental band called Audio Letter (sometimes spelled Audio Leter) formed by Sharon Gannon and Sue Ann Harkey in 1979 (but playing out more regularly by 1981). The band was a bit less bratty than Mr. Epp, and the thinking behind it more sophisticated, though still anarchist. Often employing unedited sounds and tape loops, the band was once described as "a punk-sensitive postmodern sound" (closer to Mr. Epp than the F@rtz). The band took its name reportedly from a "guy in Texas who sends mail-order cassettes where he reads his conspiracy theories." To explore their ideas, Gannon and Harkey formed the Citizens for Non-Linear Futures, which published the zine *Patio Table* (also sometimes called *Patio X Table*). There was little discussion of music in the zine. Instead, there were head-spinning discourses on feminism and the way science objectified the natural world and legitimized ecological catastrophe. Gannon and Harkey were some of the first to show interest in the Situationist International and the writings of the Frankfurt School, as well as Wilhelm Reich's theories of fascism. One of the topics that recurred in *Patio Table* was the argument for animal rights and vegetarianism. They criticized the mechanization of murder in large slaughterhouses and promoted the British movie *The Animals Film* (1981), a gross-out that showed the disemboweling of cows on a conveyor belt. What upset them the most was how Americans grew distant from the process by which their food was made. They attacked the fur industry and the laboratory testing of cosmetics on animals. This was the natural underbelly of American consumer culture, which always separated consumers from the act of production.[78]

The final zine in Seattle worth mentioning is *Desperate Times*, which was the exception to the rule here of bands and zines connecting with one another. Run out of a communal house mostly by young women (showing that though largely male, there were certainly females coming into the movement, beyond Audio Leter), the zine lasted only for the summer of 1981. But during that time, it promoted the idea that music and ideas worked best when joined together: "Music is the only real revolutionary force in this country —in terms of affecting the thought of masses of people—and punk is the only musical form to really hook into that potential power since the days of ol' Country Joe doing the first-one-on-your-block-to-have-your-boy-come-home-in-a-box." That alluded to one of the more famous antidraft protest songs heard at Woodstock in 1969. The editors agreed with Mark Arm that the biggest challenge for Seattle's burgeoning scene was a lack of venues for shows. The most well-known venues, Danceland, Showbox, and Wrex, were jacking admission prices. *Desperate Times* considered a boycott of overpriced clubs. They organized meetings for Seattle punks to discuss the possibility and argued: "By establishing our own values and demanding their worth it will force promoters to work within that standard, and attract a creative promotional system." Nothing seemed to come of this, but it suggested a growing political consciousness about DIY and its demanding ethic.[79]

XXX

Showing the Actors to Themselves Again

The air in utopia is poisoned . . .
> —Brendan Mullen, in *The Decline of Western Civilization*

On March 13, 1981, *The Decline of Western Civilization* debuted at the Hollywood Boulevard Theater. "Over 300 policemen descended on" people gathering out front, creating chaos and conflict. The theater sat 1,200, and they had to have two showings to quell the crowds that had gathered. It would seem that the movie's director, Penelope Spheeris, had touched a nerve in her portrayal of a culture war taking place in Los Angeles.[80]

Penelope Spheeris was born in 1945 and raised mostly in California by her mother, a barmaid, circus player, and alcoholic. Her father had been a wrestler, killed in Alabama when she was only six years old. She started showing an interest in psychology as an academic subject, but then fell in love with filmmaking, attending the prestigious UCLA Film School (her student films were fake documentaries, one about protestors against the Vietnam War being driven into government-run concentration camps— seemingly like Peter Watkins's 1971 *Punishment Park*). Her first job was making music videos—before they were called that—of bands like the Doobie Brothers, a not terribly uplifting experience. She then hooked up with the comedian and director Albert Brooks, who was doing some shorts for the television show *Saturday Night Live*. She helped produce Brooks's full-length movie *Real Life* (1979), a funny mockumentary about the PBS series *An American Family*, which documented the disintegration of a marriage as television cameras invaded a family's suburban home.[81]

And then, just as she was growing frustrated about her prospects in Hollywood, she found punk, right in her own backyard. Her then husband, Robert Biggs, was editor of *Slash* magazine and owner of Slash Records. Thus, she had an easy-in. But it was her own anger that propelled her. "I myself was so pissed by ten years in Hollywood," she explained, that she felt simpatico with punks. She hoped to capture their anger on film.[82]

She pitched her idea to every studio she could, only to face cold shoulders. She was saved, so to speak, by "a couple of insurance salesmen from the San Fernando Valley" who were "looking for a porno movie" but settled for a documentary about the L.A. punk scene instead. They gave her $50,000 to work with and artistic independence. She started to film shows and interviewed bands and other participants throughout the first five months of 1980. Spheeris also started to conceptualize her approach to the subject matter. First, there was her rival from UCLA film school days, Paul Schrader, who had had an illustrious career, most recently with *American Gigolo*, released when Spheeris had started filming. When Spheeris had shown her student movies to an audience, including Schrader, he criticized her confrontational, in-your-face approach. As she watched *American Gigolo*, Spheeris found the film unreal, too light, too pastel and glittery, smooth surfaced, with a cushy, soft glow. "I couldn't make something like *American Gigolo*," Spheeris explained, "it has to feel real." She wanted a neo-noir tone to her film—something that Schrader had helped pioneer with *Taxi Driver* but now drifted away from—and for some interviews she had subjects sit in a dark room with just a bare light bulb dangling above their heads.[83]

Spheeris resisted the cliché of "rock and roll movie." She did not want to present a string of performances, and she wanted the audience to get as much attention as the bands (in contrast to a movie released soon after hers: *Urgh! A Music War*). In other words, she was closer to *Debt Begins at Twenty* than *The Blank Generation*. Brad Lapin at *Damage* praised *Decline* because it came "close to documenting the excitement that is the essence of the rock'n'roll experience and, even more significantly still, the first to explore in depth the ideas and attitudes of the musicians and fans whose combined energy produces that excitement in the first place. . . . [The movie] is a spectacle but one that's in-process." Spheeris would concur; it was like filming movement. She noticed younger blood—the first wave of suburban kids—entering the scene just as she started shooting. The punk scene was fast changing, making the movie a historical document, telling about the past in a sped-up culture. Spheeris admitted that if she made the film after the explosion of suburban bands throughout 1981 she could have made a "more powerful film."[84]

Nonetheless, she saw these kids as revolutionaries of a sort. "Punk is the only form of revolution left," one participant tells her. But here was a tension. Sometimes punk came off as an acerbic form of intelligence, and at other times as stupid, anti-intellectual, and violent. At certain points, the editor of *Slash*, Claude Bessy, would blast out pronouncements about the fakeness of "new wave" and his own conceptualization of punk intellect as based around provocation: "I'm not using this contempt" as a "style," he explains in the film. He hopes instead to jumpstart and provoke his readers' thinking (these scenes also feel historical, since Bessy had left the United States before the final version of the movie was released in order to escape the Reagan presidency). This was the same Claude Bessy who a year and a half earlier became the first to encourage punks to look into the complex theoretical writings of the Situationist International. And he was notorious for giving encouragement to other zines that were just getting off the ground by 1980. There are also long shots of the bassist from Black Flag, Chuck Dukowski, who many people considered the intellectual of the band, who talks about hippies having been "neutralized" and then pondering the psychobiology he had studied in college (an area of intellectual interest he shared with Spheeris). And then at other times, there are Eugene and Michael X-Head, who sound preposterously dumb. Eugene, a young teenager who hung around the scene, talks about hating "old people" and the "buses" in Los Angeles (buses?!). Michael X-Head brags about putting a guy in the hospital and "beating people up." Spheeris never scrutinized such statements, playing the role of objective recorder.[85]

Here was the movie's risk. Some might watch it for the intelligent wit found in Bessy and Dukowski, and some might watch it for the dumbed-down violent braggadocio of X-Head. As the movie made it to a place like Washington, D.C., writers at *Capitol Crisis*—the zine that had coined the term "teeny punk"—were divided, some thinking that the film made punk into a form of "closed-mindedness." Another letter writer from Bethesda, Maryland (a suburb of Washington, D.C.), argued that the movie was realistic, that many kids have been "getting agro from cops and their peers" and thus have turned violent, like it or not (also suggesting that this might be better understood as a movie about L.A. punk, and that the scene shaping up in D.C. wasn't nearly as violent). It suggested that as much as some wanted punk to be a singular thing, it was really an ongoing conversation among participants. Brad Lapin rightfully called *Decline* a work that helped open a wider conversation in the making.[86]

XXX

The Politics of New Romance

The only positive thing about punk was that it was a revolt in style.

—Adam Ant, 1981[87]

They stood armed with nothing more than rotten eggs, readied for war, or at least a good deluge. It was just ten days after an assassination attempt on Ronald Reagan's life, which likely upped the tension in the air. Most gathered were young punks eager to vent their anger. Some wore stickers on their t-shirts that read "Black Flag Kills Ants On Contact." They had gathered at Tower Records in downtown Los Angeles on April 11, 1981, awaiting the presence of the lead singer of Adam and the Ants, the newest import from Britain intended to drive kids wild, with hopes of recreating the "Beatlemania" of 1963–1964. The talk now was of an "Ant Invasion." The band was part of something bigger, calling itself—as if pronouncing a death—"post-punk."[88]

Adam had been active in the punk scene that created the Sex Pistols, mostly interested in Malcolm McLaren's famous "Sex" Shop that sold punk T-shirts and bondage paraphernalia (McLaren managed Adam before moving onto Bow Wow Wow). Adam and the Ants were known for their "look" as much as their music—more for style than sound. During the time of the egging, the *L.A. Weekly* explained how the band would "wear Indian warpaint and feathers, pirate stripes and sashes," a sort of postmodern bricolage. They seemed to "adore Hollywood and America and especially the Wild Frontier." There were other bands growing in popularity alongside Adam and the Ants during the spring and summer of 1981, many of them remembered nostalgically today as core to the "sound" of the 1980s: Duran Duran (whose semipornographic music video of "Girls on Film" would become a huge MTV hit when reissued in 1983), Spandau Ballet (one punk zine labeled them the "electronic Glam-boys for the 80s"), Heaven 17, Depeche Mode (with its "trendy electro-disco."), and Haircut 100.[89]

Though it wasn't a coherent movement with a manifesto, new romantics shared a penchant for synthesizers and drum machines—making the music more programmable and thus mechanical sounding (a critic at the *L.A. Weekly* called it "technology-dulled music"). One zine writer believed the more chintzy and electro feel would dominate the mainstream music of the 1980s, whereby "the peppy synth has taken the place of the roaring Gibson [guitar]." Another alluded to new romanticism as "synth shit-twitching, neurotic shit." John Crawford, creator of the punk cartoon character Baboon Dooley, zeroed in on the overuse of the synthesizer in this "new romance" music, arguing that they have "HAVE to use that shit" to get their "investment. . . . Machines over music and musicians, the convenience of capital over people." The music wasn't just mechanized, it was supposed to be dance music, a return to disco. Praise for it came from the British magazine *The Face*—a slick publication that focused on "Music, Movies, Style" (and featured Adam Ant on its cover in April 1981, the time of the egging). *The Face* emphasized fashion and a "look" that had erupted within the "club culture," especially the Blitz in London. *Own the Whole World*, a zine out of Akron, Ohio, explained the history to its readers, arguing that new romanticism was for the British "aristocracy," those with money for the requisite fashion purchases: "In 1981 the 'New Romantics' came into being. Steve Strange had his fashionable 'Blitz' Club where all the chic types swirled and cooed to Spandau Ballet, Haircut 100, Ultravox, and Roberto Duran Duran," making "English 'synth-pop . . . the new musical trend" of the year.[90]

New romanticism was more than a trend, though, because it offered an implicit conservatism that went along with Thatcherite (and now Reaganite) politics. These bands and their fashion sensibilities replaced the anger of punk—heard in the curdling cry of Johnny Rotten—with a despairing quietude. Synth pop was another call for Jello Biafra's "mellow out." Duran Duran, for instance, wanted "to be the band to dance to when the Bomb drops." When Jello Biafra heard new romanticism at trendy nightclubs in Los Angeles and New York City, he could not help hearing an echo of "the cabaret culture in Berlin, pre-takeover period. People are drawing into their own cocoons." He condemned, in an interview with *Desperate Times*, the "celebration of wealth and snootery" new romanticism represented. Punk zines pilloried new romanticism's conservative narcissism. *Ripper* called it "superficial glamor." The zine *Cranial Crap*, published in the suburbs of New Jersey, shouted: "We don't need this fashion groove thang. I boycott Spandex Ballet and Durhan Durhan—it's in your own best interest." Bob Moore's *Noise* (out of Dayton, Ohio) echoed the rejection of "all these New Romantic blitz Spandau Antpeople who worship fashion and dancing to repetitive eurodisco technopop. New Romanticism is the New Wave is the New Disco."[91]

Others—like the editors of *Take It!*, based in Boston—believed the new romanticist fad repeated a refrain in American cultural history, in which Americans genuflected to anything from Britain. They rolled out a sort of "buy American" proposal without the jingoism. Jello Biafra felt compelled at this time to put together a compilation album of punk bands across the United States—including the Dead Kennedys and Black Flag, but also Feederz (originally from Arizona), Bad Brains (originally from Washington, D.C., now in New York City), Really Red (Houston, Texas), Flipper (from San Francisco), and Half Japanese (from Maryland). Biafra saw the compilation as an act of patriotism, a humble variant of national pride. But it also grew from a critique of the reign of Reagan. It was titled *Let Them Eat Jellybeans*. Jellybeans, after all, were purported to be Reagan's favorite food, and there was the obvious reference to Marie Antoinette's remark that the starving masses could eat cake. The cover of the album showed a smiling president giving the thumbs-up with an American flag behind him. Released on Biafra's Alternative Tentacles label, the album promised to promote the most creative bands in America, while at the same time confronting "America's Darker Side."[92]

So maybe those kids tossing eggs at Adam Ant thought of themselves as inheritors of the American revolutionary tradition that rejected British imports, or maybe they were just pranksters who hated celebrity culture, or maybe they rejected how new romanticists moved from "revolt" to "style." One thing for sure: Their act represented a desire for their "own culture" and screamed "no!" to the importers of chic.

XXX

A Clash of Wills (Punk History 101)

> Men make their own history, but not spontaneously, under conditions they have chosen for themselves; rather on terms immediately existing, given and handed down to them.
>
> —Karl Marx[93]

A month after the egging of Adam Ant, Tim Yohannan invited Bill Graham onto his "Maximum Rock 'n' Roll" radio show (MRR from now on), which was broadcast to San Francisco on KPFA. It became a showdown between two oldsters, whose outlooks were shaped by their different experiences in the 1960s and who now faced questions about the future of punk in the 1980s.

Perhaps even more than *Rolling Stone* magazine, Bill Graham symbolized a "rock establishment." He was a tough Polish Jew who had barely escaped the terrors of the Nazi Holocaust during his childhood. But as he emigrated to the United States and then entered the hippie scene of San Francisco in the mid-1960s, he charted a vision of "hip" capitalism that squeezed profits from the counterculture. A bicoastal jet-setter who spent most of his time barking into phones, Graham could still remember his halcyon days in San Francisco. He had helped Ken Kesey put on his "Trip Festivals" back in 1966, where the Grateful Dead played noodling guitar solos in rooms full of strobe lights and acid-fueled dancers. Those events were early money-makers for Graham (he supposedly grossed $16,000 off the Trips Festivals). Soon after the Summer of Love of 1967, with kids flocking to Haight-Ashbury with "flowers in their hair," he made his Fillmore West the mecca of psychedelic rock, grossing profits off performers like the Jefferson Airplane and Janis Joplin, with oversold, high-tech light shows. For Graham, rock was a staged, spectator form of entertainment. As the radical magazine *Scanlan's* once quipped, when Bill Graham took over the Fillmore West he turned "dances," where the audiences *did things*, into "concerts." He also started the Fillmore East (in New York City's East Village) and was called in as a consultant for the infamous Woodstock concert (in the movie Warner Brothers made about the festival, Graham can be heard shouting out for "control" over audiences he compares to "ants"). As the sixties bled into the seventies, Graham opened up the Winterland venue in San Francisco, a larger setting than the Fillmores but still smaller than the huge arenas and coliseums that now dominated rock performances. He continued to reap profits. From 1972 to 1977, Graham had grossed from 100 to 150 million dollars, which helped fuel his growing cocaine habit.[94]

When Graham heard that the Sex Pistols were coming to San Francisco to play a small club on their unorthodox tour of 1978, he pounced, seeing green. Graham went onto radio (KSAN) and asked listeners if they wanted the Sex Pistols to play a venue large enough for high demand—meaning his own Winterland. Thousands sent in postcards saying yes, and Graham used these to persuade Malcolm McLaren, the band's manager, to play his hall instead of a smaller venue. McLaren wanted the local San Francisco band Negative Trend—some of whose members would later form Flipper—to play after the Sex Pistols' set (the Sex Pistols would then appear as an "opening act" for a younger band). Graham hated the idea, even though he consented to it at the time. When the show went on, he exerted his control by kicking off the stage the rock journalist and philosopher Richard Meltzer, who had impressed John Shirley as the show's emcee, and then refusing to let on Negative Trend.[95]

Graham's penchant for control drove Tim Yohannan (from now on Tim Yo) berserk. If Graham symbolized hip capitalism, Tim Yo drew energy from remembering the 1969 struggle over People's Park in Berkeley, California, an event that framed his worldview for life (similar to the way the Paris Commune framed the worldview of late nineteenth-century radicals). Yo was six years younger than Graham (and the same age as Penelope Spheeris), having found his way to San Francisco around 1967, after attending Rutgers University in his home state of New Jersey. He was in his mid-twenties when the battles over People's Park erupted in Berkeley in 1969. People's Park, in Yo's own words, had been a "trashed square block of University of California property that served as a parking lot and was full of abandoned vehicles." Through a concerted effort at grassroots organizing and pressure, citizens turned it into "a community controlled open space." Local citizens volunteered daily to lay sod and build a park. During April, "up to three thousand people a day" volunteered. Todd Gitlin, one-time president of SDS, explained at the time, "As substance and sign of a possible participatory order, as the living and hand-made proof that necessary institutions need not be overplanned, absentee-owned, hierarchical—as such the Park came to stand in many minds as one tantalizing trace of a good society." That voluntary, free, participatory spirit energized Yo for some time to come. So too did the backlash ridden by the then governor of California, Ronald Reagan, who called in the National Guard to repossess the park for the university. Protests erupted, including one where a young man, James Rector, was shot to death. Yo drew the lesson that a participatory culture required vigilance. There was a desperate, absurdist sensibility that People's Park prompted for him, something that nurtured his own dark humor.[96]

Yo knew his radio audience and consciously reached out to the young punks Jello Biafra had seen entering the scene (Yo called them "new legions of young, pissed-off middle-class kids"). Starting in 1979, he made flyers for the MRR show to be distributed at over fifty high schools in the area. In April of that year, he organized a protest to demand that KPFA expand the MRR show, and 150 protestors showed up waving signs that read "KPFA Eats its Young," "No Wimp Rock for the 80s," and "Down with Disco."[97]

Now, with Bill Graham eyeing the burgeoning punk scene, Yo drew aghast. He first helped New Youth Productions (NYP), which wanted to boycott any show Graham organized. Now that NYP had gone belly up, Yo decided to confront the man face-to-face. On May 12, 1981, Graham sat down for a discussion, and Yo made his charge that punk in the 1980s promised a "total culture" to be controlled by its participants:

You've lost touch with the culture that the music belongs to. It's not just another pre-packaged creation by Warner Bros.—this is still an organic process that's happening. But what happens when business runs into this process? It tends to disrupt it, sterilizes it, makes it safe. This is a folk culture which music is only a part of.

Graham, to most listeners' surprise, agreed, at least to a certain extent. But then he went on to argue that punks at shows were jumping on stage, pissing in the aisles, and graffitiing the walls. He called punk "immoral and inhuman," which sort of let the cat out of the bag (why promote something immoral and inhuman?). So Yo pushed his point: What if Graham got together with nightclubs that competed with him and agreed to "get out of this scene." They could "do rock music, and leave punk alone." Graham surprisingly conceded, and Yo went to work on drawing up a more formal agreement. As spring turned to summer in San Francisco, Yo called meetings and got Graham's competitors to concede to an agreement to stay out of punk. Knowing there might be contestation as to what constituted "punk," Yo drew up a back-up plan that would simply call for "ceilings on ticket prices." To no one's surprise, Graham changed conditions and tried to weasel out of any restriction on his business activity.[98]

So Tim Yo didn't win. But he had made it clear that kids could grow some clout by threatening to create their own culture, one that they controlled and defended against those seeking profit (the protest *Desperate Times* had proposed). Punk was becoming a form of political activism that worked from the bottom up, but that also relied on leaders who had historical perspective. It was like People's Park: create something yourself, lay the sod, and then defend it against those with power. Broadcast your message, using community radio and flyers and some old-style marching, if necessary. The sixties, for Yo and his compatriots, had nurtured a "usable past" of events that came prior to the "mellow out" diagnosed by Jello Biafra. People's Park helped deepen the history of the 1960s for punks, moving beyond Raymond Pettibon's focus on psychos like Manson. Yo envisioned kids struggling to create their own cultural space, free from the pressures of a for-profit culture. It might be doomed to defeat and absurdist in its nature, but there it was.

XXX

More Oldsters Debate

> I invented punk. Everybody knows that.
>
> —Lester Bangs, 1981[99]

In the August 1981 issue of *Musician* magazine, the rock journalist Lester Bangs, who had taken down Blondie a year earlier, stewed about his middle-agedness and tried to get a sense of what was happening among young people. He gasped at a recent revival of the late sixties band the Doors, and he could see no traces around him of any vibrant youth culture. Instead, teenagers huffed the fumes of 1960s bands who dominated the radio waves (what would be called "classic rock"). Bangs never had kids, so he hit up "the younger brother of an old girlfriend" who was a recent high school graduate playing in a Detroit rock band to figure out what was going on. Bangs asked him who his favorite bands were and was shocked to hear a litany of 1960s groups—Yardbirds, Cream, and the Doors. He asked: "Can you imagine being a teenager in the 1980s and having absolutely no culture you could call your own?"[100]

Could Bangs see what was happening right in front of his eyes? After all, the previous April he had watched the Dead Kennedys perform at Irving Plaza, a medium-sized ballroom in lower Manhattan. He penned a hasty review for the *Village Voice* that channeled one of his more recent heroes, Malcolm Muggeridge, a conservative British writer. Inside Irving Plaza, Bangs felt surrounded by morons. There was a "phalanx of big ugly skinhead goons (imported from Washington [D.C.], apparently the same guys Black Flag brought up for their show) to hurl themselves on the audience with brutal but monotonous regularity." Bangs turned sloppy here, not bothering to ask any of these goons if they had been "brought up" from D.C., which they would have denied, having traveled north of their own accord. Instead, Bangs just scoffed at the Dead Kennedys performance, saying it was derivative of Iggy Pop—who had stage-dived twelve years earlier—and the Ramones. He related the Dead Kennedys to Los Angeles's Black Flag, who he labeled "stupid possibly proto-fascist/racist California nihilists" (quite a hurl of charges). He wrote it all off, without even attempting an interview with the story's subject or taking the time to see the Dead Kennedys play in their local scene of San Francisco.[101]

Bangs was repeating a mistake he had made in the past, when his career as a rock journalist was just beginning. In his first published record review for *Rolling Stone* in 1969, he panned the MC5, now known as a proto-punk band laden with radical politics (due in large part to the band's manager, John Sinclair). Bangs hated the band's first album, *Kick Out the Jams*, calling it the work of "punks on a meth power trip," being at once "intentionally crude" and "overbearing" and "pretentious." He compared the album to the youth-exploitation film *Wild in the Streets* (1968) that pandered to "the troops out there in Teenland."[102]

Embarrassment came his way when he actually visited Detroit and witnessed the MC5 playing to thronging crowds at the Grande Ballroom, one institution of many in the burgeoning counterculture area around the Cass Corridor. He saw how rooted the band was in a local "scene" (that included by 1969 bands like the Stooges and the Up and the independent record label A Squared, which had released the MC5's first single). The band's performances were, in the words of Sinclair, a "total thing" of "high energy." Bangs noted a local radical press that nurtured this homegrown culture, including the magazine he'd come to write for, *Creem*. He began to realize he had gotten everything wrong in his shoot-from-the-hip review of *Kick Out the Jams*. He now understood why John Sinclair demanded that the MC5's first album be a recording of a live performance—not only because it allowed for a more chaotic and freer sound than that distilled in a recording studio, but also because it captured the audience's role in generating the energy the performers drew on. The scene and community mattered as much as the individual members of the band (rejecting, as it were, the idea of rock stars).[103]

Biafra had taken some of his inspiration, in fact, from the MC5 and the band's history. When he read that he was labeled a "goon" or "cretin," he was angry, but confident too. Bangs looked to Biafra like a middle-aged curmudgeonly gatekeeper of "punk." After getting a question about Bangs's criticisms of the Dead Kennedys, Biafra concluded, "If all these kids start their own band, it's going to put him and everyone like him out to pasture at long last." Biafra was right, or at least shaping up to being right. For a year after Bangs dissed Biafra, there would be hundreds of bands across the country inspired by the Dead Kennedys, Black Flag, and Minor Threat, plus numerous zines besides *Ripper*, *Punk Lust*, and *The Attack*. And on April 30, 1982, Lester Bangs would be dead from an overdose, another baby boomer punk icon snuffed, his gatekeeper status now ungated.[104]

XXX

A Summer of Meanness

> Do you realize the greed that came to the forefront? The hogs were really feeding. The greed level, the level of opportunism, just got out of control.
>
> —David Stockman to William Greider, 1981[105]

Reagan's smile beamed throughout the summer of 1981, as he piled up victories. In early August, with a sweep of his hand, he broke the Federal Airline Controllers' strike. Members of PATCO (Professional Air Traffic Controllers Organization), predominantly white collar, had walked out on August 3, demanding an increase in salary and benefits. Seeing this as a national emergency and violation of an oath airline controllers took, Reagan buttressed himself by turning to history. He remembered his hero, Calvin Coolidge, who as governor of Massachusetts broke a police strike in 1919. Reagan projected an air of confidence as he faced down what might have solicited a dangerous situation (these were skilled workers, after all, who helped prevent airline accidents and secured safety). "The law is the law," Reagan would repeat as he not only broke the union by firing each and every one of the strikers, but also sent PATCO (which had ironically endorsed Reagan for president in 1980) into financial ruin.[106]

Just a few weeks later, Reagan announced his biggest and most important victory yet: A tax cut on wealthy incomes and corporate profits, including the "windfall" kind. Additionally, cuts sliced away at inheritance and estate taxes and those on capital gains. It was a tax cut for the rich. To justify it, and to downplay the fear that cuts would increase the federal deficit, the term "supply side" was used. Reagan's budget director, David Stockman, would admit that the terminology of "supply side" served as a "Trojan Horse" that covered up how the cuts represented an older, conservative faith in "trickle down"—the idea that cutting taxes on the wealthy would inherently help out the poor. That old-style argument, Stockman admitted, was "kind of hard to sell."[107]

That certainly didn't make Stockman's job at the Office of Management and Budget (OMB) any easier. But he did have something going for him—a faith in conservative ideology. When he was an undergraduate at Michigan State in the mid- to late sixties, he "became," in his own words, "a radical" who got hopped up on New Left writers like Herbert Marcuse and C. Wright Mills. But afterward, while attending Harvard, he moved to the right—always in search of some sort of overarching ideology that explained the world (and, in this case, providing a foreshadowing of the yippie to yuppie transition that marked the eighties). He worked for John Anderson (a Republican from Illinois who would run for the presidency as an Independent in 1980) before becoming a congressperson himself, serving a "rural and Republican" district in Michigan, which pushed him further rightward.[108]

It pushed him all the way to the OMB to search for a way to cut $40 billion from the federal budget, while securing tax cuts and upping military spending (the latter being a point of consternation for Stockman, who believed there was a great deal of waste at the Pentagon). He usually slumped in front of his computer making calculations based on rosy economic forecasts. He worked sixteen hours a day and drowned in trying to make sense of the numbers, sometimes losing faith in his own calculations.

Agencies scrambled as well, trying to figure out how to make cuts to their own operations. For instance, the Department of Agriculture plotted a way to deal with a 30 percent cut in the nation's school lunch program. From mid-August to Labor Day, the agency made key proposals, all of them OK'd by Stockman. That included, in the words of the *New York Times*, the hope to "call ketchup" a "vegetable," and lowering the nutritional demands the program had adhered to before budget cuts. When the idea rolled out, an aide to the head of the Department of Agriculture gave a press conference hoping to clarify what sounded like a policy that would hurt poor kids. James Johnson opened by saying, "I think it would be a mistake to say that ketchup per se was classified as a vegetable. . . . Ketchup in combination with other things was classified as a vegetable." A follow-up question came: What "other things"? He responded, "French fries or hamburgers." For anyone concerned with children's nutrition, that didn't reassure.[109]

So the White House stalled, with Stockman quipping that the Department of Agriculture "not only has egg on its face, but ketchup too." At first, Reagan surmised that "bureaucrats deliberately trying to embarrass him" had concocted the plot (those operating in what the right today would call the "deep state"). But learning that the new program was a "legitimate attempt" to play by the rules set by the White House, he back-pedaled and killed the idea of renaming condiments. Not because he believed in school lunch programs, but because the "selling" language he and Stockman embraced was no longer operational here; it sounded cruel. The cuts would remain, but no more calling ketchup a vegetable. That would have sounded like the spirit behind a report the Hunger Organizing Team in Southern California had issued the previous spring after studying Reagan's plans for "cutbacks in federal food projects." The group noted a meanness in the cuts. It titled the report *Let Them Eat Jellybeans* (just like Jello Biafra's compilation album). If updated for the moment, it could have been better titled *Let Them Eat Ketchup.*[110]

XXX

Punk Disrupts the Feed

> The greatest concept would be when the kids take over that stage and knock the shit out of all the equipment and THEY are the fucking band. The rest is nonsense.
>
> —Malcolm McLaren[111]

On Halloween night, television screens across America turned to gray snow. The beginning of the story started with an invitation from John Belushi, the king of dumb humor in the early 1980s. It's difficult disassociating him from his breakthrough role as a frat boy in National Lampoon's *Animal House* (1978), in which he stuffed his mouth full of mashed potatoes and pretended to be an exploding zit by pressing on his cheeks. Or falling off a ladder while watching sorority girls undressing. Belushi now starred on the hip television show *Saturday Night Live* (*SNL*) and in numerous movies. He had developed ties to the CBGB scene by the late 1970s, even occasionally playing drums for the Dead Boys, the club's "house" band, before they broke up in 1979. He claimed to identify with punk, though mostly attracted to its obnoxious, dumber side—the sort that Legs McNeill of *Punk* magazine and the band the Dictators had projected during the 1970s.

Belushi opened up a conversation with the Los Angeles band Fear. He hoped the band could create a soundtrack for *Neighbors*, a film he was to star in. Belushi believed the film would serve as a work of social criticism about the cul-de-sac culture of American suburbia. It had a promising source, Thomas Berger's novel of the same title, a surrealist attack on bourgeois order, told in a story of two neighbors, Ramona and Harry, moving next door to Earl Keese and his wife, Enid. The novel was full of elliptical dialogue, beginning with Keese asking Ramona politely what he could do for her. She replies, "Anything you like." Ramona, at another point, blackmails Keese and asks, "How far would you go to avoid humiliation?" Keese foresees a "perfect hell" in his future with these two neighbors. "It was new in Keese's experience (of almost fifty years) for things to get so completely out of hand," Berger writes. As things worsen, the beast in Keese erupts—the one-time man of order had "decided to murder everybody and commit suicide." By the end, Keese ponders how "manners" no longer have "meaning," his middle-class desire for normality now finished. He decides to escape with Harry and Ramona, as they leave their house that has caught on fire, only to wind up having a stroke as the newly bonded outlaw gang drives away.[112]

Unfortunately for Belushi, the director of the film, John Avildsen, didn't focus on the story's critique of suburbia's repressed decorum. Instead, as was Hollywood's wont, he played it for laughs and kicks, even changing the ending of the gloomy novel. Physical humor—the sort that Belushi had cut his teeth on—replaced the surrealist writing of Berger (punk can be seen in the character of Keese's daughter in the movie). Meanwhile, Belushi tried to sell Avildsen a soundtrack for the movie, written and performed by Fear. But Belushi was coked up out of his mind, deluding himself into thinking the movie could be fueled by angry punk music (the director did include a very quiet, in-the-background version of "Holiday in Cambodia"). When Belushi lost that battle, he tried to make it up to the band by getting them onto *SNL*.[113]

The Fear show became something of a landmark in American television history. Watching the show from the safe setting of Dayton, Ohio, *Noise* zine called it "the most revolutionary thing on TV since the Doors on ED SULLIVAN," when Jim Morrison refused to compromise with the show's producers and sang, "girl, we can't get much higher," a line Sullivan feared promoted drug use.[114]

Fear played up their dumb punk act. Tesco Vee, publisher of *Touch and Go*, recalled how "the ultra-hip-over-thirty-sophisticated-boring audience made comments and Lee cut them down with fag jokes." But the real shocker for viewers was watching the kids jump on the stage and rush around, knocking over mic stands and careening into instruments— the spontaneity and contingency of the slam. A bunch of kids from the D.C. punk scene came up to wreak havoc, with Ian MacKaye shouting out at one point, "New York Sucks!" (which expressed his anger at the

New York–centric mentality that he had combatted in his earlier fights with *Capitol Crisis*). Another kid grabbed a pumpkin near the stage and smashed it. At which point the feed was cut, with screens turning to gray snow.[115]

When the smoke cleared, it was easier to tell what was so shocking. It wasn't Lee Ving singing about his "beef bologna" (his penis) or the music that one critic called "third-rate heavy metal." What was shocking was the chaos suddenly broadcast on nationwide television, the spontaneous interruption of an otherwise controlled medium. It was the bodies rushing the stage, the audience turning active on the television screen, the suggestion that chaos and spontaneity might still invade a world of order and formula, the high energy of kids busting through. It was like watching Adam Ant get egged. It was the joy of hearing about how the hipster producer of the show, Lorne Michaels, fished around in his New York Yankees coat for more cocaine as he freaked out and shouted to cut the feed. *SNL* might have prided itself on being au courant, cool and hip—the television version of the slick magazine *Rolling Stone*. Its actors liked to see themselves as rebels who used live comedy to press on the margins. But that evening, there was joy in the screams of "New York sucks!" and hearing that John Belushi was too scared to enter the chaotic dance floor. Who knew what would happen, he likely thought to himself. And that was the point.[116]

XXX

A Punk Rimbaud for America's Suburbs

> Bored, I look over my shoulder
> into the clear youthful days.
>
> —Dennis Cooper[117]

On November 3, 1981, in one of the darkest episodes of 1980s youth culture, Anthony Jacques Broussard raped, strangled, and killed his fourteen-year-old girlfriend in Milpitas, California. Broussard took a group of friends to see the corpse. One of them used a garbage bag and leaves to cover the body that was turning blue over days. None reported the murder; the kids turned confused, fearful of the authorities and the murderer both. When eventually one kid came forward and the story broke, a moral shock moved over California and the rest of the country. After all, Milpitas, in the words of the *Washington Post*, was "a carefully planned suburb" with a strong middle class buttressed by labor unions and a functioning Ford Motor plant doling out well-paid jobs. The murder and the silence that followed suggested a sinister underbelly—a callous amoralism—in the prosperous suburban existence of manicured lawns and swimming pools.[118]

The Milpitas murder highlighted a generalized fear growing in America during the eighties—a sense that there was something wrong with young people, especially boys. Consider the spike in youth suicide during the 1970s that plateaued in 1980 but then started to rise again. The statistics on self-inflicted death were bleak. "From 1970 to 1980 the suicide rate for older teen-agers and young adults, both male and female, rose 40 percent," according to the Centers for Disease Control and Prevention (CDC). The findings about adolescent males were far worse: "The increase was fueled by a 50 percent jump in the rate for 15-year-old to 24-year-old men, while the suicide rate for women of the same age increased just 2 percent in the same decade." As the D.C. punk band Government Issue put it in their song "Teenager in a Box," "You were eighteen, now you're a statistic."[119]

Many sociologists, at the time, connected youth suicide to the collapse of the nuclear family. Certainly there was a statistical correlation between the growth of both during what Tom Wolfe called the "great Divorce Epidemic" of the 1970s. "One-parent family groups soared by 79 percent" during the decade. The divorce rate, like the youth suicide rate, spiked throughout the 1970s and reached its highest point ever in 1980 (most pronounced in the suburban areas surrounding Los Angeles and San Francisco). A popular sociologist writing in the early eighties explained, "The number of children and teenagers affected by divorce and separation more than doubled between 1970 and 1979." Another observer pointed out that "30 percent of all children growing up in the 1970s will experience the divorce of their parents." Some studies directly linked divorce and the confusion it left in its wake to growing levels of anger and depression, especially among young men. And even if two parents stayed united, there were now "latchkey kids," high school students whose parents worked long hours and were absent when kids returned home (hence, the key worn on a string around the neck). The dissolution of marriages and parental absence left many kids with a sense of mistrust. By 1982, Neil Postman, a popular sociologist, would announce the "end of childhood."[120]

Suburban despair fueled much of punk in the 1980s. One band out of the suburbs of Green Bay, Wisconsin, called themselves Suburban Mutilation and denounced "their little suburban comfort packet." A zine in the suburbs of Cleveland decried the lives of "android youth" who hang around the "shopping mall." The suburban landscape transformed young people into passive consumers, with comfort hiding a great deal of anxiety. The rock critic Craig Lee observed the inflow of young suburban punks to Los Angeles's scene and noted, "Facing a sterile, anonymous life in suburbia is as depressing to some kids as facing a life of dull labor and low wages is to the English punks."[121]

The punk-inspired poetry of Dennis Cooper during the early 1980s offered the most poignant commentary (indirectly) on the Milpitas murder and the generalized suburban dread. Cooper himself had grown up in suburbia in Southern California. His gay identity generated a sense of alienation from high school, similar to Pugmire's. He described himself as a "profoundly unpopular kid who was harassed and beaten up at school, and spent most of my time in my bedroom obsessing over rock music and television shows." Cooper knew the underbelly of suburbia, since three boys his age had been raped and murdered and dropped in the mountains close to his home. He was already writing poetry by age fourteen, having been inspired by Arthur Rimbaud. Like many an alienated kid, his life was changed by punk rock, which he turned onto by traveling to England in 1976, after a professor at Pitzer College in Claremont warned him against a career in academe. In England, he witnessed the Sex Pistols and the bands who followed in their wake and returned to the States to form a band and become a "failed lead singer." He also created his own self-published zine, *Little Caesar*, which predominantly published poetry. By 1979, just in his mid-twenties, he became director at Los Angeles's Beyond Baroque, a literary center that dated back to the late 1960s and was famous for poetry and literature readings for a wide urban public. Cooper continued in this vein but also opened the venue to the likes of the Minutemen, Johanna Went, and lesser-known punk acts. He also promoted other writers who threaded suburban themes into their poetry, including the music director for Beyond Baroque, Jack Skelley, who wrote about "the patio," "the pool," and his "middle class heritage." Cooper also promoted David Trinidad, author of "In a Suburb of Thebes," which described a young character who was a "rebellious worm" against his sedate family. Trinidad, too, included things like a "pearl-shaped pool," "carrot-colored carpet," and a "hill of trimmed hedges"—all semiotic references to suburbia's aesthetic.[122]

Cooper knew full well of a historical marriage between poetry and punk. After all, two of the most important figures in the CBGB wave of punk—Patti Smith and Richard Hell—began as poets before becoming musical performers.* Though Cooper was only seven years younger than Smith and four years younger than Hell, there appeared a generational gulf between them. While Cooper certainly admired their work (and like Smith had traveled to visit Rimbaud's birthplace in France, a romantic voyage that embarrassed him later), but before he threw off their inheritance. Smith's early poetry was just too romantic and spiritual for Cooper—too reminiscent of Beat writers like Allen Ginsberg (who Pettibon had earlier mocked). Smith shouted out lines about "fantasy" that gave her "fire," in her poem "Autobiography." She moved from this romanticism into a deification of rock stars, especially Mick Jagger, who she saw as a "human god." Her own ambitions were captured in one of the first poems she turned into a song (and self-released as a 7" record), "Piss Factory." The last words of that poem read, "I'm gonna get on that train and go to New York City and I'm gonna be so bad, I'm gonna be a big star."[123]

Smith's romanticization of rock had died for Dennis Cooper, if it had ever lived. Certainly the experience of arena rock had helped rock lose its luster. The rock star to Cooper was unworthy of praise or deification, but rather mocking deflation. When he saw Blondie at a large venue, Cooper imagined shouting, "'Sit on my face!' to the woman singer with chills on my skin, and she doesn't even see me, or deem to answer my call 'cause she's above me, far above." Against Smith's romanticism, Cooper embraced anarchism and antiheroism. Asking the question of what he would do if he "were Peter Frampton," the rock sex symbol made famous in 1976 with his hit "Show Me the Way," Cooper explained he would "hire punk bands to open my tour, give them a spotlight then play so badly crowds turn to them like surviving family." The "best part" of the plan would be "the masturbation, looking down at my own famous body."[124]

* Some cite a performance of "Oath" at a poetry reading at St. Mark's Place Church in 1971, when Patti Smith had Lenny Kaye back her up with a noisy guitar, as the origin point of punk (still up for debate about starting points). Richard Hell's punk anthem, "The Blank Generation," originated as a poem, not a song, as early as 1972.

If Smith's romanticism turned Cooper off, so too did Richard Hell's more experimental and self-conscious poetry. Cooper praised the work that Hell had done in the world of small magazines—having run a poetry zine and then joining up with the future powerhouse literary agent Andrew Wylie to form the independent publisher Telegraph Books (which published Patti Smith, among others). He also shared with Hell a fascination with urban noir, including the flat and sparse writing of Raymond Chandler. But from there differences became more pronounced, for Hell's own poetry showed off a fascination with William S. Burroughs, who Hell called an "absolutely brilliant great man" on par with Marx and Nietzsche. He was especially enamored with the cut-up technique Burroughs developed during the 1960s. Seeing language as a concrete, physical thing that could be chiseled and reformed, Hell had a tendency to equate writing with playing the game of Scrabble, punning, and playing on words. Hell filled his poetry with passages like "Juicy Lucy / Wild Blue Potatoe" or he'd ask for a "poothtick, you mean a toothpick, 'Yes. That might even do better . . . .'" Or he'd write, "There's a rut in every truth." Certainly clever, but it also tended toward insularity and self-referentiality. As Hell explained it in his journals and the writing he did for his own self-published zine, *Genesis: Grasp*, a poem was "an idea that has to do with itself." Hell's self-consciousness about writing would eventually inform the "language poetry" that dominated academic writing during the 1970s and 1980s.[125]

Cooper believed Hell's hero Burroughs to be overrated and stayed away from his "cut-up" techniques. In certain ways, Cooper embraced a more traditional view of writing. Poetry was to be a form of communication to a general reader. Language was a tool, not a plaything to have fun with. Poetry was "art" not "confession" about the self. Cooper took more inspiration from the original New York Poets of the 1950s, especially Frank O'Hara, who managed to, in the words of one critic, "elevate the prose of everyday life . . . into the stuff of lyric poetry," creating "an elastic colloquial idiom in tune with the rhythms of his city life." Cooper, though, would write poetry that had more to do with a suburban atmosphere rather than the jazzy feel of midcentury Manhattan. He wrote approachable poems that worked at the poetry readings he organized at Beyond Baroque (Hell's poems wouldn't work as spoken word, since they were tied to their physical assemblage on paper). For Cooper, poetry communicated at a time when such an act—especially in the anomie of America's suburbs—was difficult enough.[126]

If Cooper's style was less experimental than Hell's, its substance was much darker. It's best gleaned from one of his most troubling poems, "Late Friends," which he released twice, first in *Coming Attractions: An Anthology of American Poets in Their Twenties* (1980), a compilation of poems he edited with Tim Dlugos, and then again in a book he was finishing up in late 1981, *The Tenderness of the Wolves* (Cooper claimed this book was the most indebted to punk). Cooper dedicated the poem to Robert Piest, a fifteen-year-old boy who was the last victim of a serial rapist and murderer, the eerily named John Wayne Gacy (who had been a family man who dressed up as a clown for kid events, prompting a band from Tulsa, Oklahoma, to write "Dead in the Suburbs" [1980] about the mass murderer). Piest was a promising student and gymnast who lived in a suburb of Chicago, Des Plaines; he was the sort of kid, in Cooper's words, who "never gave Warhol a chance." Cooper took this gruesome story and built an atmospheric poem around it, using his own memories of suburban high schools and youth culture. He described how Piest was "raped, strangled and dropped in the Des Plaines River." He then pulled back: "Your friends are down wind at the high school: doused faces, dim shouldered . . . where jocks fire up taller and stronger each day." At first, in respect, friends wouldn't recreate on the river, but then as time moved on, "they'll water ski" on it, a nice metaphor for skimming and jumping over painful memory. Then, as more time passes, kids are obsessed with "grades" that turn in their heads like "slot machines." Beating back memory of Piest, his one-time "pals" were now "dating your girlfriends, seduced by your buddies." These young amnesia-stoned kids "roll across the things that you loved."[127]

Sometime in 1981, Cooper finished another prose poem akin to "Late Friends." Titled "A Herd," it would constitute the second part of *The Tenderness of the Wolves*. The poem's set clearly in the suburbs, mentioning the "woods" that bank up to individual houses where "no one went" (and where corpses would be dropped). There are references to "the San Diego Freeway beyond the Sepulveda Pass" and an "offramp at Ventura Blvd." that are traveled on by another psychotic murderer who takes the life of a young boy named Jay who had "been molested . . . chopped up and dropped by a freeway." The poem ends on the young man's funeral, where the father reads out a "lyric to a song Jay" and he "used to listen to when he was a boy." It's Frank Sinatra's "When I Was Seventeen." A friend of Jay's grimaces at the reading. "How selfish," his friend thinks, "of this man to pick a lyric which Jay didn't care about. When someone's a child he listens to what his god plays." The anomie of the suburbs and the distance between father and son symbolized a generalizing disconnectedness bubbling up in 1981. As Cooper would explain to the *L.A. Weekly*, "I find these pretty bleak times. People aren't able to communicate with one another very well." The suburbs—according to this punk poet—were no longer a place of safe contentedness but rather anxiety, anomie, and distrust.[128]

XXX

"We've Got a Bigger Problem Now" as We've Gotten Bigger

Always rebel and always think.

—Chuck Dukowski[129]

On December 1, 1981, Ronald Reagan OK'd a plan to use "covert aid to the Nicaraguan contras" in hopes of toppling the Sandinista government. Millions of dollars were budgeted for the effort, now that Reagan had decided that Nicaragua and the rest of Central America was to be what he called the "hot spot" for his reinvigorated Cold War (some called it Cold War 2, a break from the détente of the 1970s). No more wimpy Jimmy Carter, who almost shrugged his shoulders at the Sandinista revolution back in 1979. But there had to be caution about it. Action had to be covert, because public opinion wasn't aligning with Reagan's bellicosity.[130]

So, too, in El Salvador, probably the second most important front in Reagan's Cold War in Central America. The president kept shoveling money toward a repressive, rightist regime there. Military aid to El Salvador "amounted to six million dollars in 1980" and leaped to "$35.5 million in 1981." The problem here was that the ruling regime used what were called "death squads" to suppress a revolutionary movement. Kids and church leaders fell from bullets likely provided by the United States. In early 1981, just a few months after death squads killed Maryknoll nuns in El Salvador, *Boredom* zine printed a fake interview with Reagan saying, "Just cuz a few nuns get wasted after enticing some locals and a few coffee bean pickers start screaming 'oppressive government' the United States isn't going to back out of any deal." A number of punk kids were joining the ranks of the Committee in Solidarity with the People of El Salvador (CISPES), including the Minutemen's D. Boon (who wrote "Song for El Salvador," released on their 1981 record *The Punch Line*). Punk bands were playing benefits for CISPES. Zines like Los Angeles's *Night Voices* were detailing these benefits but also wondering if instead of raising money for the organization, they should perhaps "hop in a car, drive south for 40 hours, get out and say, 'Here I am! I want to help really I do!" The DIY spirit nurtured a penchant for direct action rather than working through representative institutions.[131]

CISPES had formed out of a church-labor alliance and those who defended undocumented workers in the United States. By the spring of 1981, it was organizing protests, including the "largest march at the Pentagon since" the "Vietnam War," with about 100,000 attending, all opposed to intervention in Latin America and budget cuts for social programs. Though Reagan was popular as ever, his foreign policy remained a soft underbelly, with a majority of Americans worried about his warlike stance and the possibility of, as CISPES would call it, "another Vietnam."[132]

While supporting these foreign interventions, Reagan was also reconsidering a campaign promise. He had opposed Carter's decision to renew the Selective Service System. After all, he was a libertarian in part. He never warmed to the self-abnegation of "sacrifice." But thinking in technical terms about a future war, he was learning that "registration could speed mobilization by six weeks." So he decided, as they say, to flip-flop on the issue and maintain the Selective Service Act. His decision, much to his chagrin, was leaked to the press early in January 1982. The ACLU quickly condemned the decision, arguing that "Reagan . . . is using the lives of young people to play a game of military and foreign policy symbols." Placed next to the growing intervention in Central America, though, it didn't look much like a symbolic gesture—as it may have been for Carter—but a serious preparation for war. Reagan promised that those who didn't register "would face criminal proceedings." This didn't stop some draft resisters who tied up lines at post offices and blocked people from registering, or sometimes registered fictional names themselves.[133]

The prospects of a ground war in Central America were overshadowed, however, by the fears of a nuclear war. On October 17, 1981, a group of fifteen-year-old kids went to the White House with a banner that read, "Children's Campaign for Nuclear Disarmament." They had 3,000 letters written by young people about their nightmares concerning nuclear war (they were going to read them out loud, only to have the White House lawn sprinklers turned on them). The day before these young protestors' arrival, Ronald Reagan had spoken with the press. He talked openly about a nuclear exchange, arguing that it could come about without "either of the major powers pushing the button." When the press followed up on this bizarre statement, he clarified it by saying that the exchange he had cited was only a "possibility." He went on, "You could have a pessimistic outlook on it or an optimistic. I always tend to be optimistic." But in reality, as he confessed to his diary during December 1981, he was "starting a Civil Defense buildup. Right now in a nuclear war, we'd lose 150 million people. The Soviets could hold their loss down." Which sounded like the planning of a "contained" nuclear war, where only a few million would die.[134]

War talk became omnipresent. By the end of December, it came out that a bureaucrat in the Defense Department, T. K. Jones, who was responsible for Civil Defense planning, had said that surviving a nuclear war was possible. "If there are enough shovels to go around, everybody's going to make it," Jones told the reporter Robert Scheer. That's because shovels could dig holes in the ground that could be covered with doors and lots of dirt. Jones explained, "It's the dirt that does it." The comment would send the editors of *The Attack* into fits of despair, grasping at whatever dark humor they could manage to summon. Peter Wick quipped:

> I am going to start carrying my personal door and shovel with me at all times. I admit I may stand out at first. . . . But when the moment comes, they'll be sorry they weren't traveling prepared also. I'll be ready for split-second digging. And just in case you think you can squeeze in after I'm secured, I'm going to hinge my door firmly to the ground and lock it from the inside.[135]

* * *

The Dead Kennedys sounded the alarm when they released the *In God We Trust* EP. Full of commentary about the Moral Majority, who Biafra called "stodgy ayatollahs in their double-knit ties," the Dead Kennedys blasted their politics, as they drove their music up-tempo (they were getting faster, having taken inspiration from younger bands). The most timely song on the EP was

"We've Got a Bigger Problem Now," a reworking of the band's "California Uber Alles." Though most of the songs on the EP were high-speed, this one slowed itself down to mimic the comatose apathy that the band saw taking over the country. Biafra played the role of a sloppy nightclub emcee, saying over lame lounge music that his audience must "drink up. Happy hour is now enforced by law." The opening monologue ends with Reagan pledging to reinstitute school prayer. And then . . . *kabamm,* the song breaks back into the thrash-sound that dominates the EP. Biafra tirades, "Vietnam won't come back you say, join the army or you will pay." And then the song moves back to the lounge music, with Biafra riffing about "World War Three," when "they'll draft you and then jail your niece." And then a move into the final blast of thrash, as Biafra rails against the "friends of President Reagan," those corporations driving the military build-up. Here he sounds as if his vocal chords would burst. In just about four and a half minutes, the band had managed to distill the anxiety and paranoia that marked American political culture for a growing number of young people at the end of 1981.

The EP's cover portrayed Jesus Christ crucified on cut-apart dollar bills (along with a universal bar code with the numbers 666). It was one of many collages done by Winston Smith, the artist who found a compatriot in Biafra, both of them sickened by the "mellow out" of the 1970s. Smith (born James Patrick Shannon Morey) took his name from the central character in George Orwell's dystopian novel *1984,* a book that nurtured his political and artistic sensibilities. He took influence from the "montage as social commentary of Max Ernst," the overtly political, anti-Nazi artist John Heartfield, and the San Francisco–based Bruce Conner, who had hung around the periphery of the San Francisco punk scene and was known for assemblages of found items (and who argued against the principle of artistic originality). One of Smith's best works had pasted Reagan's face onto a man who was looking at the viewer while mowing his lawn; a closer look, though, showed that blades of grass were really crowds of human beings, thus the title, "Mowing Down the People" (1981). The cut and paste techniques Smith used showed up in numerous zines starting up in 1981—with images and advertisements being cut out of mainstream magazines and then reassembled. Smith had his own zine entitled *Fallout.* Influence went both ways—Smith enamored with the look of current zines, and zine editors enamored with his artwork, which was usually a bit more sophisticated than theirs.[136]

Christ crucified on a cross of dollar bills was obviously targeting a central feature of American popular culture during the early 1980s—the rise of "televangelists" like Jimmy Swaggart, Jim Bakker, Pat Robertson, Jerry Falwell, and Oral Roberts. Biafra's attacks in "Religious Vomit" and "Moral Majority" sounded so astringent as to make them atheist, but he argued that what upset him wasn't religious faith but ministers who instrumentalized it for the purpose of accruing wealth (in the case of Jim Bakker that included constructing a gigantic theme park in South Carolina known as Heritage USA). He was drawing on the deep tradition of anticlericalism in America's history. Asked if he was an atheist, Biafra said he knew friends who were building "connections between Buddhism and some of the Sioux Indians and Christianity and Islam," a sort of DIY religious faith. There was a role for spirituality, he claimed. He then cited the line in "Moral Majority" that asked, "What's wrong with a mind of my own?" "That's the main kicker line in that whole thing. The thing is we're not trying to tell people how to think." That refrain echoed his philosophy of provocation.[137]

A month before the Dead Kennedys issued In God We Trust, Bullet fanzine, out of Lawrence, Kansas, had run a review of Jerry Falwell's spoken word album Where Are the Dead?, which featured performances by the Old Time Gospel Hour Choir. As expected, the review was thumbs down. "Jerry turns out to be God's gift to sleeping," Bullet expounded. "There is even a piano playing softly in the background while he converses with the audience. A very, very slick performance. No wonder Jerry captivates the masses." But there was Bullet's own punk faith to give hope: "Fortunately some people still think for themselves and aren't afraid to say so." Knowingly or not, Bullet and the Dead Kennedys had started a flurry of punk activism. It would eventually be labeled "The Falwell Game." Kids would call the Moral Majority's 1-800 number and either spend a lot of time talking to whoever answered the phone (1-800 numbers charged the company who hosted them) or request records, "free Falwell Bibles," or cassette tapes of Falwell's sermons. And then they sometimes took the cassette tapes and recorded their own music over Falwell's preaching.[138]

This highlights one of the more overlooked things that made In God We Trust important. The EP came out on Biafra's own label, Alternative Tentacles, which released a cassette version. All of the songs fit on one side of the cassette, leaving the other side blank. For that side, the band drew a pirate and the words that parroted the Recording Industry Association of America's slogan at the time: "Home taping is killing record industry profits! We left this side blank so you can help out."

The idea caught on, since, as Howard Wuelfing argued in his zine, *Discords*, cassette tapes allowed "the hot new talent" to "bypass" the music industry and "distribut[e] their music to interested consumers." Wuelfing went on: "No one in the most minimally urbanized areas cannot know someone with a tape machine and a couple cheap RadioShack connector wires." Barry Soltz, who edited *Suburban Relapse* out of Florida, concurred: "There's more in this cassette explosion than meets the eye, many people are and have been creating wild new music and releasing it on limited edition tapes. . . . The cassette market is young." He noted how *Subterranean Pop* (eventually *Sub Pop*) and *Talk Talk* were releasing cassette tape compilations in addition to their usual printed zines. As *Talk Talk* started to move into compilations of Kansas bands, in 1981, the editors wrote, "Let us talk about the recording industry with all the built-in support systems for dinosaurs and executives. A great deal of blame for the near-collapse of the industry which exists today is placed on the 'home-tapers' or those who buy blank tape and then record from borrowed records or from the radio." Indeed, Great Britain had already placed a "surcharge tax" on cassette tapes to cut down on amateur reproduction and distribution. America's music industry noted this. A year earlier, Warner Brothers had done a "home taping survey," with the hopes of helping the Recording Industry Association of America do something to curb cassette taping, following the British model. The year 1981 was one of the worst for the record industry, and the moguls blamed pesky kids with cassette recording decks.[139]

The Dead Kennedys already had good company. The label ROIR, based in New York City (and which would release the very important Bad Brains), used only cassettes and promoted sales by explaining, "If you get bored, you can easily erase them and re-record anything you want right over them." When K Records formed the next year out of Olympia, Washington, its ads would read: "cassette revolution is exploding the teenage underground into passionate revolt against the corporate ogre." Cassette taping had an "underground" feel. The best practice was literally to erase corporate music by stuffing scrunched-up balls of paper into the notches at the top of a cassette tape. People could then record over the original contents of the tape, and often scrawl their own words on the cassette's cover.[140]

So the "friends of President Reagan," those who sat atop the country's culture industry and prepared their "Save America's Music Industry" campaign, worried about an ongoing slump. Soon after *In God We Trust* was released, *Ripper* zine pointed out that Reagan had expressed anger at an "underground economy" based around a "disturbing trend" of cash sales and bartering. Around the same time, *Sluggo*, a zine then published out of San Francisco, noted Reagan's attack on a "subterranean cash economy." Direct cash trade, Reagan worried, never garnered tax revenue. The fate of major entertainment corporations, the same that helped guide the president's career, felt threatened as sales spiraled downward throughout 1981. The political conclusion was obvious for *Ripper*'s editors: Keep up the DIY underground economy—including cassette tape and zine distribution. *Ripper* justified and politicized what Ronald Reagan would call a crime: "Why should you want to pay taxes now that the government has cut back on the programs that were helping people so they can spend more on the military to kill people?" DIY practices, again, fueled a DIY politics.[141]

* * *

The end of 1981 not only witnessed the Dead Kennedys' attempt to politicize young anger, but also clarified questions surrounding "straight edge" ethics. Minor Threat's *In My Eyes* EP (issued around the time of *In God We Trust*) hoped to clarify what the philosophy stood for. Clearly, it was a moral judgment, since it purported that a person had an "edge" on another if sober rather than inebriated. But it also opened itself up to abuse. Indeed, though Biafra supported the philosophy, believing that political judgments necessitated a certain sobriety, some participants went in dangerous directions for him. In the Midwest and the city of Boston, he noticed that some kids had "taken the straight edge attitude totally the wrong way and enforced it like a bunch of junior cops on people like picking fights with people for having a beer in their hand and treating it like some new conformist attitude." One punk kid from Grand Rapids, Michigan, complained to *Touch and Go* zine that "straight edge" nurtured violence, because of its sense of individual superiority. He went on, reporting that MacKaye once boasted of hitting "some kid . . . for blowing pot smoke in his face—wow—I could get a gun and blow him off the world, does that make me the best? The only thing he taught that kid was that he'd better have better means to protect himself." But for some, like those who edited *Bad Meat* zine in Oklahoma, straight edge was, as MacKaye believed, "an anti-obsession pro-positive thinking idea."[142]

Minor Threat solicited debate more than closure. That's no surprise, considering that the band's members, like those in the Minutemen, constantly argued with one another. MacKaye explained: "We don't necessarily get along that great. We'll practice for about two, three hours at a time and maybe 20–30 minutes will be actual playing the rest of the time we'll be discussing, arguing, going off on each other." The band's guitarist, Lyle Preslar, admitted, "it's gotten to the point that we fight incredibly." But argument could serve creativity, including with straight edge. As MacKaye was writing "Out of Step"—which would become the clearest distillation of straight edge philosophy—he pissed off the band's drummer, Jeff Nelson. Instead of preaching "Don't Smoke" or "Don't Drink" (the way those words were shouted on the *In My Eyes* EP), Nelson argued the lyrics should read, "I don't smoke, I don't drink," so that the song sounded less preachy, more about individual choice. And in the end, MacKaye complied (a release of the song with the "I"s put in would come out later). But it would still sound to some like commandments, which prompted the joke: "Why'd the punk cross the road? Because Ian told him to." Humor aside, MacKaye saw this as a personal statement, not a set of rules.[143]

A new command was added as well. The original statements of straight edge philosophy—the songs "Straight Edge" and "Bottled Violence," played at the "Unheard Music Festival"—focused on alcohol and drugs. But in "Out of Step," the issue of sexuality was introduced with the words "don't fuck." This sounded almost puritanical to some. MacKaye would be asked over and over just what he meant by "don't fuck," and he would explain that he didn't reject sex per se but rather what some call "sport-fucking," the belt-notching approach to sexual conquest so prominent in young male culture, or what MacKaye called the "chalk on your bedpost, as a scorecard" approach to sex. In a long interview with *Forced Exposure*, he would say, "I don't believe in people following their penises everywhere." He suggested that television and pornography had reduced sex to a physical act when it was actually more complicated and emotional than most people cared to admit. Vic Bondi, lead singer of the band Articles of Faith (out of Chicago), would call the enemy of MacKaye's views here "cock rock" (a term Biafra used to pillory macho music). Heavy metal, especially, projected a sense of confidence about male sexual virtuosity—which ignored how so many young men had a profound insecurity when it came to sex. Bondi admitted that air-glossed porn like *Playboy* or *Penthouse* had shaped his own views of sexuality—something he hoped to change about himself. Straight edge critiqued detached and unrealistic views on sexuality that popular culture evoked.[144]

Straight edge constituted an ethic of self-inquisition. But it also demanded conversation, the sort of conversation that Minor Threat had among themselves and that they would take with them as they started to tour. It also required an ethic of responsibility—staying loyal to your own principles. Two years after *Out of Step* was released, the *Village Voice*, never a fan of much 1980s punk, admitted that Minor Threat struggled with "questions of ethics—how to live and behave inside a limbo that grows more hemmed in every day."[145]

* * *

Black Flag, the last of the trifecta of bands to constitute the birth and spread of "teeny punk" from 1980 to 1981, had its own contribution. Their record *Damaged* would be released soon, following a long dispute with Unicorn Records and MCA. As Greg Ginn explained, "Unicorn Records was an independent label that was being distributed by MCA (that national distribution appealed to the band). We had made a deal with MCA for distribution, so we went ahead and printed up 2,500 sleeves with the MCA logo, which they approved." But then along came Al Bergamo, a MCA big shot, who listened to the album and declared it "anti-parent." Which led to lawsuits. Though those were cleared up by December 1981, the band was still aggravated enough to stay away from corporate record labels and do their own thing with SST from that time onward (much as Biafra's Alternative Tentacles and MacKaye's and Nelson's Dischord would).[146]

From its start, with the anthemic song "Rise Above," *Damaged* rang out with angst. It tied together the anxieties of adolescence with public commentary, the way bands like TSOL, Social Distortion, and Agent Orange had. "Rise Above" especially built on the anger held by kids who had been picked on by bullies—jocks or rednecks. Chris Morris, a writer at the *L.A. Reader*, called it "amphetamine protest music. . . . The music on *Damaged* is critical and black-humored, but in no way does it advocate annihilation or destruction" (what Lester Bangs earlier called nihilism). Its spirit was neither hopeful nor hopeless. The band confronted "generalized misery, boredom, and despair." Morris observed the mixed sentiment behind Black Flag: " 'We're gonna rise above,' Black Flag sings . . . , but the songs that follow—tough, savage, and even self-critical songs—imply that the odds against rising above are pretty high." "Rise Above" became, in some critics' minds, a "transcendental anthem" for punk rock of the 1980s.[147]

That transcendental feel explains in part the high reputation Black Flag had, especially in the band's mounting war with the Los Angeles Police Department (LAPD). The LAPD, armed with helicopters and squad cars, continued to shut down any show they could. One of Henry Rollins's premieres as singer for Black Flag took place at the Cuckoo's Nest, a club that throughout 1981 struggled to stay open, constantly raided by the police, who would ticket punk kids for loitering (and in the process radicalize the club's owner, Jerry Roach). In late 1981, Matt Groening, a writer at the *L.A. Reader*, called the struggle over the Cuckoo's Nest "one of the last stands left in the great police-war on punk in Southern California" (it would have reminded John Shirley of Stu Cole's defense of his club against the odds). Black Flag played up their own existential battle with the LAPD by putting up Pettibon posters that depicted a gun held to a policeman's face and the words "Make Me Come Faggot" (a homophobic comment, for sure, but one intended to tweak cops about their own repressed homosexuality and macho front). On *Damaged*, the song "Police Story" offered a plaintive refrain, "They hate us, we hate them, we can't win" but followed with "motherfuckers gonna pay." There was a politics to this, but it was an anarchist and absurdist politics, more like Tim Yo's than the band cared to admit.[148]

With so many barriers to getting their music out, Black Flag decided to tour outside of Los Angeles relentlessly. They had seen the Canadian band D.O.A. zipping around the country and reporting on local scenes that could host shows. Randy from D.O.A. told the zine *Noise* during the summer of 1981, "I mean there's hardcore bands springing up all over: Chicago, Bloomington, Indiana and even down in Lexington Kentucky." Black Flag developed another route, from California to Arizona to Houston, always trying to find places for "all-ages" shows. At one point, Chuck Dukowski explained why the band refused to play a club that had high ticket prices. He offered one word: "Ethics." That from a band charged with nihilism by the music industry and as goons and fascists by Lester Bangs.[149]

Their touring was primitive and uncomfortable—centered around a cramped van. One observer called the band "masochistic," seeing how they would go from "Salt Lake City to Portland to L.A. on successive nights." Joe Carducci, who started to work at SST in 1981, called the tours "the equivalent of fighting a ground war strategy in an age of strategic nuclear forces."

Henry Rollins would explain, "I hurt myself—mentally, physically" when on the road. This was the anti–rock star ethic put into practice, self-immolation to an extent. Against the garish decadence of arena rock (symbolized in the Who's personal limousines chock-full of cognac and other goodies), Black Flag carved out a touring route that not only showed off their resiliency but also left seeds behind for burgeoning scenes. As the Canadian band D.O.A., who had originally inspired Black Flag to tour, declared, "LA has started a whole new movement of American hardcore punk that's spreading across the country like wildfire, like, it's not a bunch of limeys coming over here and shoving working class punk down our throats. It's like all these rich kids in the suburbs going out and doing it just for the fun."[150]

Whenever Dukowski was on tour and conversed with a local zine producer, he offered promising news. He'd face an anxious looking kid with a pen and perhaps a tape-recorder and say, "It can and will happen everywhere." Even if suppressed, anger would find voice in hard-to-expect places. As the last issue of *Damage* magazine out of San Francisco forecasted in 1981: "If white, suburban teenagers on the West Coast are embracing the spirit and dialectic of punk with such fire . . . isn't it conceivable that we can expect the same fire to sweep through the Great Midwest, which is far more dry, conservative, and culturally barren than even the most rabidly reactionary Orange County burg?" Black Flag was becoming, even if they didn't want to, leaders of a new counterculture. The *Village Voice* put it this way at the end of 1981: Black Flag "now finds itself at the forefront of a tiny but growing youth movement largely suburban and largely male, the basic tenet of which is that the country is totally fucked."[151]

"Largely male" here sounded like a critique, or at least suggested a sexist shortcoming. For sure, most of the bands discussed thus far were dominated by men (though by 1981 there were some all-female punk bands—Audio Leter in Seattle, the Neo Boys in Portland, and Chalk Circle in D.C.; there were also a number of female singers in bands—for instance, John Shirley was replaced by Mish Bondage as Sado-Nation headed into the 1980s). The editors of *Desperate Times* (Seattle) were largely female; the zine *Ripper* was edited by one man joined by two women (who were sisters); those who egged Adam Ant included numerous young women. *Debt Begins at Twenty* was made by a woman, and women appear in the movie throughout. Ruth Schwartz (who would eventually found her own independent record label) helped Tim Yo put on the MRR radio show. Indeed, the oral historian Stacy

Russo portrayed thirty-seven "women from the 1970s and 1980s" in Southern California who were active in punk (including Zizi "Carrot Woman" Howell, the woman who praised slamdancing's communal ethic). And far from being a macho, exclusive culture, there were plenty of bands populated by gay and bisexual members—including Gary of the Dicks, MDC, the Big Boys, Husker Du, plus the zine editors Pugmire and Cooper.[152]

Still . . . young, suburban white males dominated, and there were those who critiqued the movement for precisely that. But for Dukowski, whenever a young, suburban, white kid came up to him, he grew excited by the sense that, even with shortcomings, there seemed to be a movement opening, created by young "teeny punks."

And here a portrait might be best. Consider the zine *Noise* published in Xenia, a suburb of Dayton, Ohio. It was edited by Bob Moore, who was a student at Beavercreek High School and the quintessential "teeny punk." Late in 1981, the class president of Beavercreek wrote up a story to explain Moore to other students (and Moore reprinted the story in his zine). Moore explained his view on contemporary music by decrying "new wave" sellouts: "Bands like the B-52's, Devo, Blondie are all products of commercialization and have become very meaningless to what they say and how they say it." He credited Los Angeles bands, including Black Flag but also Agent Orange, TSOL, and the Circle Jerks. He talked about doing "punk art" for not just his own zine but also Ohio publications like *The Offense* and Michigan's *Touch and Go*. He worked with WYSO, a public radio station, to play his sort of music. And by December 1981, just as *Damaged* started to find its way into young punks' hands, he cited the growth of bands in the Dayton area—including Toxic Reasons but also Dementia Praecox, Napalm Youth, and his own band, the Delinquents. By his own count, there were now about 220 bands across the country playing music largely inspired by trailblazers like Black Flag and the Dead Kennedys. At the same time, he could point to over ninety zines publishing independently that helped establish trading and communication pathways, constituting an "underground economy" Reagan derided. Moore was fast working on a compilation tape that would include bands especially from the Midwest, making him both a chronicler and participant in the growing punk rock world. It had come to Xenia, Ohio, so perhaps Dukowski was right: It could and would happen everywhere.[153]

2

IT CAN AND WILL HAPPEN
EVERYWHERE (1982–1983)

If the system stresses anti-intellectualism, we must become intellectuals. . . . It is the idea behind the music, the dress, the zines that [is]
important.

> —the editors of *MAXIMUMROCKNROLL*,
> 1st issue, Summer of 1982[1]

XXX

THE SPREAD . . .

We've found that there's stuff popping up all over the place, like Phoenix,
Reno, Akron, Iowa City, Lawrence, Kansas, and tons of little places . . . that
are full of intelligent kids [who] are honest, sincere, helpful . . . .

> —Really Red (punk band from Houston, Texas,
> on tour in Spring 1983)[2]

Spread it did. From 1982 to 1983, Chuck Dukowski's forecasting came true.
Punk was steamrolling the country, led by the touring assaults of Black Flag
and the Dead Kennedys (followed by Minor Threat). "It's spreading like

wildfire," HR, the lead singer of the Bad Brains exclaimed in his Rastafari brogue, the same man who encouraged Ian MacKaye and his friends to form the Teen Idles and Minor Threat (and who was now nurturing a scene in New York City). Like the vision present in Woody Guthrie's radical song "This Land Is Your Land," there was traversing and movement. Punk stretched "from the redwood forest" to "that golden valley," from "the sparkling sands of her diamond deserts" to the "wheat fields waving." In this case, regions were tied together via the interstate highway system that snaked across the country, drawing out kids from the suburbs, often going into the closest city for performances. Or wound together by the postal service (an institution celebrated by turn-of-the-century populists) when kids stuffed cash into envelopes to receive a compilation album advertised in a zine. From the eastern seaboard to its epicenter, Los Angeles, new bands formed (usually with one band trailblazing, inspiring others to follow) and zines multiplied. "Scenes" across the country spread and grew, forming a network and sense of a movement. A "punk rock world," the one that Kurt Cobain entered in 1983, established its pathways.[3]

"The Midwest is happening," a writer at *Last Rites* zine explained, toward the tail end of the early 1980s explosion. From 1982 to 1983, the state of Ohio proved that case, as scenes and zines spread throughout the state. As noted, "teeny punk" Bob Moore had witnessed this already in Dayton, where Toxic Reasons (the trailblazer) helped out Dementia Precox, who would tour all the way from Dayton to San Francisco, with stops in between. Those bands inspired Napalm Youth and Moore's own band the Delinquents. *Noise* kept churning out Moore's art and criticism and became a cassette label (eventually called Version Sound) whose first release was *Charred Remains*, a cassette compilation of midwestern bands. The compilation album signified how many punk kids considered their creativity collective rather than purely individual.[4]

To the south of Dayton, Cincinnati had the band the Edge, who wrote, among other songs, "Newport Gestapo" about "the cops" who busted a "Circle Jerks show at the Jockey Club" (a venue just across the Ohio River in Newport, Kentucky). They inspired Sluggo to hit the Cincinnati scene in 1983; Sluggo had songs like "Suburban Haven" about middle-class kids out of touch with reality (it sounded like a Minor Threat song but wasn't overly serious). Zines erupted, including *Altered Statements*, whose primary aim was to oppose MOR (middle-of-the-road) radio that played "boring dinosaurs, Zeppelin, Hendrix, and the Doors." It was joined by *Soldier of Misfortune* and *Sub Cin Zine*, with the editors of the latter expressing Dukowski's democratic ethic: "Just because this isn't LA or NY it doesn't mean something can't happen here."[5]

In Ohio's Rust Belt up north, the rubber city of Akron had Zero-Defex, Agitate, and Urban Mutants. Plus the zine *Ooops*, which, like *Noise* in Dayton, formed a compilation cassette tape company that issued *This Tape Sucks*. Bob Forward also edited *Own the Whole World*, an intelligent, scrambled-looking zine with all sorts of cut-up art. Cleveland, a city whose punk rock history was rich (with 1970s bands like Rocket from the Tombs, Dead Boys, Electric Eels, and Pere Ubu), had a young scene with Starvation Army (what the Wobblies called the Salvation Army at the turn of the century), Suburban Decay, Idiot Humans, Plague, Pink Holes, Dark, Zero Defex, Agitated, Spike in Vain, PPG, No Parole, Offbeats, Death of Samantha, and Positive Violence. The zine *Negative Print*, edited in Parma Heights, a suburb of Cleveland, helped gel the scene and explained Positive Violence's enigmatic name (it justified action against property—not people—that they saw as legitimate even if against the law). *Negative Print* also reacted to growth and started putting together compilation tapes of northeastern Ohio bands.[6]

To the southeast of Cleveland, the college town of Kent suffered from a culture of "Urban Cowboys and Charlie Daniel's look-alikes," but still had bands like Big Wow, the V-Nervz, Bosch, and the Bursting Brains (who had an eerie song about how "soon we will march across desert sands.") It also had a zine edited by Tommy Strange called *Boredom*, which promoted the Progressive Student Network chapter on Kent's campus, surprisingly active amid America's swing to the right. *Boredom* called itself "a magazine for non-adults who like rebel music." But it also worried about local contemporary history, arguing that "the May 4th killings [in 1970 on Kent State's campus] are being forgotten and will soon slip away into history." The zine saw a sort of connection with 1960s democratic radicalism that was organic to midwestern egalitarianism: America, it declared, was a place of "free spaces, of pioneers, of flux." It hoped that "our bands can express this attitude of the free, innovative America regardless of media anti-hype."[7]

Even the state capital, known pejoratively as "Cowtown," had its burgeoning scene. Columbus, Ohio, had a little bohemian area known as

"High Street" (relatively close to where the state university was located). Here was Magnolia Thunderpussy, a record store that hosted bands, along with other stores like Singin Dog, Mole's record exchange, Rockarama, Schoolkids Records, and Monkey's Retreat. There was the venue known as Mr. Brown's. But the most important institution was the zine, the *Offense*, published by Tim Anstaett, a one-time law student who served up dense, rich treatments of music in and out of Ohio (he was a sort of organic intellectual for the burgeoning punk scene going on the "offense" for the cause of new music). By one count, Anstaett's publication was one of the "19 or more zines" produced in Ohio by 1982.[8]

* * *

The college towns of the Midwest turned into hotbeds of punk and intellectual debate. In Ohio's neighboring state of Michigan, Ann Arbor (a town with its own punk history centering around the late 1960s bands the MC5 and the Stooges), there were bands like State, Ground Zero, and 3D Jesus, who all played at Joe's Star Lounge. There was *Disposable Press*, a zine that circulated at local shows. *Disposable Press* would cut out stories found in the sensationalistic tabloid *Weekly World News*, and publish young writers like Bill Brown, a college dropout who was connecting his interest in the Situationist International's radical revolt against "the society of the spectacle" with his current love of fast, hardcore music. Brown celebrated how punks were creating unique venues for shows, including one that was a collaboration between a local promoter, Ralph Nader's Public Interest Research Group (PIRG), and the University of Michigan's Union Ballroom. The cooperative effort and democratic self-management of the show helped prevent the police from shutting it down, the way they often had in other cases.[9]

In Wisconsin, the one-time hotbed of the 1960s New Left, Madison, exploded with bands and zines from 1982 onward. There were Mecht Mensch, Tar Babies, Killdozer, Knucklehead, and Imminent Attack. Bands struggled over finding venues, often playing at Merlyn's, which was a bar and thus not conducive to all-ages shows. Zines were abundant though: *Brain Death, Catholic Guilt, Domestic Discharge, Mangled Efforts, Kook Knowledge Klu,* and *Rockabilly Rag.* The feistiest, *Reagan Death,* not only reported on

Madison happenings but also engaged in local politics, campaigning for the city council to lift a ban on skateboarding. The energy found in Madison spread northward to Oshkosh and Green Bay, the latter where Northside Bowling Lanes served as a venue. Bands there included Sluglords and Depo Provera, and the zines *Suburban Mutilation, Fresh Vomit, Distorted Youth*, and *Sick Teen*.[10]

Punks in Lawrence, Kansas, built a scene in the midst of Middle America. Venues included the Opera House and Off the Wall Hall until 1982, then the Outhouse after that. Mortal Micronotz (speedy but also inventive), Start, the Yard Apes, Get Smart (they explained their name: "Form a band that will use their heads"), and the Embarrassment (from Wichita) appeared on a cassette compilation called *Fresh Sounds From Middle America*. The zines that sprouted up in Lawrence, were much like those in Madison, sophisticated ventures, including *Talk Talk, Bullet*, and *Blur*. There was a plethora of independent, local record stores, including Kief's Records and Tapes, Better Day Records, Love Record and Tapes, and Pennylane Records. There was also the college radio station, KJHK, that played locally produced music, without commercial pressure, a crown gem of a larger college radio movement that helped to sustain punk during the 1982–1983 explosion.[11]

Lawrence also featured a cross-generational rebellion. For in 1981, the "Beat" writer William S. Burroughs, then in his sixties, happened to move to Lawrence, Kansas. While he wrote *The Place of Dead Roads* (1983), a sort of postmodern western, he also hooked up with the editors of *Talk Talk* and the Mortal Micronotz, for whom he wrote lyrics to "Old Lady Sloan," about a cannibalistic woman. Burroughs would also do some "spoken word" events in Lawrence, one of them discussed in *Blur*, alongside reviews of punk shows. For *Blur*, Burroughs's "spoken arts" performances were in line with punk expression.[12]

* * *

Of course, college towns might have been the usual suspects (or locations) for cultural rebellion. More surprising were conservative regions of the country, places like Salt Lake City, Utah. Punk boomed here, the pioneers being the Massacre Guys, who sang angry political songs against apathy, one that lifted a title of a novel by Sinclair Lewis: "Let's forget about the dead, think of something nice instead. let's forget about the wars . . . let's forget the starving nations . . . it can never happen here." They were soon joined by the acidic band the Atheists, and then the Bad Yodelers and Maimed for Life. There was Raunch Records as well as the "Behind the Zion Curtain" radio show—which exposed young listeners to music outside Utah. Most startling was the zine with the same name as the radio show. The editors of *Behind the Zion Curtain* seethed with anger at Mormon theocracy and the rightward tilt of American politics: "Fuck Reagan, fuck religion, fuck the police and fuck the system." Their counter-mantra: "think for yourself."[13]

The conservative Southwest also boomed with a diverse selection of punk bands. In Phoenix, Arizona, band after band emerged from 1982 to 1983. The list leaves one breathless: Sin of Detachment, the Seldoms, Civil Death, Conflict, JFA, Poets Corner, Meat Puppets, Hellfire, Junior Achievement, Sun City Girls, Mighty Sphincter, Secret Ceremony, Eddie Detroit, Domino Theory, Vic Morrow's Head, Bloody Five, Zany Guys, Our Neighbors Suck, Spot 1019, Kiwis, Response, Skeletones, Woody and Peckers, Feederz, Chain Gang, UPS, Corporate Whores, Useless Pieces of Shit (UPS), Killer Pussy, and Maybe Mental. Out of the list stand the pioneers JFA, or Jody Foster's Army, who in bad taste had named themselves just nineteen days after Reagan was shot in an assassination attempt by the delusional John Hinckley. JFA sometimes changed their name to Jellybeans for Afghanistan or Jaded Foreign Antelopes. And they played covers of surf music alongside punk. They shared a sense of humor with Sun City Girls, who had named themselves after the retirement community just north of Phoenix that was, in the words of the social critic Joel Garreau, a "privately owned development" that had its own "posse" and that seemed to hate young people (it was hard to imagine any of its community members voting for Carter in the last presidential election). Sun City Girls played a discordant, free jazz–like form of music, adding to the diversity of Phoenix bands (similar to the Meat Puppets' synthesis of gruff punk and discordant country music). Some of the diversity could be heard on the compilation album from Phoenix, hilariously entitled *This Is Phoenix, Not the Circles Jerks* (released in 1984).[14]

Further south in Tucson the band Conflict dominated a burgeoning scene. They formed in late 1981 and grew to prominence from 1982 to 1983. The band had two Asian American women (one of them gay). They issued *America's Right* on cassette tape. It included a song that confronted a growing anti-immigrant sentiment, focusing on one "incident where these people were out to make a fast buck by driving a semi down to El Salvador, and loading it up with refugees at $1,000 each, bringing them to the U.S. and then trying to burn them to death in the truck." They protested the nuclear arms race, citing their Japanese heritage and the legacy of Hiroshima and Nagasaki. An album produced in 1983 included "photographs of people taken after the Hiroshima bombing" and carried the message: *Never forget.*[15]

* * *

Even more surprising was how the conservative state of Texas boiled with punk. Austin witnessed an exodus of bands to San Francisco by 1982, but the list of those remaining in 1983 was still quite impressive: Scratch Acid, Big Boys, Butthole Surfers, Offenders, Fudge Tunnels, Crotch Rot, S'not Art, Suicide Society, Burn Center, and National Guard. That energy spread to Dallas, where The Telefones played with Stickmen with Rayguns and the very young members of the Hugh Beaumont Experience, whose Jeff Coffey published a zine called *Throbbing Cattle* (before he joined up with the Butthole Surfers). A more serious band, Bomb Squad, arose in 1983, shouting songs about Selective Service and nuclear war and how "the right to die is the only right that we're guaranteed." Finally, there was one of the best-named bands, Jerry Falwell and the Burning Crosses (perhaps that outdid the Dead Kennedys' name finally?). Even the conservative oil city of Houston exploded. In 1979, Christian Arnheiter pledged his loyalty to a local zine, *Wild Dog*: "As for me, I'm staying in Houston," rather than leaving for Los Angeles or New York City. His band the Hates continued to "combine high energy music with . . . lyrics" that "hit hard with in-sightful social criticism." The same with Really Red—a politically charged band. Both bands played early Rock Against Racism (RAR) shows. They both inspired Legionnaires Disease, the Degenerates, and Mydolls. Finally, there was Culturcide, who performed sporadically after issuing their first single in 1981, "Consider Museums as Concentration Camps," a reitera-tion of the Futurists' and Dadaists' attack on museums for making art less dangerous, shut off from everyday life, and deradicalized. *Blur*, a zine out of Lawrence, Kansas, reviewed the record, saying, "Wow, I never thought that a good experimental band would call Houston, TX home. Then again, I never thought there was a museum in Houston either."[16]

Even more surprising was Tulsa, Oklahoma, where the Sex Pistols had played one of their most outlandish and confrontational shows in 1978. The central venue was the Crystal Pistol, which reminded one reviewer of "a small cowboy bar in 'any hick-town USA.' Small, dark, narrow, low-ceilinged." It was literally a "Rodeo Cowboy Bar" that could host up to 150 people (and usually that meant urban cowboys). Sometime in 1982, punk bands organized their own shows there, drawing from a first wave of punk (or new wave) bands like Cyanide, the New Mysterians, and Los Reactors. Most importantly, None of the Above (N.O.T.A.), a band steeped in radical ideas and politics, formed and plugged into the growing national networks. None of the Above explained that they wanted to take on the "things inside people that make them shitty. Greed, and hatred, self-righteousness . . . the feeling that you have the right to tell other people how to live. That's what the real enemy is."[17]

That spirit energized an abundance of zines. *Bad Meat*, published by Craig Draper in Tulsa, documented his state's penchant for censorship, exposing how a local school banned Robert Heinlein's sci-fi classic *Stranger in a Strange Land*. It also did a story on how McDonald's hamburgers destroyed rain forests in Central America. They hoped more "non-corporate zines" would blossom, and they got their wish with *Lazy Fair, Ratsbreath*, and *Dry Heave*, the latter celebrating punk as a "non-materialistic type of music, which places the least emphasis on rock star attitudes and capitalistic practices that go along with it." This sentiment sparked the founding, in 1983, of the Positive Youth Alliance (PYA), a nonprofit organization that often put together shows in people's houses. "At PYA shows you can go in the kitchen and watch us count the money. No profit here." They did all-ages shows, and by the end of 1983 celebrated how "the scene" in Tulsa was "about 100 strong and growing."[18]

* * *

If Oklahoma could have it, the Deep South could, too. In Miami, Florida, the band the Eats had started already by the late 1970s and were soon joined by the Throbs and the Essentials. Then an explosion of bands, including Gay Cowboys in Bondage (from close-by Fort Lauderdale) as well as D.A.M., Death Before Dishonor, Speed City, Expressos, Crank, Stupids, and Nobody's Heroes. A club called Flynn's hosted most of these bands' shows, including all ages shows on Sundays (some preferred playing "The Polish American Club"). Miami also produced one of the best zines during the time, *Suburban Relapse*, edited by Barry Soltz, who reported on local bands while documenting scenes across America, including in-depth interviews with the Dead Kennedys and Black Flag. Like *Sub Pop* and *Noise* zines, *Suburban Relapse* would form a cassette company—calling itself Sublapse—that released Morbid Opera's first EP (the band was known for Lisa Hodapp's stinging voice and the hilarious song "Eat the Rich").[19]

All of this activity spilled out of Miami and spread throughout Florida. In Tampa there were pioneers like Rat Cafeteria being joined by Primitive Romance; further north in Gainesville there were Hated Youth, Terminal Fun, and Roach Motel. In 1983, the compilation album *We Can't Help It if We're from Florida!* was released. That same year, when the Dead Kennedys performed with Roach Motel and Rat Cafeteria, one thousand kids showed up.[20]

* * *

And this partial report leaves out so many other places, including North Carolina, Virginia, and West Virginia, which all had burgeoning scenes . . . places like Boise, Idaho, and Minneapolis . . . or the exploding suburbs of New Jersey . . . all the way to Boston and the entirety of America's Northeast. But enough said. Dukowski was right: It could be and *was* everywhere.[21]

XXX

Explode! . . .

to ignite the suburbs . . .
—Paul Rat, explaining the promotion of shows in the Bay Area[22]

Meanwhile, the historical centers of 1980s punk—Los Angeles, San Francisco, and Washington, D.C.—expanded. By the summer of 1982, Black Flag, Husker Du (who had been busy building a scene in Minneapolis), and the Descendents (California) played to an audience of 2,000 kids at the Olympic Auditorium, which the local zine *Destroy LA* called "a big hall downtown" that usually hosted "roller-derby and fake wrestling." The necessity of such a large venue made clear that kids were entering the scene in droves (much to the regret of the older Hollywood clique). Publicity came, in part, from *New Wave Theater*, a television show hosted by Peter Ivers, that had made it onto the USA Cable Network, and which hosted a growing number of L.A. bands. The organizers of the show believed punk was a "social movement" more than "an entertainment phenomenon" and hoped to promote it with that in mind. Add to this numerous radio shows, including Adam Bomb's "Final Countdown" on KXLU (broadcast from Loyola Marymount University) and the radio fixture of Rodney on the ROQ, who would often play punk records that bands hand-delivered to him. A growing number of zines added to the already well-established *Flipside* and younger *Destroy LA: We Got Power!* (which turned itself into a record label), *Skank* (out of Woodland Hills), *R.I.P.*, and *Ink Disease*, among others. The growth attracted more attention from the LAPD, who continued to shut down any punk venue they could. The list of lost venues—the Whisky, Godzilla's, Dancing Waters, the Galaxy—rolled off the lips of Al Flipside as he reported them to *Suburban Relapse*. He noted the irony that the L.A. scene was growing but screwed at once, due to a lack of venues and police attacks. Still, Los Angeles's energy flowed north to Bakersfield, where Primer Grey, a local band, would open for Sin 34 (most of whose members edited the *We Got Power!* zine). And it leached south to San Diego, where The Backdoor served as a venue (it was on the San Diego State University campus) and bands like Battalion of Saints played.[23]

The D.C. scene kept growing and diversifying, already captured on the January 1982 compilation album *Flex Your Head*, which sold 4,000 copies its first week of release (the title referenced the music journalist Robert Christgau, who, like Bangs earlier, criticized "muscle head" punks in D.C.). There was the straight-ahead thrash of bands like SOA and Minor Threat (the former breaking up, the latter becoming more sophisticated), but also the complex fare by Red C (whose bass player was both African American and female) and Artificial Peace (who openly dissented against Ian MacKaye's philosophy of straight edge and sang one of the first songs about conformity within punk, "Outside Looking In"). Stylistic diversity continued with the Flipper-sounding noise band No Trend (who started to play in 1982), as well as artier bands like Submensas, 9353, and Crippled Pilgrims. By 1983, Outside Records could put out a compilation album entitled *Mixed Nuts Don't Crack*, the title itself suggesting diversity in the scene and local competition with Dischord. All of this creativity was assisted by an explosion of zines, most of them from the sprawling suburbs that now constituted the "D.C./Metro area." There was *Truly Needy* (Rockville, Maryland, and edited by Barbara Rice), *If This Goes On* (Bethesda, Maryland, and edited by Sharon Cheslow), *Suburban Outcast, Chow Chow Times, W.D.C. Period, Thrillseeker, Brand New Age,* and, by 1983, *Zone V* (out of Wheaton, Maryland). D.C. was also fortunate not to suffer the fate of Los Angeles, having numerous venues for shows: Wilson Center, Newton Theater, Lansburgh, Hall of Nationals, Pierce Hall, Space II Arcade, as well as the 9:30 Club and D.C. Space. And though the Glenmont Recreational Center had closed its doors to punk, Sanctuary Hall eventually opened theirs (though for a short time). There were also the radio waves of WMUC (University of Maryland's radio station, which hosted live performances of bands at times) and the experimental WHFS.[24]

Like D.C., the San Francisco scene pushed into the suburbs. By the summer of 1982, Tim Yo, working with Jello Biafra, had forty-seven bands from the Bay Area who contributed a song to the compilation album, *Not So Quiet on the Western Front.* Biafra explained, "In the last year and a half there has been this inferiority complex about L.A., and I don't think that's justified anymore." *Ripper* continued to publish while being joined by three of the most engaging zines—*BravEar* (out of Hayward, California, and edited by Michael Miro), *Ego* (edited by Peter Belsito), and *MAXIMUMROCKNROLL* (*MRR* from now on, edited by Tim Yo). *Rabies,* a publication connected to the anarchist bookstore Bound Together, claimed, "The San Francisco Bay Area harbors one of the largest concentrations of small-circulation underground/self-published magazines in the U.S." Venues for punk performances grew in number, and places like Valencia Tool and Die and Club Foot served as combinations of art venues and punk shows. There was even a place called the Vats (an abandoned beer brewery), where numerous bands and punk kids lived for cheap.[25]

San Francisco was becoming a political punk mecca, as it outpaced the growing scene in Los Angeles, which struggled with larger shows and police attacks. MDC embarked from Austin, Texas, to San Francisco around April 1982. They were joined soon by the Dicks, a band headed by Gary Floyd, who was called "a 300 pound communist drag queen who can sing like

Janis Joplin!" and "a tremendous sized . . . street politico." And then came D.R.I. *MRR* would report: "It seems that most of Texas is moving here."[26]

XXX

Thinking Like a Producer

> He thought of music as something you do rather than something you hear.
> —Ursula Le Guin, *The Dispossessed*[27]

Scenes spread and dispersed, but they also drew together and connected with one another. That connection happened any time a mail-ordered record finally arrived, sent directly from its producer and likely chock full of graphics, lyric sheets, and sometimes even a personal note. Or perhaps it took the form of a zine dropped through a mail slot, one tracked down from a copy of a local or national publication (likely *Flipside* or *MRR*). Vic Bondi of Articles of Faith (AoF), a band who helped promote all-ages shows in Chicago (usually held at the Central American Social Club), described the magical feel of being "less alone." He had grown up in a small town and described a near mystical feeling "when you listen to this music" and "all of the sudden you realize there's somebody there. . . . There's somebody out in the darkness besides you." There grew a potlatch culture—trading and bartering tapes and zines from across the country, resisting the culture of money (evident also in a "mail art" movement at this time). This became a sort of *I'll-send-you-mine-if-you-send-me-yours* ethic. When the zine *Altered Statements*, out of Cincinnati, started up, its editor pledged to fellow zine producers: "I DO SOLEMNLY SWEAR TO ANSWER [LETTERS] AND SEND THEM A COPY OF MY NEWSLETTER/FANZINE ALONG WITH A CURRENT LETTER ANSWERING ALL INQUIRIES." The D.C. zine *Truly Needy* offered readers to "trade issue for issue for fanzines" and printed long lists of publications across the country, all of which promoted "an exchange of ideas."[28]

In other words, from 1982 to 1983 a movement was growing nationwide. As bands like the Dead Kennedys and Minor Threat toured, they requested local bands play as openers, hoping to energize scenes. The anarchist ideal of "mutual aid" took hold, and by 1982, there were directories for those who could help line up a show (often these contacts were simply

other bands). Zines helped in the process, by warning about scummy promoters to avoid. The Milwaukee band Die Kreuzen wrote a letter to the
zine *Reagan's Death*, in Madison, Wisconsin, to warn against a Milwaukee
promoter. Known as D.H., he had ripped the band off in the past. They
suggested bands contact them if planning to come to Milwaukee for a show.
Truly Needy campaigned for the 9:30 Club in D.C. to host "all ages shows,"
including out-of-state bands; such shows might not generate a lot of cash
(clubs mostly profited from the drinks they sold), but the zine appealed to
ethics, to the cause of helping support a burgeoning movement of mostly
cash-strapped kids. Zines would also criticize local bands if they went off
the rails. *Forced Exposure*, an intelligent zine from Boston, once attacked
the band Freeze, asking:

> What the fuck are the Freeze doing opening up for Fear at the Channel?
> Isn't this the band that had all their fans get the shit beat out of them by
> the bouncers at this very club just a year earlier? Weren't they so angered
> that they [wrote] the song "Broken Bones" about this incident?

Both *Truly Needy* and *Forced Exposure* critiqued putting the profit motive
above everything else. Even so, national touring remained a challenge. There
was an ethics of suffering on the part of bands. Henry Rollins said playing
in Black Flag and touring was never considered "fun," since it involved so
much "self-sacrifice." The Minutemen labeled their own touring as "econo,"
living close to the edge, what they called an "idea of scarcity." Bands on
tour lived the "strenuous life" that the philosopher William James outlined
in the early twentieth century—a faith that struggling prompted grace.[29]

The records created by these bands, hawked at shows, were released
on independent labels, stripped-down operations run directly by the producers themselves. There felt almost a return to the rock record world of
the 1950s—when small local labels proliferated before the consolidation of
the 1960s and 1970s. There was now Posh Boy, Epitaph, ICI, Subterranean,
Thermador, Touch and Go, Dischord, New Alliance, SST, Modern Method,
and more. There were all of those zines turning into cassette tape compilation producers, including Version Sound (connected to *Noise*) and *Sub
Pop*. Many sold directly to consumers, rather than through stores, so as not

to lose control over the price that was set. Dischord, for one, printed the words "Pay No More than" and the suggested price on each release (they too did a great deal of mail order). In one instance, Jeff Nelson, Minor Threat's drummer and cofounder of Dischord, had to write directly to those who claimed they hadn't received their goods, telling one person, "I don't think we got your money, but here's $6.00 back. . . . If you find the letter with $, though, sends us the $, O.K.?" No kid expected a personal response from the likes of Warner Bros. about feeling ripped off. Labels would often work with a distributor committed to their same ideals of respecting the producer. One distributor was Constant Cause, but the best was Rough Trade, which was started by Geoff Travis—a punk intellectual—in 1978 in Great Britain and who now had a store and office in San Francisco. Travis's politics trended democratic socialist, and he modeled his distribution network on that principle (Rough Trade's employees—who formed a cooperative of sorts—would debate which records to support and not). Rough Trade worked with independent record shops and even helped out bands on tour, like when they gave MDC $1,700 to get out of a Canadian jail. The business was known for its democratic ethos, one in which musicians slogged it out in a warehouse or office, becoming—with pride—what *MRR* labeled "shit workers."[30]

This proliferation of labels, touring networks, and zines created not just a "world" but a consciousness. Kids were creating their own culture, and they realized that required discipline and self-management (having fun while doing so, of course). So the anarcho-syndicalism that Mark Sten had identified in Portland and that inspired John Shirley's punk ethics started to spread across the country. In the 1980s punk started to look a lot like Pierre-Joseph Proudhon's affirmation of anarchism as a "network of voluntary understandings between free individuals." Small producers networked with small producers. Managing an independent label or zine could give a glimpse into a prefigured future, sometimes slightly utopian. For instance, the zine *Skid*, out of Milwaukee, fantasized about "some big warehouse or something—maybe like a club where people had to pay dues to keep it open." This would grow from "people who are interested in the underground. It would be a place to meet and exchange information with others with similar interests. *Skid* could have its office there." Utopian possibilities could be found in small activities. The spread of scenes suggested that even someone living in Grand Forks, North Dakota, could be "in touch with the attitudes and ideas that make punk" into a "great awareness." Or what *Sub Pop* labeled an "anti-authority network" that was "organized" as well as "savage and defiant."[31]

Or what Ronald Reagan continued to decry as the growth of an "underground economy," that he believed generated an increasing deficit. In the spring of 1982, Reagan explained that he wasn't upset with big businessmen offshoring "tax shelters" (those were his friends, after all). He really worried about "the friendly neighborhood fix-it-man, a mechanic, craftsman." All of these types "prefer to be paid in cash," he explained. Then the president turned dour: "The underground economy is a kind of cash-and-carry barter system—no checks, no records or bookkeeping, and thus no tax." Though he never mentioned it, the DIY efforts of kids across America's suburbs certainly fit this description, especially with its potlatch feel.[32]

XXX

"The In Thing Now Is Stupidity"[33]

Communication is the opposite of violence.
—Fredric Wertham, *The World of Fanzines*[34]

Even as this network of communication grew, the mainstream media remained clueless, elevating punk's sensationalistic side. In January 1982, punk came at television viewers of *CHiPs* (a weekly show centered around the adventures of two police officers patrolling on motorcycles) as a dagger-wielding psychopath named "Thrasher." Played by William Forsythe, an actor who made a career portraying gangsters, Thrasher is the head of a motorcycle gang (a plot convenience for sure, seeing as there were no punk motorcycle gangs at the time) who also headlined his own band called "Pain." The gang had a penchant for stealing, and they rip off the equipment of Snow Pink, a new wave band proclaiming itself the next Blondie. *CHiPs* viewers tuned in for the requisite chase and accident scenes, and they got what they wanted when Thrasher tossed his bass guitar into a crowded street, causing squealing tires, accidents, and pile-ups.

The show culminated in a "Battle of the Bands," where Pain faced down Snow Pink. Pain decides to lock the doors to the club as they start to play

"I Dig Pain." The slamdancing begins, and a riot ensues, and then come the beefcake heroes on their motorcycles to break up the show. To celebrate victory, Ponch, played by Erik Estrada—whose face was made for *Tiger Beat* magazine—mounts the stage and sings Kool and the Gang's 1980 hit "Celebration," with its optimistic, disco thump and cheery lyrics about having a "good time."

Soon after *CHiPs* came the infamous *Phil Donahue Show*. On January 28, 1982, Donahue hosted his talk show with a bunch of Chicago punk kids whose scene had been percolating with a number of new bands and zines. Across from the punks sat angry and conservative parents. Donahue loved this sort of thing, where he got people to yell at one another, dredging up divides often ignored. This one got what he wanted. One elderly woman looked at one of the kids and yelled, "If it were my child, he wouldn't live in my house!" They were likely all on drugs, suggested other members of the audience. But the punk kids shot back that in fact many of them rejected drugs (straight edge), which solicited a woman yelling, "I'd rather see them on drugs than looking like that!" After taking a break, Donahue explained to the audience at home that they had been listening to a record by the Dead Kennedys, titled "Nazi Punks." To which kids screamed, "Noooo!" When asked what the real title was—"Nazi Punks Fuck Off"—they got bleeped. Then came a therapist to quell the threatening mood of disarray.[35]

Serena Dank had become the go-to spokesperson about the supposed dangers of punk by 1982; she was prepped for Donahue's show. Dank was in her mid-thirties and a "youth counselor" from Southern California who organized a group called Parents of Punkers. She expressed her concern that "punk rock is spreading across the country . . . and parents feel like they are losing their children to it." Playing up the generational card, she invoked nostalgia for hippies. She advertised her one-time flower-child bona fides: "I was part of the hippie generation. We were not violent like these kids. And we were not racists. These kids are mostly white, middle-class bigots." Or as she told the *Indianapolis Star* in 1982, "With hippies, the message was happiness, love, and peace, with punkers it's hopelessness and anger. It's very destructive." Dank was perfect for her role. She conjured the feeling of what Jello Biafra and Winston Smith called the "mellow out" of the seventies and the therapeutic politics of the "me decade," all the while ignoring the darker side of the 1960s counterculture (the side Raymond

Pettibon had emphasized). When a fan of the Minneapolis punk band Husker Du, a thirteen-year-old kid named Jesse, was asked by *MRR* what he thought of Dank and her organization, he called her "ludicrous." Here was a thirteen-year-old lecturing his parents' generation: "You can't generalize about people. . . . Some people . . . wear circled A's without fully understanding what these things signify." But there were also some who were "sensible about our actions" who could think for themselves. And maybe, he implied, that was why Dank hated punk. They refused her therapeutic politics of adjustment.[36]

No surprise that around this time, several punks (including band members of the Necros, and the Minutemen) were reading Anthony Burgess's novel *A Clockwork Orange*. Burgess offered a story about a gang of violent lunkheads led by Alex, a conniving mastermind of crime and a true antihero. He gets nabbed and placed into a behavioral reconditioning program, where he is manipulated—via nonstop exposure to violence on movie screens he's forced to watch—into behaving respectfully. The novel not only dissected therapeutic politics and adjustment, it raised the question of free will. As one of the critics of the program Alex submitted to put it, "Goodness is something chosen. When a man cannot choose he ceases to be a man." The novel's dissection of psychological reprogramming spoke volumes to punk kids who witnessed Dank's therapeutic approach to punk, the sort that turned dissent and maladjustment into things that could be cured.[37]

Black Flag hated Dank, and Raymond Pettibon continuously skewered her in his zine. Both hoped that young people could see through the mischaracterization of punk as violent and recognize its legitimate anger. Greg Ginn, the guitarist for Black Flag, explained his desperate sense of hope about the whole thing: "When someone at the show goes home and sees how the media distort what happened, they begin to think about how other things, too, must get distorted."[38]

XXX

Identifying the Real Enemy

Ronald Reagan is not a good American. He allows large corporations to run rampant over our environment, huge tax breaks for the rich, while

stabbing the poor in the back with cuts in social services and then spends
$55 billion to kill teenage girls in El Salvador.

—*Sub Pop*, 1982[39]

One of the Dead Kennedys' predictions, made in "We've Got a Bigger
Problem Now," came true five or so months after the EP had been released.
Jello Biafra had written a line where he imagined Ronald Reagan saying,
"I am now your Shah today, now I command all of you, now you're gonna
pray in school, and I'll make sure they're Christian too." On May 18, the
New York Times reported that Reagan announced his endorsement of a
School Prayer Amendment, pleasing the New Right and supporters like
Jerry Falwell. One of the best punk artworks sprang from this: Winston
Smith's portrayal of Reagan wielding a chain saw above young kids' heads,
screaming, "Ya see, kids? If we had prayer in school you could pray to get
your school lunch program back."[40]

At the same time, the Reagan administration began "its long-threatened
prosecution of the 800,000 young men who failed to register" with the
Selective Service. By the spring of 1982, Ben Sasway—the first person pros-
ecuted for refusing to register—had been apprehended and would soon be
imprisoned. But even with the Selective Service strengthened, neoconservative critics like Norman Podhoretz complained that the president hadn't
installed troops in the Persian Gulf. He seemed to be wimping out.[41]

Neoconservatives were more enthused about Reagan's growing focus
on Central America. The president had already dumped huge sums of
money—$55 million to be precise—in order to support a Junta opposed
to rebel forces in El Salvador. In the words of the *LA Weekly*, the Junta
was "opposed by virtually every person . . . except the handful of families
which run the country." The historian Edmund Morris described the Junta
as "so reactionary as to make Somoza," the one-time dictator of Nicaragua
overthrown by the Sandinistas, "look benign." Reagan thought bolstering
the regime in El Salvador was justified due to his foreign policy campaign
advisor, Jean Kirkpatrick, who had made a painful distinction between "authoritarian" and autocratic regimes and communist totalitarian regimes, the
former justified, the latter not.[42]

Talk of nuclear war continued apace as well. During the spring of 1982,
the administration oversaw an exercise named "Ivy League," which explored
the possibilities of fighting a "limited nuclear war." This accompanied plans

to "nearly double" the number of cruise missiles—often called "first strike" weaponry—intended for installation in Europe. At the same time, Reagan asked for 4.2 billion dollars for civil defense programs. He was helping to propose a "Crisis Relocation Plan" in case of a nuclear war that would move people from coastal areas to the Midwest, where they'd descend into basements. The plan included the proposition to "move 2.81 million people from the Washington metropolitan area to surrounding hamlets up to 300 miles away in three days," as the *New York Times* reported. When Congress examined the details they could picture only a "panicky exodus" and "Armageddon scenarios" papered over by the bureaucratic (and Orwellian) language of "relocation."[43]

Which explains why the term "Armageddon" proliferated throughout American public discourse at the time. In the June 1982 issue of the *Atlantic*, the journalist William Martin documented a growing interest in what he called "apocalyptic prophesy." It could be found in the "rapture" theory of Jerry Falwell, who believed good Christians would be whisked to heaven, while "those left behind" would face "a seven year period of Tribulation." It wasn't just Falwell, but key figures in the Reagan administration, including the secretary of defense, Caspar Weinberger, who late that summer gave a talk at Harvard. A student asked if he believed in what became known as "end times." Weinberger's response left many worried. "I have read the Book of Revelation and, yes, I believe the world is going to end—by an act of God, I hope—but every day I think that time is running out."[44]

A growing number of Americans drew aghast at Reagan's defense build-up and the talk of "Armageddon." And on June 12, 1982, they filed through the streets of Manhattan into Central Park, holding signs that read "Choose Life" and calling for a "nuclear freeze." They numbered, by some reports, close to one million and contrasted nicely with the memories of radical, confrontational, anti-Vietnam protests of the late 1960s and early 1970s. Protest looked polite. The march was populated mostly by "white, middle class liberals." Around the same time, Congress voted on a nuclear freeze proposal marshaled by Senators Ted Kennedy and Mark Hatfield, which "narrowly missed endorsing the freeze in a 204–202 vote." That, plus the fact that there was less support in the Senate, drove the freeze movement to go local and work on passing referenda that were purely symbolic in nature. For instance, California voted for a freeze, and Governor Jerry Brown asked Senator Alan Cranston to take the results to Ronald Reagan, who ignored him. After all, Reagan believed that the nuclear freeze movement was a tool of the Soviet Union, something he confirmed by reading *Reader's Digest*. The magazine would charge that the movement was one "that has been penetrated, manipulated, and distorted to an amazing degree by people who have but one aim—to promote communist tyranny by weakening the United States." A punk band from Cleveland called Death of Samantha looked back on this time and caught the drift of the president's thinking: "Reagan was saying that anyone involved with the peace movement in this country was a member of the KGB."[45]

Punk intersected with the nuclear freeze movement, with a small contingent marching on Central Park carrying the black flag of anarchism. The connection went deeper, though, especially in intellectual terms. After all, Kennedy and Hatfield saw the freeze movement as combatting "psychic numbing" in the face of nuclear war. Helen Caldicott, an Australian physician who became a spokesperson for nuclear disarmament, denounced politicians who were "manipulated by powerful, well-financed industrial and military lobbies." It was the "huge multinational corporation" that built an "atomic industrial complex" (most punks now would have said they also built the fledgling entertainment complex). These radical perspectives echoed in the world of zines. *BravEar*, having recently started publishing, drew from the thinking of the Marxist and psychoanalytical thinker Wilhelm Reich, and argued there was a suicidal death wish infiltrating American society, "evident in the insane global allocation of its resources, its money, labor, and scientific research to the construction of weapons for the purpose of global annihilation and self-destruction." For many punks the nuclear arms race represented a cultural and psychic crisis as much as a political one.[46]

* * *

Even though Reagan embraced much of the "end times" chatter, he had no feel for fatalism—he was too much the cheery optimist. And a few days after the large freeze march, he hosted a man who captured his worldview and put it on the silver screen. The director Steven Spielberg showed his recently released "blockbuster" movie, *E.T. the Extra-Terrestrial*, at the White

House. As the movie played, Reagan cried and dreamed, practically nodding his head in affirmation.

E.T. told the story of an extraterrestrial who winds up landing in suburban Los Angeles. E.T. is rescued by a nine-year-old boy (living in a fatherless household) who entices the alien by building a trail of Reese's Pieces candy to his bedroom. There he introduces E.T. to the wonders and bounty of America's consumer culture. The boy waxes about the virtues of Coke and the delights of Pez Candy, while his older brother celebrates E.T.'s high score on the videogame *Asteroids*. E.T. marvels at the kid's *Star Wars* action figures, one of those spin-offs from the "blockbuster" that movie had become. The film equated freedom with America's lavish consumer society (all those things Carter complained about in his "malaise speech"). The film also mocked the abuses of "big government," as bureaucrats from NASA capture E.T. and, in trying to learn more about him, nearly kill him. Indeed, the adult world as a whole looks thuggish (Spielberg filmed many adults in the movie from the chest down to make them look more impersonal). Only the kids understand E.T. "Grownups can't see him," the nine-year-old savior explains. The children defy NASA and liberate E.T. and then magically fly him on their bicycles back to his rescue spot where he enters a UFO and bids farewell.[47]

When the credits rolled, Reagan clasped Spielberg's hand and let out a doozy, "There's a handful of people in this room who know that everything in this movie is completely true." Was Reagan referring to aliens or flying bicycles or functional single-mother families or governmental agencies torturing little extraterrestrials? Spielberg took it to mean the president believed in UFOs. But really the film captured the president's central faith that belief, precisely when it provided confidence, was legitimate, that dreaming was crucial to human existence. All of which would explain to the president why the movie would become, at this juncture, the "highest-grossing film of all time." There were the spin-offs, like Michael Jackson's *The Extra-Terrestrial Storybook Album* released later in November, to keep things surging. Hershey's Chocolate did a near killing by tying into the movie, developing a public relations campaign for Reese's Pieces—now advertised as "E.T.'s favorite candy." This created "the biggest PR offensive for a single brand in Hershey's history" and tripled the sales of the candy (especially when sold in movie theaters). For Reagan, Spielberg had renewed confidence in his old home of Hollywood and the culture industry more generally. A movie's blockbuster status, built on optimism and dreams, confirmed that the culture industry knew what Americans wanted and desired—be that film, music, or candy. This was Reagan's populism, his faith that the people were good, that they made the right consumer choices, that they loved what they were told that they loved. It was governing via block-buster: *That which appears is good, that which is good appears.*[48]

XXX

The Summer of Love, or at Least the "Possibility of a Positive Negativism"[49]

What do we mean by saying that existence precedes essence? We mean that man first of all exists, encounters himself, surges up in the world—and defines himself afterwards. If man as the existentialist sees him is not defin-able, it is because to begin with he is nothing. He will not be anything until later, and then he will be what he makes of himself.

—Jean Paul Sartre[50]

During the summer of 1982, the Better Youth Organization (BYO) built the case that Serena Dank was wrong: There actually *was* a positive thing happening in the punk rock world. Shawn Stern, guitarist and lead singer for the L.A. band Youth Brigade and founder of BYO stood ready for the argument. He was armed with ideas.

Stern had discovered philosophy in high school. Of course, most punk kids found little redeemable about their high school education—the sort depicted in the summer movie *Fast Times at Ridgemont High* (1982). Here teachers get hung up on teaching rote information, the kids are stoned or ditzed out, more worried about sex than learning. None, in the words of the *L.A. Reader*, question "the conspicuous consumption that rules" their "lives." Stern was a rare exception to this, which is not to say that he didn't feel alienated from his high school. How could he not while attending, of all places, Beverly Hills High School. The silver lining of such a place though was that it was well funded and could therefore offer a creative curriculum. In his senior year (1977–1978), he was fortunate to take an English class on "Existential Literature," a course that shaped his worldview. Stern be-came especially enamored with Albert Camus, including writings like *The Stranger*, "The Myth of Sisyphus," and *The Plague*. He took from the philos-ophy a profound distrust in existing institutions and a belief in the ability to will his own existence. He also understood Sartre's maxim—"hell is other people"—that existence precedes essence, that you become who you are by tearing down a false identity that others project onto you.[51]

Stern envisioned punk's DIY practice as existentialist—refuting a common perception that punk was nihilistic (or suicidal, as Serena Dank seemed to suggest). Like Camus, he saw no objective meaning in the world. The central character in *The Stranger*—one of Stern's favorites—admitted that he confronted "the benign indifference of the universe." But this didn't rule out—as absurd as it might sound—willing your own meaning through acts taken in the moment. The historian of existentialism, George Cotkin, pointed out that, especially in America, "the existential grounds of anguish and despair functioned not as benumbing forces but as goads to action and commitment," the way it had with numerous activists in the civil rights movement and the New Left. Stern was an atheist who saw the desire for creativity as inherent in human nature. He would have agreed with Husker Du, who described themselves as "angry but not nihilistic."[52]

This homespun existentialism came in handy as BYO faced down increasing media exploitation and the likes of Serena Dank. Since 1981 (the organization formed in 1979), BYO had helped create "all ages" shows for Stern's band that were run in the interest of performers rather than club owners. From 1981 to 1982, BYO organized shows at Godzilla's, a bowling alley and nightclub, where it controlled the price of admission, hired their own bouncers, and raised support money by hosting benefit shows. "We ran it and we got punks to work there," Stern explained. A reporter at the *LA Weekly* recounted a BYO show where "one kid threatened to put his foot through a wall" and "a bunch of his peers surrounded him and told" him "to lay off." The message: *This is ours to manage, don't screw it up.* But soon after this incident, BYO faced pushback from the owner of Godzilla's, who started to raise ticket prices and hired his own nasty bouncers. Rumors floated that members of BYO had threatened to beat up one of the owner's employees, making obvious, if anything, that the agreement was dead.[53]

Turning its back on Godzilla's, BYO organized a concert called "Youth Movement 82," held at the Palladium, with TSOL, Adolescents, Wasted Youth, Social Distortion, Youth Brigade, and A.K.A. Some estimates put the attendance at 3,500, illustrating the growth of punk throughout Los Angeles's suburbs. Unfortunately, one young woman fell off the Palladium's balcony, which taught Stern about the problems of insurance (they didn't have any) and the wider challenges of DIY. It also prompted Mikal Gilmore, the brother of the convicted murderer Gary Gilmore who became a journalist sympathetic to punk, to criticize the show for a "ritual display of affecting desperation" rather than any "political possibilities." Stern rejected this verdict and continued to expand BYO's activities, turning the organization into a record label that could compete with the likes of SST and releasing, in the summer of 1982, a compilation album titled *Somebody Got Their Head Kicked In* that included Youth Brigade, Aggression, Battalion of Saints, Joneses, Bad Religion, Blades, Adolescents, and Social Distortion, plus cover artwork done by the neogothic punk artist Pushead (some of whose work, though it was more complex, looked like the sort found in *Punk Lust*).[54]

The album's opening song was Youth Brigade's "Violence," perhaps one of the best in-house critiques of punk. The song sounded sharp and angular and offered a sort of sing-along component (when performed live, kids would scream out with Stern "violence, violence, violence" or sometimes playfully "violins, violins, violins" while they played on imaginary violins). The song had punch and was full of the absurdist element Stern had gleaned from existentialist writers. Its opening line rang out, "They call us fascist and then they pray to the god that made the world their way." And then the charge of hypocrisy that America, with its long history of violence, had no right to condemn what it perceived as the violence of punk: "In whose name they kill and teach the sermons and the laws they preach." And the chorus which repeated the mantra of "Violence," followed by "just for kicks . . . does it make any sense . . . can you stop it . . . do you want to?" The song brooded with realism: "Philosophy borne of the mind try to explain the problems of our lives. It can't explain away that violence is here to stay." Don't blame the kids for violence, the song suggested, look at the behavior of your leaders: "Say it's just our nature we have to fight. . . . Doesn't matter we've been taught that might makes right." The bully in the schoolyard was simply mimicking the country's leaders.

With the compilation album came the idea of making BYO a national movement, spreading the word about a "positive" vision behind punk, culminating in a tour during the summer of 1982. To carry out this expedition, Stern bought an old school bus, tore out the seats, and installed beds, where members of Youth Brigade and Social Distortion would sleep, along with roadies and a driver. The tour left on August 18, 1982, heading first to San Francisco and then all the way up to Calgary in Canada, where Youth Brigade stayed at a collective house run by punks, complete with their own skateboard ramp (this reminded Stern of a collective house he had established a year out of high school). But pretty soon problems emerged; their school bus started malfunctioning, forcing Stern and others to push it down city streets. The growing difficulty of what *MRR* would call "a down to earth independently financed adventure done for the hell of it—suffer (if) the consequences come," started to create fissures between participants. The biggest fissure was between the bands: Youth Brigade took some but not all elements of straight edge philosophy as a source for a responsible politics. Social Distortion, on the other hand, were drunk punks—hedonistic and lazy. Their song "Telling Them" talked about the joys of getting into shows for free by entering through the back door (not really the best ethic when it came to DIY and the way Stern tried to organize his own shows). Members of Social Distortion accused Stern of being a control freak—creating rules about the little bit of money they got and how it was spent. Stern retorted that some act of self-governance for the common good was necessary to make the tour work. By the time they arrived in Detroit, two members of the tour had decided to take a bus back home. By the fifth week, things had pretty much fallen apart, with Social Distortion returning home before the tour was completed. A documentary movie about the tour came out two years later, accentuating the sense of failure. The *L.A. Reader* concluded, "You are seeing . . . young men who are realizing for the first time that rock 'n' roll, for all its glory, can't triumph over things." A conclusion that could prompt frustration and futility or highlight the ethic of suffering and humility DIY demanded. Stern took the latter course, drawing again on his reading of Camus. For Camus, as for Stern, the absurd was "born at the confrontation between the human cry and the world's unreasoning silence."[55]

* * *

No matter the failed tour, the idea of BYO spread, especially during the summer of 1982. In Philadelphia, Ronald Thatcher formed his own chapter. He hoped to find ways of stopping police from shutting down shows (which took place at an alarmingly high rate). He wanted "an alternative scene,

with a permanent hall and to be rid of elitism, authoritarianism, monopolies." Not surprisingly, the reality didn't live up to the ideals. Philadelphia's
BYO, after its formation in the fall of 1982, became "a small group of active
locals" who organized "gigs with bands from elsewhere" and planned bus
trips to protests in Washington, D.C. Thatcher hooked up with those in
other scenes, including "people in California" and New York City, finding
simpatico with the band Reagan Youth.[56]

Reagan Youth were one of many bands (another being Heart Attack)
who emerged from the city's suburbs at a critical point in punk history.
There, of course, were the gigantic hovering ghosts of Patti Smith and
Richard Hell's band Television, the memories of CBGB (still around) in
its halcyon days of punk's birth (at least for some). One of Reagan Youth's
band allies, the False Prophets, believed that something changed with the
dawn of the 1980s—those ghosts no longer intimidated. By this time, the
band explained, "The first wave of New York punk bands had pretty much
all broken up. . . . The second wave was sort of all the kids and younger
adults who had been outside the initial scene, but had been really inspired
by it, and then went and started their own bands." They were helped out
by the Bad Brains (who had moved from D.C. to New York City earlier),
and by other institutions, like the independent store Rat Cage Records,
and zines like *Damaged Goods*, published out of the suburbs of Great Neck,
New York. *Damaged Goods* documented a tiny Lower East Side club, A7,
that was "founded on uncommercial ideals, known . . . as LESRMAS (the
Lower East Side Rock Music Appreciation Society)." And here is where
Reagan Youth got its start.[57]

The band formed out of a group of "teeny punks" at Forest Hills High
School (in Queens, New York). Band members initially bonded around a
shared hatred of an authoritarian gym teacher. Lead singer Dave Insurgent
(b. Rubinstein) was an A student who loved to read. He carried around
a copy of Peter Kropotkin's *Mutual Aid* with its ideas about evolution
and communal-anarchism. He balanced this optimistic philosophy with
the dystopian forecasting he found in Aldous Huxley's *Brave New World*.
Reagan Youth would start most of their shows with a reading from Huxley,
especially scenes where kids were "being conditioned in their sleep like
the alphas being conditioned" into "a caste system." The band emphasized
Huxley's ideas about "the feelies" and a "Soma Holiday," in which people
are induced into passivity via pleasure, more than repression. The band's

guitarist, Charlie, channeling Black Flag's song "TV Party," believed television promoted acquiescence in contemporary America (as soma did in
Huxley's dystopian novel). He explained, "They take television and serve it
to kids like they serve valium to their parents." As their song "Brave New
World" put it, "everybody in their place; I take a Soma Holiday, to be born
without a face. . . . Is this utopia? Living your life on a factory line . . . living
your life from nine to five," suggesting that night-time culture (supposed
leisure time) had become as enslaving as menial daytime labor. Even with
this pessimistic inclination, Dave Insurgent touted Kropotkin's hope, precisely because of what he saw taking place in the DIY culture surrounding
him. As the intellectual historian George Woodcock explained it, Kropotkin
celebrated decentralized "cooperative working associations" that influenced
the world of "leisure" with a "vast proliferation of mutual interest societies"
formed by "fervent amateurs."[58]

That countervision of anarchism drew Insurgent to the idea of BYO—
whose hopes had a certain regionalist feel to them (though Stern encouraged formation of local BYOs, he never set out any rules for people to
follow). During the fall of 1982, Insurgent tried to form an organization
he called FRONT. The array of activities envisioned was impressive. They
planned to hand out leaflets and statements at shows to raise political consciousness and hold meetings, lectures, poetry readings, rallies, and demonstrations. They already had success in helping to organize fifty punks
marching at the huge June 12 protest against the nuclear arms race. They
hoped soon to have an anarchist festival with music and art shows. As
Insurgent explained to the editors of *MRR*, "We are working on opening
an alternative space where artists and musicians can work and own coop-
eratively." These initiatives, Insurgent was certain, could create a "real anarchistic youth counter culture."[59]

* * *

Reagan Youth was one of many bands starting to make connections between music and politics during the summer of 1982, pressing the BYO
view in more radical directions. The connection might have seemed
obvious—especially if kids were reading the song lyrics that came along
with recorded releases. And yet the connection came with challenges and
an array of approaches. As Scott McLemee, editor of *Plan 9* zine out of
Austin, Texas, warned, "Mixing music and politics can be risky."[60]

Millions of Dead Cops (MDC), who had moved from their home in Austin to San Francisco, became the most notorious band to marry music to politics. Indeed, the band's roots were found in political activism more than music. During the late 1970s, band members met one another as they worked with an "Anti-Kissinger/Pro-Farm workers" organization as well as the "John Brown Anti-Klan Committee." Dictor explained: "We did some No Nukes things. We helped out. We pamphleted. . . . We were part of Yellow Rose, which was an affinity group to send people to Seabrook," a nuclear power plant under construction in New Hampshire. They saw in the Dead Kennedys and Tim Yo's activities a promise they wanted to cultivate.[61]

Some critics accused MDC of putting politics ahead of creativity. Others argued that punk bands should sing about personal feelings and emotions (especially those adolescent feelings captured in bands like Black Flag and Agent Orange). But as the band's lead singer, Dave Dictor, saw it, his song "Corporate Death Burger" (released on their first album, becoming the second punk call—at least in America—for vegetarianism after Audio Leter's in Seattle) *was* an emotional outpouring, even though it focused on international politics of multinational corporations. "I'm just giving you how I feel," Dictor would explain. "I'm just sharing my emotion about eating meat and about corporate manipulation of food and what happens to Third World countries whose land is bought up by the multinationals." Rage at injustice propelled Dictor. He *felt* his politics.[62]

Which made much of MDC's music sound like an assault more than a provocation. The song "Born to Die" (also on the first album) opened with a shouted slogan that was repeated throughout: "No War, No KKK, No Fascist USA!" The band sounded certain of itself, declarative and confident with no time for complexity or confusion; their music hammered listeners' ears and minds. Steve Albini, a key participant in Chicago's punk scene at the time, argued that the band drowned in its own preachiness and lacked "the musical muscle to make songs rather than lectures." As the Ann Arbor critic Bill Brown warned, political punk could degenerate into "didactic exercises in ethics," with sloganeering swallowing up complexity and creativity taking second seat to getting a point across.[63]

Another San Francisco band, Code of Honor (CoH), provided a contrast to MDC. The band released their single, "What Are We Gonna Do?" around the same time as MDC's first album. Though "What Are We Gonna Do" is fast, like most of MDC's fare, it is also more angular, disjointed, broken up rather than streamlined forward (the band sometimes played with the experimental musician and singer Patrick Miller of Minimal Man). As *Ripper* described it, CoH's music had a "hard drive and sharp changes in rhythm and structure." The vocalist, Johnithin Christ, had "a dramatic way of singing, with a unique style of lyrical pacing." He wasn't just shouting or preaching with certitude. A reviewer for *Ego* explained that Johnithin Christ wasn't "really singing at all, but delivering some rather mixed up but achingly sincere oratory," conveyed in the opening lines of "What Are We Going to Do": "My life, my vision, my hope and my dreams." All of these things could be destroyed by a "nuclear war," he cried. The song would slow down and become quieter and more melodic, drawing the listener in, over which Christ spoke the words, "Here we are, a small group of kids who've realized our government's fucked. But . . . " and then posed the question "what are we gonna do?" Then he screamed the line once more, melding anger with anxiety: "What are we gonna DO?" The song ended on the theme of existentialism that Shawn Stern had developed, with the provocation: "It's your choice . . . it is us." The song never provided any political roadmaps, exploring moods rather than slogans, anxiety rather than sermons, much like the Minutemen had two years earlier (and still were).[64]

Code of Honor originated as an idea, a deliberation about beliefs among its founders. It formed out of the wreckage of two earlier bands, Society Dog and Sick Pleasure. The guitarist, Mike (from Sick Pleasure), and singer, Johnithin (from Society Dog), hooked up and started not just having conversations about forming a band, but also thinking through a "code of honor" to guide their future behavior. Mike explained the difference between CoH and Sick Pleasure: "Basically, there's a lot more morality in Code of Honor. Me [*sic*] and Johnithin really dug deep together to find out what we really believe in and what was really important to us." The actual code they wrote up managed to merge communitarianism with individualism and anarchism:

> Never desert your comrades in need, in danger, or in trouble. Never minimize your strength of power. Never seek praise, approval, or sympathy. . . . Your self-determination and honor are more important than your immediate life. . . . Choose your own decisions. . . . Better to die than live a lie.

Johnithin also added an ethic of responsibility that drew from a sense of guilt about the US government's actions abroad: "We're all responsible as long as we let our government do what it's doing. That's what bothers me the most is that everyone in America just sits back while our government is doing all this stuff." "This stuff" obviously being intervention in Central America and the arms build-up. This language of guilt and honor sounded far from the characterization of punk as violent and demeaning. Though guilt and honor might have sounded like conservative principles, they weren't for Christ, who saw them as a challenge to the unhealthy "American way," that taught kids to "Lie, Cheat, and Steal."[65]

In their discussions, the band also explored ideas about regional decentralization, arguing for California to secede from the union in order to protect the area's resources from a rapacious federal government (especially the then-sitting interior secretary, James Watt). "Other people have thought about" California secession before, Johnithin would explain. This likely referred to the writer Ernest Callenbach, who had issued, in 1981, an update to his earlier *Ecotopia* (1975), which imagined a time when California (along with Oregon and Washington) seceded from the union to adopt sounder ecological policies. There were few cars in this utopia, more high-speed rail travel; Market Street in San Francisco had "become a mall planted with thousands of trees"; the work week had been cut to twenty hours. In *Ecotopia Emerging*, the follow-up, there's a substory about an amateur band who plays local and community venues and refuses to get an agent. "We don't want to be just rock stars, up there, you know. We want to play live, for real people." Meanwhile as California prospers, the rest of the country, run by large corporations, goes to war in the Middle East. The gradualist reform and decentralization Callenbach promoted appealed to CoH. They were anarchists, not revolutionaries. As they explained, "If we . . . disarmed police there'd be panic in the streets. There'd be all these crazy people robbing and hurting others."[66]

Which was not to say that the band members were pacifist or consistent in their views. One of the band's original codes included: "Never fear to hurt another as long as it is in a just cause." In fact, they got called on this, by *The Attack* zine in Seattle, when they released the song "Fight or Die" in 1982. The song prompted the sort of debate that would increasingly mark punk discussions that year. *The Attack* reprinted the lyrics: "Take away the government and you take away the lies, kill all the politicians and no one else will die, think of what you're doing children, life is in your hands, it would be all so obvious now—especially to you, so stop the government army and disarm all police, our only chance for freedom is through honesty and peace." *The Attack's* editors saw a major contradiction here (which there was) and took note, "Don't you understand, when you kill the oppressors, then you become the oppressor, and in turn, by your own set standard, you should be killed. Murder has nothing to do with either freedom, honesty or peace." This was a line nearly plagiarized from the wartime writings of Albert Camus (who counseled becoming neither victims nor executioners when faced with an enemy). It was a fair critique, although it assumed that the band sought out consistency, which they didn't. They realized that they could not preach an airtight solution to the problems faced, the way that MDC tried. "We're not saying to everyone, 'Follow us, live the way we want to live.' We're just saying live your own life," the band explained. There was confusion as much as anger and anxiety in CoH's view of politics.[67]

* * *

Starting up *MRR* in the summer of 1982, Tim Yo—the man who had battled Bill Graham on the radio airwaves earlier—wanted to make his zine into a forum to discuss answers to the questions raised by MDC and CoH (his models, in part, were two earlier and now defunct magazines, *Search and Destroy* and *Damage*). Yo placed MDC on the cover of the first issue and interviewed CoH soon afterward. Yo was "short, stocky" with a permanent "five o'clock shadow" and always wearing black "high-top sneakers." He was slightly manic, shouting his arguments but then breaking into a wide grin. He was a bundle of energy who could work a full-time job in the shipping department of the University of California at Berkeley and then return to his "big, tumble down Oakland house," where he and fellow "shit workers" assembled the magazine. The print was tiny, with text crammed everywhere, often made more difficult to read since its black ink tended to smudge.[68]

Some considered Tim Yo a Marxist ready with a doctrinaire line, but he was, by necessity, quite inclusive in those he considered his fellow "shit workers" who collectively assembled the zine. The first issue mentioned over thirty contributors whose political views ranged from libertarianism to communal anarchism to democratic socialism. Some, like Ruth Schwartz and Ray Farrell, who had worked with Tim Yo when *MRR* was still just a radio show, were more interested in music production than politics. Schwartz once explained, "I wouldn't say that I ascribe to any particular preset political realm, although I orient myself towards the anarchistic socialist blend of things." Mykel Board was a libertarian who often seemed to write pieces just to piss off Tim Yo. Board was a cynical critic of "political correctness" on the left. He had historical memories, as did Yo, but they left him with a sense of hopelessness about politics, while Yo pined for the excitement of People's Park. Board once quipped about the 1972 election, "When Nixon got elected by 60%, I said that was it. I'm not going to make a revolution for these guys. . . . People aren't worth fighting for." He stuck with a leave-me-alone sort of attitude, his columns often more predictable than provocative.[69]

The most important writer Tim Yo hooked up with was Jeff Bale, his contemporary. Bale was much more well read, his ideas had a more academic inclination (he'd provide lengthy bibliographies to the articles he wrote for *MRR*). He had grown up in Chicago, coming of age during the 1960s. When he was two years old, his father left him to a mother who descended into alcoholism (she died at age forty-four from cirrhosis). The divorce filled Bale, in his own words, with an "emotional source of . . . rage" that turned quickly into "a critical perspective on the world at large." This was an anger shared among many punk kids who were experiencing the legacy of skyrocketing divorce rates of the 1970s. Bale started listening to hard rock and roll (the Who, for instance), and found himself hiding in public libraries where he read mounds of books that provided a haven from a rough childhood. He graduated from high school in 1968, and though he was more counter-culture and hedonistic than leftist activist, he remembered the riots at the Chicago Democratic Party convention politicizing his anger. After college, he shipped off to Berkeley for graduate studies, arriving in the summer of 1979. He left graduate school for the education he hoped punk could provide, publishing some articles in *Damage* before writing regularly for *MRR* and moving into the magazine's headquarters, holding onto his day job as a messenger in the Bay Area to fund his love of punk politics and debate.[70]

Bale knew the intellectual history of punk social criticism found in *Slash* (1977–1979), *Punk* (1976–1979), and *Search and Destroy* (1977–1979), which merged punk with political ideas while rejecting "Marxist dogmatism." Bale had read numerous thinkers in the tradition of libertarian socialism, especially George Orwell. He explained his political views in an interview with *Ripper*: "I consider my form of anarchism to be very much like revolutionary socialism: a nonauthoritarian socialism. . . . I think that any kind of new structure has to be built from the ground up, and people have to be voluntarily committed to doing it." But he was also drawn to the "pessimistic Marxism" of the Frankfurt School; he had read Herbert Marcuse's *One Dimensional Man*, for instance, which led him to believe that "people are totally unaware of their real interests." Bale held low estimates of humanity, following again Orwell, who argued that "the middle class masses" historically embraced authoritarianism, including the totalitarianism found in Nazism and Stalinism. He was also aware of his internal tension—that between hope in participatory democracy and a dark view of human nature. He once explained, "My survival and sanity have rested on a terrifically black sense of humor," shaped obviously during his childhood and now shared with Tim Yo.[71]

The bond between Tim Yo and Jeff Bale forged itself from their shared historical experiences and sensibilities. "We have a historical perspective," Tim Yo explained to *Ripper*, "in terms of what happened in the 50s and 60s with outbursts of cultural rebellion, and how that was coopted or destroyed, that definitely shapes our attitude towards what's going on now." Bale concurred, arguing that "if you try to divorce the music from the context . . . you're really doing a disservice to the listeners." Tim Yo emphasized that "we are trying to enhance an attitude in the punk scene where ideas are as important as music." His and Bale's engagement in the counterculture of the 1960s could help provide historical perspective about the possibilities and predicaments of punk in the 1980s (thus, they were suggesting that the sixties weren't just what Pettibon drew about but something that offered a "usable past"). They'd also help fill a void, now that *Creep* and *Damage* had ceased to exist; additionally, *MRR* would report on scenes across America, something *Flipside* used to do but no longer did. To document a nationwide movement, to use history for understanding possibilities, and to criticize punk from within punk—such was Tim Yo's and Bale's self-imposed charge.[72]

* * *

While *MRR* started to document scenes across the United States in the summer of 1982 and connect them to a deeper sense of politics, Matt Groening, then a chief editor and writer for the *L.A. Reader*, surveyed the world of punk art. He became something of a makeshift curator, using the pages of the *L.A. Reader* to report on the linkage between visual art and punk—especially those who worked, as he did, in cartoon format.

Groening had grown up in Portland, Oregon, in a large family headed by a cartoonist and filmmaking father. Like many who would enter punk ranks during the late 1970s and into the 1980s, he started his own "underground" high school newspaper, taking early inspiration from the "hippie" cartoonist R. Crumb and the publisher Zap Comix. He embarked for Evergreen State College in Olympia, Washington, one of those rare "hippie" colleges where students developed their own curricula (and where Bruce Pavitt would later develop *Sub Pop*). He took up philosophy, enamored with the writings of Friedrich Nietzsche and Soren Kierkegaard (two thinkers who influenced the existentialists Stern read), and wrote for the student newspaper. When he graduated in 1977, he moved to Los Angeles with his then-girlfriend Lynda Weinman, with grand aspirations of becoming a writer. He worked a series of odd jobs—including as a movie extra, a chauffeur, and a ghostwriter—while pursuing his own cartooning, which became a strip entitled "Life in Hell." It centered on Binky the Rabbit who suffered from heaps of anxiety due to living in the "hell" of Los Angeles (the first name of the character was borrowed from one of Groening's favorite cartoon books from 1972, *Binky Brown Meets the Holy Virgin Mary*). "Life in Hell," in zine form, often sold five hundred copies—featured at the newsstand of the record shop Licorice Pizza, where Groening worked. He achieved a breakthrough by getting the strip into *Wet* Magazine in 1978, a publication with a larger circulation than his little zine. From there, he clinched a job at *L.A. Reader*, which printed his writings about the L.A. punk scene (he documented what he called "the great police-war on punk") as well as his comic strip, "Life in Hell," which started to develop a broader cast of characters.[73]

The idea behind "Life in Hell" was that childhood and adolescence were not uncorrupted states of innocence but a time of anxiety (heard in bands like the Adolescents and Agent Orange as well as the punk poetry of Dennis Cooper). Groening tried to plumb the sense of absurdity that young people felt about the demands of the adult world, including discipline during the school day. He explained how he came to cartooning: "I always thought the impulse to scrawl savagely went back to school days, when twitchy kids drew their way furtively out of the classroom window while the teachers droned on." No doubt, Groening got some of this from reading Kierkegaard, who explored the themes of boredom and anxiety about freedom. But it was something he also got from listening to his favorite band, the Minutemen, who he would praise for being "ambiguously intelligent." And from remembering bullies in his own past. He saw himself as part of a new generation (he was entering his late twenties at the time) and a wider world of punk cartoonists who were "too young to have been hippies and rejected drugs as a source of inspiration." Instead, his fellow punk cartoonists tried to "offer a humanistic reaction to media slickness and an almost technophobic disdain for the future." Their DIY ethic lent itself to growth—the simplicity of the drawings and the lack of training behind them advertised that anyone could do this (or at least try).[74]

Groening's survey in August of 1982 came after a spring "Punk Art Show" he attended at Contemporary Artists Space of Hollywood (C.A.S.H.), a combination art gallery and punk venue run by another transplant to Los Angeles, Janet Cunningham. Groening was delighted with the artists exhibiting, including the paintings of Lane Smith, mural paintings that were collaged and simultaneously graffitied by Brian Tucker, painted-on photographs by Ska Masda, photographs of punk shows by Ed Colver and Michael Probert, and found items (mimicking Marcel Duchamp's ready-mades) like Greg Brown's decorated television set that had the words "Kick Me" scrawled on its screen. All shared a look of desecration and deface-ment. There were also exhibits of numerous comic strips. The growing ranks of "outraged, semi-articulate" punk cartoonists seized Groening's at-tention, for obvious reasons. Raymond Pettibon, whose talents Groening praised, now appeared as a founder of things to follow, although the more recent cartooning was much more anxiety-ridden and electric-looking than Pettibon's staid noir work. Casting his eye on a recent *Flipside* magazine that documented the growth of punk cartoon art, Groening's list now spilled out, with a bundle of names: Dennis Worden, John Crawford, Jimmy Barf, Shithead, Fred Tomaselli, Jill Young, Pushead, Bob Ray, Mad Marc Rude, Chris Chalenor, Bob Moore, Shawn Kerri, Lee Ellington, and Doug Johnston. As well as himself and his friend Gary Panter.[75]

There was an aesthetic mixed with philosophical undertones in all of this work: Punk artists managed to get the energy of anxiety onto the page while drawing buzzing-looking, jolted characters (renewing the aesthetic of John Holmstrom's *Punk* magazine, an inspiration to many contemporary cartoonists, Groening pointed out). Dennis Worden would create Stick Boy, a crude character that looked like a lollipop with arms who consistently faced humiliation and adversity. Fred Tomaselli had an old man named "Stubby"—truly a grotesque—who sat in his wheelchair wearing a Camel cigarettes promotion cap and who provided useless advice in a Celine-like monologue: "Go Grind Up some glass and stick it up yer ass." John Crawford was the most well-known among the bunch, since he offered his strip for free to zines across the country. Crawford's character Baboon Dooley was a pseudo-intellectual rock critic (modeled supposedly on a very real rock journalist, Byron Coley). As Crawford explained, "I do a comic about a rock critic because I'm tired of the aesthetes and corporate taste-makers who constantly intrude upon punk. . . . Good clean hardcore punk is an anathema to the corporate greedheads." His character Baboon is some-thing of an absurdist and echoes the existentialism that fueled Groening's vision of punk art. In one strip, for instance, Baboon Dooley asks God why he exists and is unhappy. God retorts that Baboon's purpose on earth is to have people feel better about themselves since they're at least happier than him. Baboon pleads for God's help, and God says, "You just don't under-stand do you Baboon" and then hits him with a lightning bolt.[76]

Groening felt especially partial to his friend Gary Panter, their friend-ship bond blossoming soon after both men moved to Los Angeles in 1977 (Panter was four years older than Groening and had grown up in Texas). By 1982, Panter looked like the originator of an aesthetic spreading through the world of zines (and reflected in the work of John Crawford). Panter's first cartoon strip, "Jimbo," which depicted a punk often walking through a postapocalyptic world, appeared in *Slash* magazine from 1977 to 1979, and was then turned into a book in 1982. Presently, he was drawing "The Asshole" for *L.A. Reader*, about an unhinged and frantic character who had a distinct likeness to Tomaselli's Stubby. Jimbo was Panter's own "alter ego" but also modeled on Stephen Dedalus in *Ulysses* (like Groening, Panter was well read, more in literature than philosophy). Panter could now be seen as creating an energetic, hot expressionism quite different from

Raymond Pettibon's cold noir. Panter's art was more of a jumble than the clean, stark, and icy feel of Pettibon's. He wanted to get anxiety and heat into his work, to reject the coolness that pop art and Warhol had introduced into the American aesthetic. He became "part of the expressionist revival" witnessed in the New York and L.A. art scenes at the time. So Jimbo sweats, has bolts running around his head, is sometimes drawn by scratches more than clean lines, and his head moves from one side to another in one frame. And it's done in the approachable format of the comic strip—a fixture in American popular culture, even though Jimbo messed with readers' expectations. Panter shared with the gothic work of Pushead and Pugmire a penchant for the surreal. With Jimbo, that took the form of insects suddenly invading a story, insects that suggested surrealism and a hint of William S. Burroughs (who had once worked and written about being an exterminator). Panter certainly saw his work as tied to dystopian science fiction—one of his heroes being Philip K. Dick (who Panter helped interview for *Slash* in the magazine's last full issue). Panter imagined what he called a Dal Tokyo world: "a vast Martian colony a few hundred years from now where Japanese, American, and European cultures have collided," which was drawn from his "interest in J.G. Ballard's writing," especially *The Unlimited Dream Company* (1979), and "thoughts about a Texas landscape that's littered with piles of machinery and bulldozers." His art sometimes felt like it synched with the growing ranks of punk sci-fi writers.[77]

XXX

Punk Sci-Fi Finds Its Voice(s)

> [Science Fiction] is the enemy of normality, the antidote to bored sophistication and know-it-all over-refinement.
>
> —*Cheap Truth* zine[78]

A month after Groening's survey of punk art, Bruce Sterling's "movement" assembled at ArmadilloCon, a literature fest held in Austin, Texas. Sterling was joined by John Shirley and William Gibson; they called their panel "Behind the Mirrorshades: A Look at Punk SF."[79]

Gibson got most of the acclaim, even though he sometimes appeared as Shirley's understudy. The two of them had walked the streets of the Lower East Side of Manhattan (where Shirley had moved for a brief time),

often darting into punk clubs to grab a listen. Gibson had no anxiety ac-
counting for his writerly influences, including Shirley's. Like his mentor,
Gibson had read Joseph Conrad (the expression "the heart of darkness"
appeared in Gibson's writing) and others like Raymond Chandler, with his
hardboiled, noir style that explored the seedy, underground world of Los
Angeles (Chandler once quipped: "You can live a long time in Hollywood
and never see the part they use in pictures"). There was also Chandler's
hero, Dashiell Hammett, whose clipped dialogue influenced Gibson. There
was William S. Burroughs, with his literature of the hallucinatory, and the
paranoid novelist Thomas Pynchon, who had already incorporated rock
music into his now classic *The Crying of Lot 49* (1966). And though he
hadn't read very much of Philip Dick's work, when he saw the movie *Blade
Runner*, released during the summer of 1982 (based on Dick's 1968 novel
Do Androids Dream of Electric Sheep?), he grew interested in the theme of
artificial intelligence acting back on creators. But he worried that the film's
visuals—with its huge skyscrapers that blasted advertisements over rainy
streets populated by grotesque-looking characters—overpowered what he
could do with words on an inert page.[80]

Punk sci-fi had its literary canon and film works for inspiration, but it
was also influenced by contemporary observations. For instance, one of
Gibson's key concepts, "cyberspace," came from conversations with Shirley
but also from watching kids in one of the most popular institutions of early
1980s America—the video arcade (very often located at a suburban shopping mall and featured prominently in the Disney summer movie of 1982,
Tron). Gibson spent time "watching kids in video arcades" who seemed
to grow "rapt" as they "jacked into" machines with screens—the world of
Space Invaders, Asteroids, and Pac-Man—that helped create an "electronic
consensus-hallucination."[81]

Indeed, another writer closely associated with Gibson, Rudy Rucker, author of the important book *Software* (1982), wrote an entire short story
about the video game Pac-Man (though his editor, for copyright purposes,
forced him to call it Peg Man). One character plays the game insistently—
eyes glued to the screen, hands desperately grabbing a joystick that guided
Pac-Man in his search for fruit and ghosts spilling around tunnels. Eventually,
the player sees the face of Ronald Reagan appear on screen; the president
thanks him "for developing the software for some new missile system. He
said that all the Pac-Man machines are keyed into the Pentagon, and that

the monsters stand for Russian anti-missiles." Rucker had a sense of humor, for sure, but he was also making a serious observation about a major feature of youth culture of the 1980s, an addictive substitution of reality with what the French social theorist Jean Baudrillard called "hyper-reality" and the passivity it induced toward the nuclear arms race.[82]

Gibson developed this theme and others in two of his most important short stories from 1981 to 1982, "Johnny Mnemonic" and "Burning Chrome," the latter a story that Sterling called "incredible" in its resemblance to "fast moving" punk music. Gibson had rejected Shirley's focus on urbanism for the setting of suburbia, describing a "sprawl" of "malls and plazas." The story centered around two console "cowboys," Automatic Jack (the narrator, who has a prosthetic arm) and Bobby Quine, both hackers (Gibson called them "burglars"). They have no government or law to fear, as they occupy a world of "corporate galaxies and the cold spiral arms of military systems" which they must navigate via a "matrix" in cyberspace. The two cowboys aim their sights on Chrome, a corporate entity that offshores profits with the aid of conniving "bankers." They hack Chrome, giving away the money they've stolen to "a dozen world charities" and "ten percent for" themselves.[83]

This story of victory parallels another story of failure, the case of Rikki, love interest of sorts to both cowboys. Automatic Jack doesn't like the way Bobby treats Rikki, who constantly escapes abuse for "SimStim," short for "Simulated Stimuli," a virtual world populated by celebrities. Rikki has latched onto Tally Isham, planning to have plastic surgery to make her resemble her idol. In the end, Rikki has her eyes changed to look like those of Tally Isham. She has fallen prey to the lure of SimStim. In developing both stories simultaneously, Gibson explored the underbelly of a corporate entertainment culture that works through the addictive world of video screens and hyperreality.[84]

What Sterling recognized in Gibson's and Shirley's work was a theme that he had struggled to develop in his own punkish novel published two years before, *The Artificial Kid* (1980). It was a story of a young man, Arti, who filmed himself in fights for the entertainment of wealthy clients and who inhabited a "decriminalized zone," where "corporate citizens were shocked and titillated by the spontaneous anarchic violence that broke out among the small gangs of roving, idle, bored, and defiant delinquents." What Sterling saw especially in Gibson was prose that zipped along at a fast clip like punk music, while holding to narrative rather than postmodern fragmentation and self-conscious meta-writing (at the same time, John Shirley was turning to Lovecraft and grotesque horror in his book *Cellars*). This was enough inspiration for Sterling to announce at ArmadilloCon a movement. It also helped inspire him to create his own zine about punk sci-fi, *Cheap Truth*, started up later in 1983. Like the numerous punks editing and publishing zines across the country at the time, Sterling promoted the sort of writing he thought revolutionized sci-fi, and he offered this typical bullish charge: "Xerox pirates, to the barricades." Another culture war fought by punks aimed at destroying the ethic of entertainment.[85]

XXX

Stupidity Gets Stupider

> There can be no freedom outside of activity,
> and in the context of the spectacle all activity is negated.
>
> —Guy Debord[86]

Around the time of the ArmadilloCon, some young punks in Modesto, California, decided to see a movie. The poster for the film depicted characters who looked slightly like them, at least at first glance. They brought their skateboards with them, and as they pushed their way toward the theater, a prior showing let out. Suddenly a little boy pointed at them and said in a worried manner, "Mommy, there's those people in the movie." Before they knew it, rednecks jumped them. The theater management had to come out and put down the fracas. The kids were left wondering, "*What the hell* was that all about?"[87]

The movie they planned to see was *Class of 1984*, an American-Canadian feature film whose plot line portrays, in Bill Brown's accurate account, "a civil war that pits . . . punk rock youth gangs against everyone else." The movie had a star cast, including Roddy McDowell, Tim Van Patten, and, most importantly, Michael J. Fox. The movie's release coincided with the first airing of *Family Ties*—a television series where Fox starred as Alex Keaton, a preppy, young Republican who battles his hippie-hanger-on parents (the show became Reagan's favorite). The cast elevated the film, giving it a bit more credibility, though it still came across as a B-level and somewhat smudgy product.[88]

The movie echoed films about juvenile delinquency from the 1950s, especially *Blackboard Jungle* and *Rebel without a Cause* (1955). But those movies always ended with reconciliation between the adult and teenage worlds. In *Class of 1984*, the only solutions seemed to be revenge and vigilante action (the kind evident in 1970s films like *Death Wish* and *Dirty Harry*). The film depicts punk kids dealing dope and running their high school in their own interest; adults look the other way. When the "good guy" music teacher comes for his first day of class, he faces down a gang of kids who sieg heil and assault him. Eventually, they blow up his car outside his apartment and vandalize the science classroom where the character played by Roddy McDowall teaches. McDowall's character decides to teach with a loaded pistol aimed at his students. Timothy Van Patten's character, the lead punk Peter, then declares the group's motto: "Life is pain, pain is everything." And so the kids gang rape the music teacher's pregnant wife. They even take photographs and give them to the teacher, who blows his stack and descends into the school basement pursuing the punks. He uses an electric, circular saw to cut off one student's arm and then lights a gas fire that kills another. He then races onto the roof of the school, where Peter has kidnapped his wife. Battle ensues, and the teacher pushes Peter through a glass window. Before he plunges to his death, Peter asks for help, whimpering, "I'm just a kid."

"Perhaps in 20 years people will recognize," the *L.A. Weekly* explained, *Class of 1984* "for the kitsch stinkbird it really is, and laugh it off. For now, though, it's a dangerously manipulative exploitative hate the kids movie.... We're supposed to applaud as various punk rockers get crushed ... in escalating succession!" The *L.A. Reader* called the movie "crude, vicious, and morally irresponsible." Indeed, when Bill Brown saw it, he witnessed audience members cheering for the teacher. He concluded that the movie was "cliché, cynical, hysterical," and "one of the most awful, reactionary and senseless films I have ever seen." Writers at *MRR* were troubled that some punks had enabled the project. The director had put an advertisement out calling for "slamdancers" who looked the part to apply, an offering of self-exploitation. Worse yet, Fear's "Let's Have a War" provided part of the soundtrack for the movie. Was the band just offering what it always had—sensationalism and shock? *Reagan Death* zine suggested that the media elevated bands like Fear over more thoughtful ones like Minor Threat, MDC, Code of Honor, and Dead Kennedys. Maybe there was another explanation: Maybe, the band's dumb punk style fit the movie. Or perhaps Lee Ving, the lead singer of Fear, was looking for a role in Hollywood (he had an agent) and didn't want to bite the hand that might eventually feed him.[89]

Whatever the case, it wasn't the only movie exhibiting punk at this moment. Just a month earlier, *Ladies and Gentlemen the Fabulous Stains* had come out, a movie that charted a female punk band's rise to fame. The band winds up touring with another older band composed of ex-Clash and Sex Pistols members (who appear washed out, nearly decrepit). The new band stinks at first but then they get a new look—including a painted-on mohawk (like a skunk's marking) and garish make-up, almost resembling the band Kiss (or perhaps the goth group the Misfits from New Jersey). The band's leader, Corinne, also announces a straight edge proclamation: "I don't put out." The band starts catching on, especially among younger women, drawn to the band's feminism. As they get big, their audiences accuse them of selling out, and after being ripped off by a sleazy manager, they break up. . . . But that sad ending isn't really the end.

In what feels like one of the longest endings to a film, the camera turns its attention to the band's MTV video. Audiences watch as the band members dance around and lip-synch and then, lo and behold, they hold up their gold record and the camera pans to their images gracing the cover of *People* magazine. They have obtained fame, which the movie suggests every punk kid secretly wants.* So with the *Class of 1984* and now *Ladies and Gentlemen the Fabulous Stains*, the underground was either populated by dangerous rapists or wannabe celebrities.[90]

* * *

Television was worse. On December 1, 1982, the series *Quincy* aired an episode on punk titled "Next Stop, Nowhere," which was more subdued than *Class of 1984*—no electric saws severing limbs from bodies, for instance—but just as sensationalistic and exploitative in its own way. The series followed the adventures of a medical examiner, Quincy (played by

---

* Much like the central character in another movie that came out around the same time, *Smithereens*, whose female lead Wren is interested in only one thing—making it as a star, a narcissist who makes the underground her entry point to the entertainment industry (though she fails, unlike the Stains).

Jack Klugman), who worked as a sleuth on murder cases in Los Angeles. As Tim Tanooka, editor of *Ripper*, noted, "The show is praised for its attention to details" and has "a reputation in the entertainment industry for technical accuracy." He also noted that some L.A. punks helped the show's production out. Which only made *Quincy's* off-the-rails treatment of punk more painful to watch.[91]

The show begins with a murder at a punk concert. Quincy suspects, visiting the club himself, that punk music led to the murder. The show's punk band is named Mayhem and they play, in the words of Tanooka, music that "sounds maybe like Fear but more like Rocky Horror." Meaning—like the movie and play *The Rocky Horror Picture Show*—even more campy and cartoonish. Indeed, Mayhem's song "I Want to See You Choke"—with its line, "Saw a blind man the other day, took his pencils and ran away"—could be considered a rip-off of Fear's "I Don't Care about You." Except that Fear's song expresses self-interest and indifference; "Choke" celebrates physical violence. Whatever the case, a young adolescent female punk, who lives with her single mom, becomes the prime suspect. The sleuthing proceeds, as Quincy and his perky assistant, who reminded Tanooka of Serena Dank, go on a talk show and rail against punk, linking it to murder. Extending a generational cudgel, Quincy celebrates the 1960s when, according to him, everyone was protesting and believed in peace and love, in contrast to today, when "all" kids do "is gripe." After this episode of finger wagging, we learn that the prime suspect had been framed by a nasty friend, and the daughter returns home to reconcile with her mother. The show ends with Quincy and his assistant listening to sweet jazz (it sounds like Glen Miller or Tom Dorsey). He turns to her as they wind down, asking, "Why listen to music that makes you hate when you can listen to music that makes you love?"

Soon after *Quincy* hit the airwaves, a local L.A. television station, KABC, did a special on punk titled "We Destroy the Family." The show didn't fictionalize punk characters but took a documentary approach. It opened with Fear doing a soundcheck in which Lee Ving shouts into the microphone, "Kill Your Mother and Father" over and over again, the lyrics to the band's song, "We Destroy the Family." The voice-over recognized that the band deployed "satire" but still wondered whether kids might be too stupid to get it. The show focuses its first part on a suburban family, in which a son and daughter have turned to punk (intoning that punk has spread from grimy London to America's suburbs). The parents cry about their kids; the kids roll their eyes. At one point, the son is filmed in his room, listening to the English band Crass. The lyrics are barely audible, but they plead, "Fight war, not wars." Not exactly a song in favor of violence. The *L.A. Weekly* concluded that the show was a "ridiculous bit of re-actionary garbage" that "featured the ever inane do-gooder Serena Dank," who dominated the last portion of the report. By this point, Dank equated punk with "self-mutilation." It was all danger and violence, and a hatred that threatened parents. No surprise that the venue where Fear was taped playing, the Galaxy, soon halted all punk shows. One more venue bit the dust.[92]

The belief in something "positive" emanating from the punk rock world was becoming harder and harder to find on television screens. Many critics noted how much influence these media treatments of punk garnered, and how they operated in a circular fashion. Jeff Bale noted that as television portrayed punk as violent, it helped attract violent kids to enter scenes. These kids would be called "Quincy Punks" or "video punks," those who "were watching 'Quincy' one week and then dancing the next." Bale's colleagues at *MRR*, Jerod Poor and Noizebush, warned soon after *The Class of 1984* debuted, that the media hungered for "sensationalism," driven by advertising revenue. "The population must be entertained, not informed," they wrote. "Show punks as a bunch of chain-ladden [sic] maniacs who want to die young. . . . It sells." And it seemed to.[93]

XXX

"As the World Becomes a Bomb Factory . . . "[94]

The world can be destroyed instantly. Count your jellybeans.
—*Age Home* (zine out of Visalia, California)[95]

Ronald Reagan's daughter Patti Davis, a frustrated nuclear freeze proponent, brought Helen Caldicott to the White House on December 6, 1982. She hoped that maybe, just maybe, sitting down face-to-face for a conversation might check her father's tendency to see all opposition to the nuclear arms race as communist-inspired. But as Caldicott remembered the meeting, Reagan "said that Communist and left-wing groups organized the huge June 12, 1982 rally in New York City, alluding to [the liberal group] Americans for Democratic Action and others," and cited once again a *Reader's Digest* story. That point shows how much Reagan was freaked by the nuclear freeze campaign—that he was still talking about an event more than half a year earlier. Now he faced the spokesperson for the movement. Tension held in the air, and Reagan concluded that Caldicott was uppity; he recorded in his diary that she was "a round the clock anti-nuke lecturer and writer. She seems like a nice, caring person but is all steamed up and knows an awful lot of things that aren't true." In other words, a stereotype: Typical, hysterical female, easy to dismiss.[96]

Just two days after meeting Caldicott, the nuclear freeze movement's worst nightmare came true, its growing sense of desperation turned bizarre. A van that Reagan described in his diary as "full of dynamite," which it wasn't, drove up to the Washington Monument with big letters on its side that read, "#1 PRIORITY: BAN NUCLEAR WEAPONS." Inside the van sat Norman Mayer, a sixty-six-year-old man desperate to vocalize his opposition to the arms race. Wearing a jump suit and motorcycle helmet, he leaped out of the van clutching a model airplane controller that he told Monument guards could set off the TNT in his truck (which didn't exist). He demanded the president create a "national dialogue" about the arms race or else. Talks opened up with Mayer, as Reagan was shuttled to a safe location. After ten hours, Mayer jumped back into his van—as guards opened fire on him. FBI agents who approached the van could hear Mayer say, "They shot me in the head," as he collapsed.[97]

Mayer symbolized for many a cynicism creeping into the peace movement. June's optimism with the huge Central Park protest turned into winter's despair with Mayer's van. The sci-fi writer and one-time teacher of John Shirley, Harlan Ellison, argued that Reagan could only see Mayer as part of a "communist conspiracy." Ellison admitted that Mayer "was an extremist" and "bereft of his senses," but his cause was not. He feared that America was losing its "common sense and compassion," and that we were now "no better than Richard Nixon, who went to the windows of the White House, saw hundreds of thousands massed in the streets to protest [the Vietnam War], snickered, and went back to watch the Super Bowl." Soon after Mayer passed, the band the Crucifucks, out of Lansing, Michigan, penned a song with the line "I love Norm. You should too." It was titled "Official Terrorism," and it imagined an alliance between gutter drunks, Native Americans, and punk kids against nuclear ruin. Funny perhaps, but really a reflection of the frustration settling in about a president who never even pretended to listen.[98]

* * *

By December 1982, Reagan had shut down open political discussion, both around the nuclear arms race and the hot spots of his renewed Cold War— El Salvador and Nicaragua. He faced growing opposition from groups like the Committee in Solidarity with the People of El Salvador (CISPES). As he did with the nuclear freeze movement, Reagan dismissed opposition as Soviet propaganda. He argued, "The propaganda has been worldwide. And you find the same slogans being used in demonstrations in European countries about the United States in El Salvador. You find it here." It was international propaganda (originating from Moscow) that inspired those who disagreed with his foreign policy, for there could be no other rationale. Which confirmed for Reagan the need for covert action—something his advisors kept pushing. Five days after Norman Mayer was killed, Reagan reported in his diaries a "hush hush meeting with NSC [National Security Council] to complete report on covert activities by C.I.A. [Central Intelligence Agency]." Meaning support for El Salvador's corrupt rule and aid to the Contras battling the Sandinista Regime in Nicaragua, but the sort of support that didn't look like America was behind it.[99]

That's not to deny the overt side of Reagan's war footing. Throughout December and into January, Reagan firmed up the Selective Service System. He announced that the government would target the 564,000 young men who had not registered, while proclaiming that 97 percent of those who should have registered had (some were suspicious about these numbers). Reagan now made registration for the Selective Service a requirement for any federal assistance to go to college. Simultaneously, the president made sweeping cuts in higher education funding, including to Pell Grants and loans. The journalist and popular historian Theodore H. White concluded that Reagan's cuts to higher education seemed "directly contrary to an expectation that is built into the thinking of young Americans," that they would go to college and do better than their parents.[100]

To add insult to injury, the Selective Service System worked out a plan for drafting young men in the aftermath of a nuclear attack on US soil—an imagined land war in post-apocalyptic America. The hope was, in the words of *Nuclear Times*, to "coax 100,000 young men to straggle into their local draft boards within 30 days" of a nuclear strike. The program was titled "Continuity of Operations Plan." It sounded like something Gary Panter would draw about in "Jimbo," its essence captured in Raymond Pettibon's "You Are Necessary" printed over a horizon of gravesites.[101]

Amid all of this preparation for war, Reagan made note of the other side of the ledger—the need for sacrifice at home, as mobilization seemed to be readied. Visiting Boston around the time of his State of the Union speech in late January 1983, the president let slip that, if he had his way, he would cut taxes on corporations altogether. While announcing this dream, Reagan convinced himself that there'd be no "loss to the Government," in terms of revenue. Reporting on his statement, the *New York Times* admitted that the White House "could add no details" to Reagan's quip. No surprise, since it was Reagan's dreaming about questions of sacrifice (maybe seizing revenue from the underground economy could make up for the loss). If coupled with tightening up the Selective Service's preparation for ground battle in a nuclear aftermath, it suggested Reagan's political vision: sacrifice for the many, not the few.[102]

XXX

Becoming Creators Again

> Why are they doing this to us?
> —overheard words from punk kid at the Mendiola's police riot,
> February 11, 1983[103]

Two weeks after Reagan called for obliterating corporate taxes, Jack Grisham, the ever-smiling but tough guy singer for TSOL, stood on the stage at S.I.R. studios in Los Angeles. He watched as a handful of police entered the venue that held about 2,000 punks. Realizing his de facto leadership position—a curse for any anarchist—Grisham now looked at the scene unraveling and made a quick decision. He announced, "If a cop comes at you, hit the floor and go limp. Everybody sit down." The audience sat down while the police started to approach the stage, whacking kids or pulling prone bodies off the floor. The band played three numbers and then were cut off—ironically—when they started "Abolish Government." Recognizing that their nonviolent approach had failed, Grisham yelled, "There's more of us than there is of them!" And then: "Watch yourselves, be careful—let's go get 'em." As the *We Got Power!* zine described the police action: "They had to stop a punk rock riot (as seen on Quincy & Chips) but there was no riot, so they decided they would create one." And so kids faced off against police.[104]

Though defeated, Grisham restated what it meant to be a producer of one's own culture—that you had to defend that culture against foes, or at least go down fighting. Political and collective action and the playing of music now linked arms. And in explaining what he was doing to *BravEar*, Grisham situated himself within the history of American radicalism, not the Marxist left but the more anarchist, nonviolent direct-action left. He explained that civil disobedience was "safer and it shows more sense. Anyone can fight back a cop. That's doesn't take nothin', but to actually sit there and calmly show him what a fool he's been demonstrates quite a bit of sense." Grisham channeled Martin Luther King Jr., arguing not to descend to the enemy's level of violence and use direct appeal to reveal your own humanity to those who denied it. Soon after the event took place, Grisham called his band "innovators of the sit-down strike—ripping off Martin Luther King."[105]

*   *   *

The confrontations kept coming. One month after S.I.R., another police riot erupted, this time at Mendiola's Ballroom, located in Huntington Park, a suburban area just south of Los Angeles. The line-up was the Exploited (from England), Vandals, Aggression, Suicidal Tendencies, and Youth Brigade. The BYO had organized the show, working with the promo company Goldenvoice, then operating out of Santa Barbara. The police report asserted the show had been oversold, but Shawn Stern denied that. Whatever the case, about 1,500 people showed up. Employees of the Ballroom drew back when they saw the number of kids coming in and then locked the doors, leaving many stranded outside. Right then, the police arrived.[106]

They rushed the kids locked outside the ballroom. When the smoke cleared, there were forty-one arrests. But stats don't tell the entire story—certainly not the feel of the event. Jeff Mitchell, who drove to the concert from Long Beach, remembered diving into his car, as police used batons to smash his rear window. Cops battered one person trying to film the incident. Kids were terrified, running away in droves. As *We Got Power!* asserted, "Highlights of the evening were the two police officers who took it into their hands to smash store front windows so it would look nice and violent on t.v." There was something disproportionate about it all. Al Flipside pondered, "I couldn't help but wonder what made those cops at Mendiola's so fucking mad. . . . They beat more kids for a longer time than they did even at Elks Lodge," the police riot back in 1979 that many saw as the origin point of police-on-punk violence in Los Angeles.[107]

And then the irony: the event resulted in one of the least sensationalistic and more balanced media reports on punk yet. Having filmed parts of the Mendiola's Ballroom riot, KTTV, Channel 11 in Los Angeles decided to do some investigative reporting into the relationship between punk and violence. The five-part series opened with the Ballroom show, providing a Rashomon effect, where the kids said one thing, the cops another. But in this case, the show gave time for kids to explain their plight, with an African American roadie for Youth Brigade claiming that the charging police called him a "nigger." The show then examined slamdancing, concluding that most of it was a communal affair where young kids let off steam and had fun. The second chapter showed how nuclear war propelled so much punk anxiety, heard in numerous lyrics that the reporters quoted. With a bunch of kids sitting together for an interview, Shawn Stern, recognizing a rare opportunity, explained how punks saw themselves as "the future of the world" and would like a hearing. Like a KRON show about San Francisco punk, run about the same time, the KTTV episodes were "remarkably positive" in their "attempt to show punk rockers as 'normal everyday kids,'" meaning they sounded angry and confused but were not violent or nihilistic and certainly not seeking celebrity.[108]

* * *

Late January 1983 would be the one-year anniversary of the Phil Donahue show about punk. It seemed an opportune moment to make a statement about the long record of the entertainment industry's mockery. A young woman named Nancy, a graduate of Columbia College in Chicago, had been there when Donahue got audience members to say they'd disown their kids. Now that the *Quincy* punk show had aired just a month ago, she flashbacked to her showdown with "screaming maniac housewives." And she decided to write a scorching letter to NBC's president Brandon

Tartikoff. After all, NBC had broadcast *CHiPs* and *Quincy*. She hoped to set the record straight.

She wrote as if to answer the bogus question posed at the end of *Quincy*: "Why listen to music that makes you hate when you can listen to music that makes you love?" She explained, "We see the real side of love" in increasing "divorce rates." Talk of love from the boomer generation sounded at best contradictory. Boomers who stereotyped punk as violence also ignored how something like "slam dancing is a way to release pent up energy, as are a lot of other dances." She lashed out at the therapeutic politics of Serena Dank, who played up the idea that "impressionable . . . young kids . . . aren't sophisticated enough to understand what we are saying." The media made "scapegoats" of young punks, offering only sensationalism rather than a conversation or debate.

And here her argument started to sound almost conservative in its critique of popular culture, conservative in the strange, mixed-up way that "straight edge" sounded conservative at times. In contrast with punk lyrics that served as social criticism (she included examples from songs by the Dead Kennedys and Minor Threat), she highlighted the luridness of popular, mainstream bands. There was a whole host of songs she could have cited, but she chose the Knack's 1979 hit song "Good Girls Don't (But I Do)," about a "teenage sadness . . . you know you can't erase til she's sitting on your face." (She could have gone to the Knack's earlier hit, "My Sharona" with its line, "I always get it up, for the touch of the younger kind.") In revisiting the music industry's rush to promote the Knack—seen in 1979 as a new wave, "skinny tie" band that might rescue the industry from its doldrums (like Blondie)—Nancy smirked: "Now who would you say is corrupting the youth?" The culture industry had no shame, its only goal was to build markets and sell anything, including underage sex. Nancy was repeating the findings of popular sociological treatises at the time, like Marie Winn's *Children without Childhood* and Vance Packard's *Our Endangered Children* (both published in 1983). Like these studies' authors, Nancy reasoned that punk kids grew up into a culture that abandoned its young as it feasted on sexualized television, movies, and music.

Nancy ended her tirade by demanding that Tartikoff take responsibility for the cultural fare he provided. "The more dumb things you show on TV, the more dumb ideas you're giving to the kids," she lamented. Of course, it

was unlikely that Tartikoff even read the letter or thought about its implications. But it stood as a statement about how conscious punk was about
its mistreatment in the mainstream media. Nancy (and others) hated how
sensationalism not only sold but also created "Quincy punks" acting out
their own stupidity. She closed her letter by assuring her readers that punks
possessed a "good sense of humor" in their battle to be understood. She
explained, "After all, look what we have to go through to get a point across."
It must have felt like "screaming at a wall" (a Minor Threat song). How
could kids ever fight such a corporate juggernaut that only cared about the
bottom line?[109]

XXX

God, Mammon, and the Queen

> The audience takes up the refrain as they surge into the streets screaming
> "BUGGER THE QUEEN!"
>
> —William Burroughs[110]

One of the most interesting zines out of San Francisco, *Ego*, was about to
publish its last issue in April 1983, having failed to raise sufficient funds
through advertising. Its editor, Peter Belsito, had cut his teeth a number of
years earlier by curating a gallery at the University of Massachusetts. He
was taken by the provocations of conceptual art, especially the experimental
work of Vito Acconci, who told him about the punk scene at CBGB. Though
Belsito checked out the New York punk scene, he eventually embarked for
San Francisco and started *Damage* with Brad Lapin as well as his own club,
Valencia Tool & Die, which became a key punk venue in the heart of the
city's Mission District. Belsito lived at Valencia Tool & Die, in an upstairs
apartment, and created an art gallery on the first floor and a performance
space in a basement soundproofed with copious amounts of sand. After a
year of focusing on running shows, he met Karl Hinz, who had a print shop
and promised to publish *Ego* so long as he was reserved the back cover for
his own publicity.[111]

Belsito, thinking himself more an artist than writer (although he was really both), hired, among others, Marian Kester, who he knew from *Damage*.
She had a background in art history and had studied with the historian and

social critic Christopher Lasch. To call Kester well read was an understatement; she had made her way through everything from Friedrich Nietzsche to Dostoyevsky to T. S. Eliot to D. H. Lawrence, and then some. Her articles for *Ego* reflected her wide reading. She poured out essays on Dadaism and surrealism plus feminism and semiotics. Punk appealed to Kester for its "attempt to fight free of the pompous conventions, dynasties, and reptilian mannerist decade of latter day Rock" of the 1970s. It promised, for her, a return to "the raw basics." For Kester, punk had taken on the "society of the spectacle" that the Situationists had diagnosed (and that Christopher Lasch used in his book *The Culture of Narcissism*, to explain the nature of corporate consumerism).[112]

A month before the last issue of *Ego* was published, an event erupted that seemed made for the zine. On March 3, 1983, Ronald Reagan welcomed the queen of England to a celebration at the de Young Museum in Golden Gate Park, creating scenes that reminded some of Reagan's garish inauguration. Here's the typical surface-treatment in the *New York Times* story about the event: "The queen wore a champagne taffeta Hardy Amies dress with ecru and gold lace sleeves trimmed with bows. . . . Mrs. Reagan was in a Galanos design of emerald green satin crepe embroidered with matching crystal mirrors and a crystal choker by Tess Sholom." After the guests mingled, they sat down to dinner, which consisted of "lobster terrine with golden caviar, double consommé of pheasant with quenelles of goose liver, loin of veal with morel sauce, vegetables, truffle potatoes . . . ." Besides Reagan, the First Lady, and the queen, the guest list included CEOs of major corporations, including Stephen Bechtel Jr., chairman of "Bechtel Group"; Philip Caldwell, chairman of the Ford Motor Company; and Gordon Getty, director of Getty Oil. Billy Graham was also present— symbolizing the marriage of wealth and muscular Christianity that Reagan embraced (the sort of faith that ignored moral reflection or, fortunately for Reagan, church attendance).[113]

Outside the event, it felt like a police state. A perimeter around the museum served as "an armed camp for the night . . . floodlights lighting up, the park as bright as day," as *MRR* remembered it. That didn't stop 5,000 protestors from showing up, some in opposition to England's policies toward Ireland, but many sickened by the garishness of the event itself—all that food inside when the numbers of hungry, homeless people skyrocketed on San Francisco's streets. Belsito wrote that the event "made my stomach turn." Its "conspicuous consumption" tried to outshine the reality of Reagan's presidency: "He's cut back public services by billions of dollars, asked that we send hundreds of millions to El Salvador to support a corrupt government, demonstrated a desire to dismantle the EPA [Environmental Protection Agency], asked that the countries of Europe be used as garages for nuclear missiles." Meanwhile, millions are spent, Belsito pointed out, to put on a spectacular gala in a publicly owned park. "We are asked to let pompous protocol take precedence over common sense," Belsito wrote about Reagan's smiley-faced gala. The mainstream news media "played up the pomp," too busy discussing "evening gowns" to notice the protestors in the streets.[114]

* * *

Soon after his San Francisco gala, Reagan flew to Florida to make a historic set of speeches. The first took place in a perfect setting for him—outdoors and on a sunny day at the Epcot Center theme park in Disney World, March 8, 1983. His audience consisted of eager-looking high schoolers, many of them exchange students, watching as he mounted the podium. He opened up with a joke about the weather before eventually expressing his alarm about how the Soviet Union was outperforming America's high schools when it came to mathematics and engineering. Cold War 2 required smarter kids, Reagan explained, those who got down to the grind and learned about the hard sciences and geometry.

But rest assured, the president went on, this didn't have to turn all kids into bookish nerds. After all, there were "video games" out there that could help educate kids about their future. Reagan beamed with a smile and explained:

Many young people have developed incredible hand, eye, and brain coordination in playing these [video] games. The Air Force believes these kids will be outstanding pilots should they fly our jets. The computerized radar screen in the cockpit is not unlike the computerized video screen. Watch a 12-year-old take evasive action and score multiple hits while playing "Space Invaders," and you will appreciate the skills of tomorrow's pilot.

So staring into a video game "prepared" kids "for tomorrow." It almost sounded like something from punk sci-fi, like Rudy Rucker having Reagan's face appear on the screen of a video game. Young psyches were preparing for militarization and magically via entertainment. Reports were heard of Armed Forces recruiters hanging out around video arcades.[115]

After his Epcot speech, Reagan found himself at the Citrus Crown Ballroom at the Sheraton Twin Towers Hotel in Orlando. Here he delivered one of his most apocalyptic speeches yet to the National Association of Evangelicals. The president interested in biblical stories and Armageddon was just about to give a true stemwinder, extending on his belief that those calling for nuclear disarmament were simply stooges for the Soviet Union, traitors all.

Reagan outperformed the expectations of evangelicals—pointing out his attempt to get prayer into public schools and condemning abortion, as part of his war against "modern-day secularism." He explained that America was undergoing "a great spiritual awakening" that could rekindle "the story of hopes fulfilled and dreams made into reality." But spiritual rebirth demanded that America face down "the aggressive impulses of an evil empire," also known as the Soviet Union. It sounded almost like something from the blockbuster movie *Star Wars*, the virtuous believers versus the godless warriors. Reagan cited Whittaker Chambers, who back in 1952, as the Cold War ratcheted up, called for Americans to discover "a power of faith which will provide man's mind, at the same intensity, with the same two certainties: a reason to live and a reason to die." Reagan saw the Cold War as absolutist and religious. The real zinger came when he chastised the nuclear freeze movement. Naive and traitorous at once, the movement hoped, in Reagan's words, "to remove" itself "from the struggle between right and wrong and good and evil." That was that. And then thunderous applause rang out as "Onward Christian Soldiers" played to the happy crowd.[116]

Jerry Falwell wore a wide grin when he visited Reagan in the White House, just one week after the "Evil Empire" speech. The leader of the Moral Majority joined ranks with the president to paint antinuclear protestors as stooges of Russia. Falwell loved the bomb, for it ensured the rapture. His compatriots echoed his faith. Phyllis Schlafly called the bomb a "marvelous gift that was given to our country by a wise God." Hal Lindsey, in his bestseller *The 1980s: Countdown to Armageddon*, explained that "the Bible supports building a powerful military force." Falwell pressed these ideas the hardest, practically mimicking the president. In his campaign against "freeze-nicks," Falwell once sermonized, "In the Kremlin, Andropov or somebody decides that we need 300,000 to march in Stockholm or Berlin or New York, and the robots stand up and start marching for a nuclear freeze." For Falwell, protestors weren't just traitors, they were automatons controlled by international puppet strings.[117]

The punk press lit up, renewing a proud (but largely forgotten) tradition of anticlericalism in American thought. *Existential Rage* out of Orange County California reported about the use of "Onward Christian Soldiers" and called Reagan's speech to evangelicals "a twisted dream," turning the president's own words against him. The zine *Revealin Da Lies* warned that Falwell gave "the follower a sense of power and identity, plus an absolute authority to turn to for all the 'answers.' It provides a belief system for those who are too weak to think for themselves." Reagan's relationship with Falwell—who *Reagan Death* called an American "Ayatollah"—deeply troubled them. *Negative Print*, out of Parma Heights, Ohio, reprinted a letter written by a conservative Republican who freaked out over Reagan's relationship with fundamentalists. The writer pointed out that Jerry Falwell said he needed no cemetery plot since he was assured of floating to the heavens after nuclear war. Does such a man, the question went, deserve the ear of the president?[118]

Toward the end of March, Reagan gave another speech denouncing the freeze movement. This time he channeled the great polarizer Richard Nixon (whose terms "the silent majority" and "law and order" were some of Reagan's favorites). Reagan insinuated that those who opposed the arms race were setting up America for defeat. Protest made the country look weak in the eyes of the Soviets, for dissent didn't suggest a strength of American democracy but rather a country losing its will and declining. "If we appear to be divided—if the Soviets suspect that domestic, political pressure will undercut our position—they will dig in their heels. And that can only delay an agreement and may destroy all hope for an agreement." Peace through strength again. For zine writers across the country, it felt circular and maddening at once.[119]

XXX

The Growing Danger of Demanding the Impossible

Most of the people spraying anarchy symbols on the walls don't know what it really means, but a few do: the most furious dedication to responsibility for one's own behavior, and a fierce love for life to fight for it against death.
—Jonathan Formula in opening to *California Hardcore* (1983)[120]

The federal government invaded the punk rock world on April 18, 1983. An FBI agent contacted Dan Mazewski and Alan Brown, publishers of *Destroy L.A.* (based out of Van Nuys, California). The agent, James Kellogg, had received reports from the postmaster general about an "inflammatory" publication. Kellogg asked Brown, "Who are your readers? . . . Why do you do the mag?" Kellogg was clearly interested in something wider than the zine itself, which showed up in his other questions: "What's the difference between New Wave and Punk?" And "Why do" punks "look that way?" And, of course, why did the title of the zine sound so menacing? To which Brown explained he was "bored" and hated "this city," laughing nervously. To which Kellogg, in dour FBI style, said, "I'm glad you think this is funny. I don't."[121]

Kellogg warned Brown that he was going to send a report to the US attorney general for further action. He laid out a roadmap for the zine to follow, if it wanted good standing with the law. The demands were, as reported in the *L.A. Weekly* and *MRR*: "(a) change the name of the magazine (b) send a letter of apology to the postmaster general (c) send letters to all contributors and subscribers telling them of the name change and (d) place an ad in a local music trade publication announcing the name change." In other words, shut it down, cease to exist, for what zine publisher could afford such initiatives, especially having to take what would be an expensive advertisement in the mainstream music press, where no one read about zines in the first place. Alan contacted the ACLU to see if they could help, but he was told that until the attorney general made a move, there was little to be done. In the end, Alan stopped publishing *Destroy L.A.* And *MRR*, in reporting the incident, concluded, "Oh well, so much for the First Amendment."[122]

* * *

A few days later, a dangerous art show debuted in Washington, D.C., next door to a major punk venue, the 9:30 Club. It was organized by the Washington Project for the Arts (WPA) and an organization based out of New York City known as Colab (short for collaboration). Colab had been behind the "Times Square Show" of 1980, where artists displayed their work in a decaying building they had occupied. They had also, earlier in the year, organized the "real estate show," where, in the words of the art critic Lucy Lippard, they had "taken over a derelict city-owned storefront right on teeming Delancey Street on the Lower East Side of Manhattan, . . . and filled the space with art protesting absentee landlordism, eviction, developers, the city's waste of space, greed . . . ." As for the nonprofit WPA, it had hosted in 1978 a "Punk Art Show," curated by its director Alice Denney with great assistance from John Holmstrom, editor and illustrator of *Punk* magazine. Denney was on the perpetual search for the next avant-garde, especially the sort connected to punk.[123]

The result of this collaboration between Colab and WPA, "The Ritz Hotel Project," was fueled by three hundred artists who took over the dilapidated building and filled it with art in all forty rooms available. Reviewing the show, the art critic for the *Washington Post* documented its "anti-establishment, anti-elitist, anti-cash, anti-quiet and anti-government" feel. "When they portray Reagan, as they often do, they put fangs in his mouth or blood on his hands." One artist offered a " 'jelly bean brain award to James Watt [Reagan's secretary of the interior] for service in strip mining our forests for coal.' " Another participant hoped " 'the black flag of anarchy will fly over the capitol.' " To see these works, attendees had to walk past broken windows and use rickety staircases, all the while hearing a tape loop of Reagan's voice that gave the show a "sleazy and chaotic" feel.[124]

Barbara Rice, editor of the D.C. zine *Truly Needy*, attended the show. She had read Roger Shattuck's *The Banquet Years*, a book about the European avant-garde from 1885 to World War I. Rice learned an important lesson from the book, namely that "any active avant-garde is so rapidly absorbed by the cultural market that it scarcely has time to form and find a name." Though the Ritz Hotel show was a bit overhyped for her, she noticed how art had merged with the act of illegal occupation, an attack on the principle of private property. Which might explain why the fire marshal shut down the show days before it was intended to close. This wasn't just art, it was an act of occupation, remaking abandoned space into an arena of anarchist expression.[125]

* * *

By the spring of 1983, the art of occupation, that is, of squatting abandoned buildings, was becoming more prominent in San Francisco's punk scene. Admittedly, squatting was more an international movement than an American one (there was the universal symbol for squatting, an electric bolt through a circle). When MDC toured Europe, they returned with news about a huge number of squats, especially in Germany. One squat in Amsterdam, the band reported, had 3,000 residents. So too Britain, which already by 1973 was reporting upward of 10,000 people engaged in squatting. Of course, these were countries with stronger welfare states and less obsession about private property, which made importing these examples of mass squats into the States precarious.[126]

Against the odds, a number of kids based in San Francisco (and New York City) were learning how to work crowbars and bolt cutters to enter abandoned buildings. They were learning that a drum-type lock was better than a dead bolt for protecting seized property, and they were discovering the skills of electrical wiring. They were learning to enter buildings from the rear, to evade detection by the authorities. They were diving into dumpsters to scrounge for food and cooking on camp stoves. More importantly, they were *organizing*, having formed Squatters Anonymous six months earlier. The group's membership consisted of "street people, housing activists, and community people who were tired of old forms of organizing for people's housing rights." They merged the DIY spirit of squatting into an essential act of anarchism.[127]

For sure, they didn't always succeed; by the spring of 1983 they faced as many defeats as victories. Back in February, thirty squatters got ejected from Polytechnic High School, a building that had stood empty for a number of years before squatters took it over. They turned their eviction into a protest that included marching on Haight Street and taking over an empty building and hanging banners out of windows. A month later, squatters tried to "break open the Empress Hotel in Tenderloin." But landlords spotted them and chased them away.[128]

Even with these defeats, squatting reflected the growing politicization of the DIY ethic and a wider punk aesthetic. Peter Plate, along with Jim Squatter, provided intellectual ballast to the movement in San Francisco, as they explained the act's aesthetics and ethics simultaneously. Plate had embraced punk back in 1979, making connections with his anger. He once explained: "Punk rock is an integral facet of an anti-authoritarian rebellious stance against big business and ruling class interests. That music moves me, it moves my anger." Anger at a city where empty buildings existed alongside rising numbers of homeless people—that idea burned inside him. But there was also an aesthetic connection to history and the past and something almost conservative (in the literal sense of the term *conserve*). "I am very interested," Plate would later write, "in discovering the merits of abandoned buildings, the sweet and sour odors of debris, the huge broken down warehouses across America, like architectural dinosaurs from prehistory." Squatting for him was an act of preservation, even conservation, as much as revolt. He explained in forlorn, almost romantic terms, "I want to enter forgotten gardens." To pre-serve, to cultivate, and to break the law of private property—such was the politics of squatting, the art of demanding the impossible.[129]

* * *

The impossible . . . like finding a venue in Los Angeles for a punk show in the spring of 1983. Clubs continued to shut down; police raids be-came the standard. This prompted some to search for different venues (the way BYO had tried earlier). Two of the best Southern California bands, the Minutemen and Savage Republic, struck up a conversation about where they could put on a show free from cops and bouncers. It immediately dawned on them: *the desert*. Close to Los Angeles, the Mojave Desert provided a stark and open landscape just right for a show.[130]

Savage Republic—the name connoting a self-governing political unit driven by primitive desires—had a leg up on the Minutemen in one way. Some members of the band studied at the UCLA Fine Arts Department, which gave them a source of revenue, namely university grants for exhibitions and performances. They started to experiment with alternative venues by playing in underground tunnels on UCLA's campus and then approached their advisor, Chris Burden, who by then was a notorious performance artist. Burden was famous for an array of pieces—like "Shoot," in which a friend shot him, and "Shout Piece," where he screamed at people entering the gallery, "get the fuck out, get out immediately." Burden wanted to make his performance art into an "existential arena of self-creative, death-defying acts" and a way to eschew the art market (his work "could not be sold" as his performances were "one-time event[s]"). Though Savage Republic (and certainly the Minutemen) lacked the pretension that art could revolutionize the world, they shared Burden's hunger for sites outside the normal venues of performance.[131]

So, with the OK of Burden, on April 24, 1983, 150 people boarded buses that drove them to the Mojave Desert. A writer from *BravEar* accompanied them. During the drive, one participant was overheard saying, "It seems like there's something new happening." Other passengers hushed up to hear him say, "I mean the club scene. . . . But—like this, going to hear music in the desert. People are starting to do something, to try new things." The bands arrived early and then welcomed, as equals, those coming off the buses. Conversations ensued. And then they listened to the "primitive rhythm" of both bands as their songs bounced off the stripped-down landscape of the desert.[132]

* * *

At the same time as this desert performance, *MRR* was taking note of what looked like an even more radical project. In its March–April 1983 issue, *MRR* discussed the far-out escapades of the San Antonio, Texas, punk band called No Way Muffo. The band had announced a "mall tour," which had originated during a Christmas show at Wonderland Mall in 1982. The band had pushed its way into the mall and mounted a stage (probably intended for Santa Claus) and started playing. Mall patrons freaked out. "It was so loud," said the marketing director of Wonderland. "They were obnoxious. They were wearing weird pants, hospital orderly shirts, makeup, earrings, and one had on a surgical mask. It was like something I've never heard." She cut the power on them, called the cops, and had them arrested. The band simply posted bond and planned for a wider "mall tour." They had assaulted, and hoped to continue to assault, the quintessential institution of America's suburbs.[133]

* * *

Then there was street art. Imagine these visuals: The Marlboro Man, the tough cowboy perched against a red, southwestern canyon wall, lighting up a cigarette. Below him the words: "Cancer is Macho." Or an army recruitment advertisement that read, "We'll pay you $288 a month to kill." Or just these words spray-painted on a blank wall: "A society of sheep must in time beget a government of wolves."[134]

Another space for graffiti could be found on a ubiquitous set of boxes spreading through suburban America in 1983—boxes that looked like television sets that sold the newspaper *USA Today*. The publication debuted in the fall of 1982 and in two years stood as "the third largest daily in the United States." It was written at a sixth-grade level and tried to be very "visual," receiving the nickname, "McPaper." Here was Jello Biafra's take: "*U.S.* [*sic*] *Today* is a corporation newspaper full of Reagan's 'happy news.'" Each colorful (not black and white) issue of the paper shone through a clear plastic screen—thereby mimicking television—and had the words "the Nation's Newspaper" featured prominently. But sometimes vandals armed with black magic markers erased the "ati" and the apostrophe "s" in Nation's to make it read "the Non Newspaper." Or sometimes they'd fill the slots (where quarters were to go) with glue and scrawl on the screen: "Sorry: TV on the blink."[135]

This sort of graffiti was growing more conscious and organized by 1983, especially in San Francisco. Sometime around the spring of 1983, Bound Together Books—which published a zine that discussed squatting and other anarchist practices—gave advice on how to alter billboard advertisements. There was an art and technique to it. If you wanted to cover up text with your own, you had to calculate precisely the size of letters in the original. You needed to consider how absorptive billboards were, since they usually had been papered over again and again (some watched as paint soaked into a billboard, literally disappearing). You had to post lookouts to complete the job, making this a collective rather than an individual action and increasingly self-conscious. *BravEar* reported on a "guy down on 6th Street" who had held "a party recently where he had photos of graffiti from all over town, and these huge sheets of paper for people to write on all night" in order to practice for future opportunities. *Ego*, in its last issue in the spring of 1983, discussed a group called Incites! who had taken direct inspiration from the anti-Nazi collage artist John Heartfield (an inspiration also for Winston Smith). They did Xerox art and photo-montage with political messages, wheat-pasting their wares throughout San Francisco. The group had once been involved in the Revolutionary Communist Party (RCP) but now rejected doctrinaire Maoism for a politics of provocation—more open-ended than sloganeering. They considered their work as coming from the "youthful intelligentsia" who had been the "catalyst for the anti-war movement." Mark Chambers explained to *Ego*: "We intend to create an oppositional landscape without deference to the media."[136]

Street art mixed tones of existential freedom and desperation. The writer Norman Mailer had commented on graffiti art in 1970s New York City. Juiced on his own home-spun existential philosophy of rebellion, Mailer described the graffiti artist as "all the schizophrenia of the powerless and all-powerful in one psyche." When the French sociologist Jean Baudrillard wrote on spray-painting, he cited a *New York Times* reporter who saw the act as "the indestructible survival of the individual in an inhuman environment." Now Jeff Bale picked up on this philosophy of graffiti. He explained to *Ripper*, "We're in a situation where the only way we can express ourselves is by doing something outside the existing communication networks. And that is by . . . writing things on walls—let's face it, for a person who's powerless, if you write something on a wall, thousands of people are gonna see it, going by in a car or train or whatever." Existential and absurd, for sure, but also, at least for some, fun and exhilarating, energized by a sense of danger and joy at the act of leaving a mark on an otherwise desultory landscape. Graffiti art offered a politics of interruption, altering the messages of a culture built on screens and billboards.[137]

XXX

Can't Beat the Stupid?

There can be no negation on MTV.

—Greil Marcus[138]

Would there be a repeat of *Class of 1984* as the summer movie season beckoned? Fortunately not. But that didn't make things better, in terms of the representations of punk on the silver screen. It just meant fare like *Valley Girl*, a movie that starred Nicholas Cage as a "punk" (or "new wave") adolescent. The movie was pure screwball comedy, where the punk kid beats up the jock and seduces the wealthy and always-at-the-shopping-mall Valley Girl (meaning someone who lived in the posh section of the San Fernando Valley of Los Angeles and known for her studied vapidness). The critic Bill Brown believed the movie to be a less "negative" treatment of punk on the silver screen, but in reality it was another lame Hollywood attempt to provide fare about youth culture, the way it had with *Fast Times at Ridgemont High* a year earlier, except the types were more clearly outlined and diced. Outfits defined the differences: our hero in skinny tie and black leather, his love interest in a dress and pastels, the jocks and preppies in Izods with collars pulled up. Hair mattered too: his was cut jagged and dyed, hers was permed and coiffed, the jocks' and preppies' feathered and blow-dried. All served as symbols of style and semiotic cues. Nothing more, because it might get in the way of telling the unbelievable story of the alienated outsider getting the girl. *Romeo and Juliet* redux, except with a much happier ending.[139]

What made the movie different from *Fast Times* was that its soundtrack blasted, sometimes taking over the movie. Songs took center-stage over the development of characters and dialogue, especially with Modern English's "I Melt with You," played twice during the course of the film. The song receives full play as the two love-birds flock around, hold hands, look into one another's eyes, and kiss. Nary a spoken bit of dialogue just jump-cut video flashes that signify the act of falling in love. The music was standardized electronic new wave synth pop found on the lower ranks of the music charts. There was Josie Cottin's "Johnny Are You Queer" (the Go-Gos had originally performed the song), the Psychedelic Furs "Love My Way," and the Plimsouls' "A Million Miles Away." Catchy ear-worm material, these songs synched with images to develop the story in a way that dialogue and character development couldn't.

* * *

Call it the MTV effect. The Music Television Network—with its 24/7 showing of music videos hosted by "VJs"—had been around for two years by now, but it wasn't until 1983 that it reached the New York and

L.A. television markets and started to realize its cultural impact. Some critics saw MTV as part of a longer aesthetic history. A writer in Tucson, Arizona, stretched the historical lens quite far, stating, "The roots of the rock video evolved from the musical extravaganzas of Busby Berkeley in the thirties." But this creative, aesthetic history couldn't ignore the bald fact that MTV, in reality, was a marketing mechanism for corporate music. In the words of John Leland, it "played nothing but promotional videos that were produced and paid for by record companies or performers in order to sell records." Bottom line: its aesthetic style and history mattered only so much. MTV was, after all, "the indirect progeny of American Express and Warner Cable Corporation." Its mission was to turn around plummeting record sales, helping the culture industry come out of its slump. It was starting to work. The Nielsen Survey reported in March 1983 that "MTV . . . is already a bigger factor than radio airplay in record sales."[140]

For the rock critic Richard Meltzer, MTV got music all wrong, because it prioritized visuals over sound, when it should be, for him, the other way around. MTV grafted images onto music, rather than allowing the viewer's imagination to work for itself. It also raised the entrance fees for bands to break big (now it meant not only expensive studio recording time, but also good looks and high-cost video production). The cable channel created "awesomely larger upfront promotional expenses." One scholar noted that "the moment of music video" coincided with "rise of the New Pop—those acts (such as Duran Duran, Culture Club, Wham!, Howard Jones) who refused the downbeat style and oppositional politics of punk" (and acts that many people now look on with nostalgia). MTV aligned with what some call a "second British invasion of synth pop," the sort stemming from the earlier "new romanticism" flurry (like Adam Ant). After all, one of the most popular videos in 1983 had been first issued in 1981 by Duran Duran, "Girls on Film"—with its lurid visuals of buxom women sliding around in kiddie swimming pools. Imagery worked well with the synth pop of these bands, relaxing to both ear and mind. MTV always moved things horizontally and sideways, sliding from one image to another, as if everything was equal in worth, nothing requiring excavation or sustained attention. This is why Greil Marcus, a rock journalist who was reading everything he could by the Situationist International, proclaimed in 1983 that "there can be no negation on MTV." The critic Jim Farber would later equate MTV with "walking into a shopping mall where we can try on a whole range of identities." Its aesthetic, therefore, was the exact opposite of Raymond Pettibon's artistic style, which turned image and text disjunctive, provoking disgruntled understandings and necessitating imagination and excavation on the part of the viewer. Kristine McKenna, a music writer for the *L.A. Times* who often promoted punk, drew aghast at MTV's capture of young peoples' imagination. She almost described the feel of *Valley Girl* when discussing MTV. "Rock video" had created "the Punk Lolita." You could see this "in videos by the Go-Go's, the Flirts, Bananarama and countless others, this swinging gal wears sunglasses and mini-skirts, drives a convertible, is madcap and kooky and an untouchable tease." Men are "uniformly depicted as misunderstood toughs, James Dean is the role model of choice and black leather is an absolute must." Stylized, semiotic rebellion easy to cue up for jaded and conditioned eyes.[141]

* * *

The MTV effect could be seen in a movie released at the same time as *Valley Girl*—*Flashdance*. It was another screwball comedy where a young working-class welder, Alex Owens (played by Jennifer Beals), falls in love with her rich boss. Alex wants to be a professional dancer, and she is making some extra income as an exotic performer who ends her shows with a giant bucket of water splashed over her body. The music of Giorgio Moroder, the man who created so much of the *American Gigolo* soundtrack, plays throughout. His song "Flashdance . . . What a Feeling!" is featured twice. Once again, electro-synth pop, with a new wave tinge. The scenes of Alex were edited for the movie but also for MTV, which helped promote the film and its soundtrack, showing off the expanding power of "synergy."

Plus, *Flashdance* was Lee Ving's Hollywood premiere. The singer from Fear played a carnival barker who stood outside a strip joint and shouted "All Nude!" His mashed-in face and angry mannerisms would remind punk kids of his performances with Fear. Ving had cut short a Fear tour to come home to Hollywood and break into the big leagues, and after *Flashdance* he starred in *Get Crazy* (1983) as a shirtless angry punk, replicating his "role" on stage with Fear, just a bit more slapstick and exaggerated. He had become a semiotic rebel.

* * *

So how to get at anything deeper about punk in a culture succumbing to images and stylized "types"? Maybe a movie about kids who were actually punks. That idea seized the imagination of Penelope Spheeris, who released her second major film in the summer of 1983, *The Wild Side*, known eventually as *Suburbia*. For Spheeris, punk was about attitude more than style. She explained, "You can turn a punk into an actor but you can't turn an actor into a punk." She had recruited punks who would play out a fictionalized story about squatting abandoned houses in a first-ring suburb of Los Angeles, what the leader of the group (known as The Rejected, or TR, for short) called the "slums of the future."[142]

The movie had a certain accuracy about it. Most of the characters came from broken families, including one kid who had just left his alcoholic, abusive mother. The punks confront what a reviewer called "a group of laid-off Lockheed worker rednecks who, besides harassing the hardcores, get their kicks hanging out at topless bars and shooting the wild dogs that roam around the suburban decay." When the punks aren't at war, they go on food drives, raiding suburban garages full of boxed and canned goods (suggesting a survivalist mentality had settled into suburbia by 1983). In one of the funnier scenes, punks rolled up a suburban home's front-yard sod and brought it to the shopping mall, where they sat on it to watch television at RadioShack. Except for these bright scenes of lighted up malls and sunny suburban streets, the film had a somber and neo-noir feel to it, a low-budget grittiness that enhanced the film's realism.[143]

Except for one thing. When the film depicted punk concerts featuring TSOL, D.I., and the Vandals, it turned more sensationalistic than real. A young punk reviewer of the film, Lori Peacock of Tipp City, Ohio, saw the movie sometime late in the summer of 1983, at a showing in Dayton. She believed that the film's realism fell apart throughout:

> The scenes of the gigs—a girl stripped of all her clothes by a group of guys and no one helps her. They all just laugh. A guy sneaks drugs into a kid's drink. I guess for kicks. Rednecks come into a show and knife a security guard. A kid gets into a fight, he falls, and a gang of people surround him, kicking and beating him. Come on!

Peacock pointed out that Spheeris had done an interview with a local Dayton newspaper around the time of the screening. The director reportedly said, "Given the choice between art and exploitation, I'll choose exploitation." Which just aggravated Peacock, for obvious reasons: "I don't appreciate something that is so much a part of my life being exploited."[144]

* * *

Peacock would not have known, but the band Flipper had refused to let their music be used in Spheeris's movie. Usually thought of as beer-swilling nihilists, Flipper actually had a long-standing affiliation with punk ethics. Back in 1979, two members of the band, Will Shatter and Bruce Loose, had worked with the New Youth Organization, a group that tried to put on not-for-profit shows and create a more egalitarian community for San Francisco punk. When Spheeris approached the band about using their song "Sex Bomb," with its monotonous lyrics sung over the band's dirge-cycle, they refused, citing the film's "exploitative rape scene," the one where a young woman gets her clothes ripped off and fondled. They complained that the movie would become a "bastardization" of what the punk scene was all about, pure sensationalism. After seeing the final product, the band concluded that Spheeris was an "exploiter."[145]

By this time, the band could offer up its own film, or at least one that their guitarist, Ted Falconi, had helped to write and acted in. *Emerald Cities*, directed by Rick Schmidt, spun a bizarre story centered around a young woman living in a broken-down trailer park in Death Valley. Her father is an alcoholic whose only skill in life is playing Santa Claus during the holiday season (he has a natural, white beard). When at one moment he asks her to get him a drink, and she refuses, he complains about how he had worked so hard to raise her. She retorts that she was actually raised by television, and she winds up leaving him to travel with a punk (played by Falconi) to San Francisco. The father hitches a ride with an ex-convict to try to hunt his daughter down (he has a postcard he hopes will lead him to her). Meanwhile, the story is broken up with scenes of a roving reporter doing television interviews on the streets of San Francisco about people's belief in Santa Claus—which of course implies their faith in fantasy. Interspersed with all of this are television appearances by Ronald Reagan and other members of his administration talking about a "winnable" nuclear war, with

Caspar Weinberger and Alexander Haig justifying the need for a massive military build-up, including the MX missile. The idea of winning a nuclear war seems equated with a belief in Santa. Though at times incoherent, the film congealed to form a sharp critique of a country off the rails, living in a fantasy world of passive television watching, while tuning out the possibility of a nuclear apocalypse. In other words, America in 1983.

XXX

Caravan the Crisis-Ridden White House!

> People like Sinatra and Dean Martin are still considered "far out" in Vegas... A week in Vegas is like stumbling into a Time Warp, a regression to the late fifties.
>
> —Hunter S. Thompson[146]

During the summer of 1983, Americans were fast learning what it meant to be ruled by a president who believed that "government" was not "the solution" but the "problem." Reagan put people in charge of government agencies who didn't believe in their founding mission. Case in point, Emanuel S. Savas's resignation as assistant secretary of the Department of Housing and Urban Development (HUD). As the journalist Haynes Johnson explained, "Before entering federal service, [Savas] had received $33,000 in consulting fees from a firm that later was awarded a $495,000 HUD contract. Savas himself selected the panel that awarded the contract, and it was granted even though two competing firms submitted bids at least $190,000 lower." He had also worked on government time to write *Privatizing the Public Sector*, a dry, wonky book that, if the title wasn't clear enough, examined ways to get government out of business regulation.[147]

Another prominent member of Reagan's cabinet was sitting on the cusp of a crisis. James Watt, the secretary of the interior, was a quintessential Reagan appointee. Having come out of antienvironmentalist activism in the American West (referred to as the "Sagebrush Rebellion"), Watt hoped to turn public lands over to timber, oil, and mining companies. He explained his mission: "We will mine more, drill more, cut more timber," and try to "open the wilderness." A true hardliner, Watt was known to call environmentalists a "left-wing cult" bent on destroying "our very form of government." And he managed to marry his prodevelopment politics to his Christian faith, especially his belief in an impending Armageddon. He explained one rationale for not preserving public land: "I do not know how many future generations we can count on before the Lord returns," making environmental protection futile as the "end days" approached. A perfect fit for Ronald Reagan. As the critic Mark Miller once quipped, "Reagan has suggested that forests cause lung cancer, but next to Watt he starts to look like Johnny Appleseed."[148]

There was only one problem with Watt for the Reagan revolution. The man was too doctrinaire, too prudish, too hung up and serious. He was totally unhip, and this unraveled as the July 4 celebration on the nation's mall approached. The Beach Boys—a sclerotic band who sang about the California marvels of surfing and "girls"—were scheduled to play. Watt decided the band didn't offer "patriotic, family-based entertainment," nor were they "wholesome." He made an executive decision to replace the Beach Boys with Wayne Newton. Newton was the avatar of contemporary Las Vegas–based entertainment and a big Republican donor. He had connections with the mafia and was famous for his splashy decadence, living in a garish mansion with a swimming pool for his horses and his own private plane called the Eagle. When the zine *Own the Whole World* learned about Watt's decision, the editors chuckled about the secretary of the interior being a "nationally known music critic," as if he could assess the worth of an artist (the zine included a fake interview with Watt commenting on bands he would have never heard of—like Captain Beefheart and DNA—who he promised to ban from the mall as well). The real problem with Watt's choice wasn't Newton per se, but rather not checking with the boss. The Reagans happened to be big fans of the Beach Boys, and the band had played fundraisers for Vice President George Bush in the past. Watt didn't understand the first ethic of Reaganism: Feelgood entertainment trumped Christian prudishness.[149]

* * *

As Watt fumbled, a caravan was fast approaching the nation's capital. It consisted of a school bus with its seats torn out; a bunch of bands, including MDC, the Crucifucks, Reagan Youth, and the Dicks; T-shirts with antidraft and antiwar slogans painted on them; speakers ready for soap box oratory against Reagan; and representatives from the political organization called the Youth International Party (YIP), known as yippies, who held onto their 1960s radicalism even into the dawn of the eighties. The caravan was called Rock Against Reagan (RAR), and it planned to arrive in Washington, D.C., at the same time as Wayne Newton, after having traveled the punk circuit, starting in May in Wisconsin, moving to Carbondale, Illinois; then Cincinnati, Columbus, and Kent, Ohio; then to upstate New York; down to Pittsburgh; then West Virginia; then up to New England (even making it to Burlington, Vermont). A true whirlwind of a tour.[150]

RAR had a history to it, one that went back to large concerts and rallies against the National Front during the late 1970s in Great Britain (when it was known as Rock Against Racism). The idea was imported into America, especially in San Francisco, but also Dayton, Ohio. Jim Alias, the editor of the Dayton-based zine *I Wanna*, recounted how he had made contact with Syd Sheldon, chief organizer of Britain's RAR. Hearing about the National Front's racism and anti-immigrant sentiments, Alias couldn't help but compare that to his "shock at seeing 2,000 people showing up for a cross-burning in Middletown, Ohio." Alias also cited the heavy levels of unemployment in the midwestern Rust Belt, and being something of a Marxist, he worried race might divide the dwindling solidarity of America's working class. Still, even with this attempt to import RAR, there was always something British-feeling about it, something that didn't fit the political culture of America in the 1980s. By the spring of 1982, Alias had opened up RAR to an array of issues. That's when he changed the name Rock Against Racism to Rock Against Reagan. His targets now included "Reagan, Radiation, Racism, the Right, Repression, Registration, and Recession." He explained: "It's time to show our opposition to Reagan's policies of nuclear war and radiation poisoning, his involvement in El Salvador and the draft, the growing repressive strength of the religious new Right and other Bonzos running around in this grade-B movie we call home."[151]

Around this time, the Yippies were reconceiving their own annual "smoke in," which had included a July 1982 concert on the national mall featuring Fear and some local D.C. punk bands. Dana Beal, the unspoken leader of YIP, couldn't help but notice that many of the punks turning up at the smoke-in were straight edge, with little to no interest in the cause of decriminalizing marijuana (often stomping on joints tossed from the stage into the crowd for people to get high). When approached by members of MDC, who knew full-well just how pervasive straight edge had become, the Yippies decided to reframe their event as "Rock Against Reagan."[152]

When MDC announced the Rock Against Reagan tour in the spring of 1983, they provided rationale and expanded on Alias's vision. They derided how Reagan said America had become "a second-rate power" that needed to arm itself to the hilt to defeat the Soviet Union, while making cuts in domestic policies that hurt the poor. They condemned the growing power of the CIA and covert operations in American foreign policy. Their statement of purpose, written before the Savas and Watt troubles, aimed at a scandal at the Environmental Protection Agency (EPA). "Rita Lavelle," the band explained, "has just resigned after being caught showing evidence collected against polluters to the culprit companies to help them prepare their cases, and then erasing governments [sic] evidence from computers." Lavelle had been an assistant to Anne Gorsuch Burford, who had been in charge of the EPA, even though she had "a record of opposing controls over hazardous waste and auto pollution control devices." Gorsuch Burford would resign, handing the reins of power to William Ruckelshaus, vice president of Weyerhaeuser (a paper manufacturing corporation). All of this annoyed Ronald Reagan, who fumed—in strident terms—about "the media . . . lynch mob that thinks it smells blood" and a "lynching by headline hunting Congressmen" who wanted to ruin Gorsuch Buford's career. Others simply labeled it "Sewergate."[153]

Just a month before RAR hit the nation's mall, the Dead Kennedys had played at the Lansburgh Building (an abandoned department store close to the "Ritz Hotel Project" and the 9:30 Club). Many complained the show was overpriced (eight bucks). Worse, the Fire Marshall entered the premises just as the openers, No Trend, had played and the band Void was going on. Realizing that D.C. punks rarely had problems with law enforcement, Biafra considered calling the show off. But the kids on the floor refused to leave; they sat down in peaceful protest (the way some had at the TSOL show at S.I.R.). Biafra approached the stage and did a sing-along of "Nazi Punks Fuck Off," but he changed the lyrics to, "When you ape the fire marshall it ain't anarchy." But some chanted back, "Let's Lynch the Fire Marshall," a play on the Dead Kennedys' song "Let's Lynch the Landlord." Jello insisted to keep cool and warned: "This is a test. We can't lose our tempers or they'll make it impossible for us at other shows." Parents started coming in to retrieve their kids and bring them home, and outside there was a "line of cop cars from one side of the block to the other." Then they got word they could play until 12 midnight. Some kids believed they had fought a political battle and won. The zine *Suburban Outcast* claimed, "We showed those bastards that we don't have to riot or beat people with clubs or go around fighting in general to prove our point and make a stand."[154]

When the Dead Kennedys performed on the mall a month later, Biafra was his usual self, rapping with the audience throughout the show, about boycotting Coors beer because its CEO had connections with James Watt. He pointed to the Washington Monument, calling it a "giant Klansman" whose eyes shone bright red throughout the night. He riffed about the CIA's covert operations while performing "I Am the Owl." But he saved the best for last. Smelling the lingering whiff of hypocrisy about James Watt's decision to have Wayne Newton perform in place of the Beach Boys, Biafra called out: "So, Wayne, this is for you." The band broke into a slightly altered version of Elvis Presley's "Viva Las Vegas," a song that equated contingency of luck and chance with the "American Dream" (and that had appeared on the band's *Fresh Fruit for Rotting Vegetables*). The final set of revised lyrics sounded particularly funny, considering the proximity to Newton: "Gotta keep on running, gonna have me some fun, if it costs me my very last dime. . . . Gotta coke up my nose to draw away the snot, so Viva Las Vegas!"[155]

Less than three months after the Dead Kennedys played on the mall, James Watt would leave office. Not because of his hypocritical reasoning that Newton was somehow more moral than the Beach Boys. Certainly not because the policies he stood for would run roughshod over the American environment. No, it was because he was too crude, too vulgar, lacking the sprightly entertainment ethic of the president. A few months after Rock Against Reagan hit the mall, Watt found himself battling critics who suggested he didn't do enough on issues of affirmative action. He rebuffed the critique by saying that he had "every kind of mixture you can have. I have a black, I have a woman, two Jews and a cripple. And we have talent." Too backward sounding, the man lacked the skill of his boss. When the chips fell, Reagan expressed his permanent state of victimhood and described Watt as falling to an "environmental lynch mob." But really the man never fit the aesthetic of Reaganism.[156]

XXX

Ground Enemies Spotted as Culture Wars Rage On

> Yes kiddies the real clubs close while the rock discos are just clothes.
> —*Damaged Goods* zine (New York)[157]

The Big Chill hit theaters on September 23, 1983. It told the story of a bunch of one-time supposed activists who had lived through the 1960s, coming to terms with a friend's suicide in the 1980s. The film suggested a singular story line: The movement *from yippie to yuppie*, from the 1960s to the 1980s. The movie mimicked the "peace and love" nostalgia that the antipunk episode of *Quincy* articulated. The film's director, Lawrence Kasdan, insisted on a 1960s music soundtrack, which became just as popular as the movie itself (once again, synergy elevated profit margins). In typical baby boom gloat, Kasdan explained that "rock 'n' roll hasn't since equaled that period in terms of richness or emotional impact." It could now be called "classic rock." The historian Gil Troy believed the film was not "just a movie, but an event, a defining moment in the collective annals of the baby boom generation and the 1980s." It sounded a generational cudgeling (a gentler version of Serena Dank), with baby boomers gloating about their mythical past.[158]

The *we-were-once-so-good* message the movie projected remained blurry in many viewers' minds. It was never clear what the characters in the film had actually accomplished during the 1960s. There are references to activism and Vietnam, but rarely anything concrete. It is clear however what they do in the present. One central character, Harold Cooper (played by Kevin Kline), gathers friends into his large and plush house in the wake of the funeral. He is, in the words of contemporary critics, a "hip capitalist" who markets running shoes and "worries more about SEC regulation than global issues." One character is a television star, another a writer for *People* magazine. In other words, sellouts to the entertainment industry, adults tossing aside the supposed ideals of the 1960s for contemporary material advantage, while growing nostalgic for a past growing ever hazier. One of the most evocative scenes is when a popular TV actor named Sam commiserates with Karen about his life purpose (while she, though married, tries to seduce him). He tells her that what he does now is "garbage" (when the group watches an episode of his show, the opinion is confirmed). But Karen recoils at this negativity, "That's not true. You're entertaining people. God knows we need that now." If anything was foolish, it was believing in the cause of yesteryear. Entertainment was more important than politics.[159]

The movie's reference points in historical reality were easy to find. There was Jane Fonda, who had turned herself from radical activist, pejoratively called "Hanoi Jane," to the nation's leading exercise video coach. Her VHS exercise tapes sold like hotcakes during the 1980s. (One punk band out of Fresno, California, even wrote a song called "Jane Fonda Genocide" about "the constant pressure to achieve a horribly distorted feminine ideal.") There were other yippie-to-yuppie stories. The punk cartoonist John Crawford documented "hippy [sic] radicals" who "cut their hair" and "joined the system." He rattled off numerous examples: "Jerry Rubin," who "went through forty trendy therapies then went to work on Wall Street"; the black nationalist Eldridge Cleaver, who "went on to preach the fascist variety of Christianity"; Abbie Hoffman, who became "a fugitive from a cocaine bust"; and antiwar organizer Rennie Davis, who now "peddled life insurance in Colorado." This mantra of yippie to yuppie became a foundation for a peculiar brand of 1980s conservatism. The meme became: one-time radical recognizes the errors of his or her way, shuns the past, while still glorying in it, creating a strange variant of quietism. It was part of what Jello Biafra had diagnosed earlier as the "mellow out" syndrome, except that by now, any doubt or malaise of the 1970s vanished.[160]

* * *

Jim Fouratt provided another yippie-to-yuppie story, and one that changed the landscape of New York City's nightlife and nurtured a burgeoning yuppie culture nationwide. Fouratt had grown up in the Midwest and moved to Manhattan as soon as he possibly could in order to escape his working-class background. In the early 1960s, he became a beatnik who hung around Greenwich Village. By the late 1960s, like Hoffman and Rubin (and unlike Fonda), Fouratt became an *actual* yippie—helping form the Youth International Party (YIP) when it got off the ground back in 1967 (he supposedly came up with the idea of dropping dollar bills on the floor of the Wall Street Stock Exchange to create havoc—a famous yippie action). From there, Fouratt became a gay activist, having been a firsthand witness to the Stonewall riot of 1969. During the 1970s, a time he described as "dark," he moved to Los Angeles, working as "an actor and union activist." Returning to New York City in 1978, Fouratt morphed into one of the most important architects of New York City's "club culture." He started at a place called Hurrah's (where the "beautiful people" went) and then moved onto one of the most famous institutions of 1980s Manhattan—Danceteria.[161]

Danceteria became the house that Fouratt helped build. It had multiple floors, each with a different function. Though bands performed gigs at Danceteria, there was growing emphasis on fashion shows and music videos—some by local artists, but increasingly MTV fare. Danceteria was less a rock club than a dance club, with a new wave, new romanticist, and disco feel to the music selected (though Fouratt sometimes played the Dead Kennedys and other high-profile punk bands). By late 1982, after Fouratt had left for other venues, Danceteria debuted its most important star, Madonna, whose late 1982 single "Everybody" fit the sounds of chintzy, synth pop that dominated 1980s music (and that some would proclaim the true "sound" of the 1980s). And by 1983, Danceteria's accomplishments were being touted by the hip, trendy, new romanticist British publication *The Face*. Indeed, *The Face* would celebrate its third-year anniversary at Danceteria, confirming that it held out the new wave disco of the future. It had successfully filled the hole left by Studio 54—the glitzy discotheque full of mirrors and scantily clad young men—that had collapsed in 1979. In the form of Danceteria, Fouratt had helped build a central institution for fashion, new wave, and dance—now features of a burgeoning yuppie culture defined by its hedonism.[162]

As imagined, many punks didn't take well to what they saw in Danceteria. *Zone V* zine, published in Wheaton, Maryland, denounced Danceteria as a "fashionite, douchebag of a club" that was "run by fat-cat corporate types." The *L.A. Weekly*, by October 1983, connected the rise of yuppie dance clubs with the shuttering of punk venues throughout the city. Dance clubs were, quite simply, safer than punk shows—and capable of generating revenue. Over the last few years, the *L.A. Weekly* reported, fifty-six punk clubs had been shut down, in addition to eighteen in Orange County. Presently, there seemed only the Cathay de Grande and the Anti-Club. Dance-based discotheques were growing in number and having a comeback since the collapse of disco in 1979.[163]

Kim Gordon, bass player in the New York City punk and experimental band Sonic Youth, saw the future that Danceteria (and other rock clubs at the time) portended. In 1983, she focused her attention on Danceteria's "sterility." She elaborated, "Video monitors are standard design apparatus; the images are there to sustain the customers, as business dealings become mingled with fantasies—sexual, career, or otherwise. . . . The images shown on the videos are more or less unseen, and function much like televisions left on." People transformed themselves into screens, losing depth or individual identity, becoming more like "channels" for networks buzzing around, as the French sociologist Jean Baudrillard had suggested. The individual turned into a "pure screen, a switching center for all the networks of influence." This hyperreal environment, with its mixture of images and sounds, created what Gordon called a "rapid crowding of changing images" that nurtured a "blasé attitude," both overstimulated and spectatorial (she borrowed here from the German sociologist Georg Simmel). Rock clubs created a "playground environment" and an army of blanded-out spectators moving to the "disco sound system" like a controlled machine, much like kids losing themselves in front of screens in video arcades or whatever a corporatized culture offered them.[164]

XXX

The Great Debate of 1983/Consciousness Distilled

> The dreams of your youth will become the firm convictions of your mature age. You will wish to have wide, human education for all, in school and out of school. And seeing that this is impossible in existing conditions, you will attack the very foundations of bourgeois society.
>
> —Prince Peter Kropotkin, "An Appeal to the Young"[165]

As the year 1983 wound down, it would be fair to say what punk wasn't. It wasn't knife-wielding rapists in pursuit of a teacher's pregnant wife. It wasn't a form of music that drove kids to kill one another. It wasn't stylized rebels who became romantic heroes courting Valley Girls. It wasn't some mental illness that kids could be weaned from by psychological counselors. It wasn't screened out blasé young club kids. It wasn't . . . But what was it?

What was this thing that was spreading across the country? Or better yet, what *could* it be?

There was never, of course, any unitary philosophy of punk, only threads and recurring themes found within zine writing and interviews with bands. Punks disagreed with one another (even bandmates would argue). Matt Groening spotted the conversations of punk when discussing *MRR* and *Flipside*, in which "the smartest kids in the history of adolescence" took "page after page" to "debate the throes and cons of punkish behavior." There were conversations and debates *among* the editors of publications, with *MRR*'s shit workers possessing "a variety of progressive opinion, ranging from petit bourgeoise to utopian anarchy." Tim Yo's household became a place for heated debates, especially when visitors—bands on tour and writers for the zine—descended on it and pushed conversation into the wee hours of the morning, often when the best collisions arrived, animated by delirious exhaustion as well as a feeling of connection. When Articles of Faith entered *MRR*'s ramshackle Oakland residence, for instance, they talked until six in the morning almost every night, about "politics, music, life, death, genetics, socialization, LSD, God, dreams—you name it." Like the spread of punk itself at the time, discussions went in all sorts of directions.[166]

But there was one overarching theme shared by practically all punks— a conscious rejection of the fares hawked by a corporate entertainment industry. The ethic of DIY—young people making their own culture— naturally pushed in that direction. The sense that corporations were face-less entities that dumped product on a passive audience drew visceral contempt of big business. But what it meant to be anticorporate required some sharper thinking to make it more than just an attitude and something more political in nature.

Enter Peter Titus, a writer who created his own syndicated column, "Analyzing Pop," for the punk press (his writing appeared in *Disposable Press, Own the Whole World*, and multiple issues of *MRR*). Titus was an old-ster whose biographical background informed his writing. He had studied literature as an undergraduate and got a master's degree from City College in Manhattan in 1977. From there, he transitioned into the book business. This experience provided him with special insight into the corporatization of American culture, where commercial success—sales—outweighed crea-tivity or imagination. Titus took what he learned from the book industry to write about the politics of music. He wrote, "The sophisticated technology

of record pressing is far more productive with high volume." But technology could not explain everything. The music industry rested on a flawed
idea: that big-name, secure rock acts would trickle down, so to speak, and
help elevate lesser-known acts riding on the back of the already successful.
Titus called this the "logic of the blockbuster." Expecting a large record
company to help promote an artist who was perceived as creative and imag-
inative never materialized, because there had to be a "significant market"
for an act's appeal "already or . . . easily created." Here was a catch-22. Risk-
taking was verboten; this is what made corporate capitalism conservative,
so to speak. Titus concluded, "The blockbuster syndrome codifies the logic
of today's music industry. Here its money-making identity collides head on
with its role as an avenue between creative talent and the public." Seeing
this as a structural problem, Titus explained, "This bitter truth cannot be
changed by any amount of public relations manipulation." Titus recognized
that corporate control of the record industry had fallen into tough times
during the recession of 1979–1983, threatened by the practices of a punk
DIY culture, including independent labels and the rise of cassette tape releases being traded directly through the mail.[167]

Titus warned that the culture industry's leaders recognized the threat that
punk kids exhibited. Especially important were home taping and noncommercial distribution of music (what some would call "trading" and what
Reagan would have described as an "underground economy"). In late 1983,
Titus noted congressional "legislation . . . aimed at regulating the use of both
home video recorders, used to tape TV shows, and the cassette decks that
music fans are using to copy records they buy, borrow, or rent." The plan was
afoot to place a "surcharge" on blank cassette tapes (Titus's own Marxism
would have labeled these the "means of production"). He cited the "Home
Recording Act of 1983" that would punish "home tapers" who would be
"made to pay." Titus pointed out the politics behind all of this: "Very clearly
big money is at stake. With some 23 million audio tape players imported
in 1981 alone—and with about 228 million tape units shipped for sale that
year—even a nominal fee (and the surcharge is likely to be considerable)
will generate hundreds of millions of dollars in revenue." The culture industry had its front group ready for action, ironically named the Coalition
to Save America's Music, which "issued reams of 'fact sheets' and studies,
purporting to prove that home taping was killing the business, causing a . . .
decline in the number of new recordings, and most of all harming legions

of struggling artists and composers." Warner Communications—the most majestic of entertainment oligopolies—did its own study, "citing evidence to the effect that some 52.5 million Americans buy blank tapes and use about 75 percent of them to record music at home." Titus spelled it out for his readers, "The real reason people tape at home is simple. The price of prerecorded music has skyrocketed. Cassettes jumped 52 percent in eight years and in 1981 average $7.70 list." The culture industry's CEOs were waging a culture war against the DIY ethic and communal sharing of cassettes and zines so central to punk. And they were finding friends in the White House, with Alan Greenspan, chairman of the President's Council of Economic Advisers, testifying to the Senate on behalf of the Recording Industry Association of America in favor of stopping home recording.[168]

Punks *had* to see themselves, Titus suggested, as waging a political and cultural war against corporate control. What masqueraded as "entertainment" was in fact *political*—because of the dynamic of power and control that Titus saw behind the corporate curtain. Here Titus was joined by Winston Smith, who made direct linkages between the ideology of the culture industry and the world of politics. Smith alerted readers to an "industry composite that was put together from polls taken to determine what the majority of America wanted to hear," which in circular fashion legitimated the decisions of record industry leaders. Smith proceeded, "Reagan did the same in formulating his political platform. . . . Whether it's government or the record industry, keeping control of Pop Youth is in the interests of the Powers That Be—and those interests are keeping their powers and raking in $$$. . . . Keep 'em quiet and buying lots of records and we'll all be happy." Reaganism, for Smith, worked in tandem with corporate power—be it in the manufacturing of weapons or entertaining the masses. Earlier, in its second issue, *MRR* tied things together the way Smith had by focusing on the huge conglomerate Bechtel, which held a government contract to help build MX missiles. The *MRR* story began with, "I pledge allegiance to the flag of the United State of Bechtel and to the tyranny for which it stands, one corporation, under God, indivisible with profits and power for Stephen" (that being Stephen Bechtel, the man sitting at dinner with Reagan and the queen in San Francisco).[169]

* * *

In openly waging a culture war, punks broached the looming question: Just *how* political should it get (and what was meant by the term *politics* in the first place)? Black Flag, for instance, argued that their music was intended to be "personal, emotional . . . about . . . passion and intensity," not politics. It was "gut emotion." Minor Threat concurred, believing that change came from below in the realm of face-to-face exchanges. Lyle Preslar, the band's guitarist, argued that "if you change the way you deal with the guy down the block he may change the way he's gonna deal with the next guy. If that happens, the System's gonna change." The midwestern band Necros agreed. Their singer Barry explained: "Personal politics is a decent phrase; the songs are mostly about personal feelings and experiences." Dave Smalley, of the band DYS in Boston, once elaborated, "[W]e're dealing with our own small level." The band couldn't be a "bunch of junior Karl Marx's [*sic*] trying to lead a revolution on the White House. Just trying to get people to deal with things in a more open way."[170]

But as MDC had argued earlier, this came down to a false binary—the idea that emotions had no place in politics. Both MDC and AoF, two of the most political bands at the time, were racked by a politics of guilt (notice: not shame) over the condition of worldwide poverty. They *felt* the anger it prompted as the result of their own privileged status. Whereas earlier in the 1980s, punks were politicized by the reinstitution of Selective Service registration—driven in part by libertarianism—now there seemed to be a growing awareness about pain and suffering in the wider world, all relying on a sense of empathy. Now known mostly as Multi-Death Corporations, MDC explained to a Chicago zine, *Bullshit Detector*, that "the United States happens to be dictating a lot of the misery in the world. We feel like as American citizens, we have a responsibility to see what our country has been doing to the rest of the world in our name." Vic Bondi of AoF grew up a military brat, seeing conditions far removed from America' prosperity. This heated up his empathy and sense of responsibility. "When I lived in Puerto Rico," Bondi explained, "I couldn't believe the poverty those people live in. I mean they live terribly." Meanwhile, wealthy people at home "build their rhetoric to protect their ass. I wish kids, instead of taking drugs for kicks, would go shit on the IBM President's front lawn." Anger at worldwide disparities was a legitimate, heartfelt emotion at the same time it was political. This was not a *theory* of social injustice—Marxism for instance—but a visceral response to corporate exploitation and an embrace of radical empathy.[171]

This politics of guilt and empathy prompted a heated debate between MDC, AoF, and Minor Threat. For MacKaye, 1983 had been a year of touring and debating (and then by the fall, breaking up the band for the second time). In the course of a discussion, facilitated by *MRR*, MDC and AoF criticized Minor Threat's song "Guilty of Being White," on their *In My Eyes* EP, in which MacKaye in tones of anger screamed, "You blame me for slavery, a hundred years before I was born." Ian explained that growing up white in a largely African American school setting (being literally a "white minority") drove him to write the song. Talking about his history classes, he griped, "When we get to slavery, they'd drag it all the way out." He said he was forced to read only African American authors and gave a lame excuse for the term "nigger" standing for a "black asshole," the way people would use words like "jock" or "redneck" as standing for "white assholes." Both MDC and AoF believed MacKaye mistook subjective experience for actual history. Dave Dictor from MDC lamented, "What happened to the black people that got kidnapped out of Africa and shipped over here is really horrible. It's really scarring." He went on to cite the high number of black men in prisons and hinted at the principle of reparations (without using the term). For Vic Bondi of AoF, MacKaye ignored the wider structures of history by overemphasizing his own high school experiences. "You have to take responsibility for yourself as an individual within a system," Bondi explained, "and in recognizing that things are incurred in the system. And trying to do something about it." Only radical empathy and guilt could secure a responsible politics, including guilt about America's history of exploitation and racism.[172]

Bondi—much more than Dave Dictor of MDC—recognized the danger of emotions curdling into spew and dogma, especially once turned political. There was always the danger of becoming pedantic (and this could certainly be heard in some of MDC's hammering songs). Bondi spotted it in a suburban Milwaukee band, the Clit Boys, who would issue an EP at the time entitled *We Don't Play the Game* (1983). Their songs tended toward fast-paced, explicit critiques of sexism, the Ku Klux Klan, and homophobia. When they played live, the band often explained what their lyrics meant. For Bondi, "going to people before a song and saying, 'This is what I mean

by this song,' you limit their ability to interpret it to their own satisfaction."
Provocation yes, preaching no.[173]

One of the best bands who searched for a balance between complexity
and emotion was Boston's the Proletariat. The band rejected hardcore
diatribes for minimalist lyrics featured on 1983's *Soma Holiday*, the title
showing the influence of Aldous Huxley (as it had for Reagan Youth).
Like Minor Threat, the Minutemen, and AoF, the band's members turned
their internal argument outward—rather than trying to repress conflict.
The guitarist for the band, Frank Michaels, explained that "we're a political band." He went on: "There's probably a million other things I'd rather
be thinking about or doing, you know? Politics is a bore, . . . but . . .
a necessary bore." When the band members described their political
views, arguments ensued. The vocalist, Rick Brown, described himself
as a "communist," to which Michaels retorted that he hated all political
systems and ideologies, being suspicious of totalitarianism on the left.
Rick shot back: "Frank, that's because there's never been real communism." To which Frank explained, "That's what every theorist always says.
And the reason for that is that there never could be. You're hoping for
something that could never happen." He then set out a more circumspect view of a punk band's ability to transform American politics, with
this dour note: "[T]here is absolutely nothing this band can accomplish
politically," except, he hinted, to write songs with political meaning that
might energize others to engage some sort of action.[174]

The band was often asked about their song "Religion Is the Opium of
the Masses," which expressed a potent anticlericalism (an intellectual tradition that goes back to thinkers surrounding nineteenth-century American
transcendentalism—including Ralph Waldo Emerson and the more radical Orestes S. Brownson). The song rang out: "Priests are men, men are
mortal, not better than you or I [sic]." Michaels explained the song had
no theory behind it, not even Marxism. "It pretty much summed up our
feeling about organized religion. We were all products of strict Catholic
upbringing." Experience mattered more than theory. Michaels recalled a
parish priest who drove young people to tears about God and sinfulness.
"The ironic part is that the same priest was excommunicated because he
was found molesting an altar boy." Like the band the Dicks (and the Dils
and the Avengers before them), the Proletariat's radicalism was nurtured

more by personal experiences than abstract theory. They *felt* their politics without letting go of complexity.[175]

* * *

The most bitter debate about punk politics sprang from the mind of one of Matt Groening's favorite cartoon writers, John Crawford, creator of Baboon Dooley. Crawford had grown up during the 1960s in New Jersey, where he first heard of Tim Yo, the editor of *MRR*, who at that point was a hippie activist (before moving to San Francisco). Crawford agreed with Tim Yo's anticorporate views, and he drew Dooley to deride "corporate taste makers" and "corporate greedheads." But by 1983, Crawford lashed out at what he called *MRR*'s "stupid violent politics." He did this the way a punk would be expected to, by issuing his own zine, *All the Drugs You Can Eat* (a 1960s picture of Tim Yo with long hair graced its cover).[176]

Crawford had a peculiar obsession with Tim Yo, having been seduced at first by his hippie radicalism. Tim Yo, Crawford recalled, "had long hair, he had an underground newspaper with cartoons in it, he talked tough, he went to Rutgers University. He was New Jersey's big radical." Crawford, showing off his humility as much as his anger, admitted that he had once "wanted to be a revolutionary" like Yo. He had "dreamed of fighting and killing pigs in the street." But then he watched as the hippies sold out, as yippie turned yuppie. Hippie had "all that bullshit about drugs and riots." He didn't buy any of that. "I mean at least we were realistic enough to know you didn't save the world by smoking pot, chanting enemy slogans and freaking out at Woodstock." But now, *MRR* threatened to politicize punk, the way the yippies had tried to politicize the counterculture of the 1960s. Crawford decried the "attempt to take control of the scene away from the musicians and their friends and place it in the hands of [M]arxist politicians." Worried that *MRR* perceived its role as "taking over and telling you this for your own good . . . to help you," Crawford argued that the publication suppressed free discussion and indoctrinated kids into its ideology.

There was special danger, Crawford went on, in turning music into a political statement. "In the past 20 years radical politics in America have been reduced to little more than a form of entertainment, a business, a game played by college hippies in the sixties (and punks in the 80s?), the Great Rock and Roll Swindle." Crawford complained, "Showbiz radicalism is to real radicalism what *Hustler* magazine is to sex, one big greasy wank." He reminded readers of "backlash" against 1960s activism. "The tactics used by the hippy [*sic*] radicals to protest the war only helped to get Richard Nixon elected president and, I add, Ronald Reagan elected governor of California." Crawford imagined a "Joe not so smart Citizen" who might have hated the Vietnam War, since his kids were serving, but he grew diverted by the crazy hippies and wound up pulling the lever for Nixon. His fear of backlash didn't turn Crawford into a neoconservative; he identified with the left, just not the cultural left. "Give up your positions as . . . moral authorities of punk," he explained, "and go out and join a labor union and organize workers like the real radicals." Then he let loose what could sound like an equation of *MRR* and Reaganism. "You two," meaning Yo and Bale, "seem to be under the misconception that entertainment and politics are the same thing."[177]

No surprise Ian MacKaye celebrated Crawford's takedown. When asked about *MRR* and a "new punk morality," by the zine *Suburban Relapse* (itself seemingly sympathetic to Crawford), MacKaye argued, "Read *MRR*, but also read John Crawford's *All the Drugs You Can Eat*. I personally found that 100,000 times more interesting than *MRR*, just because it's a turnaround, a shock to read." MacKaye rejoiced in debate: "I think it's good to have a good war like that."[178]

Others found Crawford's critique overbearing and out of proportion. Virus X, who played drums in AoF, called Crawford "petty." He argued that the cartoonist's sweeping depiction of the 1960s hippies and drugs missed the civil rights and "black liberation movement" (simultaneously, Vic Bondi's own political realism showed up when he argued that Martin Luther King Jr. might not have been as successful "if the men in power didn't have to deal with somebody like Malcolm X"). By solely focusing on the idea of backlash, Crawford missed different political possibilities that existed in the past. Nor did Virus X find compelling Crawford's fictionalized character of Joe Average. Virus X wanted an agonistic model of politics where people struggled against one another, even if that aggravated the working class. "You can't have it both ways," he explained. "You can't really oppose the fucked up way the world is and not anger Joe Average, cause he thinks he got a stake in it. Living in one of the most rapacious nations the world has brought Joe Average a life known as the 'American Way,' and there are many Joe Averages whose vision is clouded by the few illusory benefits that they have, be it paid vacations or the freedom to choose between the Big Mac or the Whopper." Crawford missed this and, more importantly, he missed the intellectual pluralism at *MRR*, with different views expressed by different shit workers, not just a bunch of cloned "Marxist politicians." The publication wanted a "forum for discussing and debating a lot of the different views that have emerged around music, and also its reflection on politics." It's why Tim Yo would continue to print Mykel Board's column even though he consistently hated what Board wrote.[179]

When Tim Yo provided his own counter-response to Crawford, he admitted that he had a "Marxist perspective," but the magazine wasn't populated by a bunch of "Marxist politicians." Yo explained, "Out of our whole group of staff . . . that number well over 50, there is only one other who I know shares [my] view" about Marxism. "The prevalent perspective presented in our zine is anarchist."[180]

* * *

Which prompts the term heard in so many discussions among punk kids in the 1980s—"anarchism," represented by a circled A. When Crawford accused "marxist politicians" who hoodwinked punks, he missed just how organically many punk artists—bands, writers of zines, organizers of shows and demonstrations—went from making their own culture to pronouncing their own anarcho-democratic politics. Mark Sten in Portland said punk was "shot through with a lot of anarchist-communist sentiments." That's because many envisioned themselves as local producers of culture situated within networks of "mutual aid." And now there was evidence of pushback from the powers that be—senators backing the "Save Our Music" campaign, the FBI looking for homegrown terrorists, and a president complaining about the dangers of an "underground economy."[181]

Anarchism offered a language of liberty that buttressed the early 1980s anti–Selective Service registration movement. But it started—after experiments in DIY exploded—to synch with a language of communal producerism. Anarchism was not just utopian but also *prefigurative*, that is, the act of writing the future in present-day activities. Increasingly, punks looked at the sixties as a time not just of the insanity of Charlie Manson but also of organizations like the Diggers—those who fed homeless runaways in the Haight-Ashbury District while projecting a bigger vision of political transformation. Jon Jolles saw this in the activities of the "Georgetown [Washington, D.C.] Anarchist Group" that was "sponsoring a show where 25% of the proceeds go to a Volunteer Food Assistance Program." The organization witnessed cuts in public assistance and school lunch programs, and they wanted to address this immediate problem (by distributing food to the poor) while simultaneously arguing for a broader set of policies that ensured more economic equality. Concrete action nurtured a debate that went to higher levels. Sometimes the term "libertarian socialism" was used instead of "anarchism" (after all, a desire for the redistribution of wealth was part of anarcho-communalism). Bob Soltz of *Suburban Relapse* called for "libertarian socialism" and quoted Bakunin: "Liberty without socialism is exploitation; socialism without liberty is tyranny."[182]

Anarchism or libertarian socialism provided an important check on any tendency toward left-wing authoritarianism—the sort that Crawford heard in Tim Yo's fulminations. As the zine *Own the Whole World* explained, "Anarchy is the only form of political thought that does not seek to control the individual through the use of force. . . . Anarchy isn't about state control, it's about people seeking a life of personal responsibility." Rarely would punks embrace revolution. They had pessimism about the historical record in which revolutions installed new forms of dominance. As MDC explained in 1983, "It's a vicious circle because usually people are governed by dictatorships, and then there's a revolution, and they end up with another dictatorship." One rarity here was MDC's compatriots, the Dicks. The lead singer, Gary, endorsed the "basic Marxist philosophy," more out of "living poor" than "studying Marxism." But Steve Kiviat of *Thrillseeker*, a zine out of Washington, D.C., asked about a comment Gary made on MRR's radio show that insinuated an apology for Stalinism and Maoism. Jeff Bale responded, "Let me emphasize that 'police state communism' represents no part of my philosophy." Bale called Gary "naïve." Yet, he went on, "I happen to subscribe to most of his critiques of contemporary American society. One can accept certain elements of a person's views without incorporating his entire world view."[183]

Jeff Bale was always someone who thought through his political views, the most intellectually sophisticated in connecting political theory to the practices of punk. His arguments also paralleled Colin Ward's *Anarchy in Action* (1973), a book that others in punk circles drew from. Ward saw anarchism as a set of practices committed by ordinary citizens. A Brit, Ward cited a mass squatting movement that erupted in England in the years following World War II. He documented how citizens took over army compounds and organized them into self-governing units that combatted homelessness as men returned from war. He also discussed "the French revolutionary syndicalists of the turn of the century" (workers who wanted self-management as much as better pay). Ward took note of a "deschooling" movement where families tried to decentralize and deinstitutionalize the process of schooling (Ivan Illich's classic book *Deschooling Society* was published just three years before *Anarchy in Action*). All of Ward's examples captured a broader vision of anarchism as "the breakdown of institutions into small units . . . based on self-help and mutual support."[184]

Holding out a sort of reformist anarchism, Bale attacked "monopoly capitalism" for allowing "unchecked profit seeking of multinational corporations" rather than "larger social needs." Except Marxists in fact celebrated the advances of capitalism, hoping to use private industries' efficiencies and large-scale structures for communal purposes. Bale made it clear, "I am not a Communist. I consider most contemporary Communist states to be repressive, and I vehemently oppose highly centralized bureaucratic 'elites' which claim to make decisions in the name of 'the People,' then crush all popular dissent." Part of the problem of "monopoly capitalism" was not just its exploitative nature but its *bigness* and centralized power—similar to Peter Titus's critique of the blockbuster. Bale argued, "I view monopoly capitalism as an exploitative system, but I support the establishment of decentralized, non-authoritarian structures that permit popular participation in political decision-making." That sounded like the anarchist vision of Colin Ward. He could also, by birthright, remember the New Left of the 1960s, especially how Students for a Democratic Society (SDS), in its early rendition, developed a vision of participatory democracy. His political theory became a bricolage of anti-monopoly capitalism, "classical anarchist thought," and "the early New Left's humanistic critique of modern Western society." Only such a polyglot philosophy could manage to critique the unfairness of monopoly capitalism without descending into a left authoritarianism hyped on revolutionary delusions. But it left in its wake its own tensions and contradictions.[185]

* * *

Those contradictions were best expressed by punk's leading "organic" or "public intellectual," the man who spelled out the internal tensions within the anarchist worldview. If Ian MacKaye was learning new things by touring in 1983, Jello Biafra was taking what he had learned from Bale and others at *MRR* into his conversations on the road. When asked, he too would set out anarchism as a superior political philosophy, with its emphasis on personal responsibility. But here emerged the rub: how to envision an anarchist transformation? Over and over, like a mantra, Biafra told zines, "If suddenly there was anarchy and there were no more cops and no more laws when we wake up tomorrow, everyone with a rifle in the back of their pick-up truck would go around playing king of the neighborhood" (like the atmosphere captured in the movie *Suburbia*). For Biafra, the abstract ideal of anarchism conflicted with the realities of humans as they actually were: "Americans are much too . . . insecure to handle anarchy on a mass-scale right now." He even wondered whether "human beings are genetically incapable of real anarchy—taking responsibility for their own lives—or that we're hundreds of years away from it on a societal scale." Sometimes Biafra wondered if it wasn't human nature but something endemic to *America's* political culture that raised the most doubts about anarchism. "Anarchy is the opposite of greed and this is a very greedy country," Biafra lamented. Be it human nature or the culture of Americanism, none of these statements boded well for anarchism as a political theory or the immediate practices of DIY.[186]

As his audiences grew over the years, Biafra would often hand the microphone over to a young kid to make a statement, usually dismayed by what was said. He'd break up fights on the floor. It was his way of exerting an ethics of responsibility and realizing his unspoken leadership—responsibilities that demanded self-policing via organizations like BYO. But this stood in strong contrast to the other key band spreading punk into the hinterland—the band whose name itself symbolized anarchism as much as the circled A. Black Flag took their libertarian questioning of authority to an extreme. Chuck Dukowski, the bassist and resident intellectual of the band, explained: "Do we have a right to act as leaders, to tell people how to act?" He explained that he and his bandmates never wanted to become "authority figures" who would "tell people what to do." The one-time vocalist for the band (before Henry Rollins) and now second guitarist, Dez Cadena, concurred, "We don't want to be police. Eventually that turns out to be very fascist." Black Flag had expressed the traps of anti-authoritarian thinking here: Their rejection of authority could, if not necessarily justify violence, at least do nothing to prevent it. A philosophy of liberation, anarchism could degenerate into a de facto authoritarianism of violence, where fists drowned out all else.[187]

Anarchism couldn't provide punks with a roadmap, especially when it came to its anticorporate philosophy. After all, how could "small units" of "decentralized structures" combat the power of large, multinational corporations? Jeff Bale, as smart as he was, never answered that question, nor even really asked it. How was allowing fights and irresponsible behavior to erupt at shows akin to "mutual aid" and assistance? Black Flag evaded this question entirely. For sure, anarchism prefigured itself in the local actions of punk activists and the debates and conversations they were having at the time. In 1983, when *BravEar* zine announced it would have to shut down due to lack of advertising revenue (it would emerge again a year later, only to disappear again quickly), the editors hoped that their efforts envisioned a wider ethic: "If *BravEar* demonstrated anything . . . it was that people with no experience can take an active part in generating their own culture and that people can work with people much different than themselves and make something that benefits everyone." That was the essence of connecting punk activism—the making of a zine in this case—to a wider goal of making society more democratic, more anarchistic, more reliant on local initiatives of young people. But the pronouncement also captured the challenge of punk activism. After all, *BravEar* admitted that its ethic of DIY could not survive in a for-profit corporate culture. Quite simply, it had run out of money. If anarchism was the philosophy of small actors trying to make change in a world where bigness reigned, it felt like a revolt of desperation, an impossible revolt, absurdist at its heart.[188]

XXX

"Cold War Reborn"[189]

> You know I turn back to your ancient prophets in the old Testament and the signs foretelling Armageddon, and I find myself wondering if . . . we're the generation that's going to see that come about. I don't know if you've

noted any of these prophecies lately, but believe me, they certainly describe the times we're going through.

—Ronald Reagan, to Thomas Dine, executive director of the
American-Israel Public Affairs Committee, October 1983[190]

Meanwhile, Ronald Reagan decided to go to war. On October 27, 1983, he rallied the country by speaking into television cameras about his new battle. He began on a somber note, recognizing the death of Marines stationed in Lebanon and the earlier shooting down of a South Korean airliner on which sixty Americans perished. The Soviet Union stood behind both horrific acts, the president argued. But then came the fun part. America had just invaded Grenada, a Caribbean island "twice the size of the District of Columbia, with a total population of about 110,000 people." Radicals hopped up on the aid of Fidel Castro had killed their prime minister, Maurice Bishop. A thousand Americans populated the island, many of them students, prompting fears of another hostage crisis. So the invasion. The best part of it all was that it was over in just a few days, and the troops would be coming home soon. America had triumphed.[191]

The press concurred that this was a "lovely little war." The *Washington Post* headline screamed: "TIDY U.S. WAR ENDS: 'WE BLEW THEM AWAY.'" Grenada served also as a spectacular war, with its images of helicopters landing and troops descending to liberate the black citizens from the slavery of communism (a "Splendid War," as the Proletariat would have called it facetiously). Tim Yo synopsized: "Reagan has been looking for a short, winnable war for some time now, and found one."[192]

Most Americans applauded Reagan's militarized patriotism, pollsters reported. Americans felt like winners again. But the invasion also prompted the peace movement to radicalize, with religious activists declaring a "pledge of resistance" to prevent a potential invasion in Central America. Direct action now beckoned, as activists planned to travel "to Nicaragua to stand unarmed as a loving barrier in the path of any attempted invasion." The war in Grenada also inspired one of the best punk protest songs, the Dicks' "I Hope You Get Drafted." Opening with a cheesy Chuck Berry–sounding riff, the song spewed anger at couch potato patriots cheering the easy war in Grenada. "I hope you get drafted, I hope you carry a gun, when you come back with no arms or legs, then you can say war is fun! Cause you don't care what happens to me, as long as it don't happen to you." As a member of the political punk band from New York City's Lower East Side, Cause for Alarm, explained, "There's an old saying: You may not be interested in politics, but politics are interested in you."[193]

Regardless, Reagan just kept rallying, and victories mounted. Soon after his speech on Grenada, the Senate rejected an amendment on the nuclear freeze, with twelve Democrats breaking ranks. By early November, despite huge protests consisting of "two million Europeans," Germany welcomed the so-called Euromissiles. It was a bruising defeat for the dwindling nuclear freeze movement—which for Reagan, of course, was populated by little more than communist dupes.[194]

Television intervened to stall Reagan's reborn Cold War in the last few days of 1983. On November 20, one hundred million American television viewers watched *The Day After*, a long and scary movie about a family in Lawrence, Kansas, living after nuclear apocalypse. It showed ordinary citizens descending into chaotic, vigilante, and barbaric attempts at survival, all the while suffering from the horrors of mass radiation. What made it scarier was that the movie opened with news flashes in the background talking about the installation of missiles in Germany. But the punk press dismissed it as just another television show, as really part of the problem. An organizer of Wisconsin punk shows explained: "A media piece of junk to keep people from thinking, similar to a football game or a visit to a religious shrine. There will be NO day after and everyone should know that!" The zine *Skid*, whose editor moved from Milwaukee to Buford, Georgia, where he continued publishing, argued that the show—which his high school teachers said was a communist plot—could not stop Ronald Reagan, who seemed "set on starting a new cold war and bringing our cultural consciousness down to a more manageable New Dark Ages level."[195]

In fact, Reagan was "greatly depressed" by *The Day After*. Unlike the annoying voice of someone like a Helen Caldicott yelling in his ear, he could relate to visual depictions centering around the sufferings of a middle-class American family. But he was certainly not going to reconsider the installation of the Euromissiles or a nuclear freeze. Instead, his new pet cause was for "Star Wars," an elaborate satellite system that would be positioned in space to shoot down incoming missiles. He didn't like the name "Star Wars"; instead, he called it "a defense weapon that would render nuclear missiles obsolete." Reagan's New Right ally, Phyllis Schlafly, pressed him to stick with "Star Wars," since it suggested a "drama of the battle between good and evil, and of the triumphs of good over evil through adventure, courage, and confrontation," the sort of vision he had set out in his Evil Empire speech. Whatever the case, "Star Wars" promised to drive the arms race into space, taking it to new levels, literally and figuratively.[196]

The clouds of nuclear winter shown in *The Day After* cleared eventually, giving way to a real winter, as the Christmas holiday beckoned, and as the White House was decked with bows and trees. The feel of the holidays gave Reagan an opportunity to champion the ethic of war, this time at the Congressional Medal of Honor Society in New York City on December 12, 1983. He announced that "the last of the combat troops in Grenada" were returning home. The triumphant return confirmed for Reagan his idea that "our days of weakness are over. Our military forces are back on their feet and standing tall." Raising the military budget was paying off, he suggested. And then the president broke into storytelling mode, finding his "memory going back to those things" he had read about World War II, including about another Congressional Medal of Honor recipient. It was a story about a "young ball-turret gunner" in a plane that had taken a hit, leaving the young man wounded, incapable of escaping his position. Reagan went for the drama, explaining that "over the channel, the plane began to lose altitude, and the commander had to order bail out." Many started to prepare to ditch their plummeting plane, leaving "the boy, . . . knowing he was left behind, to go down." Instead of disembarking with the others, the commander in charge sat down on the floor, took the turret gunner's hand, and said, "'Never mind, son, we'll ride it down together.' Congressional Medal of Honor, posthumously awarded."[197]

The journalist Lars Erik Nelson found these remarks particularly strange (how could there be a record of a conversation between these two deceased men?). He searched for the original story and thought that it either came from *Reader's Digest* (one of Reagan's favorite publications) or perhaps, and not surprisingly, a movie, *A Wing and a Prayer*, released in 1944, that starred Dana Andrews. One thing for sure, Reagan had spun a tale of heroism out of his imagination, his dreams, and cobwebbed memories of stories. When asked about this, White House spokesman Larry Speakes shrugged his shoulders and explained, "If you tell the same story five times, it's true." There couldn't be a better statement about Reagan's governing philosophy than that, especially now as the year turned to 1984.[198]

IT'S 1984! (1984)

ARE YOU READY FOR 1984?: Are you ready . . . to "die for your country" all because it had to keep meddling in the affairs of . . . El Salvador? To be blown away by our friendly "peacekeeper," the MX Missile? For Boy George drag to become the fashion rage?

—*Negative Print*, October 1983[1]

XXX

The Year of Fear

You go to school for twelve years where you learn just one thing: how not to mind being bossed . . . just where you're going to work for the next fifty years, that's your freedom of choice . . . 1984 knocking on your door; will you let it run your life?

—Feederz, "1984," on *Ever Feel Like Killing Your Boss?* (1984)

The zine *Warning* worried in its January 1984 issue: "It's finally here—the year of the great and horrible Orwellian vision of the future!" That sounded ominous, but behind the words of fear stood hope. *Warning's* sheer existence illustrated how punk had made it all the way to the great frontier of Alaska, nurtured by the hard work of Bill Bored (aka Frank Harlan) whose zine helped forge a local scene in Anchorage. There were bands like the Angry Nuns, the Urban Tribe, Ten Ten, and Skate Death, playing often at the Carpenter's Hall. Bored helped organize and promote shows based on an ethic for "all ages": "no alcohol, no drugs, no promoting of physical abuse." The zine built a following, with its circulation by 1984 reaching 2,500, due largely to Bored's success at recruiting advertisers. He even made it onto the radio to publicize what punk was to wary audiences. He argued that punk drew from "alienation" that took on an "explosive force" ripe with "defiance." Punk, he explained, "stubbornly resists cooptation and commercialization. It cannot be sold as a bland and inoffensive commodity."[2]

Making it out to the frontier suggests punk continued growing and spreading as the year 1984 dawned (there were even glimmerings of it in Hawaii). With that spread came more nationwide coverage. *MRR*, for instance, watched as its numbers of readers grew. Starting in 1982 with a circulation of 1,000, by 1984 it had 10,000 and was being printed on a monthly basis, rather than bimonthly. On the East Coast, Bruce Gallanter could rifle off the name of sixty bands in his small state of New Jersey. It wasn't just quantity, either, it was the feel of the movement that managed to "balance . . . humor and seriousness, . . . control and letting go, and the throttling intensity" that brought participants to it in the first place. Al of *Flipside*, who had been at it for seven years now, saw "something more constructive and positive coming out of punk" as 1984 dawned. Zines like *Truly Needy* kept publishing contact information for a growing number of zines spreading across the country. Punk even started receiving some friendly treatments in the mass media (as happened in the wake of the Mendiola's Ballroom show), especially from Charles M. Young, a writer who once worked for *Rolling Stone* (where he had gotten the magazine to pay attention to the Sex Pistols earlier). Young tagged along with the Dead Kennedys and MDC as they toured and penned a salutary treatment of punk published in *Playboy*. Young championed the movement, comparing it to "early Christian Gnosticism in that there is no central, unchangeable Scripture. Adherents are encouraged to experience the Truth for themselves and to write their own Gospel in photocopied . . . fanzines . . . or scream it over their own dissonant guitars, as opposed to accepting their Gospel on faith from a priest or Mick Jagger." (Young would also go on the Phil Donahue show in 1984 and defend the movement from another round of fretful middle-aged parents.) Optimism, ironic as it might sound, animated some punk circles—a belief that the positive dimensions of punk were finally getting a hearing. A New York City zine called *Sense of Purpose* (an interesting name for a punk publication) drew back to assess what was going on as 1983 turned to 1984: "More than at any time in quite a bundle of years, there's a whole slew of bands filled with guts and heart pitted against a totally soulless streamlined mainstream. . . . It's been placed there by writers, programmers, and just plain folks" who oppose the "Velveeta trash" of new wave disco bands like Spandau Ballet or Boy George.[3]

* * *

And yet . . . The year 1984 prompted fear as much as hope, seen in *Warning's* dread of an "Orwellian" present. After all, for the last thirty-six years George Orwell's *1984* (1948) had nagged at readers about a dystopian, totalitarian future where the individual had been eradicated ("The Last Man in Europe" was the book's original title). Orwell imagined an all-powerful state—run by "Big Brother"—that probed the internalized fears of anyone considering rebellion (in the case of the main character, Winston Smith, his fear of rats) and used propaganda to control thought. There were "Hate Weeks" in which new enemies of the state would be declared and switched around, keeping citizens bamboozled while stoked with fervor and fear. The government dominated its citizens by creating an official history bereft of stable facts ("it never happened," an evocative statement made about the past in the novel). Propaganda played on inverted logic (or ideology) with slogans like "War is Peace" and "Freedom is Slavery." Any opposition to the state was forged by the state itself. And now, a growing number of readers looked at their wall calendars—wondering, are we there yet?[4]

At the time *Warning* expressed its worries about 1984, the Soviet Union tried to turn a book that had clearly condemned Stalinism into a critique of everything wrong in America. The novel, the Soviet leadership explained in a communique issued in January, was "a grim warning precisely to bourgeois society, bourgeois civilization, bourgeois democracy—in which, as [Orwell] feared, the poisonous roots of antihumanism, all-devouring militarism and oppression have today thrust up truly monstrous shoots." Ronald Reagan was "Big Brother," who used the "thought police" in the United States and ginned up "hate broadcasts" that created a "continuous frenzy . . . for foreign enemies and internal traitors." That prompted Vice President George Bush to use a series of university addresses to turn 1984 into an endorsement of the administration's aggressive policy toward Central America. "Big Brother may be all-powerful in Havana," Bush would explain, "but the United States will not stand idly by while Big Brother tries to extend his power and influence over our freedom-loving neighbors in Central America." Americans must "stand together, firm and strong, in defense of our freedom." So a book suspicious about power squared itself with the rhetoric of reigning power, be it the United States or USSR.[5]

What better person to ask than a man who had lifted his name from 1984? Winston Smith, the artist for the Dead Kennedys, believed Orwell's novel held insights into contemporary America. He was asked to elaborate on these in the January issue of MRR. He went back to the Iranian hostage crisis, when television news showed "pictures of millions of [Iranians] pushing their arms in the air, fists clenched, yelling 'Death to America.' TV made millions of Americans froth at the mouth, that was Hate Week." There was Reagan's equation of dissent with Soviet propaganda. And what could be more Orwellian than the president's use of the term "peacekeeper" for the MX Missile, Smith asked. Reagan himself spoke in a dreamlike way about nuclear war (and more recently "Star Wars"), Smith pointed out. It all numbed people out, leaving them in a state of fear and passivity.[6]

One reader of MRR responded to Smith's interview and suggested people read 1984 Revisited, a collection of essays edited by the democratic socialist writer Irving Howe, including one by a college professor who had assigned Orwell to his students. These young readers didn't lose themselves in the details of the book; instead, they thought through some of their own personal experiences in relation to the major story line—the state breaking down the resistance of a lone individual. One student wrote, "Orwell has me convinced that with proper condition[ing] and absence of truth I could be made to rationalize or could be made to hate that which is good." The novel conjured a fear about personal strength in the face of adversity. Another wrote, "I can't believe that they set people up so they can torture them. But then again I do know people who would intentionally play mind games and scheme to hurt other people emotionally." Indeed, Orwell had written 1984 simultaneously with an essay about his own fears about attending a boarding school, "Such, Such Were the Joys." Young readers picked up on that, as they squared off against bullies in their own schoolyards while reading the novel. *1984* made sense to younger readers, not in its specific details, but in giving expression to fears and anxieties about being complicit with corrupt power.[7]

Even with this interest of Winston Smith and readers of *MRR*, many punks would balk at the idea that *1984* got things right about the society they inhabited. Orwell's predictions, after all, clashed with the forecasts of another widely discussed book among punks, Aldous Huxley's *Brave New World*, a book Reagan Youth read from when performing and that provided the title for the Proletariat's 1983 release, *Soma Holiday*. In fact, something of an unarticulated debate began when George Orwell, just before his death, sent Huxley a copy of *1984*. Huxley reacted negatively to the book's arguments, especially in assessing "Western capitalist democracies." For Huxley, Orwell focused too much on top-down domination and the repression of individualistic instincts. In *Brave New World*, citizens consume soma and dance communally to celebrate the industrialists and corporate leadership class. They engage in orgies and experience unbridled sexual pleasure. Huxley himself made the point in *Brave New World Revisited* (1958): "It has become clear that control through the punishment of undesirable behavior is less effective, in the long run, than control through the reinforcement of desirable behavior by rewards." Huxley believed passivity and ignorance spawned from a consumer culture, one where entertainment was the highest measure. He explained that many "did not foresee what in fact has happened, above all in our Western capitalist democracies—the development of a vast mass communications industry, concerned in the main neither with the true or the false, but with the unreal, the more or less totally irrelevant. In a word, they failed to take into account man's almost infinite appetite for distractions." These words sounded much more prescient than Orwell's warning about repression and state directives, at least in America, circa 1984.[8]

Besides, all this dystopian talk about the future ignored the hopefulness punks clutched as they watched their movement continue to grow, making it to the American frontier. *1984* might have suggested the potential to crush the individual, and Huxley might have shown that pleasure could be as much a sedative as state power (in the process forecasting the rise of the "yuppie"), but even with those warnings in mind, Chuck Dukowski's earlier claim could now be updated: Punk could be and was now *everywhere*.

XXX

Blockbuster Revenge

> Ever notice how much Michael Jackson looks like a stained-glass saint on his Michael Bubble Gum Cards? Especially the stick-ons. The way his head is always outlined in design makes him look like he's wearing a halo. When you stick him on things they become blessed by Saint Michael.
>
> —*Bang!* zine, 1983[9]

No hope in the hearts of young punks, as they watched scenes erupt on the American frontier, could match the cash-ridden grins in the corporate offices of CBS, MTV, Michael Jackson's talent agency, and the Pepsi Corporation. All were enthused by an album that turned itself into a history-changing phenomenon. Michael Jackson's *Thriller* was released in late 1982, became a hit-machine over the course of 1983 (with "Billie Jean," a single that stayed number one for seven weeks), and then transformed itself into a "block-buster," according to the *New York Times*, by January 1984. The *Guinness Book of World Records* proclaimed *Thriller* the "biggest selling album of all time." Its eponymous video—which ran up to fourteen minutes, a sort of masterwork for MTV—had been released a month before and now was everywhere. "Prior to airing of the fourteen minute long videoclip 'Thriller,'" two historians report, "its album sales were down to quarter of a million. . . . The first week MTV played [the video] sales jumped from 250,000 to 657,000 copies, next week to a million and the third week in excess of a million." Meanwhile, Jackson signed a contract with Pepsi to brand their soda as a "generation's" drink (ironically, Jackson didn't consume the cola, since he refused all caffeine). In return, Pepsi would print its name and logo on cups sold at future Jackson concerts (among other things). Jay Coleman, the marketeer who cooked up the deal, called it "a multifaceted marketing campaign with lots of touch points: big-time advertising, tour sponsorship, logos on the cans, displays in the supermarkets and PR-friendly events." The Pepsi commercial, filmed in January 1984—and resulting in Jackson's highly coiffed hair catching fire while on set—would become "the first and only commercial to ever be included in the *TV Guide* listings." MTV secured a premiere of the commercial, believing the ad to be a work of art. As Roger Enrico, the CEO of Pepsi, asserted: "97 percent of the American public watched" the commercial "at least a dozen times." Synergy worked to create a "blockbuster" and a "spectacle"; Jackson seemed to be *everywhere*, much like Big Brother in *1984*.[10]

It's purported that when Quincy Jones, the record producer, started to work on *Thriller*, he announced: "Okay, guys, we're here to save the recording industry!" Whether true or not, by 1984, the sentiment among the CEOs perched on top of the industry beamed with hope. Gil Friesen, president of A&M Records, told *Time* magazine, "The whole industry has a stake in this success." *Time* gushed that Jackson's album had "given the business its best year since the heady days of 1978, when it had an estimated total domestic revenue of $4.1 billion," before the crash of 1979. As Michael Jackson dolls started to roll off the assembly line, *Time* sounded like it channeled the spirit of the popular and "positive" preacher Norman Vincent Peale: "For a record industry stuck on the border between the ruins of punk and the chic regions of synthesizer pop, *Thriller* was a thorough restoration of confidence, a rejuvenation." *Thriller* managed to draw "people into record stores," something entertainment CEOs were starting to worry would never happen again (while blaming it mostly on cassette taping). Which explains why one program director at a New York City rock station could express with relief to the *New York Times* that "Michael Jackson is mass culture, not pop culture—he appeals to everybody." In late February, Jackson would sweep the Grammys, piling up eight wins. His presence at the televised Grammy Awards show, the *L.A. Reader* later reported, helped skyrocket "the cost of half a minute's advertising." And with the Pepsi commercial, the soft drink company watched as its "sales" pushed to "record levels." No surprise that when planning a tour following *Thriller's* long reign of popularity—a tour sponsored by Pepsi—it was called appropriately "Victory."[11]

* * *

The movie industry also felt wind in its sails, as it solidified its partnership with MTV. It aimed its sights on a younger audience—hoping to become a voice for teenage rebellion and angst, the way it had in the 1950s. After the wild success of *Risky Business* in the summer of 1983, where a young wealthy suburbanite (Tom Cruise) uses his parents' house for a brothel that makes him temporarily rich, came *Footloose*, a movie released at the same time Michael Jackson swept the Grammys. Starring Kevin Bacon (a marginal member in what would become known as the "Brat Pack"), the movie told the story of a young man moving from Chicago to a rural area—facing the standard enemies of Hollywood: small-town provincialism and dogmatic, puritanical religion. Bacon's character, Ren McCormack, decks himself out with a leather coat and skinny tie and pledges affinity for new wave bands like Men Without Hats and the Police. He faces down a hung up, hokey, closed-minded preacher who condemns "obscene" music and "lax morality" and who backs an ordinance against dancing in town. The preacher happens to have a daughter, and McCormack falls for her. Ren winds up beating the boyfriend of the preacher's daughter in a tractor "chickee" run (a scene almost directly lifted from *Rebel without a Cause* [1955]). And then he dances to the song "Never Hide Your Heart" in what seems a scene made for MTV. Indeed, better than the previous year's *Flashdance*, the movie scored four music videos on MTV.[12]

After the preacher beats his daughter, she leaves home. Meanwhile, Ren challenges the dance ordinance by going to the city council. "Let's Hear It for the Boy," an electro-pop song that sounded an awful lot like Madonna (though it's Deniece Williams) blasts the obvious message here: Bacon champions the music sold by the entertainment industry and upholds the virtues and rights of dancing to it. Makers of the film hoped that its "mild-mannered rebellion," as two historians called it, "appealed to teens." Revolt now could be fun and simple. The message from Hollywood, MTV, and the entertainment industry as a whole was: we give you the things you need in order to rebel against the prudes. That's provided not just in the movie, but in the MTV videos, the soundtrack album, the hype. Nina Blackwood, a video jockey (VJ), explained around this time that MTV provided young people their "own culture, which was empowering." MTV and movies like *Footloose* constituted now for Blackwood "a celebration of youth."[13]

The unlikely love story between Ren and the preacher's daughter replicated *Valley Girl*'s Romeo and Juliet meme. And a few months after *Footloose* hit, came the quintessential screwball comedy and debut of the director John Hughes—*Sixteen Candles*. The film's story was easy: there's an artsy, new wave (ish) girl who is unpopular in school. Her family forgets it's her sixteenth birthday, distracted by the wedding of her older sister. This outsider girl ("Sam," played by Molly Ringwald) falls for a football-playing, cheerleader-dating hunk. And then, of course, *he* falls for *her*.

Hughes, who is now celebrated for the fare he offered during the 1980s (often quite nostalgically), had climbed the Hollywood ladder, moving from screenwriter to director (his previous background was actually in advertising). His biggest inspiration was Frank Capra, a director known for Great Depression movies that projected sentimental populism. Capra had perfected the formula for screwball comedy in his classic *It Happened One Night* (1934), where a wealthy socialite falls for an unemployed journalist. Hughes simply translated this 1930s storyline to 1980s suburbia. Like Capra earlier, he wanted to get emotions and feelings onto the screen, including teenage angst, romantic dreaming, and sexual desire. So he would tease out the awkwardness of a high school dance, the raging and libidinal desires of adolescent males, as well as the status system and cliques of suburban youth. Like Capra, Hughes was reported to be a Republican. Like Capra and Reagan, he was a believer in the power of dreams and desires. No surprise he relied on music in *Sixteen Candles*—including "new romanticists" like Spandau Ballet and new wave dance music by the likes of Billy Idol and the Thompson Twins. In *Sixteen Candles*, with its romantic music droning in the background, Hughes developed what one critic called "anything is possible depictions of teenage romance" that fit Reagan's dreamland America.[14]

XXX

A President with Secrets

> The frightening thing was that it might all be true. If the Party could thrust its hand into the past and say of this or that event, it *never happened.*
> —George Orwell, *1984*[15]

Ronald Reagan opened a new front in the second Cold War. By 1984, the Euromissiles were getting installed, and "Star Wars," or SDI, had derailed the nuclear freeze movement. Now he could turn his attention to Central America, particularly Nicaragua, whose Sandinista government Reagan saw as an extension of Cuban and Soviet power, and whose opponents—usually referred to as "the contras"—he called "freedom fighters." Reagan hoped to enter that civil war and give aid to the Sandinistas' military enemy. The problem was that as much as he hoped to overcome the "Vietnam syndrome," public opinion hadn't. And Congress was fast in backing, in late 1982, what were called the Boland Amendments that made illegal any covert operations "for the purpose of overthrowing the government of Nicaragua."[16]

On April 9, 1984, a *Wall Street Journal* story explained what Reagan did when faced with opposition. He gave the go-ahead to the CIA to work with the contras and to mine the harbors of Nicaragua (at the same time, he considered, in his own words, "possible covert operation (CIA) in El Salvador"). When news broke, the message was obvious: *Congress and protest be damned.* When Reagan's one-time hero Barry Goldwater found out about the action, he wrote to his fellow senator Daniel Patrick Moynihan: "I've been trying to figure out how I can most easily tell you my feelings about the discovery of the president having approved mining some of the harbors off Central America. It gets down to one, little, simple phrase: I am pissed off!" No supporter of the Sandinistas, of course, Goldwater feared the growth of an imperial presidency, the extension of executive power defying congressional legislation.[17]

If Barry Goldwater was pissed, the world of punk zines seethed. The zine *Hard Times* (out of New Jersey) blistered at the situation: "The US cannot use democratic methods to overthrow the Sandinista Government." That meant the Reagan administration would follow the teachings of Henry Kissinger on Chile and the Allende government. The editors quoted Kissinger: "I don't see why we have to stand by and watch a country go Communist just because of the irresponsibility of its own people." The zine pointed to history, arguing that "the U.S. was involved militarily in Nicaragua for sixty-seven years prior to the founding of the USSR, what rationalization did they use then?" America was just bullying in its backyard, intervention fueled by national hubris. The zine *Silence*, out of Boise, Idaho, found the whole thing Orwellian—how can you oppose something when it's being secretly hidden from you, they wondered. The mining of the harbors destroyed the "right to question," what *Silence* took as a fundamental principle rooted in the Constitution. Now the right to question included a responsibility to be "informed." "It involves going down to your library and reading. It involves talking to others about important issues. It involves the ability to create your own opinion." Some punks started reading *CovertAction Information Bulletin* to try to get to useful information, but they did so with a sense of frustration about how hard Reagan made it to be an informed citizen.[18]

XXX

A Return to Neo-Noir

Fuck that!

—Otto in *Repo Man*

Covert operations. Secret military action. CIA. Lying. Covering up. . . . Sounded like a good time to rejuvenate noir movie-making, the "hardboiled" fare that usually centered around murder and that dominated American cinema in the 1940s (*The Blue Dahlia* and *Double Indemnity* are premiere examples). And that Paul Schrader predicted would have a comeback in the era of Nixon and Watergate, as evidenced in his own screenplay for *Taxi Driver* (1976). Noir explored themes of entrapment and secrets pushed aside, of people not knowing their motivations. Its darkness expressed a mood of despair about human nature (there were no heroes in noir). Which explains why *Repo Man*, a movie released in the spring of 1984, became a testimony to how punk kids felt living in the age of Reagan.

The movie came by way of a British ex-pat, Alex Cox, who had moved to America to attend film school in Los Angeles and got involved in the punk scene there (he witnessed the infamous police riot at Elks Lodge in 1979). He completed his student film, *Edge City*, in 1980, a herky-jerky movie about an "artist" living in Los Angeles, and one that showed the influence of the director Bunuel (and shared some themes with Matt Groening's "Life in Hell"). The movie was arty with a droll sense of humor, no entry ticket to the studio system of Hollywood.

Cox threw himself into numerous projects that failed. He penned a screenplay based on William S. Burroughs's "Exterminator," which never materialized. He wound up writing a script for the British director Adrian Lyne, who wanted to make a movie akin to "The War Game," a scary depiction of nuclear war's aftermath in England. Lyne wanted Cox to set the movie "in America." Cox wrote a script "about the last 60 minutes in this

French Restaurant in Seattle—just before the bomb is dropped." It was to be titled *The Happy Hour*. Once Lyne saw the script he killed the idea and moved onto directing *Flashdance*, while Cox decided to stop writing undeveloped screenplays and start writing and directing his own film.[19]

Cox got lucky when Michael Nesmith—probably best known for *The Monkees*, the 1960s television show revolving around a concocted rock band—befriended him. Nesmith promised to produce the film and hawked it to Universal. Execs at Universal hated the movie, with one of them supposedly screaming, "I hope they never show this film in Russia!" Cox was saved, ironically, by the principle of "synergy" now so central to the entertainment industry (made explicit in Michael Jackson's *Thriller*). For just as doubts set in about the film's viability, the sales offices at MCA records, which had already released the film's soundtrack, reported that sales were booming (the album included Black Flag, the Circle Jerks, and Fear among others). The bottom line of sales quelled the fears of Universal's execs, an ironic turn in the history of punk.[20]

The film demanded close watching, with subtle points made often in the background. But it eschewed any "avant-garde" or "experimental" pretensions, for the most part staying with a narrative—albeit a quirky one that took twists and turns. Unlike the "no wave" filmmakers of the late 1970s, Cox didn't employ metacommentary about making a movie while making a movie; he just presented his story. Cox also (consciously or not) rejected what was called "the Cinema of Transgression" that Nick Zedd and Richard Kern—both directors heavily influenced by punk—were busy developing at the time of *Repo Man*, emphasizing shock and sex and violence.[21]

The movie centers around Otto (Emilio Estevez), a young man audiences first meet when he is working at the local grocery store, where nearly every item comes in a can labeled "Food." Alongside him is "Kevin the Nerd" (played by Zander Schloss) who moronically sings the jingle for 7-Up ("feeling 7-Up!") and then denies doing so—suggesting how invasive and ubiquitous advertising had become for young people. Otto curses out his boss, quits, and hits the streets where he's approached by a repo man (Harry Dean Stanton) who tricks him into stealing a car. When Otto finds out that he's been rooked, he heads home to ask his hippie parents for money. His dad and mom look like those kitschy hippies Jello Biafra encountered in Boulder, Colorado: They smoke pot and have mellowed out so much that they're now couch potatoes who stare at the television. When Otto queries them about their savings, they admit to giving their money to a right-wing televangelist who appears on their television screen fulminating against "communism abroad" and "liberal humanism at home." Learning that they're broke, Otto hits the streets again, this time becoming a full-blown repossession agent.

Here the movie's critique of macho gels (most noir films from the past show men who think they can control their destiny only to learn the opposite). Harry Dean Stanton plays the character "Bud," who is fast to recruit Otto. He provides a hilarious portrait of the deranged hardboiled antihero—belligerent and declarative, sounding like a street version of Friedrich Nietzsche as he barks out how he hates "ordinary fucking people" and won't let "commies" or "Christians" in his car. When Otto expresses doubt about Bud, Stanton turns misty-eyed and tries to win back the young man's respect. There's also the macho joshing that takes place back at the repo office. During one exchange, the character Miller, a mechanic, tells the repo men gathered around that "John Wayne was a fag." The repo guys— including one who's decked out in a police uniform—look startled and demand that he explain his derision toward their hero. Miller recounts how he once went to Wayne's house, only to find the star wearing a dress and asking to have two-way mirrors installed in his bedroom so he could watch himself and his friends screw one another. "Well that doesn't make him a fag," they shoot back. "A lotta guys like to watch their friends fuck. I know I do," says one of them in mindless retort. The men in the film—hiding behind a flank of hardboiled toughness—come across as suckers.

Suckers especially for the big prize on the streets: a Chevy Malibu that's been winding around the surface roads of Los Angeles. Uranium is packed into its trunk and when it is opened victims literally evaporate from the heat. Cox admitted that he stole this from one of the most bizarre noir films from the 1950s, *Kiss Me Deadly*, which centered around the hardboiled character Mike Hammer's search for a suitcase packed with uranium. In Cox's rewrite, Otto tracks down the car and gets in with its eccentric driver, J. Frank Parnell, who proceeds to monologue. "Radiation, yes indeed," Parnell says. He derides the "lies" that "do-gooders" tell about it. Just as the Dead Kennedys sang about the neutron bomb in "Kill the Poor" (1980), Parnell praises a weapon that can kill people but leave property intact. And then he starts rambling about a "project" he worked for (perhaps the Manhattan Project or the attempt to build a neutron bomb at Lawrence Livermore Labs?). "Working on the thing will make you mad," he tells Otto. So mad, he had to have a "lobotomy," Otto learns just before Parnell slumps dead onto his steering wheel. The message—somewhat akin to that of *Emerald Cities*—becomes explicit: Designing nuclear weapons in the first place was an act of madness, as the zine *BravEar* had suggested two years before. Rationality begat something entirely irrational and suicidal.

These themes and the film's dark humor that made the execs at Universal so nervous are developed through zingy dialogue, much that sounds like it was cribbed from the "hardboiled" writing of Raymond Chandler and Dashiell Hammett (with a humorous twist). One-liners make the film sprint. When his punk friends come into a bar and misbehave, Otto's girlfriend says, "Nice friends, Otto." His retort: "Thanks, I made them myself." When one of Otto's friends, Duke, is irradiated by the trunk of the car, his girlfriend leans in and says, "Let's go do some crimes." Duke says, "Yeah, let's get sushi and not pay." When Duke lies on the floor of a liquor store he tried to rob, with blood running from his mouth, Otto hears him say, "I blame society." To which Otto quips, "That's bullshit, you're a white suburban punk just like me." The mechanic Miller standing amid Los Angeles's suburban sprawl explains, "The more you drive, the less intelligent you are." Perhaps best of all, considering the soundtrack did so well, was the worrying line Otto spoke when he sees the Circle Jerks playing at a nightclub decked out in pretentious tuxedoes and singing, "Shoobee de doo-wop." Otto looks grimaced and says, "I can't believe I used to like these guys."

The movie served as noirish social critique crammed full of ideas about the miseries of car culture in Los Angeles, nuclear war, the stupidities of macho, the "sell out" of punk bands. And yet it also laughed at itself. The *L.A. Weekly* called it a work of "anti-heroism" in the tradition of the independent director Samuel Fuller (famous for his noir offerings). Declaring it the best movie of 1984, the Seattle zine *The Attack* explained that the film was "so good it hurts." When *MRR* finally published a review of the film almost a year after it was released, the sentiment was mixed. The magazine declared the movie "hilarious" and said that it "worked," but it worried that it wasn't really an independent movie—rather a product of Universal (along with the soundtrack on MCA). So while the film offered a humorous form of social criticism, it also symbolized the possibility of punk abandoning its DIY ethic.[22]

XXX

The Savior Arrives at the White House

> The Michael Jackson of American politics is . . . Ronald Reagan. Like Jackson, Ronald Reagan has a sound that's inescapably conservative but produced with a polished gleam that makes it seem new.
>
> —*L.A. Reader*, March 1984[23]

On May 14, 1984, Michael Jackson walked onto the South Lawn of the White House, decked out in a sequined blue jacket and trademark, single, white glove (Bloomingdale's would soon be selling a "Michael Jackson inspired rhinestone-studded white glove" for $9.95). Jackson faced a beaming Ronald Reagan. Purportedly the celebrity was there to receive an award for allowing one of his hit songs off *Thriller*, "Beat It," to be used in an anti-drunk-driving public message for radio. But Reagan had other things on his mind.[24]

"Isn't this a thriller?" the president gushed as he introduced Jackson. He took note of Jackson's "deep faith in God and adherence to traditional values," but quickly explained that he was also a "fan" of Jackson, enamored with the star's commercial success with *Thriller*. As the president noted in his diary, Jackson was a "sensation of the pop music world—believed to have earned $120 mi. last year." That the man had saved the music industry from its slump and that he made lucrative deals with the Pepsi corporation to help brand the soft drink, and that he earned a boatload of money from all of this—*that's* what thrilled Reagan the most.[25]

Which freaked out the president's legal counsel. The president appeared to be shilling for a celebrity, blurring the line between public service and commercial entertainment (a divide the president, by nature, couldn't understand). Reagan's correspondence aide, James Coyne, had written a letter for Jackson after the White House visit. It celebrated Jackson's "accomplishments in the entertainment business" as much as his service to public announcements denouncing drunk driving. Coyne hoped it could be used by *Billboard* magazine, the music industry's trade publication. John Roberts, an associate in the White House counsel office, saw the drafted letter and bugged out. "The Office of Presidential correspondence is not yet an adjunct of Michael Jackson's law firm. 'Billboard' can quite adequately cover the event by reproducing the award citation," Roberts scolded.

Three months later the Jackson craze was still going strong, and Reagan received an invite to a Jackson concert at RFK Stadium. Reagan wanted to go big on this and celebrate Jackson's Victory Tour, which garnered another explosion from Roberts: "Whatever its status as a cultural phenomenon, the Jackson concert tour is a massive commercial undertaking. The tour will do quite well financially by coming to Washington, and there is no need for the President to applaud such enlightened self-interest." It was a struggle to get the entertainer-in-chief to just say no.[26]

All of which explains why Ronald Reagan and Michael Jackson were such deserved compatriots. They saw the world similarly. Both men fetishized confidence. When asked how he thought of himself as a performer two years before his White House appearance, Jackson explained, "I always hated the word 'acting'—to say, 'I'm an actor.' It should be more than that. It should be more like a believer." That sounded an awful lot like Reagan's love of dreams and the right to believe in them. More so, both men celebrated wealth, celebrity, and the power of large corporations, yet somehow squared this with "traditional" values (Jackson constantly advertised that he didn't smoke or do drugs, since he was a Jehovah's Witness). Call it puritanical garishness, a peculiar variant of their shared brand of conservatism. Both men also celebrated the importance of the visual, the facade they both presented to their audiences. For Jackson, this included a growing reliance not just on his garish dress but also on plastic surgery (something he denied); Reagan was a devotee of Brylcreem, to keep his hair shiny and youthful, and he wore oversized shirts to look bigger than he was (one of his speechwriters said, "The White House always seemed like a set"). As Jello Biafra quipped, Reagan worried less about policy and more about getting mentioned in *People* magazine or the *National Enquirer*. Both Jackson and Reagan held a confidence in the rightness of the culture industry—the idea that entertainment came first, that democracy equated with consumerism. They both celebrated Jackson's commitment to saving the entertainment industry, as a reminder of Guy Debord's principle about the spectacle: *That which is good appears; that which appears is good.* And the Kalamazoo-based zine *Free Beer Press* described Michael Jackson this way: "He is the prince of rock videos. Great imagery. Lots of hair spray. Yes, he did have a nose job. . . . Now shut up and dance."[27]

XXX

Minds Still on Fire during a Summer of Creativity

> Future observers will look to our time as a cauldron of creative energy. They will marvel at a dramatic verve of Elizabethan intensity and an aesthetic boldness to rival German Expressionism or the Russian avant-garde.
> —Peter Titus in *Own the Whole World*[28]

In July 1984, the Minutemen released "Political Song for Michael Jackson." Like most of the songs the bassist Mike Watt wrote, it wasn't a straightforward protest song, too complex and multilayered for that (although musically very simple, mostly two chords played and Boon's straightforward vocals). Watt claimed that he actually wrote the song for Jackson "to sing." He went on: "I don't know if he knows of it. He's Jehovah's Witness and stuff. He'd probably think it is wicked, just at the sight of it." One underlying theme of the song was about young men marching off to war, having learned militarism from serving in the Boy Scouts. It was also a song that rejected the happy-making of Michael Jackson. "If we heard mortar shells," D. Boon would sing, "we'd cuss more in our songs, and cut down on guitar solos." For sure, that sounded like a commentary on the flashy 30-second, virtuoso guitar solo played by Eddie Van Halen for Jackson's song "Beat It!" (and it was followed by a spastic guitar solo from Boon). Resistance to Reagan's and Jackson's culture of happiness required both thoughtful self-assertion and self-defacement. "Me, I'm fighting with my head," Watt would write. "I'm not ambiguous . . . "—a silent pause was built into the song here—and then "I must look like a dork." Watt found himself "naked, with textbook poems" shouting at the "iron-fisted philosophy" of contemporary America.[29]

The song appeared as one of forty-three others on the double album *Double Nickels on the Dime*, certainly a high watermark of punk creativity. The album, Watt explained to *Ink Disease*, "cost about 1,200 dollars total and took 50 hours all together." The Minutemen were still a "one-take band" who would always go "econo" with their minimalist approach to recording. Still, their audience was growing, with 10,000 copies of the album sold upon release.[30]

The album was full of rich intellectual sources—in large part an ongoing conversation with others (the album had a participatory feel, since the band's friends wrote songs for it). Though the gendered language might not have been to their liking, *Flipside* was right to call the Minutemen the "thinking man's band." The D.C. zine *Truly Needy* explained that the band's "songs make you think, not feel. They do not strike with sledgehammers, they worm their way through memories." So for instance, numerous conversations with Raymond Pettibon (whose art appeared in the liner notes for *Double Nickels*) about linguistics introduced the band to Ludwig Wittgenstein, the philosopher who saw language as a performative act that could never obtain "objective truth." Wittgenstein argued humans play "language games" that never find "transcendent certainty." "A meaning of a word," he wrote, "is a kind of employment of it" and "the difficulty is to realize the groundlessness of our believing." Those ideas seeped into the song "Do You Want New Wave or Do You Want the Truth?," which explored the multiplicity of meanings: "Should words serve the truth?" Boon asks. "I stand for language. I speak for truth," he went on, the sort of truth that still could never eradicate doubt. "I am a cesspool for all the shit to run down in," Boon pondered.[31]

Through conversations with Chuck Dukowski, the band solicited song lyrics for "Nature without Man." Dukowski's existentialism worked well with Pettibon's questioning of language. As he explained, "I was thinking about morality and the intellectual impositions we place upon existence that I feel is without purpose or morality." As much as Dukowski's philosophizing mattered here, so too did Mike Watt's rereading of James Joyce's *Ulysses*—one of his favorite books, chock full of language experimentation. He was inspired by the fractured nature of the book, which often broke from stream of consciousness into a formal question-answer format into internal monologues. Watt tried out this technique with songs like "One Reporter's Opinion" and "Retreat."[32]

All this pondering about language and certainty shouldn't cover up the album's politics. Indeed, "The World According to Nouns" suggested how language could defend the existing order. "The state, the church, the plans, the waste, the dead, what's the verb behind it all? The do, the how, the why, the where, the when, the what, can these words find the truth?" As the rock critic Tom Carson, writing for the *Village Voice*, noted, "The Minutemen have a style . . . call it the analytical-demotic. In their explicitly sociopolitical songs, the interest is in the way they use the terminology of leftism to create effects that are grunged-out lowlife-nihilistic, as American as film noir, instead of militant." In other words, there was no screaming or whining about Reagan, but there was the song "Viet Nam," which challenged the president's growing faith that America could have won that war. "Executive order, congressional decision," Boon would sing, "The working masses are manipulated. Was this our policy? Ten long years, not one domino shall fall." At other points, the band's anger at Reagan grew more explicit: "Fear of death is so close, crimes on our heads. Are we ignorant, blind? Afraid to swallow our pride." Numerous songs on the double album attacked the white working class that was presently bolting toward the Republican Party and Reagan's cheery leadership. Boon again, in "Themselves": "Can't they see beyond the rhetoric? The lies and promises that don't mean shit." Boon wrote about his own working-class identity on the album. For instance, the upbeat "This Ain't No Picnic," in which he expressed frustration at working dead-end jobs with stupid bosses, went: "Working on the edge, losing my self-respect for a man who presides over me." As the band admitted in *MRR*, they understood the humiliation faced by working-class people, being working class themselves. But on the other hand, "most of the working class is [*sic*] rednecks." They had no Marxist illusions about the working class as an agent of revolutionary change. The band held out what one zine editor called "their personal and social commentary" that "spoke out of caring, not out of blind hatred" or any sort of rigid ideology. *Double Nickels* thus struck a balance between "humanism and humor."[33]

The title of the double album itself provoked head-scratching. But here there was a clear referent. *Double Nickels on the Dime* alluded to the I-10 interstate highway and also to a song by Sammy Hagar, a brazen and conservative rock star akin to Ted Nugent. Hagar's 1984 hit song "I Can't Drive 55" balked and barked at the speed limit that Jimmy Carter endorsed as part of a wider energy conservation program that encouraged drivers to use less gas. The song's MTV video provided quintessential conservative rebellion. Hagar recklessly drives his revved-up sports car, with one foot on the brake, the other on the gas, getting stuck behind a truck on a two-lane road. He nearly careens into a highway patrolman, who Hagar defies until he's cuffed and brought to court, where there's a judge who looks like a British magistrate, wig and all. Hagar's fellow band members disrupt the court proceedings, as Hagar jumps on top of the judge's desk and pushes him aside. A member of his band tosses him an electric guitar and Hagar goes to town soloing on top of the judge's desk. An old lady (of course) in the jury starts to beat him with her umbrella, and the cops manage to tackle him into jail. Hagar, though, busts out, and the final scene shows him in defiant rebellion, driving his car in the three-digit mile per hour range.

The video was the culmination of what Jello Biafra—a friend to the Minutemen—called "the cock rock" politics of heavy metal music. It was a hurly burly macho appeal to white working-class fans (as against the critique of macho that Alex Cox had developed in *Repo Man*). Biafra explained, "Many of the heavy metal bands are openly rightwing, openly racist; Foreigner with DIRTY WHITE BOY, Sammy Hagar on the Fourth of July during the hostage crisis, 'Now there's somebody we'd all like to kill' and Ayatollah Khomeini lights up on the screen, the whole crowd cheers." What the Minutemen offered with *Double Nickels* extended Biafra's critique: They were happy to drive 55, as the cover picture on the album shows Mike Watt doing. A tad late, of course, but it felt like a nod to Jimmy Carter's conservationist politics rather than Reagan's libertarianism. And most certainly it was a jest at the baby antics, pseudo-rebellion, and macho "cock-rock" of Sammy Hagar.[34]

* * *

Inspiration for a double album also came from the Minutemen's partners and sometime rivals, Husker Du, a band who helped inspire a local scene in Minneapolis, hooking up with the pioneering band the Replacements and others to come, like Final Conflict, Man Sized Action, and Rifle Sport. The band's second release on the Minutemen's label, *Land Speed Record* (1982), was frantic and minimalist, a continuous string of songs played live without pause, with a frenetic shouting against impending war ("Casualties will be gigantic, run down the street and panic"). It was easy from this to see the alliance between Husker Du and the Minutemen—both pioneers of frantic protest songs fueled by anxiety. Bob Mould, guitarist and sometimes lead singer, explained soon after *Land Speed Record* was released that he saw punk as "the protest music of the 80s," being "anti-war and anti-establishment," like folk songs of the past. But two years later, he was starting to have his doubts about the efficacy of such protest.[35]

Having toured for quite some time now, Mould met numerous punks he thought were way in above their heads when it came to politics. He suggested to *Ink Disease* that MDC was a band that went to a library to write a song rather than *feel* a song (of course, MDC would argue that point). In general, the spirit behind *Land Speed Record* had passed for Mould. He had once told *Destroy L.A.* zine, "You can't change the whole world with a song." He found himself turning his back on politics, more to everyday emotions and the like.[36]

SST released Husker Du's *Zen Arcade* at the same time as *Double Nickels*. It was much more unified than the Minutemen's, more truly a concept album with a narrative story (sort of like the Who's *Quadrophenia* or Genesis's *The Lamb Lies Down on Broadway*). The songs managed to fuse together a much more poppy feel (including the song "Hare Krsna," modeled on the pop song of the mid-sixties "I Want Candy"), while still being angular sounding, with heavy guitar playing and feedback fusing with more melodic singing, but singing that often turned into screaming still. To many it had a sound of buzz saws.

Its story centered around a young man running from his "broken home" and into the streets. One review suggested the album sounded like the "raves of a pissed off street bum." Bob Mould explained that *Zen Arcade* was "about a kid who runs away from home and then goes through a number of experiences in order to try to stay alive and just keep going." Sort of an updated version of John Bunyan's *Pilgrim's Progress* (once the most-read book in America), where the sins of the world—including the crudeness of the marketplace known as Vanity Fair—tempt a young man who holds to his faith (the story was told as a dream in part). At the core of the double album is the theme of communication breakdown, of people not being able to connect and talk with one another (the theme that Dennis Cooper prompted in much of his poetry). The story starts, as it almost has to, with one of the saddest punk songs ever, "Broken Home, Broken Heart," the first side's second song (which is punchy and features Mould's screaming and sounding like his vocal cords had been torn—capturing the sound of a young person screaming in anguish about failed family life). The fighting among the character's family—Mould envisioned the father as a high-strung, well paid doctor who shuts off from his family at night— leads to fighting among peers. Both family and friends fail the protagonist, and in "Chartered Trips," the main character has everything he owns in a "nylon carry-all" destined for a trip with no return, "out there on the desert" (suggesting military service in Afghanistan or Iran). But generally, "indecision" and the character's ability to "daydream" overpowers any temporary closure. Some try to grab his attention like the "Hare Krsna" (the song that sounded like "I Want Candy"). Listeners could hear bells and chanting in the song, representing the public sound of Hare Krishna proselytizing in their search for spiritual meaning (many a punk kid had chowed down on Krishna soup kitchen fare, after all it was free). The protagonist sinks further into a state of impotent solitude ("Standing by the Sea"): "I was talking when I should have been listening." The character experiments with sex—including masochism—to which he concludes: "I love it, I hate it. Why is it so confusing?" Like the Minutemen's doubt about logic and language, the search for identity never landed on secure ground: "Trying to find identity but I just find a disguise." And then the young protagonist falls in love with a woman who scores drugs for him and then overdoses ("Pink Turns to Blue").[37]

Once again, the central character is alone, but now draws back to consider the state of the wider world. The political anguish the band was known for creeps back in here, with the central character crying out, "A world where science went too far, there's no way to survive—Why can't we get this thing straightened out cause I wanna stay alive." Then the character returns to his family, "I'm not the son you wanted but what could you expect, I've made my world of happiness to combat your neglect." And then in a slightly disappointing way, the listener learns that this was just a reoccurring dream and that the protagonist had simply fallen asleep. Shouts of "Wake Up!" and "Turn on the News" come at him. The young man then comes full circle to the major theme of the double album: "If there's one thing that I can't explain is why the world has to have so much pain. With all the ways of communicating we can't get in touch with who we're hating." Though less hopeful about political change, the band remained committed to the principles of exchange, communication, empathy, and open conversation.

Husker Du embarked on an extensive tour to promote the double album months after its release. It started to receive mostly positive reviews in the punk press, many zines finding the melodic, slower pace of the album—without leaving off sharp edges—an enjoyable listen. The sound was rough and tough but more approachable than their first album. Some found the album's story line compelling and fairly realistic (what punk zine editor had not had experience with broken families or the Hare Krishnas?). The album documented the challenges of coming of age during the 1980s. But there were also some concerns. From the perspective of *Own the Whole World* zine, the first three sides of the album were superb, but when it came to "side four (the jam side), with 'Turn on the News' and 'Reoccurring Dreams,'" the album became "unsuccessful." "Reoccurring Dreams" was "an instrumental of gross proportions," *Own the Whole World* complained. "It's a pity they had to end it so self-indulgently." Commenting on *Zen Arcade* and the Minutemen's *Double Nickels*, the *L.A. Reader* couldn't help reflecting on the double album's meaning in rock 'n' roll history (missing that the British anarcho punk band, Crass, had released a double album in 1979). There was an irony here, seeing that "the shorter is the better ethic of punkdom did much to bury the bacchanalian spirit of the double album." In other words: Some were worrying that these bands might be repeating the errors of their elders, becoming bloated and pretentious as they got older.[38]

* * *

The summer movie for L.A. punks was *Desperate Teenage Lovedolls*. Its director was Dave Markey, who played in a band called Sin 34 and who for the last three years had edited the zine *We Got Power* out of his bedroom in Isla Vista, California. *We Got Power*—the title itself recognizing the growing impact of punk—committed itself to documenting scenes throughout the United States. It grimaced at Serena Dank (Parents of Punkers) and the shuttering of punk venues in Southern California. And it honed a type of humorous social criticism, for instance, rating (on a star system, one to five) police raids on punk shows, "best band names" (Jews from the Valley and Ethel and the Mertz Killers were among the winners), and "breakfast cereals." Eventually, the zine would start putting out compilation albums, before falling apart in late 1983. Markey had made a documentary about

Southern California punk, the *Slog Movie* in 1982, and he decided now to make a movie about a female band rising to popularity—sort of a better version (because it didn't take itself so seriously) of *Ladies and Gentlemen, the Fabulous Stains.*[39]

Desperate Teenage Lovedolls was clearly indebted to Russ Meyer's "classic" *Beyond the Valley of the Dolls,* which told the story of a female rock band trying to break big (there were also traces of Warhol's campy movies, where characters overacted their roles). The movie told a story that replicated the history of the Runaways, a band designed and managed by Kim Fowley who played up the members' youthful sex appeal. Indeed, so similar was *Desperate Teenage Lovedolls* to the story of the Runaways that Fowley purportedly threatened to blow up any theater that showed it.[40]

The movie relished in its amateur status (shot in Super-8), parodying the rise to fame of *A Star Is Born* (1937) and its many remakes. The film focused on two young women who had a band, one member recently escaped from a hospital. They are thrown out of the house where they rehearse by a completely antic mother (played by Markey's coeditor of *We Got Power,* Jordan Schwartz, wearing a wig that flops around as he gesticulates). Hitting the streets, the band members talk about how they want to become rock stars. They turn to drugs (since all rock stars do that) and steal guitars and play them on sidewalks. The audience listens to pathetic renditions of "Louie Louie," perhaps one of the most covered songs in history, and the Beach Boys' "Let Me Go Home." It's on the streets where the band meets Johnny Tremaine (the Fowley equivalent), played by Steven Macdonald of the band Redd Kross (one of the funnier bands out of southern California, whose songs often referenced popular culture in a comical manner). Tremaine symbolizes all the lecherous sleaze of the music industry and serves as the consummate confidence man. He displays in salesman talk, the language of overpromise and lust for power: "Johnny Tremaine's the name and making rock stars is my game." And his eye-rolling line: "I think I can do for you girls what God did for mankind." Tremaine then invites one of the Lovedolls back to his swank apartment, where he tries to rape her. When she resists, Tremaine blurts out, "Listen bitch, fame has a price."

The film follows the rise of the band to fame after Tremaine plots a media blitz. Their performances look like MTV videos and earn them screaming crowds of fans and boatloads of money. And then there's the ultimate revenge, when the two Lovedolls go to Tremaine's apartment to party. They plead for "some heroin," and as Tremaine fetches some, the women drop drugs into his drink. They start to leave and say, "Have a good twip [trip] Johnny." At one point, he looks at his tight pants that are blue and screams, "Oh my god, my legs are blue," and then hurls himself down the streets of Los Angeles, freaked out of his mind while the Jimi Hendrix song "Purple Haze" blasts (a cover version done by Redd Kross, that is). Then in the final scenes one of the Lovedolls is shot to death, and the other moves into a state of depression, becoming a street wino. As the line went, "fame has a price." And as the movie closes, the take-away becomes: be careful what you wish for (making it again counter to *Ladies and Gentlemen, the Fabulous Stains*, where fame is exactly what makes a young female punk band happy in the end).

* * *

Desperate Teenage Lovedolls provided a snickering critique of the music industry as lecherous, decadent, abusive, and grotesque. That message could be seen in one of Raymond Pettibon's drawings included on *Double Nickels on the Dime*. The drawing showed a crowd of people shouting over a wall at what appears to be a bodyguard. The drawing depicts the mid-1970s, when Elvis Presley had bloated out on drugs as he made a comeback in Las Vegas. He was known to have his bodyguards snag women from the audience to have sex with him. "Hey Elvis," one of the crowd is saying in Pettibon's drawing. "Can you hear me? A young girl killed herself because you had her for a night and couldn't return her love. Why don't you have them write a song about that?" The rock empire, its edifice of power projected in celebrity and blockbuster sales, deserved nothing more than derision and mocking laughter, especially as it made its comeback.

* * *

The summer of 1984 continued to explode with punk creativity. In July, William Gibson successfully made the move from short story writer to novelist, paralleling the double albums of the Minutemen and Husker Du (the latter of whom Gibson sounded like in his writing, according to Bruce Sterling). The novel *Neuromancer*—which drew on his previous short stories—became a highwater mark for punk sci-fi, both for its creativity and for its capacity to dissect a dystopia that appeared closer to the American reality of 1984 than George Orwell's novel.

Gibson's central character is twenty-four-year-old Henry Case—the last name suggesting from the beginning a sense of dehumanization (he's a "case" not a human being). Like Raymond Chandler's antihero Philip Marlowe, Case tries to solve a mystery that is murky and cobwebbed. He is recruited by Molly Millions—a character Gibson had developed in "Johnny Mnemonic." She bears a striking resemblance to those femme fatales who populate noir fiction and film. She has retractable razors built into her hands, artificially remaking her body. And even as she recruits Case to work for Armitage, the leader of the expedition, she hints about evil lurking within the boss, who we eventually learn had been injured as a Green Beret on a mission into Russia and then rebuilt by "a congressional cabal with certain vested interests in saving particular portions of the Pentagon infrastructure." Armitage is heartless and cold and knew that Case was a drug addict as well as someone who stole from his previous boss. He promises to provide Case with new blood and a pancreas, but with a twist. Stealing from one of his favorite movies, *Escape from New York* (1981), Gibson has Armitage place "fifteen toxic sacs" in Case's "main arteries." These will kill him, unless he moves fast. "You have time to do what I'm hiring you for, Case, but that's all. Do the job and I can inject you with an enzyme" that would keep the sacs closed. In other words, Case is no hero or free actor, but rather something of a pawn, a lowly worker.[41]

The mission centers around finding "Wintermute" so it can be fused with "Neuromancer," since these are "two halves which when joined will create a new entity" of artificial intelligence (AI). Case's primary goal is to hack and break down the Tessier-Ashpool's computer defenses to acquire Wintermute. Regulations prevented AIs that were so large. These regulations are enforced by the Turing police, who arrest Case at one point in the novel (Wintermute kills the police in order to further its planned reunification). AIs project more power than expected—they are literally becoming self-conscious—and here is where some influence of *Blade Runner* (the movie released in 1982) leaked into the novel. Itself neo-noir, *Blade Runner* (1982) depicted a type of artificial intelligence—"replicants" invented to do dirty work for society now consciously fighting their own makers. Gibson's story repeats this theme of the created revenging the creator. And so along with the personal disintegration of Armitage comes the reunification of the two AIs, and the disbanding of the group of characters surrounding Case. Most poignantly, Molly leaves Case as the mission closes down. There was to be no romance here.[42]

This summation doesn't do service to the narrative's strange turns, or its collage-style writing where Case "flips" in and out of cyberspace during his mission. Case's confusion—especially about Armitage's identity—makes for intentional disorientation. Like the music and lyrics of the Minutemen and the elliptical artwork of Raymond Pettibon, this novel wasn't straightforward or easy. Gibson's friend and critic Tom Maddox, a professor of English at Virginia State University and writer of sci-fi himself, argued that the book—much like works of high modernism, including *Ulysses*—was "strenuous" and that it required multiple readings.[43]

True, but there are also some clear themes that turned the novel into a work of social criticism and not just storytelling. There is the lack of trust between characters (Molly and Case especially). Trust—a major theme of noir writing (and a major theme of Husker Du's double album)—appears fleeting. In addition, characters face a dehumanized world of nowhereness and geographical homogeneity, as Gibson describes "the sprawl" that constitutes BAMA (the Boston Atlanta Metropolitan Axis), which is dotted by shopping malls and little to no nature. Indeed, the novel is full of environmental warnings, such as how the "the sky was that mean shade of gray. The air had gotten worse; it seemed to have teeth." There is very little government left to police such problems. Multinational corporations dominate.* Toward the end of the novel, Gibson himself pulls back and makes the following observation:

> Power, in Case's world, meant corporate power. . . . The multinationals that shaped the course of human history, had transcended old barriers. Viewed as organisms, they had attained a kind of immortality. You

---

* Another book associated with the spread of sci-fi punk came out the same year as Gibson's (but was overlooked as Gibson's work received fanfare). Lewis Shiner's *Frontera* had even a harsher dystopian view. Here a huge corporation known as Pulsystem moves its offices from D.C. to Houston because "one job after another had disappeared as the government tried desperately to cut itself down to a size that its tiny budget could support." Shiner describes a society where government shrinks, resources die out, and large corporations rule. Lewis Shiner, *Frontera* (New York: Baen, 1984), 52.

couldn't . . . assassinat[e] a dozen key executives; there were others waiting to step up the ladder, assume the vacated position, access the vast banks of corporate memory. . . . Case had always taken for granted that the real bosses, the kingpins in a given industry, would be both more and less than *people*. . . . It had allowed him to accept Armitage's flatness and accommodation of the machine, the system, the parent organism.

And joined to this theme of corporate power, Gibson depicted a society constantly distracted, its attention span shortened, with all sorts of pleasure immediately at hand. There was simstim (an idea developed in Gibson's earlier stories) and a walled- off "pleasure dome," a resort in space for wealthy people that was named Freeside. And a society where image and screens replace reality, the world of cyberspace versus what Gibson called the "meat world." *Neuromancer* became *Brave New World* updated for America in the Reagan era.[44]

XXX

Protest Kids

> Street art is free expression . . .
> the streets are the gallery
> public art
> to evoke a response in people.
> jolt them out of their numb state.
>
> —*Cerebral Discourse* zine, 1984[45]

July 16, 1984: Scenes of the Democratic Party Convention held in the Moscone Center in San Francisco broadcast to a national television audience. Though there would be impassioned speeches by the likes of Jesse Jackson and Mario Cuomo, there were no debates about policy or philosophy and no tension about the nomination. Instead, attention focused on the "spectacle" of the Convention. Audiences were directed toward "giant video screens." Delegates could barely see the podium because television cameras stood on platforms, blocking their view. "It was as if the delegates themselves had been reduced at last to part of the television audience," the liberal historian Alan Brinkley noted. Instead of "Happy Days are

Here Again," "Celebrate Good Times"—the song played on *CHiPs* after cops drove punks away from the club—blasted its thumping disco beat to those on the floor. The Convention, like much of American politics, had become scripted, set within a sanitized version of San Francisco. Mayor Dianne Feinstein (considered a potential vice-presidential pick by Walter Mondale) had approved "sweeps" that cleared downtown of prostitutes, drug dealers, and homeless people. That added to the feeling of watching a "careful . . . upbeat . . . spectacle" free from diversions.[46]

Almost. On the streets of San Francisco, in the heart of its business district, punks were banging so hard on the windows of corporations like Bank of America and Diamond Shamrock that they shook and warbled. Banded together in "affinity groups" and taking part in what were called "War Chest Tours," kids would run from one business to another, often shut out by locked doors. Protestors would throw themselves on the ground in major intersections, performing "die-ins," where they writhed in mock mass death from nuclear war. Many chanted, "Do the police a favor—beat yourself up." Others screamed, "Democracy in Action!" They handed out leaflets about each business they targeted—for instance, exposing that Diamond Shamrock produced Agent Orange, that Bank of America funded repressive regimes abroad, and that Wells Fargo "invested in over 32 major nuclear corporations." One activist remembered a "very informative leaflet" on corporate "dealings in nuclear waste, warheads, and munitions trading." Offering leaflets to passers-by, punks chanted and ran from the police, even "unarresting" some of those snagged by the cops. Reports put the number of arrests at over 200, and that number would climb as the Convention proceeded (reaching 455). The reports about the ruckus suggested something new was happening here. "The punks have become the street opposition of the 1980s," as the *Village Voice* would explain. Another magazine published a story that was clipped and reprinted in *MRR*: "The punkers, in torn T-shirts and polychromatic hair styles, are a relatively new force on the political scene, part of a new generation of protestors who prefer street theater and spontaneous action to marching with placards." But as with anything that appears new, sudden, or spontaneous, there was a back story.[47]

* * *

The great debate among punks of 1982–1983 had addressed numerous questions regarding politics, including the effectiveness of nonviolent direct action. Now, during the spring and summer of 1984, debates maintained that focus but also took up questions surrounding the nature of corporate power, protest, and the idea of anarcho-existentialism.

The hatred punks harbored about the entertainment industry transformed itself into a larger suspicion about corporate power, the sort Gibson's character Case articulated. David Solnit, a twenty-year-old punk activist who became a central figure during the Democratic Convention protests, explained it this way: Punks "already reject corporate music and fashion. Why wouldn't they want to join a protest at corporate offices?" Besides, corporations had all the power, albeit shadowy and lurking behind the beaming glass façades of skyscrapers. Why protest government but not corporations, some were asking. The punk zine *Protest and Survive*, released in July 1984, criticized the more mainstream organization "Vote For Peace," which hoped to protest at the Convention and call for Democrats to renew their support for a nuclear freeze. Pressing politicians was useless, the editors reasoned, because the real power of the defense industry sat in the hands of large corporations. Protest had to show, in the words of *MRR*, "how the Democrats and the electoral system" were "run by big money and multi-national corporations." Some participants constructed a large "Trojan Donkey." It was "fed ballots, money, and a globe and then excreted missiles, tanks, and skeletons." The first steps toward the raucous protests in July of 1984 started months earlier with a research phase (earlier on there was what was called a "Hall of Shame" that exposed the corporate-military complex), prompting a process of self-education to learn more about the extent of corporate power, especially in relation to the growth of the nuclear arms race. A zine calling itself *Absolutely No Corporations* compiled a list of businesses and how they aided and abetted the growth of nuclear weapon systems. It listed and analyzed the ties among Northrop, Texas Instruments, Lockheed, Boeing, General Dynamics, DuPont, General Electric, Bechtel, and Exxon. Protest had to become an act of exposure, of companies guilty of plotting mass death to the sound of shuffling papers in skyscrapers.[48]

As much as identifying the real enemy, young dissenters were also rethinking protest. By the 1980s, protest looked tame (like the famous nuclear freeze event in Manhattan that stayed on Reagan's mind a long time afterward). Even when engaging in acts of civil disobedience, protestors no longer seemed dangerous or disruptive; they seemed formulaic and routine. Organizers would acquire official permits and plan their event (including the number of expected arrests) with the police. A series of discussions held at Bound Together Books, the small independent bookstore that had hosted debates about squatting a year earlier, noted how organizations like the Committee in Solidarity with the People of El Salvador (CISPES) assigned certain "monitors" who were to herd participants. John Hennessy, a police inspector, explained how protests had been organized in the past and would hopefully (from his perspective) be organized during the Convention: "The organizer met us before hand; we agreed upon guidelines and they cooperated. They monitored their own people." Some activists noted that at an April 1984 protest against Casper Weinberger, Reagan's secretary of defense, monitors squashed all spontaneity. Protest was becoming "passive." Participants at Bound Together discussions called it a "parody of protest." The alternative to acting like cattle would require more spontaneity, more movement (the term "roving" was often used). The anarchist dilemma was broached in the conversations at Bound Together: "Direct action that involves head to head confrontation with the police is both stupid and suicidal, but any actions which disrupt business as usual will draw the police in a hurry." A conundrum never solved, one hinted at earlier by Jack Grisham and others.[49]

These debates erupted also within the ranks of the Livermore Action Group (LAG), a group David Solnit worked with. During the year 1982, LAG had protested against Lawrence Livermore National Laboratory, a federally supported and classified research center that worked on developing nuclear weapons. LAG had a number of older Christian pacifists who believed in "moral witness" and "personal responsibility." During 1982 to 1983, they engaged in "direct action" (also the title of their newsletter) to try to shut down the Laboratory, or at least disrupt its activities. In 1982, one protest action saw 1,300 people arrested, a year later, 1,000. They started developing what became known as "affinity groups" (an idea that some trace back to the Spanish Civil War, when young men organized themselves into small groups—sometimes called brigades—and self-managed their military activities). In this case, clusters of people would discuss next steps in a protest, governed by the principle of consensus as best as possible (with the idea of not having visible leaders). Some had clever names like "Communist Dupes," referencing Reagan's penchant to see all antiwar activism as Soviet inspired. "Domestic Terrorists" was the name of David Solnit's affinity group. By 1984, there were some in LAG who thought the huge arrests had become more theatrical than anything else; some hoped they could actually *shut down* the Lab. They wanted direct action that could disrupt business as usual, and they started to develop strategies like "die-ins" that could serve as blockades. But as the convention approached, a rift opened in LAG (representative of a wider divide in the nuclear freeze movement). Some members recollected the Chicago Democratic Convention of 1968—where violence erupted and that, in part, helped send Richard Nixon to the presidency (seen as the "law and order" candidate, as John Crawford had asserted a year before). Patrick Diehl of LAG, a self-professed anarchist, explained, "We don't want a pitched, 1968, Chicago-style battle." Some members of LAG thought younger activists wanted to create a situation "just like Europe," when mass protests erupted against "euromissiles." LAG was being taken over, some feared, by what they called "anarcho-romanticists."[50]

Such were the challenges of "Do It Yourself Anarchy," reasoned one San Francisco zine eager for direct action. To reinvent protest as something that provoked while being self-managed and self-governed—squaring anarchist and existential ethics—was no easy charge. In the act of confronting power, participants would free themselves from the "bad faith" and "self-deception" that those marching in step to a formula fell prey to. All done with a sense of dark humor (like Tim Yo's) and an acceptance of absurdity (like Shawn Stern's existentialism) and the very likely case of losing, still going down with a fight (just as Jack Grisham recollected his S.I.R. performance and police riot more than a year earlier).[51]

* * *

On July 19, 1984, the link between music and protest came together. Rock Against Reagan (RAR), having raced across the country as it had in 1983, now drove its school bus close to San Francisco's Convention Center (for many on the bus, this was a homecoming). The RAR caravan had traveled from Washington, D.C., on the Fourth of July through the Midwest, putting on shows and registering young people to vote, distributing zines and literature, and showing political movies.

At least 5,000 people showed for the gig at the Convention Center, which featured Reagan Youth, the Dicks, MDC, and the Dead Kennedys. David Solnit was frantic, calling for a march on the Hall of Justice to free those in the City Jail. And so after listening to the Dead Kennedys and Biafra's usual call for kids to do something more than just attend a concert, around 2,000 kids started to march. The police freaked out about "reports that the demonstrators would come down and try to shut down the hall, free the prisoners, and trash the building" (a wild report that). Kids started chanting lyrics from a 1981 TSOL song: "America, Land of the Free, Free to the Power of People in Uniforms!" But soon the fear heard in discussions at Bound Together played out. The police, often on horseback, surrounded the marchers, while undercover cops made their own moves. The arrests began. Bludgeoned, the punks resorted to the only thing they could—"running away," while 369 people left behind got arrested.[52]

Not to be stopped, one month later, a smaller number of activists and musicians descended on Dallas, Texas, for the Republican Party Convention. RAR was there, along with the Dead Kennedys (who found it odd to perform so close to where JFK had been assassinated). Once again, the band's performance transitioned into a "War Chest Tour," this one even more frantic than any of those held in San Francisco, right in the heart of conservative America. There was a surreal feel to it: "Punks with mohawks, hippies with face paint, transvestites with pig masks" marching together. Kids pounded on windows and made funny faces to those inside. As with San Francisco, they drew on their research to target Diamond Shamrock and Bank of America. They spray-painted these businesses' entrances. All the while, they were "keeping mobile, fast-paced and scattering when necessary, to regroup at the next target." A big score happened when the tour entered the swank flagship business of Neiman Marcus (whose headquarters were in Dallas). Chants of "Let's Go Shopping" erupted as punks entered the store. Riot cops were called in to protect the perfume counter. Supposedly Senator Goldwater was in the store and screamed, "They're a bunch of goddam nuts." There were ninety-seven arrests, most importantly of Gary Johnson, who wound up burning an American flag during the War Chest Tour, prompting a legal battle that made it all the way to the Supreme Court five years later (decided narrowly in favor of the principle of free speech and expression).[53]

* * *

All of these actions were so spontaneous as to become fleeting. Indeed, that RAR show in Dallas would be the *last* RAR show. And that was partially the point—to erupt and die rather than become formula and ossify. Anarcho-existentialism lived from moment to moment. And yet there were some in the ranks of RAR and anticorporate protest who thought they saw glimmerings of a sustainable movement.

Dave Dictor of MDC committed himself to sustainability by creating the *P.E.A.C.E.* compilation album, released through his own independent label R Radical Records. It was a double album with a booklet inside (produced in collaboration with *MRR*). The booklet offered advice about activist organizations (there was also an extensive bibliography for further reading). The double album crammed itself full of bands from overseas, including Japan, Spain, Denmark, Holland, Italy, West Germany, Sweden, England, Canada, and even South Africa. The American bands included the RAR usuals: Reagan Youth, the Dicks, Dead Kennedys, and MDC. Most of the other US bands were from San Francisco. But there were also bands from Ohio (O.D.F.X. and P.P.G.) and one from Houston (White Lie) and another from Austin (the Butthole Surfers, who offered the evocative song "100 Million People Dead"). All in all, fifty-five songs, and almost every band producing a single-paged statement, usually with song lyrics, printed in the booklet.[54]

A tension emerged between the emotional nature of the songs (two of the most riveting being "Uneasy Peace" by the Proletariat and "Up Against the Wall" by Articles of Faith) and the rational advice given in the booklet. This was a central tension in punk more generally, of course. The booklet sprawled over numerous topics but focused especially on the nuclear arms race, with an emphasis on the dangerous development of "first strike" capacity (the recent installation of "Euromissiles"). Following the spirit of the War Chest Tours the booklet emphasized how multinational corporations turned a profit manufacturing weaponry. There was also attention paid to the New Right's and Reagan's views on Armageddon. There were sections on feminism and personal politics. Though support was shown for the Vancouver Five, from Canada (which included Gerry Hannah, bass player for the punk band The Subhumans), a group who bombed Litton Industries for the company's cruise missile production, emphasis fell on nonviolent activism. And surprisingly there was little mention of anarchism (on their page for the booklet, the Proletariat republished an interview with *MRR* where some members denounced anarchism as "impossible"), encouraging kids to work either through representative institutions (the booklet praised Senator Alan Cranston from California, for instance) or direct action. This reflected Dictor's vision of political activism. A year before *P.E.A.C.E.* was issued, Vic Bondi of AoF asked Dictor, "You believe in force of opinion as a viable means of political change?" Dictor shook his head vigorously and said, "I really do. Because I've seen it successful in the anti-nuclear activities in this country. There have been no new orders for nuclear plants in the last seven years." Of course, Dictor ignored the role that local and state government played in slowing down the building of nuclear plants. But he felt compelled to emphasize citizen protest as something that could be sustained and made effective. In the end, the *P.E.A.C.E.* album raised over $10,000 for peace movement organizations. And it outlined a vision of grassroots activism that carried beyond the moment of the summer of 1984.[55]

* * *

Dictor likely cheered when he learned that some young punks in Las Vegas, Nevada, had started up Positive Force during the summer of 1984. The name of the organization itself held intrigue. "Positive" likely alluded to Shawn Stern's vision and a growing sense that punk should turn activist. The second word had more ambivalence to it—perhaps a cry for militancy, or else a belief that nothing would change unless *force* was used to challenge those with power? Whatever the case, the group's call to action echoed the *P.E.A.C.E.* booklet (led by its chief organizer, Michelle Cali). The group planned to work on "human rights, nuclear militarism, animal rights, wilderness preservation, ecology, and hunger issues." They hoped to create a "thriving activist community" while working within the sprawl of Las Vegas. Though mostly atheists themselves, they worked with local Franciscans who were feeding the homeless while taking a pledge of Christian sacrifice and vow of poverty. Organizers would also work with numerous nonprofit community organizations dedicated to peace, the sort that Dictor funded with his booklet and album. They pledged to educate themselves and tried to get "kids in school aware of what's going on in the world." One member believed handing out leaflets at schools solved a quandary for her. She explained, "I am informing people without lecturing." The group wanted provocation, not preaching.[56]

Las Vegas was not hospitable for young people to find public spaces to organize (similar to the experiences a few years earlier of the editors of *Ripper*, who tried to carve out conversational space in a shopping mall). The group resorted to having meetings in casinos. Finally, it found a "warehouse" suitable for all-ages shows and where they could circulate their zine, *Civil Disobedience*. They worked with KUNV (the University of Nevada's radio station) to advertise local events. The group's key ally was the band Seven Seconds, headlined by a charismatic lead singer, Kevin Seconds. In 1984, the band released their song "Clenched Fists, Black Eyes," which became something of an anthem for the energy swirling behind the formation of Positive Force. Seconds would fuse together "straight edge" with the politics of MDC: "We're aiming for a different goal, succeeding where the hippies failed. But one thing's for sure and you can bet, we'll be more than a drugged-out threat."[57]

XXX

DIY Was Never So Easy

There were pilgrims walking to the Celestial City . . . through this town of Vanity . . . moreover, at this Fair there is at all times to be seen jugglings, cheats, games, plays, fools, apes, knaves, and rogues.

—John Bunyan, *A Pilgrim's Progress*[58]

Just as War Chest Tours hit the streets of San Francisco, one hundred people gathered in Olympia, Washington, to participate in a conference about the making of independent music. An organization called the Lost Music Network (LMN) and a national publication, *Op*, organized the event. There were workshops on the nuts and bolts of producing and distributing music, and one on "small radio networking" where independent label owners complained that stations threw out or sold their product, without even considering playing it on the air. *Op* promoted cassette tape activism, and so there was a workshop on how to do cassette duplication and distribution. Another workshop focused on "DIY magazines and production techniques." All in all, participants discussed the challenges of making their "own culture."[59]

The problem was that the LMN was not in great shape, struggling to get along as a "non-profit Volunteer organization." Worse, *Op* had already announced that it would fold later that year. Part of this was a self-destruct plan of sorts. Each issue of the magazine had a letter that it centered around (so, for instance, the "L" issue had a story about Arto Lindsay, the "N" issue a story on the Neo Boys from Portland, etc.). They were running out of letters in the alphabet by 1984 (both LMN and the magazine had started five years earlier). But there was another reason for the magazine to go belly-up. Its editor, John Foster, a thoughtful man who hoped to assist "independent artists and labels," explained the situation to the Seattle magazine *The Rocket*: "After the Z issue, it's all over, at least for me. There is a burn out factor." It took a lot of energy to sustain a noncommercial publication that helped spread word on independently produced music. It was especially challenging, as the oligopolistic record industry—Foster's foe—was making a comeback from its earlier slump.[60]

In contrast to Foster's "burn out," there was nothing but excitement at New York City's annual New Music Seminar (NMS). Madonna would participate, having risen from the dance floors of Danceteria to sign with a major label (Sire Records, owned by Warner). She was now creating hit material (electro-synth pop) and videos shown constantly on MTV. NMS had been around for the same amount of time as *Op* and the Lost Music Network, but unlike them its energy continued to bubble through the years. As opposed to the amateurism that charmed the hearts of a John Foster, NMS was all about rock professionalism and trying to get young musicians into the big leagues of corporate labels, snatched from places like Danceteria or from independent record companies. DIY, for NMS, was declassé. By 1984, participants paid $150 for entrance to NMS, a good way to lock out small fry. Exhibitors laid down $1,000, and the rule now was that "only [they could] hand out or distribute samples, flyers, records, cassettes." During discussions, NMS leaders promoted music videos. Madonna herself, serving on a panel, would argue that without video there was no future; kids were sucked into television, she argued, a sort of circular, inescapable conclusion. Some noticed that the founder of NMS, Mark Josephson, who had started off as a College Radio Promoter at RCA, had a "silver stretch limousine" at his "disposal." "New Music," it would appear, was part of a general upswing in the industry writ large.[61]

XXX

USA! USA!

> The Patriot did not know just how or when or where he got his opinions, neither did he care, so long as he was with what seemed the majority— which was the main thing, the safe thing, the comfortable thing.
>
> —Mark Twain[62]

It goes without saying that most Americans were more interested in the Summer Olympics than the New Music Seminar or the Lost Music Network. The games, played in Los Angeles, started in late July and sprawled into mid-August and could be best remembered as the Reagan Olympics. For two reasons: The games helped fuel the patriotism Reagan would gin up for his upcoming re-election—with chants of "USA! USA!" heard day after day— and because this was the first Olympics with no governmental assistance— raising all its money from corporations, which saw grand opportunities in television advertising. Its chief organizer (or perhaps the term "entrepreneur" would be better) was Peter Ueberroth, who had a background in the airlines industry and who would become, due to his organizing skills, *Time* magazine's man of the year. He explained that this was to be the first "free enterprise, private sector Olympics, with no taxpayer money." An Olympics made for Reagan, who opened the Games and hoped to become the chief welcomer to the American team (Ueberroth placed limits on his role, as he did on the mayor of Los Angeles). Most cheerful of all, the Soviet Union, by the spring of 1984, had announced it would boycott the games. Ueberroth figured Reagan wouldn't care much about the boycott; indeed, it would likely help him electorally, he reasoned. With the Soviet pull-out, this would become a one-country show for Americans to cheer for.[63]

Reagan did well by the Olympics. He welcomed the athletes with a line from a movie he had starred in, *Knute Rockne, All American* (1940): "Win one for the Gipper." But in reality those athletes were winning one for the entertainment industry. After all, ABC, which won exclusive rights to broadcast the games on national television, would watch its ratings sky-rocket. Coca Cola—still reeling from Michael Jackson's ads for Pepsi as the drink of a new generation—put $30 million into the Olympic coffers to fight the ongoing cola wars. McDonald's branded the Olympics Burger, leaving Burger King in the dust. Those working on logistics studied

Disneyland as their model of stagecraft. Fearful of leaks, they kept press conferences to a minimum (as had Reagan), and many of those who knew him found Ueberroth a tightlipped control freak, and his discipline served him well. One historian determined that the 1984 Games "returned a larger profit than any other sporting event in the history of the world."[64]

The chants of "USA! USA!" that dominated the Olympics distracted athletes from other countries, but they also hammered home the idea that this was more than a sporting event, it was corporate "blockbuster" patriotism. A young punk band calling itself Body Count, out of Lakewood, California, observed that the Olympics "were a pro-war conditioning event overrun with nationalistic ideas." Reagan's opening of the games, as he beamed his grin, suggested the athletes were his ground soldiers. The zine *RAD* from Morro Bay, California, placed the games in a wider context, including "the Invasion of Grenada, the CIA involvement in Central America (including the mining of Nicaragua's Shores), stationing of Nuclear Missiles in Germany, and other cute little things that the Reagan Administration sanctioned in it's [*sic*] efforts to make the world safe for 'democracy.'" The Olympics were Reaganism perfected—corporate-funded patriotism and deafening chants and cheers whooped up from the masses.[65]

* * *

Two days before the Olympics ended, Ronald Reagan's sense of humor got the best of him. He prepped his weekly radio address to the country, this one endorsing the rights of religious organizations to use school facilities for meetings, a tip of the hat to the evangelical right. After all, Reagan was gunning for evangelical turnout, now that he faced not Jimmy Carter (who happened to be an evangelical) but the dour Walter Mondale. Reagan practiced his radio address by reading and riffing on it. His opening was all-riffed, and he came out with a doozy: "Good evening. I am pleased to announce that I have just signed legislation outlawing Russia forever. We begin bombing in five minutes." That line didn't go out over the airwaves, but the press leaked it. Those ominous and joking words quickly found their way onto the front cover of *Mutual Oblivion*, a punk zine out of New Mexico, with goth drawings of Reagan and a skeletal grim reaper. Soon activists made posters showing Reagan's face and a clock set to five minutes to midnight, and of course the words, "We Begin Bombing in Five Minutes."[66]

XXX

A Salesman at His Best

> A salesman is got to dream, boy. It comes with the territory.
> —Arthur Miller, *Death of a Salesman*[67]

Reagan chose Labor Day to kick-off his re-election campaign. If there was the evangelical vote to worry about there were also those "Reagan Democrats," many of them union members who wound up voting for one of the most anti-union presidents since Calvin Coolidge (a hero to Reagan). The location for the re-election rally spoke volumes—it would be in Orange County, California, the heart of Reaganland. The county provided the core of West Coast conservatism, much of its wealth coming from federal money poured into the region's many defense industries. To Reagan's delight, this was to be a *rally*, not a press conference or debate about policy. It was to be masses of people—more than 50,000 showed up—chanting for their leader as they filled up Fountain Valley's Mile Square Park. Though the park was hot and lacked toilet facilities, Reagan's fans just kept coming in. Looking out at that sea of believers, Reagan beamed: "When people need a little sunshine in their lives and a feel for the optimism that fills the soul of this beautiful country, then I can assure them, they'll find it in Orange County."[68]

Outside the gates of Mile Square Park, a journalist from the *Los Angeles Times* witnessed "a group of youths wearing punk-rock clothes," there to protest. Mayhem broke out, the *Times* explained: "The Reagan defenders tore up several of the demonstrators' signs, hurled rocks, bloodied a few noses and chased the anti-Reagan group back to the parking lot." Participants found this a sanitized story: "It was not just 'young' Reagan supporters that attacked the group of anti-Reagan protesters. The aggressor group included middle-aged men who, rather than calm the situation" used "sticks and rocks (as well as fists and feet) as weapons." The story also downplayed the extent of the damage. "Matt Viking, a young black protester mentioned in your article," a letter to the editor clarified, "was the victim of an assault by a group of Reagan 'defenders.' . . . He was beaten so severely that he passed in and out of consciousness and required emergency hospitalization." Another letter writer said, "It was a case of about ten 'adults' attacking a younger person . . . and sending him to the hospital." Some of those adults had been energized less by Reagan and more by a local political talk-show host, Wally George, who was organizing "Peace through Strength" rallies in support of the president. George's television show mostly consisted of him shouting down liberals and often physically attacking them or having them forcefully removed by his bodyguards. As George explained it, he'd invite "the wildest, craziest lunatic liberals I could find as guests. I'd find some jerk who believed exactly the opposite as I do, then I'd go at him." Television-watching hate fests spilled over into the streets of Orange County, all part of a self-ordained vigilante defense of the nation's leader.[69]

Whatever the age of the attackers, Reagan was going for the youth vote, as he was the evangelicals and Reagan Democrats. Reagan youth—the term, not the band—were becoming identifiable. When Walter Mondale campaigned at the University of Southern California, he was jeered by young Reagan supporters, who booed and heckled him, drowning him out. Some of them called themselves "Fritzbusters." The term referred to the most popular movie of the previous summer, *Ghostbusters*, which focused on a small business that exorcised haunting spirits from Manhattan apartment houses. A "government bureaucrat," Walter Peck of the EPA, becomes the villain who hunts down the inventive business and pesters them about all sorts of silly regulations. Reagan watched the film at Camp David "as his campaign for re-election was revving up" and loved it. Kids at Reagan rallies now waved "Fritzbuster" signs with a sense of confidence that popular culture had their back.[70]

More strident than the Fritzbusters were the Wolverines. They were featured in *Red Dawn*, a movie released toward the end of the summer of 1984. The film had an odd backdrop to it. After serving as secretary of state under Reagan, Alexander Haig had moved on to advise the Hollywood studio MGM, and he took up the movie as a personal project, producing and promoting it when released. The movie could have been made by the president himself. It opened with the Soviet Union, Cuba, and Nicaragua invading the United States, sticking parents in concentration camps, leaving a band of high school jocks to become guerrilla warriors, much like the mujahideen in Afghanistan (indeed, Soviet leaders in the movie compare their invasion of the United States to Afghanistan). *The Rocket* magazine reported: "The teen freedom fighters" as they engage in battle spray paint the name of their "high school football team," the Wolverines. They will of course lose this impossible battle, but that just clarified the movie's message: Arm now or face invasion later. As Reagan put it on the stump after seeing the movie, "Our country's days of apologizing are over. America is standing tall again, and don't let anyone tell you we're any less dedicated to peace because we want a strong America." Another message of the film: That there was a constituency of young people fervently anti-communist, ready to fight it out if necessary. Or as the band Reagan Youth sang: "We are the sons of Reagan . . . Heil! Want another war? Forward to El Salvador! Gonna kill some communists!" Wolverines and Fritzbusters now constituted part of the backbone and shock troops of Reagan's re-election campaign as well as serving as the foot soldiers for the triumphal entertainment industry.[71]

* * *

Reagan campaigned with his eyes open and ears out for popular culture that confirmed his worldview. And soon it latched onto the unceasing radio play of Bruce Springsteen's song "Born in the USA," which was climbing the charts (the album by the same name was one of the first released as a compact disc (CD), a new technology that helped the recording industry make a comeback, since suddenly people had to replace their vinyl collection with new-fangled CDs). Springsteen was first discovered by the conservative columnist George Will. The rock star's appeal to Will (and later Reagan) was multifold: First off, there was none of the poofy, glam feel to Springsteen, no "androgynous" look, more the look of a macho working-class dude, wearing jeans and boots. Attending one of Springsteen's concerts, Will admitted that he didn't know what marijuana smelled like and maybe some of the kids were using it, but in general he found himself "surrounded by orderly young adults earnestly—and correctly—insisting that Springsteen is a wholesome cultural portent." Unsure of what Springsteen's politics were (supposedly Springsteen hadn't voted since 1972), Will argued that attendees could not miss the "flags" that "get waved at his concerts while he sings songs about hard times. He is no whiner, and the recitation of closed factories and other problems always seems punctuated by a grand, cheerful affirmation: 'Born in the U.S.A.!' " Rock star celebrity and corporate-backed patriotism—like the fumes from the Olympic games. And after all, Will reasoned, Springsteen's popularity was confirmed by his record sales (music, pun intended, to Reagan's ears).[72]

Soon after Will's column was published, Reagan campaigned in Hammonton, New Jersey. He spoke, as usual, about the right to dream: "America's future rests in a thousand dreams inside your hearts. It rests in the message of hope in the songs of a man so many young Americans admire—New Jersey's own, Bruce Springsteen." Followed with the closing sales line: "And helping you make these dreams come true is what this job of mine is all about."[73]

It was like the Minutemen's song "If Reagan Played Disco" (1982) come true, where Reagan was portrayed on a "white horse," singing "lame lyrics" and trying "to reach the working man." Henry Rollins would later imagine seeing "troops . . . bounding over the fields in a war singing, 'Born in the USA' while they catch bullets." And Raymond Pettibon published an imagined story about a bunch of kids who went to Springsteen concerts seeking "tail-gate parties, post-concert rallies, cigarette lighter vigils." One character gushed, "America's so great I get all choked up and start crying in my beer. Say 'Born in the USA'!" Kids, in his story, claim to have voted for Ronald Reagan, because "Bruce was for him." They keep chanting "Born in the USA," as they move onto a store that is run by what they call "slants" (i.e., a racist slur for Asians). Pettibon was picking up on the nativist feel to Springsteen's song, which was, after all, "*Born in* the U.S.A." Reagan and Springsteen—no matter what each of them thought—seemed made for one another, or at least Reagan hoped.[74]

Springsteen countered the president, arguing that his song wasn't intended as a conservative anthem but rather a song about the plight of working-class Vietnam Vets (the brother of the central character in the song, in fact, dies in Vietnam). But Reagan's branded patriotism and talk of dreams swept up Springsteen's song into their gale winds that had been unleashed at the Olympics and replayed during rallies. This was, after all, about "dreams," not intentions. Reagan's world was one in which popular culture could be re-made by leaders who listened for what they wanted and who could conjure a spiritual feel behind fare like *ET* or *Thriller*. Reagan campaigned on the right to believe, as he stated when he endorsed Springsteen. He was stoked, and thus far it was securing his re-election campaign a path to victory. He was reaching people in the realm of what they heard on the radio or saw on television or listened to on their shiny CDs. It was becoming, as his advertisements for re-election would ensure, "morning again in America."

XXX

I Want My MTV

We are no longer a part of the drama of alienation; we live in the ecstasy
of communication . . . a whole pornography of information and communication, . . . of circuits and networks, a pornography of all functions and
objects in their readability, their fluidity, their availability . . . in their poly-
valence, in their free expression.

—Jean Baudrillard[75]

To be on par with Hollywood and the major broadcasters on television,
MTV announced its own "Video Music Awards" show to be held on
September 14, 1984, at Radio City Music Hall in Manhattan. The year 1984
had so far been very good for MTV, both expanding its reach and watching
as its influence on record sales grew. The "Awards" show pretended that
sales and promotion activities could be considered art. It drew on the optimism across all sectors of the music industry that a comeback was in the air.

The star of the show was, in the words of *Own the Whole World*, Madonna,
who sang her hit song "Like a Virgin"—"in a wedding dress . . . while rolling
around on the stage." Punk critics noted how Madonna backed her "thin-
voiced" singing with standard electro-pop-synth music—that is, the typical
sound of 1980s popular music. That made the visuals in her performance
and videos so important to her brand. She had honed a "look": "dressed in
several rosaries, bangles, black mesh, a wrap-around mini skirt, and most
memorably, a bare belly" (projecting the image and attitude that Kristine
McKenna had earlier suggested MTV reduced all young women to).
Now the white wedding dress worn for the Awards ceremony projected
her pseudo-rebel side: she had donned an iconic symbol of purity and
sexed it all up (with skyrocketing divorce rates in place, who would say
the desanctification of marriage was all that rebellious?). Nonetheless, her
"rebel" performance sent a big thank you to MTV for elevating her celebrity
to a mass audience. The two parties needed one another.[76]

* * *

By the time of the MTV Awards, a punk band had actually done what no
one thought possible: They got play on MTV. Kraut had started up back

in 1981 at the small club A7, part of a punk revival in the New York City area (alongside other bands like Heart Attack and Reagan Youth). They now turned their catchy and stripped-down song "All Twisted" pixilated. They shot the video themselves, and explained, "We're not really big on MTV—they've helped us out a lot and they've promoted us. We're the only band on there with an independent video—every band on there belongs to a major record label." What attracted MTV to Kraut was that the band had shot their video on the cheap. There was little risk in airing it, and no overhead cost. DIY started to look too good to be true from the music industry's vantage point—maybe the underground could become the farming ground for the overground, the way *Repo Man* had in a sense. Kraut's video depicted cops abducting the band and tossing them into jail, while the band sings from behind prison bars. There was a whiff of rebellion, but it was no more threatening than having auto-erotic relationships in a wedding dress (in fact, the lyrics of "All Twisted" sounded defeatist if anything).[77]

The zine *End Times* made the most prescient observation about seeing Kraut on MTV. "Amazing how harmless it all seems when Eurythmics [a British synth-pop-dance band] comes up right afterwards, I'm afraid it's a disaster in the making." For in the world of MTV, consumers didn't dig down into each video, but rather allowed everything to move sideways past their eyes and ears, going from one video to another, creating a field of fleeting images, all equally sellable. MTV appeared the direct opposite of Raymond Pettibon's artwork, which required viewer excavation and thinking. Sure, MTV hoped viewers would turn into buyers of albums. But in the process of having one advertisement zing past another, MTV generated the blasé attitude that Kim Gordon had identified in New York City's club culture (where, after all, Madonna got her start, and where video screens had become omnipresent). Kraut offered just one more fleeting image placed alongside the others. MTV resembled a suburban shopping mall experience. Choice was fine—just so long as nothing threatened the power of MTV as arbitrator of that choice. So viewers watched as Kraut's hard-edged music and jail scenes transitioned into the lilting, feathery sounds and airbrushed images of the Eurythmics. MTV offered a cultural pastiche and a banquet of abundance.[78]

XXX

Viva La Sewage!

> . . .a million bureaucrats are diligently plotting death
> and some of them even know it.
>
> —Thomas Pynchon, *Gravity's Rainbow*[79]

A month after the MTV Awards, the Associated Press broke a story whose noir qualities outdid the one about mining Nicaragua's harbors back in April. It was discovered that the CIA had prepared a manual for Nicaraguan rebels that taught how to blackmail, kill, and torture in order to overthrow the Sandinista regime. There was also a graphic book that illustrated for ordinary citizens how to set fires and plug up sewers to tear down the civic fiber of Nicaragua. At first, Reagan claimed ignorance about all this, and he dreaded the prospect of getting a question regarding the issue in his second and last debate with Walter Mondale.[80]

The question came, however, and in responding, Reagan looked unwound. He sputtered, "We have a gentleman down there in Nicaragua who is on contract with the CIA, advising supposedly on military tactics with the Contras." But the CIA had been prohibited from doing this, as the Boland Amendments had made clear. "Are you implying, then, that the CIA is directing the Contras?" a journalist asked. Reagan looked ashen and started to backpedal. "I'm afraid I misspoke," he said. There were "CIA men" stationed in different places but not Nicaragua, and somehow the manual got into the hands of a "CIA man" who sent it up to Langley. It didn't sound very convincing. And Reagan seemed to be angry with the media reporting on the matter and obsessing about its dark implications (one journalist at the debate called the booklet an example of "state-sanctioned terrorism").[81]

Reagan turned angry and doddering at once. And it looked, for a moment, that perhaps he was going to "lose" this debate, the way he felt he had the first, against a "fierce Fritz" Mondale. Reagan was always better at rallies than he was handling press inquiries about policy or debating issues with opponents. But maybe digging back in his memory about the one debate he had with Carter, he could remember how a one-liner, a humorous quip, could entertain and soothe and build on his innate talents. He got his chance when a journalist reminded him that if he won he'd be the oldest president in history and that there were reports that he suffered from exhaustion (and after all, he looked exhausted in his exchanges with Mondale around the Nicaragua manual). Reagan pounced: "I want you to know that also I will not make age an issue of this campaign. I am not going to exploit, for political purposes, my opponent's youth and inexperience." The whole room erupted into laughter, including Mondale, who would soon confess that, at that moment, he knew he had lost the election.[82]

But that didn't change the fact that the CIA was directing Nicaraguans to use dirty tactics, including murder, to overthrow the Sandinista regime. A cartoonish book deserved a cartoonish counter claim. Matt Groening, now offering his "Life in Hell" cartoon in an increasing number of venues, had just the right type of dark humor to do the job. He printed the headline "CIA Also Linked to a Comic Book," which he then proceeded to illustrate for readers. It opened with Groening's standard bunny-eared character (this time with a moustache and sombrero) explaining, "We're going to learn how to liberate ourselves from oppression with some useful sabotage and assassination." The first thing to do was "stop up toilets with sponges," to which the narrator, looking at an overflowing toilet, exclaimed, "Viva La Sewage!" And then "neutralize—heh heh—Sandinista officials." Orwell to the rescue on this one. Groening showed a man being shot through his back and chest—that's what the euphemistic "neutralize" meant. Groening's character explained how to make prank calls or blackmail enemies or leave lights on to waste electricity. And then he closed: "Remember, Amigos, don't let this manual fall into the hands of subversive journalists. Our sacred cause might then be misconstrued." Groening was trying to fire a shot in the culture war Reagan's reelection campaign had ignited—rejecting Reagan's use of jokes and hyperpatriotism to elide over difficult issues, and instead using laughter as angry protest, renewing the need for noir humor and doubt in the face of sunshine and optimism.[83]

* * *

October 1984 witnessed students at Brown University voting for a "suicide pill referendum." They wanted the right to kill themselves instead of facing the dreadful conditions of any postnuclear apocalypse. In essence, the organizers equated "nuclear war with suicide." The vote was two to one in favor of providing students the pills. The Health Services Department at Brown refused to stock the pills, but the case had been made. The students who led the referendum turned their attention then to activism to prevent "World War III," hoping to "stop business" nationwide next year—working with figures like Jim Squatter in hopes of taking the demonstrations in San Francisco and Dallas to the next level. *MRR* followed what was happening here, seeing it connected to the growth of "peace punks" in San Francisco at the same time. But it also represented the sense of desperation and darkness of the antiwar movement.[84]

* * *

October 1984 also saw the last "high profile" squat in San Francisco shut down by the city. It was called the Hotel Owners Laundry Company (HOLC, pronounced "hole see"). Since spring, participants had organized the squat democratically, with twice-weekly meetings. There were rules against drug use. And the squat became a hangout and planning space for RAR and the War Chest Tours, when meetings got too big for Bound Together Books. They'd also show political movies and distribute free food mostly gotten from dumpster diving. It took a while for the owners of the HOLC building to fill out the requisite paperwork for eviction. But then it happened mid-October. Warren Hinckle, a radical journalist whose days went back to his editorship at *Ramparts* in the late sixties, observed the eviction and saw its dark humor. The evicted simply "set up housekeeping outside. They had rugs on the sidewalk, and couches and coffee tables set up like it was a god damn living room." They had "plants and easy chairs and someone had drawn a clock and a telephone in chalk on the wall of the building to make it seem more like home."[85]

A few months before the eviction, a writer for the *Village Voice* had interviewed a group of HOLC squatters, trying to figure out the inspiration for the radicalism brimming up in San Francisco. One person interviewed offered up a fusion of existentialism and desperation:

> We will do our thing in our time. It could be called existential. We are in a way orphans of this society—abandoned and not cared for by society in general. I observed it from being an infant and growing up in it. I see the way people really are. I see their ways. They're so proper and so beautiful. They go to church on Sunday and molest their daughters

on Monday. They're all puritan. At the same time the most perverse institutions exist. I think we're living in the dark ages.

Add to those words the images of evicted squatters and furniture on sidewalks, and what better statement of existential anxiety can there be but that?[86]

* * *

Neo-noir and punk continued to flourish, as witnessed in the premiere film of October 1984, *Stranger than Paradise*. Its director, Jim Jarmusch, had jumped first into the Cleveland punk scene of the late-seventies then into the one surrounding CBGB (paralleling Alex Cox's experience in the L.A. punk scene). As Jarmusch told Peter Belsito, he learned from punk that "you didn't have to be a virtuoso musician to form a rock band," and that the same held true for being a movie director or an actor. Intrigued by the "no wave" directors who surrounded the music scene in New York City, Jarmusch hung out at the Squat Theatre (which was "an avant-garde theater company from Budapest" that had relocated to Manhattan). Here he met Eszter Balint (who would star in *Stranger*). He showed some of his early films alongside those by Eric Mitchell, known for his droll approach in making films that were self-conscious of their artificiality. Jarmusch was more attracted to traditional narrative filmmaking (like Alex Cox). He completed his first movie at New York University's film school, in the same year that Cox released *Edge City*. *Permanent Vacation* focused on a young man who is both a "kid" and "an adult." Scenes were filmed against the ruins and rubble of New York City. "I do have a very dismal view of the future," Jarmusch explained soon after *Permanent Vacation* debuted. He wanted to depict "the world as post-depression, post-industrial . . . a set of lapsed systems." He wanted to show people down the rungs of America's social ladder, to provide "an economic viewpoint and a critique of American capitalism."[87]

Stranger than Paradise centered around three characters locked in a struggle for communication, all of them suffering from an "inexpressible loneliness," but more comic than tragic. There was Willie (John Lurie of the band the Lounge Lizards), Eva (Balint), and Eddie (Richard Edson, who once played drums with Sonic Youth). Eva comes from Hungary to stay with her Aunt Lotte, who asks Willie to take Eva into his tiny apartment because she needed to enter the hospital. Willie's hipster style is cramped by Eva's presence. She watches as he eats his TV dinner and then asks him, "Where does that meat come from?" She then shoplifts a TV dinner for him, which he finds endearing, knocking down his wall of coolness. But just as his fondness grows, she leaves for Cleveland. A year later, Willie and Eddie go to visit her and rekindle their friendship. When she takes them to see Lake Erie, a snowstorm moves in and blinds them, but this doesn't stop Eddie, who says about every place he goes, "It's beautiful." The threesome then leaves for Florida, getting a hotel room, and the two men betting and losing their money on dog races. Eva is mistaken for a drug dealer's girlfriend and is given a suitcase full of cash. Meanwhile, Eddie and Willie win back their money and come for Eva at the hotel. She leaves a note for them that says she will catch a plane back to Hungary, and they race to the airport. The final scenes show Willie buying a ticket to Hungary, while Eddie protests his decision, and Eva returns to the hotel they've abandoned, all of them in their separate corners.[88]

Jarmusch's film evaded politics, in the strictest sense of that term. Unlike *Repo Man*, there was no mention of nuclear war, Central America, or Reaganism. But it's hard to miss the broader theme that all the characters lack "ambition." When the two men seek wealth, they gamble, dependent on contingency rather than hard work. Eva succeeds by sheer misidentification. *Stranger* challenged the optimism that Reagan projected. The storyline isn't the only thing that matters here, there's the technique of shooting the movie "in grainy black and white, in the most depressing urban and rural locations in America, with . . . minimalist long takes," creating a "forbidding form" but with a sense of humor. The *L.A. Reader* reported, "The characters are hilariously oblivious to the nightmare world they live in, and the blank stare of Jarmusch's camera pushes the gap between their reactions and ours to outrageous proportions." Jarmusch intentionally slowed down the pace of his film. He used black leader to separate scenes so viewers could think a moment about what they just saw. In this way, the movie felt like a rejection of the MTV experience. It was more akin to the excavation that Pettibon's drawings had prompted or the enigmatic lyrics the Minutemen wrote or the dense cyberpunk writing of William Gibson.[89]

Stranger shared a sensibility a bit less manic than *Repo Man*. And it shared another feature. Though Jarmusch independently directed the film, it was distributed by the Samuel Goldwyn Company, meaning that it was not entirely independent of the Hollywood corporate studio system. The film cost a meager $100,000 to make and took in $2,436,000 at the box office. Clearly the punk rock world could create product sold by the very same entertainment industry it once conceived as an enemy.[90]

XXX

Maybe a Little Situationism Might Help

> There's a tendency now to try and organize and establish punk rock as a *thing* within American society. . . . That's why the hippie thing is dead. Because it became a *thing* and became established like that.
>
> —Chuck Dukowski[91]

Throughout 1984, starting in the spring, *MRR* had prompted debate on the question, "Does Punk Suck?" Letters poured in over the course of many months. Some complained there were too many stupid people in scenes, leading to violence. Others claimed, quite the opposite, that there was too much elitism, that punks were a bunch of purists holding the world at bay. Others argued that "hardcore" and what was called "thrash" music had become so formulaic and repetitive that it was unlistenable. Tim Yo even seemed uncertain. He wondered if punk "will be able to survive (at a grassroots level) the new corporate attempts to co-opt it," pointing to how bands like the Dead Kennedys and Suicidal Tendencies were receiving radio time (Suicidal Tendencies would, like Kraut, get play on MTV; the Dead Kennedys resisted that sinkhole). And now instead of truly independent movies like *Emerald Cities* and *Desperate Teenage Lovedolls*, there was *Repo Man* and *Stranger than Paradise*, both punk-influenced movies but absorbed into the studio system.[92]

Bill Brown, the critic from Michigan who had been schooling himself about a group of radical French intellectuals called the Situationist International (SI), stepped forth. He believed SI writings could inform debate about punk's future. After all, he had been reading SI material over the past few years, and he wanted to share his learning, which he hoped could offer intellectual intervention for worried readers about the future of punk.

Punk and situationism intersected throughout the 1970s (soon after the SI collapsed, having expelled nearly all members). Some thought Malcolm McLaren, an art school devotee before becoming the Sex Pistols' manager, had toyed around with situationist ideas. He'd sometimes talk about crashing the spectacle and decry the boredom of modern life and its passivity—key SI themes. He talked about overthrowing the entertainment culture and his hope, when he was most idealistic, was that the Sex Pistols' eruption would empower young people, "if they are ever so smart," to "destroy a culture that has nothing to do with them." And he had explained earlier to *Rolling Stone*, "I'm not a communist. I'm rather anarchistic." Though SI thinkers were not necessarily anarchist, they expressed fondness for workers' councils and direct self-management as means to oppose passivity (and Guy Debord, leading intellect of the SI, claimed he didn't read much Marx and loathed the French Communist Party for its Stalinism). But then McLaren's situationism faded. When he made the tell-all movie about his supposed masterminding of the Sex Pistols' rise to fame, *The Great Rock and Roll Swindle* (1980), he changed his tune to "cash from chaos." Every time a scene showed cash registers ring, as the band signed contracts for larger amounts of money, the idea that McLaren was a situationist grew preposterous. He looked more like a profit-seeking con artist.[93]

Not surprisingly Claude Bessy, chief writer and editor of *Slash*, raised awareness of the SI. Bessy was French and during his years at *Slash* (1977–1980), a lot of SI writing had not yet been translated. He would make cryptic references to a "Southern California Situationist Movement" as early as February 1978 (just in the wake of the Sex Pistols' infamous tour of America). He dedicated the May 1978 issue of *Slash* to the Parisian revolt of 1968, which many believed had taken at least some inspiration from SI writings; Bessy praised "the handful of enrages (French for maniacs, fanatics, crazies) who, ten years ago (May '68), tried to change life." And then in the summer of 1979, he dedicated a long article to explaining SI ideas. He described how the SI was "started by a bunch of European intellectuals (don't snigger—everybody got to come from somewhere) . . . in the late fifties as the ONLY viable revolutionary alternative to stifling dogmatic 'established' revolutionary movements (mainly Marxism)." Bessy explained that the SI's aim was to "CHANGE LIFE ITSELF, not the structures hiding it. In other words don't vote for the lesser of two evils, but tear down the fuckin' machinery that tells you such a choice is freedom." But it wasn't all fiery radicalism, he explained. Though they "REALLY meant to go to the roots of the matter, . . . they meant to have a hell of a time in the process." Such a combination of critique and humor offered "inspiration" that punks could draw from in their battles against boredom and the entertainment industry.[94]

Bessy mattered to Brown but not as much as Greil Marcus, a rock journalist and friend of Lester Bangs. Marcus was more scholarly than Bangs; he had studied American studies and political science at the University of California–Berkeley. He participated in the free speech movement there in 1964 and was politically engaged even while becoming a "professional" rock writer for magazines like *Rolling Stone*. His writing was more straightforward than the "gonzo" and sprawling prose of Bangs. After all, Marcus had always been more of a tweedy pipe-smoking professor type, and when Altamont erupted in 1969 he turned his back on any counterculture temptations he might have had. He became a model for someone like Bill Brown—scholarly, yet engaged, more than just a fan but a critic who buttressed his opinions with loads of reading. Another thing about Marcus, he was more receptive to 1980s punk than Bangs. Reviewing an Adolescents album from 1981, Marcus made a distinction between the years of 1977–1979 ("punk") with the 1980s (which he saw as "postpunk.") He elaborated: "If punk says, 'Life stinks,' post punk says, 'Why does life stink?'" For Marcus that was a legitimate question.[95]

As with anyone who comes to the SI fresh, Marcus found the organization's barbed theoretical writing, sectarianism, and bombastic rhetoric off-putting (one SI writer claimed the organization would "wreck this world"). He managed to distill the most important insights of the SI, rather than drown in the weeds, and make their ideas more approachable for readers who might not have a great deal of background in continental (French and German) philosophy. Marcus was helped out greatly by Ken Knabb's 1981 compilation of SI writings—*The Situationist Anthology*—translated into English and self-published. The book served as a source for an extended review-essay Marcus did for the *Village Voice* in 1982. He explained in broad strokes how the SI had shed nineteenth-century Marxism, which emphasized the contradictions of production (labor, work, capital). The SI instead focused on the realm of consumption, which "had come to define happiness and to suppress all other possibilities of freedom and selfhood." So as much as the SI would endorse workers' councils, most of their attention and ire were directed toward the entertainment industry. Marcus discussed how the Lettrists (a group that preceded and then folded into the SI), showed up at a press conference Charlie Chaplin gave in 1952, where he promoted his recent movie *Limelight* and derided mistreatment on the part of the US government (he had been banned from re-entering the country, seen as a communist sympathizer). The Lettrists explained their protest against Chaplin: "We believe that the most urgent expression of freedom is the destruction of idols, especially when they present themselves in the name of freedom." In whole for Marcus, "The spectacle"—key word that—was "not merely advertising, or propaganda, or television, it is a world" in which people are enclosed and made passive in favor of what a bloated entertainment industry provided them.[96]

Brown followed Marcus's lead. "What has happened since the 1940s is that aesthetic production has become fully integrated into commodity production generally," Brown wrote in *MRR*. Commodity production had exploded as a new form of "multinational capitalism" grew. Brown homed in on a "capitalist imperative to produce fresh waves of ever-more novel-seeming goods, at ever greater rates of turnover." Sounding much like Kim Gordon (who had learned a great deal from Marcus as well), Brown said, "We now live in a perpetual present." Anything and everything could be turned into a commodity, becoming next week's "spectacle," then tossed for another. This included punk rock. If some were saying that punk sucked in the pages of *MRR*, Brown went further: "Punk is dead . . . no longer at all shocking to the middle-class culture." It could "now be seen with increasing frequency on MTV."[97]

If punk was becoming absorbed, Brown pondered, perhaps it should dive deeper underground. He quoted an SI writing: "One of the classic weapons of the old world, perhaps the one most used against groups attempting to alter the organization of life, is to single out and isolate a few of the participants as 'stars.'" Sounding like the Lettrists who attacked Chaplin, Brown had nothing good to say for one of the few SI-inspired bands, Feederz, once based in Arizona, now San Francisco. Frank Discussion, lead singer of the band, would often show up in conversations at *MRR*, and he usually sounded like he was spouting slogans more than engaging in deliberation. For instance, a year before Brown wrote his article, Discussion was "shooting the shit" with Jello Biafra, V. Vale, Jeff Bale, and Tim Yo. Whereas the other participants had longish disquisitions about the topic of discussion, the Feederz leader offered one-line quips like "that is what's called the standard of living" or "they're only interested in extending a miserable past into a boring and miserable future." It sounded like bumper-sticker exposition. For Brown, Discussion had tried to turn SI ideas into an "ideology," into slogans with little thought.[98]

Brown's solution paled to his analysis here. He exclaimed, "The hardcore movement must revolt against its own leaders, which means dumping people like Frank Discussion and Ian MacKaye" (who were starting to feel like rock stars to him). Here Brown called for doing what the original SI did: "reduce its numbers . . . which means that each person should be able to understand his or her own relationship to the totality of social life." He called to link up "with the revolutionary forces of the modern proletariat," a variant of Marxism that would likely fall on deaf ears, seeing how few punks identified with the working class as a revolutionary change agent (including the working-class bands like the Minutemen and the Proletariat). Whatever the remedy, Brown had outlined the challenges of revolt within a consumer society. What it signified more than anything was that the hope of early 1984 had grown a bit tattered.[99]

XXX

Mourning Again in America

> He still had his anger.
>
> —William Gibson, *Neuromancer*[100]

While Brown argued to sharpen punk's edge, the editors of *MRR* faced a more pressing question: Whether or not to vote in the upcoming presidential election. There was the old anarchist adage that voting ratified state power. That showed up in political buttons worn on some coats at the time: "No matter who you vote for, the government wins." Besides as the War Chest Tours made clear, corporations held more power than politicians ever would. Money, after all, ran the show. The SI, as Claude Bessy argued, would have viewed voting as the equivalence of passive consumer choice. Or as Debbie Dub, a longtime organizer of shows in both San Francisco and Los Angeles, now writing a column for *MRR*, put it, "The notion that changing the figurehead on the top of the totem pole is going to make any difference is naïve to the extreme."[101]

Necessarily so?, asked other editors and letter writers at *MRR*. Did someone voting really embrace a naive view of the world? For Tim Yo, who obviously agreed with the political sentiment among War Chest Tour organizers, voting was an ethical responsibility, and it made a wider statement than just the choice of one candidate over another. Not voting in fact was morally defeatist to him. "If re-elected Reagan will murder (in my name) thousands of Latin American peasants and freedom fighters," he explained (the words in parentheses the most important). He refuted the idea that voting negated other approaches to engagement and rearticulated the politics of guilt developed earlier by MDC and AoF. Those on the left, he argued, "should use all the tools available to them. It is not contradictory to demonstrate in the streets, participate in direct actions, form collectives, organize at the grassroots level, sing about the horrors of the world . . . and to vote for the lesser of two evils" (sounding like the call for rounded political engagement in the *P.E.A.C.E.* booklet). Jeff Bale concurred and suggested that punks should conceive their vote as a vote *against* Reagan, not necessarily an endorsement of Mondale (though he'd punch that hole when the time came). An editor at *RAD* zine (out of Morro Bay, California) pushed these arguments further, suggesting that not voting was itself an active endorsement of Ronald Reagan. *RAD* raged: "Reagan wants you to believe a vote for Mondale is a waste of a vote. Bullshit! The only way to waste a vote is not to vote at all!!!"[102]

So some punks voted, others didn't. No matter which choice they made, they all learned on November 6 of the brutality of the election, as some of them watched the television host Dan Rather pronounce the election over even before polling booths had shut down on the West Coast (some suggested this might have suppressed anti-Reagan votes). The election was a Reagan landslide. Mondale was whupped, having just barely won his home state of Minnesota and Washington, D.C. Reagan got 525 electoral votes to Mondale's 13, and the president won nearly 59 percent of the popular vote. There would quickly be talk of a "mandate" based on such a victory. The president had shored up support from Reagan Democrats and evangelicals. Like Michael Jackson before him, Reagan had become a "blockbuster."[103]

Frustration hummed through the world of zines. *The Attack* condemned the winner-takes-all principle behind America's electoral system. Peter Wick argued that "the election did result in an electoral vote landslide for Reagan, but this only reflects the glitch in our elections process which effectively mutes the voices of 41%, that is slightly more than 2/5, with under 3/5 for Reagan." Wick suggested that Reagan's foreign policy had not been endorsed by the election. "Nearly half of our nation appears to have recognized Reagan's foreign policy muscle as little more than a 'Make my day' American ego trip" (a reference to the Cint Eastwood film, *Sudden Impact* (1983), a movie Reagan quoted). The zine went on to cite how Jerry Falwell supposedly "prayed" for a Reagan victory, hinting at a scary sense of presidential divinity. Especially twisted was how Reagan's re-election was preceded by open knowledge that the CIA had given "3,000 Nicaraguan guerillas tips on how to kill government leaders." *The Attack* went further in its jeremiad; it widened its scope on what had happened by late 1984. The editors related Reagan's landslide to Michael Jackson's blockbuster status. It felt by November that punks had lost a two-front war: One against Reagan, the other against the entertainment industry—which was now booming. So how was Michael Jackson related to Reagan? Jackson was "worthless in every way shape and form. America, who loves this man, deserves Reagan as President. . . pointless drivel such as 'Thriller' is only overproduced elevator music." So the entertainment industry boomed, as Reagan beamed. And then even sadder news from the zine: This would be their last issue. Another fragile DIY project bit the dust, just as Reagan swept back into the White House and the record industry grew lush again.[104]

A similar tone came from *RAD*. It rang out: "The youth of today has really disappointed me. Last night, election night, 18–24 year olds gave Ronald Reagan the biggest landslide victory in U.S. history." Like *The Attack*, the editors here saw a connection between the smiley-faced conservatism of Reagan and the lilting, synth, dance music coming from radio and MTV. "I think the youth, the same youth, that listens to . . . Michael Jackson are being sold out. They of course are sucking it up." Though *RAD* would remain active in local political struggles against a nuclear power plant in San

Luis Obispo (Diablo Canyon), their activism now carried with it a sense of frustration as much as anger.[105]

The Minutemen gave expression to the feel of late 1984 in their first-ever music video, based on "This Ain't No Picnic" (a song on *Double Nickels on the Dime*). It was a DIY affair, much like Kraut's. The whole thing cost $450 and was helped along by Randall Jahnson, who had studied film at UCLA. The Minutemen had caved to the pressures of music video culture while preserving their "econo" philosophy and complexity. The band was shown playing in a setting of rubble, just holding their instruments with no amplifiers (George Hurley had just one small drum, for instance). They sang their song about dehumanization of labor (with historical and documentary shots of workers during the Great Depression), and then suddenly the video cut to a World War II training film that starred Ronald Reagan as a pilot and bomber. Reagan beams his trademark smile as he flies far above, and splicing scenes together made it look like Reagan was shooting down at the Minutemen. Boon looks up and sings the line, "Hey, mister, don't look down on me for what I believe." Reagan drives his plane down and drops bombs on the band, burying them in rubble. The final shot shows Reagan reporting back to his commanders: "It was a helluva explosion. I guess that's all sir."

As with everything the Minutemen did, it held varying meanings that could be peeled back. The first and most literal: the feeling of being blown up by Ronald Reagan, that sense a landslide election conjured. But those watching closely might also figure that this was Reagan as an actor, not a real pilot, a line that the president often blurred. Some viewers might have known that Reagan did not serve overseas during World War II, due to bad eyesight. The term "chickenhawk" would subsequently be a label that some applied to Reagan (one that his mythical hero John Wayne couldn't dodge either). Here Reagan was performing imagined, image-based patriotism. And perhaps one more message to be added: Reagan could have symbolized the entirety of the entertainment industry shooting down the Minutemen and its DIY "econo" culture. His big military plane and huge bombs against the Minutemen's unplugged instruments in the rubble. There was no contest here. The video also symbolized a transition for the band: they were looking to break open the gates of MTV, repeating the attempt that Kraut pioneered.

XXX

"Becoming Everything I Used to Hate . . . "[106]

> I really get pissed when I read articles on bands and they say, "We're just a rock n roll band." Think about it guys, in the beginning punk was made to fuck over the big business cokehead groups and record companies by making raw noise and selling it cheap.
>
> —letter to *MRR*, December 1984[107]

In December 1984, Black Flag released their album (and single), *Slip It In*. Around this time, the Minutemen were asked what they thought about their mentors—the band they opened for at their first show close to four years ago. Black Flag had embraced heavy metal or what would be called "crossover" between punk and metal (both of these categories can become capacious at times), already witnessed earlier in 1984 with the release of *My War* (which *Who Owns the World* called "heavy, and I mean heavy, metal" to that point it became "schlock"). Was slowing down the pace of their music (*The Rocket* said it sounded like "the band members had all taken elephant tranquilizers") symbolic of progression? *Ink Disease* asked Watt. He immediately shot back, "Degression." He followed up with: "They write more lame songs than good ones."[108]

Take the single "Slip It In." Black Flag had mastered long ago tongue-in-cheek social commentary in songs like "TV Party!," "White Minority," and "Six Pack." Perhaps "Slip It In" was intended as humor about American macho and sexual prowess, but that was lost in the grossness of what sounded like a young woman resisting unwanted sex while being labeled "loose." The song's refrain, "And you say you don't want it, then you slip it in," sounded an awful lot like Fear's dumb song "Beef Bologna," where a man lived through the prowess of his cock. The fact that the song ran over six minutes and was full of guitar solos added to an argument made earlier by Jello Biafra that there was a strong connection between heavy metal and male, macho politics or what he called "cock rock" (Jeff Bale simply labeled heavy metal "reactionary.") Commenting on crossover, *Flipside* correlated heavy metal with a decline in the DIY spirit (the reproduction of rock stardom) and declared that many punk bands were "out of touch with their own business" (which sounded a lot like Bill Brown's complaint). More ironically, Harley Flanagan, whose Cro-Mags were certainly crossover, stated it baldly: "Hardcore [punk] is 'of the people,' while metal is more of a 'we think we're hot shit' type thing."[109]

The video Black Flag made of "Slip It In" (with the help of Dave Markey) was even worse. It bore remarkable resemblance to Van Halen's video hit of the summer of 1984, in which nerdy students get "Hot for Teacher" as a model strips down to a skimpy bathing suit in front of them. Guitar solos abounded in that one as well. "Slip It In," which starred numerous "actors" who appeared in *Desperate Teenage Lovedolls*, focused on a teacher (played by Jordan Schwartz) who sings along to the song with the girls in the front row, one of whom is licking a lollipop in seductive play. The teacher is then seduced by one young woman who takes a long time at the pencil sharpener, making grinding motions, and pouting; he takes off his suit and, while the song has descended into the sounds of male orgasm, sheds all clothes and charges. Meanwhile, outside the school, a gaggle of adolescents look through a fence at a young woman who mimics *Playboy* photo shoots, fingering her lips, caressing her breasts, sucking on a crucifix that hangs around her neck (suggesting rebellion along Madonna's lines); eventually the men break down the fence and run after her in a roving pack, looking prepared for gang rape. In between both "stories" there are shots of Black Flag performing live, swirling their long hair to the music; Rollins appears in his dark tight shorts, barechested and belligerent—his weightlifting body pulsing, his long black hair whisking away sweat as he shakes. The whole thing spoke of "degression."

Funny thing is that Henry Rollins knew by this time that the band had run its course, that it had turned into something it never intended to be. By the summer of 1984, he would record in his diary, "I think that Black Flag has reached its high point. . . . I think that the new songs bum people out." He had a sinking feeling that Greg Ginn didn't like him (which was true), and band members descended into argument and the silent treatment even while packed into a van. Whereas argument among band members might elevate creativity—the way it had for Minor Threat (who had broken up by this point) and still did for the Minutemen—here it seemed to calcify. Worse yet, Rollins couldn't figure out what was happening to him when the band toured—how he was being turned into a rock star celebrity against his will. He pondered: "A man that welds steel doesn't get asked for his autograph, but I do. I can't see it as anything other than bullshit." Later he'd complain, "I can't see why all these people like me. . . . I wouldn't like me." Performing bare-chested drove the growing perception that he was in line with cock rock. He explained to one zine that he played shirtless because he sweated so much: "I hope people don't think of me as some sort of David Lee Roth [lead singer for Van Halen] tough guy. I'm not like that; I'm not tough." But the persona that surrounded him suggested to fans otherwise. Throughout his diaries, he noted how some came to shows just to punch him in the nose, to do as much physical harm as possible. No longer was there rapport between performer and floor participant. Rollins found himself becoming what Bill Brown had warned about: a rock star— elevated above those who saw him as either a celebrity or a thing to take their frustrations out on.[110]

* * *

Black Flag was not alone. Other bands adopted "crossover" with heavy metal, including DRI (San Francisco), Corrosion of Conformity (a North Carolina band who played "punk metal" to "headbangers"), the Necros (Michigan), Government Issue (D.C.), and Void (D.C.). Most notoriously, bands in Boston like Gang Green, DYS, Jerry's Kids (who played "generic thrash" with "ultra powerful, heavy metal oriented attack"), and especially SS Decontrol went full-on metal. It wasn't just a different style of playing, something changed about the attitudes that stood behind the music.[111]

For instance, Al Barile, the guitarist in SSD, had always been a macho jock in most people's estimation, his sport of choice being hockey (he sometimes sported Boston Bruins stickers at shows). As he saw it, rock was all about boys expressing themselves, once suggesting that girls went to new wave shows, boys to punk shows (which furthered the view that suburban punk in the 1980s was male-dominated). This sort of macho politics could be heard in the 1984 release of How We Rock, an album that The Noise labeled "hardcore with power chord laden heavy metal." A letter writer to MRR said the album sounded like the metal band AC/DC. The D.C. zine Truly Needy would eventually conclude, "Yes, SSD has gone heavy metal . . . all the way." Band members argued that they were graduating from punk hardcore to metal because now they knew how to play their instruments. Which prompted a retort from Kevin of Seven Seconds: "I don't see why you have to become heavy metal to play your instruments." It was telling that as they became virtuosos, DIY was tossed to the side. SSD's lead singer, Springa, said they no longer organized their own shows because it's a "big headache that we don't need." Nor did they play in Boston very often by 1984, seeking national stature rather than local support. Springa complained, "I don't see why people say 'Oh, they've sold out' and all this shit. What is wrong with trying to be the best you can be?"[112]

* * *

That same year, Heart Attack, a suburban teeny punk band who started alongside Reagan Youth and Kraut, broke up, while the Cro-Mags charted their rise to popularity. One of the reasons for Heart Attack's breakup was the band's dislike of so much "knuckleheaded, cement-head music"— code for metal. The Cro-Mags embraced crossover, combining aggressive metal-fused music and the teachings of Hare Krishna of all things. The band's venue remained CBGB but more and more the Rock Hotel, a place described in MRR as "pretty big," literally and figuratively. The Cro-Mags manager, Chris Williamson, ran the Rock Hotel shows, where he often put metal and punk bands on the same bill (including Motorhead and the Cro-Mags). One letter writer to MRR recounted an experience that suggested what was shaping up in New York City. He had gone to see Kraut—who were not only getting MTV play but also trending metal—at the Rock Hotel. The band "used some blinding intense lights that panned the audience." The experience provided "hallucinogenic flashbacks of Foghat," one of those dinosaur, arena bands. The letter writer concluded that it was one big boring "heavy metal concert," like the ones the Minutemen had hoped to escape permanently back in the day.[113]

* * *

Seattle, Washington, became a hotbed of crossover in 1984. That year Mark Arm disbanded Mr. Epp and the Calculations—one of the more clever bands in Seattle's history. He also stopped writing for The Attack, which collapsed the same year. Arm moved quickly to form Green River, one band, in a critic's words, created by "punks" who "wanted to sound like Aerosmith" (although the influence of the Stooges was present as well). Green River had compatriots in their cause. There was the already-formed

Melvins, who Krist Novoselic, future bass player in Nirvana, remembered as being Black Flag–influenced (meaning especially by 1984, metal). There was also Soundgarden, an exemplary metal band who played interminable guitar solos and whose lead singer, Chris Cornell, sounded like Robert Plant of Led Zeppelin. Also, like Plant (and Rollins), he performed bare-chested (Mark Arm claimed Cornell wore tear-away shirts to pretend his clothes had been ripped off, looking more macho).[114]

* * *

It would be overreach to think there was direct connection between the growing prominence of a heavy metal style in a variety of punk scenes and the conservative ascendancy Reagan's landslide reelection suggested. But . . . observations of a "skinhead" invasion into numerous punk scenes occurred, just as "crossover" became more popular. Skinhead was a look (shaved heads, bleached jeans rolled up, Doc Marten boots if the cash was available) and a subculture imported from England. The style went back to the 1960s but was now informed by the reactionary politics of the National Front and white supremacy. As it came to America, often through sales of cassette releases by the band Skrewdriver, skinheadism, if such a thing could be clearly diagnosed, consisted of a solidarity with Reagan (and conservatism more broadly), a love of punk music (including metal crossover), a hatred of the left, an affiliation with white nationalism, and an aggressive, violent form of expressing patriotism. As T. J. Leyden, once a white nationalist skinhead himself, put it, "As punks became more anti-American, skinheads became more nationalist. Ronald Reagan was president, and there was a lot of 'Love America or Leave It' sentiment in the air." Mostly this took the form of fights, usually directed against what skins pejoratively called "peace punks." By 1984, a prominent skinhead presence was noted in San Francisco, where Bay Area Skinheads (BASH) arose, often cajoled along by Marc Dagger (who was sent to jail by the end of 1984); Chicago (instigated by Clark Martell, a fierce white nationalist who would also be sent to prison); New York City (where *Zat* magazine documented how skins had pledged to "beat up 'positive punks'"); Oklahoma; Florida; Texas; Denver (where one participant who called himself Nazi Jeff had a penchant for beating up hippies); and Washington D.C. (bizarrely led by an African American woman nicknamed Lefty).

The worst nightmare of Jello Biafra came true: the Nazi Punks were not fucking off, they were invading scenes across the country.[115]

Skinheads acted like the vigilante types who had beaten up protestors at Reagan's Labor Day re-election rally (and like the Wolverines in *Red Dawn*). Of course, Reagan didn't directly inspire skinheads (and he distanced himself from those who were crashing Mondale rallies and booing and heckling). But it's fair to say that by 1984 "Reagan youth" now included an angrier, more aggressive type. Letters sent to *MRR* by the end of the year repeated over and over how it was no longer "fun" to go to shows—the threat of fighting and violence on the part of skinheads had created an atmosphere of fear.

By the end of 1984, Tim Yo addressed both the growing skinhead presence in the scene and a sense that "peace punks" were on the decline (or perhaps just despairing). He invited skinheads onto the MRR radio show, to argue why they were wrong; it was noble but, of course, doomed— rational arguments were not in the domain of skins. It felt like things were crashing. David Solnit, the chief organizer of the War Chest Tours, recalled both the heady feel during the summer of 1984 and the sense of decline in the months to follow: "I had survived two weeks out on the street, getting battered, dodging the San Francisco Police Department and then at Club Foot, I tried to break up a fight and I got pummeled by some skinheads. I stopped going to shows." Drawing on an ethic of violence, skinheads offered a form of vigilante patriotism that had long roots in America's past. They often saw themselves as Reagan's foot soldiers—echoing the chants of "USA! USA!" at the Summer Olympics and then Reagan's re-election rallies. Their growing presence certainly dampened the hopefulness of so many punks earlier in the year.[116]

XXX

The Victors of 1984

> I simply accepted the basic greed and selfishness of human beings.
> I recognized that they are always going to act in their own interests...
> —*Diary of a Yuppie*[117]

At its end, *Newsweek* magazine declared 1984 the "year of the yuppie." Young urban professionals had managed to carve out a "social type" that fit the times. Yuppies, in the magazine's "special report," had developed a "state of Transcendental Acquisition, in which the perfection of their possessions enables them to rise above the messy turmoil of their emotional lives." The novelist Jay McInerney, in his 1984 bestseller *Bright Lights, Big City*, announced the yuppie ethic this way: a "refusal to acknowledge any goal higher than the pursuit of pleasure." Yuppies worked hard during the day (likely in finance or real estate) but partied hard at night (what Daniel Bell called a "disjunction of the realms" endemic to postwar capitalism). Self-confessed hedonists, yuppies gushed about their material possessions, the way the conservative intellectual William F. Buckley did in *Overdrive* (1984), a book with little to say about political principles and more about his indoor swimming pool and the wine he chose for lunch. The yuppie lived for fancy "pasta and the proliferation of raspberry vinegar" but always managed to stay fit, learning from Jane Fonda's workout tapes or joining a private gym (and, if truly sycophantic, turning to the *Yuppie Handbook* (1984) for tips in "lifestyle," a term heard ad nauseum). If drugs were used, they were not pot or LSD (the hallmarks of the hippie tune-out), but rather flake cocaine that boosted energy for work and sex (what McInerney called "the Bolivian Marching Powder"). If fortunate enough, a yuppie might reside at a place like Trump Tower, erected a year earlier, with its "$200 million chrome, brass, and glass tower," "six story atrium shopping arcade," and "ninety one condominiums starting at one million dollars." Its builder, Donald Trump, was a yuppie confidence man extraordinaire.[118]

Newsweek reported that yuppies, by the end of 1984, had successfully gentrified San Francisco's Haight-Ashbury neighborhood—once the mecca of the 1960s counterculture (further concretizing the "yippie to yuppie" meme). The neighborhood was transformed, as "young professionals have flocked to take advantage of the roomy, affordable housing, proximity to Golden Gate Park and pleasant climate that once attracted the flower children." In the process they generated a real estate boom, driving out "lower income families" and creating numerous "chic shops" (aka boutiques). *Newsweek* reported that a house in Haight Ashbury "bought for $87,000 in 1977 and refurbished sold two years ago [1982] for $385,000." Commenting on the cultural status of Haight-Ashbury, the artist Bruce Conner (who had engaged the San Francisco punk scene) called it "real estate with a legend attached to it." Once an enclave for hippies and bohemians, it now became a zone of high finance.[119]

Yuppies had helped return Ronald Reagan to the seat of power. They served as the foot soldiers of the Reagan Revolution, pushing the country to escape the malaise associated with Jimmy Carter (and the dour spirit of Walter Mondale). The yuppie—with his search for pleasure—stood in contrast to the likes of James Watt, the uptight, Puritanical conservative. *Newsweek* noted that yuppies first latched onto Gary Hart's run for the Democratic Party nomination as a "neoliberal." They were uncomfortable with the cultural conservatism of the New Right and its influence on the president. But once Hart was out of the picture, the Reagan campaign "courted" yuppies. This "reached some sort of milestone in shamelessness last September, when they sent Reagan forth to cloak himself in the mantle of rockmeister Bruce Springsteen." Still, that seemed to work. The politics of the pleasure principle won over the yuppie vote, the idea, as a pollster explained to *Newsweek*, that "there has been an erosion of the sense of obligation to others. . . . Mondale embodied some of those traditional values, and the rejection of him is one of the signs of the times." As 1984 came to a close, yuppies toasted their leader with a glass of chardonnay, recognizing Reagan as, in the words of the *Wall Street Journal*, "the most aged Yuppie."[120]

MARCHING TOWARD THE "ALTERNATIVE" (1985–?)

In the 80s truth passes into fiction and out again, history is recycled into the present without a context, and the present has become a leap of faith, as we sit back and enjoy the ultrafast life of MTV.

—Kim Gordon, 1985[1]

XXX

Reagan's In Again

Prayer should be the habit of everyone on this team we call America.
—Reverend Billy Graham, during Reagan's second Inauguration[2]

It was one of the coldest winters D.C. had witnessed. So cold that the inaugural parade was canceled. The streets of Washington, D.C., lay empty, as strong winds gusted through the bleacher seats set up for an event that never happened, creating what the *Washington Post* termed "eerie, empty stillness."[3]

But, as the saying goes, the show must go on. And it did by moving indoors, starting the evening of January 19, with an Inaugural Gala held at the D.C. Convention Center. Donna Summer, usually considered the high queen of American disco, performed, as did the Reagans' favorite, the Beach Boys, the band James Watt chased away from the national mall more than a year earlier. And, of course, the obligatory Frank Sinatra, the crooner who once championed JFK but now loved to fete the Reagans. There were plenty of photo ops with numerous retro celebrities and friends of the president, the likes of Elizabeth Taylor, Zsa Zsa Gabor, Charlton Heston, and Jimmy Stewart.

Reagan's speech, given inside the Congress Rotunda, offered little that was new. The president celebrated the comeback of the economy and restated his and his fellow citizens' faith that "there are no limits to growth and human progress when men and women are free to follow their dreams." Listeners had to have expected at least one mention of dreams. Reagan then went on to square, as was his wont, free markets with traditional values and institutions of the family and church. Coining an odd turn of phrase, he celebrated not just "confidence" but also "tradition of progress." Like his first inaugural address, he didn't have much good to say about government, condemning a "bloated federal establishment." Then he said something about hoping to get rid of nuclear weapons, which could have been a jawdropper, except that it segued into an endorsement of Star Wars, that satellite system that could shoot down incoming Russian missiles. That, of course, was one of his own biggest dreams, for which he could see no limits.[4]

All day on January 21 there were numerous galas throughout D.C., usually held in high-priced hotels. During the evening, inaugural balls took place. The Reagans would whisk themselves away in limousines to get from one to another. It was like a blur of celebrities checking their fur coats and dancing in honor of the entertainer-in-chief. At one inaugural brunch at the Four Seasons Hotel, David Hasselhoff, star of the television series *Knight Rider* (a show where the good guy gets the bad guy by using his souped-up car with its artificial intelligence) arrived to much fanfare. As he walked into the brunch, he faced numerous beggars for his autograph. He was heard saying, "It's just like Hollywood."[5]

* * *

Not far from one of the inaugural balls on the evening of January 21, there assembled a scraggly group of young punk kids, many of them members of the Revolutionary Youth Brigade (the youth wing of the Revolutionary Communist Party, a wacky group of Maoists). Most wore strong boots. They also had bags of Twinkies with cardboard wings jammed into them, intended to look like cruise missiles. As limousines started approaching an evening ball in the Dupont Circle area of the city, these kids swept down and pelted the limos with the Twinkies. Some jumped up on the hoods of the limos, others kicked at windows, and when the police showed up with batons and shields, the kids scattered to the winds. It was a desperate protest.

The evening before, the yippies and local punks held a "Counter-Inaugural Ball" at the Warner Theater. It was like a last gasp of Rock Against Reagan, and it promised—after the roster of bands changed around—to host a group flown in from England, the Poison Girls. They were one of the more important anarcho-feminist bands at the time and had never before performed in America (the original invite went to the anarchist band Crass, but they had broken up by this point). Practically no one showed up, due in part to a lack of publicity and to bad weather. It felt like something more than just the weather had chilled.[6]

* * *

Soon after Reagan's inauguration, a song started climbing the charts, and it seemed anthemic, for it captured the spirit of the times even better than the president's smile that beamed through his second inauguration. Madonna's "Material Girl" served as a yuppie anthem and celebration of consumer hedonism. It explained, in Madonna's nasal whine, that "the boy with the cold hard cash is always Mister Right; cause we're living in a material world, and I am a material girl." Of course, only hardworking and wealthy men need apply to Madonna's boudoir, those "boys who save their pennies" and "make" her "rainy day." Some heard strains of feminism here, the strong female making demands of her men, and it certainly was no celebration of monogamy: "Boys may come and boys may go, and that's all right you see. Experience has made me rich, and now they're after me." But the female empowerment theme couldn't displace *the addiction-to-things* theme. As it closed out with the monotonous repetition of the words "living in a material world" over and over as the synthesizer pumped, it became hypnotic about the benefits of ramped-up consumer capitalism in the age of the yuppie. Meaning it was obvious hit material.

The video, now all over MTV, cinched the message. The synthesizer (a must) blasts a beat and then comes Madonna, dressed in imitation of Marilyn Monroe in *Gentlemen Prefer Blondes* (1953). She occupies a bright red stage and is surrounded by men in long coats and bow ties, slaving over her, offering her a variety of goods, from jewelry to furs. The many men who pursue Madonna help drive home the song's suspicion of monogamy (keep the playing field open, it suggests), she flirts with every guy on the stage, indiscriminately, grabbing for what they dangle in front of her. The men pick her up and dance with her, suggesting back that she's an object they hope to acquire. She picks the men's pockets, in a sort of pseudo-rebellious way, and waves dollar bills at the camera. Madonna had become, in the words of *The Rocket* (Seattle), "the female role model of the know-nothing '80s" who "epitomizes her own brand of benign, heartless hedonism." Perfect for the re-election of Reagan. Perfect for the celebration of yuppies cheering the president's victory. Madonna's "material girl" was one of those who in Reagan's second inaugural symbolized that "there are no limits to growth and human progress when men and women are free to follow their dreams." Especially if you were a celebrity.[7]

XXX

"We Care a Lot!"[8]

> There comes a time when rock stars beg for cash, and that's how the world's supposed to come together as one. There are people dying, whoa, and they just noticed. And they think they're the greatest gift of all.
>
> —Culturcide[9]

On January 28, 1985, Michael Jackson, once again, made history. He took the next step in making celebrity and the entertainment industry into the new heroes and saviors of the 1980s. The celebrity was now a *moral* leader, as Jackson wrote the music and lyrics for "We Are the World" with Lionel Richie, a song that called on Americans to notice famine and despair throughout Africa. In actuality, Harry Belafonte came up with the idea, but he was more than happy to step aside and let high-profile stars take over, especially as Quincy Jones promised to produce (the same Jones who once supposedly pledged to save the music industry). Inspiration also came from the late 1984 success of the song and video "Do They Know It's

Christmas?," which was performed by British rock stars (calling themselves Band Aid) in order to raise money and awareness for victims of African famine. Jackson was largely copycatting here.

The song "We Are the World" was intended as an "anthem" and required multiple tracks laid down and then topped off by a celebrity chorus (that was how it was done in "Do They Know It's Christmas?"). While they were listening to a take, Jackson and Richie had an awkward moment, recounted in the publicity book for "We Are the World." The two maestros had been reading the *National Enquirer* as taping proceeded. They found out that Joanna Carson—ex-wife of television host Johnny Carson—had confessed she couldn't "live on $44,600 a month." The promo book went on: "Everyone runs down [Carson's] list of monthly expenses, clothing and jewelry and so on. The story becomes an absurd motif for the evening, an extreme counterpoint between the extravagant world the performers themselves live in and the purpose of the project at hand."[10]

After days of laying tracks, the celebrities descended. January 28 was the same day as the American Music Awards in Los Angeles. All it took was an array of limousines to whisk the bounty of stars to Kenny Rogers's recording studio in Hollywood. As they arrived, Quincy Jones announced that they should change out of their glamorous attire for the Awards show and into regular clothes. "Cause we don't want to make a hunger record in tuxedos," he explained. It turned into an all-night session where one celebrity after another was invited into the recording studio to sing a line for the song. People hobnobbed around outside the studio. There was Cyndi Lauper, Whitney Houston, Willie Nelson, Huey Lewis, Bruce Springsteen . . . the list went on and on, up to at least forty-six performers. It was a blockbuster just in its making. Soon after the single and the video were released, HBO made a documentary, narrated by the yuppie Jane Fonda. It offered interviews with participants, most of whom, in the words of the *New York Times*, tended "toward the self-serving and sincerely simplistic."[11]

"We Are the World" stood within a long history of private charity. Almost one hundred years before Jackson wrote up the song, Andrew Carnegie had argued—amid the populist revolt and radical unionism of his times—that those who made wealth out of their own acumen should be those who decide how to spend surplus profits charitably (an argument informed by "social Darwinism"). "We Are the World" suggested that celebrities should direct the public toward the causes they saw fit, "to lend a hand to life," as the lyrics went. "We are the ones who make a better day, so let's start giving," the celebrities sang, sounding a lot like Carnegie. Greil Marcus thought such lyrics suggested a profound conservatism: "There is a 'we'—you and I—who should help a 'them,' who are not like us; that as we help them we gain points for admission to heaven ('We're saving our own lives.')" There was no call for regime change—right as a movement against South African apartheid was hitting college campuses—or permanent re-distribution of wealth. That would have sunk the whole project in the first place. "We Are the World" was a narcissistic performance. There was that strange line that Marcus had quoted: "We're saving our own lives." And there was that synch between the way Michael Jackson saw the world and the way Ronald Reagan did (and the president admitted to being moved by the song after hearing it aboard Air Force One). No doubt the presi-dent might have smiled at the line that captured Jackson's optimism and Carnegie's philosophy: "When you're down and out, there seems no hope at all. But if you just believe there's no way we can fail." Celebrities dreamed of making the world in their own image, basking in their own glory.[12]

The most telling moment of the evening of January 28 came after the Awards show closed. Word was in that Michael Jackson's white, stretch lim-ousine had made its way to the studio. When hearing this, Quincy Jones blurted: "God has arrived."[13]

* * *

Meanwhile, Hollywood reaffirmed for the youth market that they "cared a lot" too. John Hughes's *The Breakfast Club*, a follow-up to his *Sixteen Candles*, became the "authentic" youth culture flick of the year (very likely for the decade as a whole, with Courtney Love later calling it "the defining moment for the alternative generation"). It told the story of high school students defined by their stereotype and clique: The Valley Girlish and pampered Claire, macho wrestler Andrew, nerdy Brian, new wave outsider Allison, and tough delinquent John. They are all serving detention on a weekend day in 1984, supervised by an assistant principal, who's a lunkhead, authority figure (both mean and feckless). The unimaginable happens: Characters open up (marijuana helps) to one another about their fears, the limits of the stereotypes they inhabit, and the suffocating peer pressure they face. They all realize they hate their parents. Brian admits to considering suicide;

John talks about an abusive family situation (played by Judd Nelson, who tries a bit too hard to be the next James Dean or Marlon Brando). And after this confessional therapy session, more of the unimaginable: Allison, now coiffed and cleaned up by Claire, kisses Andrew; Claire and John kiss and pledge their love. It was screwball comedy set in 1980s suburbia.[14]

But the story doesn't capture the feeling of the movie, which consistently breaks out of its conversational narrative into dance scenes backed with new wave music. The kids sneak out of the library, where their detention convenes, and as they run from the vice principal through high school hallways, they dance in synch with songs. The movie bursts with new romantic, new wave hits: the Scottish band Simple Minds' "Don't You (Forget about Me)" plays as the kids run through the school halls, and Karla DeVito's "We Are Not Alone" blasts while the kids dance, do cartwheels, play "air guitar," smash windows by shouting into them, and jump around the library. Most viewers would feel like they were watching MTV, and they were. All of these songs played on MTV as "videoclips" from the movie (depicting slices of a story scrambled together). Synergy perfected, MTV's power confirmed. After all, around the time of the movie's release, "68 percent of music video viewers chose a movie to see as a result of cable exposure." Universal Studios based their marketing campaign on videoclips played by MTV. Hollywood showed that in the course of a half day, kids could overthrow peer pressure and the clutches of cliques (Claire and John especially). Rebellion was made happy and easy here, packaged by Hollywood, the booming record industry, and MTV.[15]

* * *

The year 1985 had a different feeling to it from the earlier 1980s. Joe Carducci, who had worked at SST for about four years now, suggested to the Minutemen that they were getting a good amount of college radio play (it was true for Husker Du, too). They had tried that whole video thing. And now maybe, if they toned down their high decibel and high up the neck squealy guitar, they could acquire more college radio play that could leapfrog them into the mainstream. The band agreed to the challenge (and even got a friend to play trumpet to soften their sound a bit more), and in February they started to record a record they'd call *Project Mersh* (short for commercial).[16]

The whole thing came across as a joke, heaving with postmodern irony. The album's cover included a D. Boon painting of three hip capitalists together, with one saying, "I got it! We'll have them write hit songs!" The best song on the EP would become "King of the Hill," a rather profound lament about American foreign policy, and the closest to a hit the band could have expected. In the song, Boon analogized the kids' game—where one person stood on a hill and fought off others who tried to take his place—to the bullying tactics America had used in Central America. "We would run with all our might, push the king off to take the hill, and to learn who was king and who makes the better serf." The judgment came swift: "And I can't believe it was good for humankind. And I have to read the lies between the lines." The band even made their second video for the song, showing D. Boon wearing a king's crown and barbecuing and gorging himself with buckets of food. Kids try for the top, as Boon tosses a single hotdog for them to swarm after (the "let them eat jellybeans" idea). Eventually Boon faces a coup d'état and is dethroned, his rotund body rolls down the hill as kids run away.

When the Minutemen released the *Project Mersh* EP, its sales were about half of what *Double Nickels* earned. So much for going mersh.

* * *

Around this time, a fairly major punk publication called it quits. *No Mag*, edited by Bruce Kalberg and his partner Ewa Wojciak, had started in Los Angeles, during that first wave of punk bands like X, the Germs, and the Bags (most of those bands got coverage in early issues). Unlike *Slash*, *No Mag* managed to sustain itself as the 1970s turned to the 1980s, although like most zines it was sporadically published over those years. Kalberg took inspiration from the secessionist movements in modern art during the first years of the twentieth century, especially the surrealists, cubists, and expressionists. He believed—and here he was close to Raymond Pettibon—that punk could draw from that past in developing its own aesthetic. So, from the beginning, Kalberg was interested in publishing artists who he believed related to the music he wrote about (or more often, interviewed bands about). He consistently published artists like Gary Panter, Pettibon, and Fred Tomaselli (those who Matt Groening had anointed leading punk visual artists). He sometimes gave way to a politics of shock (the sort practiced also by the "cinema of transgression" promoted by directors Nick Zed and Richard Kern), including close-up images of hardcore porn and mangled bodies (the televangelist Jimmy Swaggart once waved copies at his television audience and condemned moral depravity, giving Kalberg a brief burst of popularity). As his interest in imagery grew, so grew the range of that imagery.[17]

In its last double issue (perhaps a nod to the Minutemen and Husker Du), *No Mag* offered a long story about Gary Panter, who the previous year had released his comic book *The Invasion of the Elvis Zombies*. There was an interview with organizers of the Zero Gallery, who had held a Raymond Pettibon exhibit. There were references to other artists who seemed to contribute to a punk aesthetic—especially the work of Sue Coe and Savage Pencil. There was discussion of bands like Thelonious Monster, among others. Standard fare so far. But then a reader encountered not bands but Europa's Fashions and the "scene at 'the Lingerie,' 'the Zero,' and 'the Veil,'" where people were "dressing up" and "living their fantasies." And then another story about "Texas Tattoo Terri," described as "a different kind of hairdresser." This double issue looked like a slummed-up version of Andy Warhol's *Interview* or maybe even *People* magazine. In sifting through the last issue, a reader could watch a transpiration, moving from what the critic George Melly called "revolt into style."[18]

* * *

The March 25, 1985, issue of *People* magazine showcased Jennifer Cunningham, a woman with roots in the Los Angeles punk scene. She was chief organizer of C.A.S.H. (Contemporary Artists Space of Hollywood), a venue that started up in 1981 for punk shows, film showings, and art exhibits (including the one that Matt Groening had praised three years ago). Like other clubs, Cunningham's faced police raids that she found exhausting and disruptive. She shut the club down as a venue for punk shows and moved in a different direction.

Any treatment in *People* brought with it natural trepidation. A previous portrayal of punk in this glossy magazine had appeared two years ago. It focused on the New York scene (not surprisingly) and a performance by the False Prophets, going for the shock value. Words like "menacing" and "mayhem" and "scatological" and "aggression" rang out to readers in that story. Some of the kids who were interviewed said ridiculous things just to screw with the reporter (some punks read the article out loud during performances, mocking its dire tones). Now with Cunningham in 1985, things were quite different.[19]

Cunningham had turned C.A.S.H. from a punk venue into a Hollywood agency. She was getting punk kids small-bit roles in movies—including by this point *Fast Forward*, *Protocol*, and one of Reagan's favorites, *Ghostbusters*—and popular television shows—like *Hill Street Blues*, *Night Court*, and *Cagney and Lacey*. She realized that punks were exotic-looking and could add flavor to films and television shows and get paid in return (and she'd skim earnings as the agent). *People* explained in its typical way of turning everything into a trend: "Cunningham . . . knows that although punk is passé in the era of the yuppie, the leather and chains crowd is still in demand for big and little screens." The story then quoted Cunningham, "Punks are hot now. It might be dead as a cultural movement, but it's marketable in the mainstream." She hoped that her well-behaved punks on sets could change how they had been "portrayed" (the *Quincy–Class of 1984* syndrome). It was like what Shawn Stern had tried to do with the television news show after Mendiola's, or what Charles M. Young had tried to do a year before on the Donahue show—to push back against a reigning stereotype. Except that in the case of Cunningham, she was turning punk into a decoration. Punk was no longer a threat, it was a "look" that entertained and whizzed by viewers' jaded eyes. A style made for a world of images playing out on screens.[20]

* * *

At the same time *People* hit newsstands, Raymond Pettibon released another one of his small zines, this one entitled *Short Teats, Bloody Milk*. He had grasped something that was going on at the moment in the world of consumer capitalism. One illustration showed three packs of cigarettes, Vantage, Kool, and Salem. Then the words: "Which is America's Best? Our system of healthy competition lets you decide." The use of the word "healthy" was, of course, something to make a reader laugh. But what also made a reader laugh was the idea of choice, mediated by large corporations. This was Reagan's vision of monopoly capitalism: That large multinationals could give us whatever our hearts desired with "choice" granted by big business, "alternatives" offered by capitalism itself. Pettibon had caught and distilled the feel of 1985 as the hyperkinetic consumer capitalism Reagan had dreamed of was becoming a reality.[21]

<h1 style="text-align:center">XXX</h1>

The Impossible Protest

> I don't know what I've been told, have no chance of growing old;
> if Ronald Reagan has his way, we'll all die for the USA.
> —Chant heard at numerous protests[22]

Tim Yo's "peace punks" hadn't quite disappeared as he thought. They were busy organizing for a nationwide series of protests against the nuclear arms race and the possibility of World War III. They named April 29 "No Business as Usual Day" (NBAU). It was a cross between the War Chest Tour protests from the previous summer—direct action and affinity groups—and the dark mood Brown University students expressed in their suicide pill referendum. The national call for action sounded militant, nearly desperate: "They won't listen to reason. They won't be bound by votes. The governments must be stopped from launching World War III, no matter what it takes."[23]

Actions, some sizable, took place in San Francisco (the site of NBAU's national office, no surprise), Chicago, and New York City. The movement even made it to the small burg of Ann Arbor, Michigan, the college town where Bill Brown wrote from. Here a little group of suburban peace punks organized what they called "No Briarwood As Usual." Briarwood being one of the many regional malls that dotted the suburban outskirts of town. Organizers equated the zombie-like quality of mall shopping with passivity toward the nuclear arms race. They explained, "The shopping mall embodies a creeping sameness conquering diversity bit by bit." They wanted to interrupt the controlled experience of a shopping mall as an act of art (the way No Way Muffo had two years before). Stephan from the False Prophets had explained the spirit of NBAU to Jello Biafra this way: this wasn't "a grim demo people had out of guilt" but rather a "celebration of subversion and alternative thought in action." Punks publicized the day of protest by handing out leaflets and selling copies of their zine, *Going Under*, at "schools and at concerts."[24]

Only about twenty-five people showed up. April 29 was a Monday, and most kids didn't see the point in playing hooky for the sake of protest. Those who did show up prepared to rush the mall to perform a die-in, and as they did, mall security guards immediately swept down on them. All twenty-five were booted from the mall and pushed back into the parking lot. The guards were in their legal right, seeing as there was no protection of free speech in Michigan's shopping malls, conceived as private rather than public space (in contrast to California). The protest was over within minutes, and zombie culture proceeded.[25]

* * *

Meanwhile, *RAD* zine in Morro Bay, California, was also trying to keep up the cause of protest. After bemoaning Reagan's landslide, they turned their attention and energy to a local protest against the building of Diablo Canyon, a nuclear power plant. They published articles about the risk of radioactivity, arguing that "Diablo Canyon Nuclear Power Plant will produce each year an amount of radioactive waste products equal to that produced by 2000 Hiroshima bombs." Editors engaged in multiple protests, including civil disobedience during the summer of 1984, where police had to shut down an attempted blockade. They also used more conventional outlets for activism, like attending public hearings about the plant (much in the spirit of the *P.E.A.C.E.* compilation booklet— embracing a variety of approaches). They wore "Charles Stokes Fan Club T-Shirts" (Stokes was the first to whistle-blow about the threat of radio-active dangers at Diablo). They circulated their zine at high schools and leafleted shows to get support, often organizing punk benefit concerts for the Abalone Alliance, the chief organization doing most of the leg work.[26]

The same month as the NBAU action, *RAD*'s editors learned that the power plant was on-line and up and running. And the Abalone Alliance, having been protesting for about four years now, went belly-up. DIY pro-test was defeated.[27]

XXX

Yuppie Thump Thump Keeps Churning

> Take a look at the Eighties and find that nothing succeeds like success.
> It's the credo of the decade. Scratch the surface and find, not cynicism
> of the Seventies, but a self-conviction that is the only faith left. The new
> Romantics hyped their way out of a recession. The government hypes self-
> help. Poke the decade a little deeper and find . . . the collapse of resources
> and ideals. Success and failure: these are the motors that drive the decade.
> —*The Face* magazine, May 1985[28]

The Palladium nightclub opened in May 1985, with lines of people trying
to get in, stretching entire blocks in lower Manhattan. Just four years earlier, the director of the Palladium, Steve Rubell, had been in prison for tax
evasion. As chief executive of the most famous discotheque of all time—
Studio 54—Rubell had, during the late 1970s, "skimmed" the cash his discotheque took in (he supposedly fondled himself in big pools of dollar
bills). He found illicit drugs for his celebrity clientele (Quaaludes and cocaine mostly). He lied and covered up. But seemingly few who came to
dance at the Palladium cared about Rubell's past, so long as he delivered
what they wanted—a large yuppie outpost in a city that thump thumped
to an electro-synth soundtrack and Wall Street money.[29]

Rubell studied his competition and ripped off his predecessors at
Danceteria and the Limelight. He installed a dance floor larger than his competitors. He emphasized recorded music over live performances. Instead of
the gigantic wall mirrors that framed the inside of Studio 54, so that people
could watch themselves and one another dance, Rubell had twenty-five syn-
chronized video screens throughout, again topping his predecessors. Unlike
Studio 54, located in mid-Manhattan, the Palladium was on 14th street,
close to the "downtown" scene in the East Village. The Palladium made hipness a ticket for entry, policed by a doorperson who determined who could
and couldn't get in. Yeh Jong Son had once been doorperson at Studio 54
and saw it as an honor to do the same at the Palladium. As she recounted
to *People*, her main aim was to cut down on "Grade C's," meaning those "not
fashionably aware, not that classy . . . usually out-of-towners . . . from Staten
Island and New Jersey"; on the other hand, celebrities were admitted for
free. Those locked outside would be the same type who couldn't appreciate

all the art that populated the club. Rubell felt it necessary to hire an "art adviser," to fill in space not occupied by video screens.[30]

Most of the paintings purchased came from the exploding East Village art scene—two artists particularly, Keith Haring and Jean-Michel Basquiat, who were on a stellar rise to fame at the time. Both had started as graffiti artists whose works appeared on the streets and subways of Manhattan. In his earlier years, Basquiat was a high school dropout who sold his postcards and painted sweatshirts on the streets of SoHo, while playing in a "no wave" band called Gray and sleeping on friends' couches. Haring came to the city in 1978 to study at the School for Visual Arts, when he first came across Basquiat's spray-painted art, calling it "literary graffiti," a "condensed poetry which would stop you in your tracks and make you think" (akin to Pettibon's one-liners). Haring started to draw bubbly looking characters on subway station walls. As the 1980s moved apace, both graduated from street art to the East Village galleries, and from there to the more expensive SoHo neighborhood scene and finally a nationwide art market that boomed with the rest of the economy. Basquiat moved into the arms of the SoHo gallery maven Mary Boone, who could get $20,000 for one of his works by 1984. Haring too was selling his goods to the highest bidder. As the *Village Voice* columnist Michael Musto would write, "Haring has clearly masterminded his ascent from the subways to the world of big business." And as Steve Rubell explained to the *Washington Post* close to the opening of the Palladium, "Artists are the stars of the 80s. They are as rock stars were to the 60s and designers were to the 70s."[31]

Art was selling, and so too was real estate in the East Village, the area of Manhattan the Palladium banked up on (paralleling the yuppie invasion of Haight-Ashbury documented earlier by *Newsweek*). Rent prices seemed to correlate with Basquiat's and Haring's sales, all skyrocketing. The art critic Craig Owens had noted the connection between the celebrities of the art world doing well and the gentrification of the East Village. He ridiculed "the East Village scene as a 'surrender . . . to the means of the marketplace' and as a 'culture-industry outpost' where 'subcultural' forms are fed to that marketplace as products of consumption, their vital resistance to dominant culture thereby defeated." The small galleries that dotted the East Village were now farming grounds for the bigger leagues—for Wall Street traders as much as the Palladium. By October 1985, the alternative publication the *East Village Eye* pronounced a funeral: There was no counterculture left in the East Village. "East Village art is dead. . . . Greed and envy have disbanded our beautiful community. . . . The East Village will continue to exist as the simulacrum of itself." The neighborhood once known to be a seedy and affordable area for artists and writers was now branded as hip and trendy, a whiff of bohemianism giving way to aftershave. In other words, yuppies were winning the culture wars of the 1980s in the heart of Manhattan. Their victory blared in the lines of people waiting to get into the Palladium every night.[32]

* * *

It blared nationwide in Madonna's "Virgin Tour" of April to mid-June that year. Madonna had become "blockbuster," with her album *Like a Virgin* (which included "Material Girl") charting to number one, chock full of hit singles and thus making it like *Thriller*, with its ability to sustain itself in sales after its original release. Madonna made the cover of *Rolling Stone* in May, where there was a story on one of the two movies she recently starred in—*Desperately Seeking Susan* (a screwball comedy, which contrasted the colorful, hip East Village with the conformity and boredom of suburbia, where the major character resides). She also appeared in *Vision Quest* (where she performed as a singer in a bar set within a teen romance story). Both movies' soundtracks included Madonna songs, of course, and when the videoclips from these films hit MTV, it goes without saying they added sustenance to her synergy, her appearance seemingly everywhere. When she announced the "Virgin Tour," sponsored by Warner Bros. Records, tickets sold out immediately. Her audience was mostly young girls who decked themselves out in the Madonna look (dyed blonde hair, leather jacket, and midriff exposed), and like those attending Bruce Springsteen concerts, they were, in the words of James Wolcott, "the best-behaved rock audience . . . ever seen," genuflecting to their idol. Though Madonna found the transition a little overwhelming, she had moved successfully from the performance and dance floor space of Danceteria to the world of playing live in sports arenas to throngs of fans.[33]

Which might explain why she could stick to her choice for her opening act—the Beastie Boys (which supposedly stood for "Boys Entering Anarchic States"). The band came out of the tiny club A7 and the Lower

East Side Rock Music Appreciation Society (LESRMAS) that included bands like Reagan Youth, Heart Attack, and Kraut. Started in 1981, the band sounded like many a thrash band, but by 1983 they had "crossed over," not into heavy metal but rap music, becoming white boy hip-hop. Just at the right moment, too. With roots going back to the early 1970s and the dangerous streets of the South Bronx, where disc jockeys spun and "scratched" records for local audiences gathered often in community recreation centers, rap moved to mainstream success, most clearly with Run DMC going gold by 1984. The Beastie Boys cultivated their own image as white outlaws, macho as could be, and even booted their one-time drummer, precisely because she was a woman and therefore didn't "fit into" the band's "tough-rapper-guy identity." They didn't go over well with Madonna's audiences, but they offered another example of how in 1985, what was once underground now seemed moving into the overground.[34]

XXX

The Yuppie Brat Pack

> The overgrown children who still protested bedtime, the drunk, the doped up, the hangers on, the hangers out, the young, the hip, the insomniacs, trying to make the night, the party last forever. Dancing, dealing, falling on each other, falling away from each other.
> —Emily Listfield, *It Was Gonna Be Like Paris* (1984)[35]

The celebrity face of yuppie-dom by June 1985 was the "Brat Pack" of actors, two of whom starred in John Hughes's *Breakfast Club*, Emilio Estevez (who was also the star of *Repo Man*) and Judd Nelson, and one of whom hadn't, Rob Lowe. All three found themselves part of a portrait article that ran June 10, 1985, in the pages of the (very yuppie) *New York* magazine. The threesome's movie was announced in the piece: *St. Elmo's Fire*, expected to be the yuppie movie of the summer.

The movie was something of a disaster, a sprawling soap opera as much as a coming-of-age romance about a group of Georgetown University graduates. The film tried to cover seven main characters, flitting from one to another, becoming bloated (often characters felt listless, even though the movie announcement claimed, in clichéd form, "The passion burns deep"). It captured multiple affairs between the characters, a good amount of infidelity, cocaine abuse, failed romances, multiple gatherings at the characters' favorite bar (which provided the title of the movie), and even an attempt at suicide on the part of a character named Jules (played by Demi Moore), a shopaholic who loses her job and can't pay off her credit card—truly a yuppie's worst nightmare.

If the movie was too self-conscious and didn't work, the portrait in *New York* did. It captured the high-glam element of this group of male actors, what it called "a roving band of famous young stars on the prowl for parties, women, and a good time." The author of the piece, David Blum, followed the threesome around, first as they hung out at the Hard Rock Café, where "the prettiest of the girls would find some excuse to walk by the table," eyeing the three men "as languorously as they could." Clearly, these weren't just actors playing yuppies, they were actual mega-yuppies who lived for a nighttime club culture. We learn that Emilio Estevez had "summoned a young writer he'd always wanted to meet, Jay McInerney," the author of *Bright Lights, Big City*, the yuppie novel of 1984 (Estevez hoped to turn the novel into a movie and was working with the director of *St. Elmo's Fire* to do so). McInerney joined the Brat Pack for the evening, and soon they decided: "There's a punk club open tonight across the street. Let's go." They face a line of people waiting to get in, but when the manager learns of their presence, they are immediately summoned inside (one line-stander says, "I guess we're not as important as *they* are"). Here the story turns comical. "McInerney, somewhat of an expert on nightclubs—his book is filled with tales of late-night New York crawl— remarked upon entering the crowded club that there did not seem to be a VIP lounge on the premises." A VIP lounge at a punk club, now that was funny. The man who wrote about club-hopping and name-dropped Danceteria now explained what he must have meant by his enigmatic statement about "the inevitable disappointment of clubs."[36]

* * *

John Hughes's movies, *St. Elmo's Fire*, and McInerney's novel all helped explain a new generation coming into adulthood in the 1980s (what would eventually be termed Generation X). There was an upstart in that cause, Bret Easton Ellis, whose novel *Less Than Zero*, was becoming the summer read of 1985, helping to grow a "literary brat pack."

Less Than Zero was indebted to the punk scene of Los Angeles (there are mentions of bands like Fear and X), but more so to the new wave, yuppie culture that was cresting in 1985 at places like the Palladium or in the haunts of the Brat Pack out west (like Hard Rock Café). The book has two of its characters shop at a "punk clothing store" (a boutique), and others get their knowledge about new wave fashion from reading *The Face*.

The novel follows the central character, Clay, who has returned to Los Angeles from his first year in college in New England. He is searching for Julian, who has become addicted to heroin while turning tricks as a male prostitute. Clay drifts from party to party, witnessing the depravity of snuff films (where women are raped and killed) and a dead boy's corpse rotting in an alley. After seeing a gang rape of a twelve-year-old girl, Clay recoils. His drug dealer Rip lays out the ethics of the situation: "What's right? If you want something you have the right to take it." Which sounded like a yuppie slogan.[37]

Clay passively records events and carnage, signifying a desensitized and anesthetized culture. Characters zone out on MTV, usually helped along with Quaaludes. Images spin past viewers losing their critical acumen, turning them "blasé," to use Kim Gordon's term. A culture of screens depleted any depth or emotional resonance for characters. That's accentuated by the experience of driving the highways of Los Angeles, high above surface streets and where people are "afraid to merge" (there are parallels here to John Shirley's "city" with its collective unconscious). To cope, Clay grows indebted to the teachings of Deborah Harry, pronouncing his own philosophy of life: "If I care about things, it'll just be worse, it'll just be another thing to worry about. It's less painful if I don't care." Ellis managed to fuse here the classic novel of youth, *Catcher in the Rye* (1952), whose central character dreams of becoming a deaf mute able to turn off the world, with Blondie's 1979 breakthrough song, "Heart of Glass." Realizing he had written what some might call a "dispassionate, cold book" he struggled with the novel's moral implications. One critic suggested that Ellis's novel "concealed a harsh, stony faced puritanism" (a similar critique was often lobbed at the straight edge movement). Ellis himself thought of his novel was "a very political book in the sense that it is 'anti-eighties youth.'" Ellis had tracked the aftermath and the dark underbelly of the yuppie revolution, a hedonism devouring its young.[38]

XXX

Nostalgia Already?

> Nostalgia does not entail the exercise of memory at all, since the past it
> idealizes stands outside time, frozen in unchanging perfection.
>
> —Christopher Lasch[39]

It was to be "Revolution Summer." But it wasn't always clear what that meant. For some punks in the nation's capital, it suggested that their scene had grown bleak and needed a revolution from within. Things felt like they were falling apart. Skinheads kept coming to shows; violence and destruction erupted in a scene historically free of such things (especially in comparison to Los Angeles). A show held at the Wilson Center early in 1985 symbolized what was wrong. It featured Madhouse (an artier band than most and headed by Monica Richards), Marginal Man (a local D.C. group two years old), Corrosion of Conformity (a metal-punk fusion band from North Carolina), and the old timers, the Circle Jerks (who had appeared in *Repo Man*—as did its new member, Alexander Schloss—and who were about to release their fourth album, *Wonderful*). The show was big, with some reporting that 1,000 kids showed up, and it turned violent, with slamdancing breaking into fights (like scenes from *Quincy*), and then vandals punched through a partition, causing a hefty amount of damage. The decision came swiftly: The Wilson Center, a not-for-profit venue, would no longer host punk shows (the co-founder of Positive Force, Mark Andersen, would call this event "the end of an era"). Around the same time, a new venue for punk opened called Sanctuary Theater. After violence erupted there, it too banned punk.[40]

Such bleakness showed up on a Dischord release during the summer of 1985. It was a Minor Threat song that had been recorded two years earlier, around the time the band broke up (it required that Ian MacKaye lay down a new vocal track before it could be issued). "Salad Days" had been performed at one of the band's last shows, and now it would find its way onto vinyl. The song combined the spirit of a Jeremiad—with its sense of a fall from grace—with hopeless, near-existential despair about the art of revolt. Its opening line was pure nostalgia: "Wishing for the days when I first wore this suit. Baby has grown older. It's no longer cute." It verged on a punk rock version of *The Big Chill* with a *then-we-were-good-and-now-we-are-confused* feel to it. MacKaye complained about "too many voices" that have "made me mute," a sense of things getting out of hand. And then MacKaye sounded a jeremiad that promised no redemption, admitting that he had grown "soft and fat" and was "waiting for the moment it's just not coming back." Now was the time to "dwell upon our memories." MacKaye almost sounded like those oldsters at *Capitol Crisis* who clung to nostalgia when faced with "teeny punks" like him. The song's conclusion came in the line "the core has gotten soft."

For *The Rocket*, the record's release symbolized going to "the vault," retrieving something from the past. It certainly suggested that a moment had passed, that perhaps things weren't progressing or getting better but slipping into turmoil and lack of direction. Whether that attitude could energize a revolt within a revolt—what "Revolution Summer" suggested at the time of the record's release—wasn't clear. There were still those "greener pastures" that kept MacKaye staying on, but more telling was just how much it felt and sounded like a requiem, especially as listeners heard chimes throughout the song. Still, MacKaye talked about a potential "renaissance of sorts" within the D.C. scene, clinging to his ethics of personal politics. "I'm not into political protest," he told the *Washington Weekly* at the time, "but I do consider my life a protest." Personal politics and individual acts—which after all were the bases of his earlier straight edge philosophy—now seemed the only hope for bleak times.[41]

But at the time, there was a group pulling in different directions.* Positive Force—the name borrowed from the Nevada organization formed a year ago—now had a collective of sorts set up in Washington, D.C. The group consisted of punks and some nonpunk high school–aged kids (with some oldsters in the mix as well, and fairly balanced in terms of men and women) who had started to try to politicize the D.C. scene and put an emphasis on protest politics—the sort that MacKaye rejected. The group met on a weekly basis in a Quaker meeting house near Dupont Circle, which also hosted the Washington Peace Center (an organization that had worked on antidraft and antinuclear activism). Some had participated in the counter-inaugural protests in the streets of D.C. at the beginning of the year. A report about Positive Force in the zine *WDC Period*, #12 (probably published sometime in late summer) provided a long list of actions the group had organized: they held a local Rock Against Reagan

---

* A new musical group had also started up in D.C. by this time: Beefeater. They had classic political songs like "Assholes" and the hilariously mocking song "Fred's Song (Skinhead Guys Turn Me On)." The latter roasted the skinheads who were fast invading the scene.

event (different from the nationwide tours of 1983–1984), engaged in the NBAU day of national protest against World War III, held numerous teach-ins about an array of subjects, including the situation in Nicaragua and the nuclear arms build-up, and organized a protest where they threw rotten vegetables at limousines that entered a D.C.-based event known as the "Arms Bazaar," essentially a trade show for defense contractors.[42]

The group sought out direct action for young people, like feeding the homeless at soup kitchens usually organized by the Community for Creative Non-Violence (CCNV) or designing a political zine (entitled *Off Center*) distributed to high schools in the area. This sort of "hands-on" politics synched to the culture of DIY. Meanwhile, the conversations at the weekly meetings ranged widely and went well beyond immediate practical tasks as they took up the merits and demerits of pacifism and the philosophy of anarcho-communalism. There were open discussions about the Situationist International, prompted in part by Bill Brown's writing. Both pie-in-the-sky conversations and immediate acts promised a way to move beyond the "personal politics" offered by MacKaye.

XXX

A Summer of Secrets

Can we win this time?

—Rambo

On June 30, 1985, thirty-nine American hostages were released after TWA Flight 847—which had flown from Cairo to Athens and intended to debark for Rome on June 14—was hijacked eventually to Lebanon (landing three times in Beirut and twice in Algiers). This hostage crisis created a chaotic and frightening two weeks, with terrorists armed with grenades and a pistol commandeering their difficult to follow route. At one point, the hijackers murdered Robert Stethem, a US naval officer. But with the help of Israel (who promised to release hostages the terrorists wanted to liberate), diplomacy won the freedom of many of those who had suffered a frightening ordeal.

That evening, Reagan went on national television to announce victory. As he practiced his words in front of live microphones he had another "we begin bombing" slip. He let out this line, "Boy, after seeing 'Rambo' last night,

I know what to do the next time this happens." That was a tip of the hat to Sylvester Stallone, who cowrote and starred in a movie playing in theaters at the time, *Rambo: First Blood Part II* (the top-grossing film for the month of June). The movie told the story of John Rambo, who in the previous release (Part I) had been sent to prison. He is popped from the clink in order to pursue a renegade operation to document the existence of prisoners of war (POWs) held in Vietnam. He's directed to take photographs if POWS are found (coached by a bureaucratic, desk-sitter, Marshall Murdock). This doesn't stop Rambo from freeing POWs, but soon he's thrown into a Russian-controlled prison. Of course, Rambo escapes, blowing up everything he can. With POWs at his side, he returns to base camp and Marshall Murdock, who had been actively suppressing knowledge of the number of POWs. Rambo's final monologue amps up the patriotism that courses through the movie, when he explains that he "wants for our country to love" those veterans who served in Vietnam "as much as we love it."[43]

This was a recipe for a hostage crisis? Perhaps for the seven American hostages still held in Lebanon, who Reagan would cite in his speech? Or perhaps the dream of sending one mercenary who distrusts diplomacy and projects pure physical strength? Or maybe it was the desire to refight the Vietnam War, which Rambo asks if "we" could "win" this time (to which his commanding officer says "this time it's up to you"—meaning that if grunts on the ground took things into their own hands and ignored all those wimpy politicians, they could refight the war and win this time, for sure).

Oddly enough, there seemed a Rambo referent who worked for the White House and who the press was making inquiries about. Oliver North, who worked for the National Security Council (NSC), was a man who—unlike Stallone—served in Vietnam. Returning in 1974, North suffered a "mental breakdown" (what could have been labeled post-traumatic stress disorder, a term first used in 1980). He embraced fundamentalist Christianity and became a hardened cold warrior who—like Stallone—believed the Vietnam War could have been won if the politicians hadn't gotten in the way (Peggy Noonan, a Reagan speechwriter, said he "had the sunny, undimmed confidence of a man who lacks insight into his own weaknesses"). He was the perfect fit for a White House committing itself to covert action.[44]

* * *

North's presence helps explain the secrets that were being hushed at the White House during the summer of 1985. Through backdoor discussions, Robert McFarlane, head of the NSC, concocted another way to get the remaining hostages out of Lebanon: Send missiles to Israel, which would ship them to Iran—a nation Reagan rebuked for sponsoring terrorism—which needed them for its war with Iraq. Since the hostage-takers in Lebanon were allied with Iran, armaments shipped might free the remaining hostages.

McFarlane hoped to find a way to have this sort of activity benefit not just Iran but also the Contras—Reagan's "freedom fighters"—in their fight against the Sandinistas. Here's where North entered the dim picture. By early 1985, North was creating "the Enterprise." He approached countries for funds to purchase weapons for the Contras (Saudi Arabia was an early supporter). He would generate revenue by upping the costs of those missiles sent to Israel and then Iran. These earnings could be skimmed and earmarked for Reagan's "freedom fighters" in Nicaragua.

As Reagan went under the scalpel on July 13, to remove part of his colon, his minions scurried. When the president returned to the White House, McFarlane and Reagan agreed on a go-ahead. By August 20, 1985, close to a hundred TOW missiles (tube launched and optically tracked) were sent to Israel, eventually passing into Iran's possession. The press that same month inquired about what Oliver North was up to, and the administration ensured reporters that there was nothing wrong or illegal going on. A shroud surrounded the White House, led by a man who knew he couldn't have accomplished what he wanted if he had gone to Congress—full of pesky politicians slumped in Vietnam malaise—or to the public (his pollster, Dick Wirthlin, back in March, showed him that up to 90 percent of Americans opposed US intervention in Latin America, and that included supporting the Contras). As Tim Yo put it in July 1985, "popular opinion" was against "clandestine operations," so Reagan was "trying to find 'private' ways of funding the mercenaries [Contras]." When Reagan discussed the project in his diary, he said the whole thing was "complex" and "I won't even write in my diary what we're up to." It had become better to protect against leaks and to spin the matter. Maybe something in the world of popular culture would come their way to boost their spirits of hushed secrecy.[45]

* * *

It came the month the first hostage was released, in the form of *Invasion U.S.A.*, a movie that mixed *Rambo* and *Red Dawn* together. This time Cubans invade the United States through the porous borders of Florida, led by a Soviet operative named Mikhail Rostov. Chuck Norris plays a one-time CIA operative named Matt Hunter, who leads the counterforce against the Cubans after invaders burned down his Florida house and killed his friend (a hero must always look reluctant). Audiences watch as the Cubans rip through America's suburbs, blowing up ranch houses on leafy streets. The Cubans even plan to destroy a shopping mall during the Christmas season. Here Norris puts his foot down, Rambo-style, by entering the mall and killing all the guerrilla soldiers, single-handedly. The battles continue, and soon citizens are arming themselves to drive away the guerrilla forces. Hunter tricks Rostov, in a final twist, and then blows the Soviet agent away.

Norris saw his role as providing a pillar of Reaganism. The tough-guy actor explained, in homespun language, "everything is so doggone negative. We didn't win the Vietnam War, and we didn't really get much out of it. But the fact is, Americans went over there and fought." He cited a movie he had help make the year prior, *Missing in Action* (remarkably similar to *Rambo: First Blood II*). His lesson fit the more recent *Invasion U.S.A.* He projected a "positive attitude" that aimed at the national bummer of Vietnam. Norris, like Stallone and North, explained, "We could have won the war in the very early stages if we had gone in to win it." Optimism was the key. Norris hated "depressing movies . . . that deal with tragedies." He liked Reagan's worldview. The president was honest and straightforward. "What I like about Reagan is that he doesn't pussyfoot around. Like Grenada." The president, Norris cheered, "says what he feels." And taking his inspiration from Reagan, Norris blurred the line between entertainment and politics—showing off why America could win just about any war it wanted to.[46]

XXX

The Industry Rag Takes Note

> Those among us who aspired to the role of stars . . . had to be rejected.
> —Bill Brown quoting SI writing[47]

Rolling Stone magazine had become perhaps *the* force in the world of the rock industry and celebrityhood since its founding in 1967. At its helm sat Jann Wenner, who had originally conceptualized the magazine as a voice for the burgeoning counterculture in San Francisco. From being a Kennedy Democrat who dated debutantes, Wenner transformed himself into a one-time student radical, engaging in the Free Speech Movement at the University of California–Berkeley and some early protests against the Vietnam War. He also came to love the psychedelic music played at the Fillmore (Bill Graham's club), especially the Grateful Dead and Jefferson Airplane (his biggest fondness, though, tended toward the British bands, especially the Beatles and the Rolling Stones). As the bright side of the sixties crashed with the murders of Altamont and Charles Manson, *Rolling Stone* limped along into the dreary 1970s. By 1977, the publication's offices moved from San Francisco to New York City. In the process the magazine got cozier with the music and movie industry, now celebrating "hip" celebrities and consistently putting faces of stars on its cover (like Madonna's), and printing more advertisements as much as researched and journalistic stories.[48]

By the 1980s, Wenner resembled other yippie-to-yuppie figures, like Jerry Rubin, Jim Fouratt, and Jane Fonda. He loved sports cars, cocaine, and lavish excess. In 1985, Wenner played himself in the summer movie *Perfect*, which centered on a journalist (played by John Travolta) who covered the second most important yuppie institution next to the nightclub: the workout gym, where wanna-be Jane Fondas dressed in tights and did calisthenics (the movie posters copied the font and style used on the cover of *Rolling Stone*, trying for synergy). At the same time, Wenner started to rethink his politics. Though most of his writers remained liberals, he found Reagan's "sunny" performance as entertainer-in-chief difficult to debunk and admitted he benefited from Reagan's tax cuts on the wealthy. As his magazine's readership continued to grow, closing in on one million, he grasped his new demographic. An in-house poll suggested that the "under twenty-five readership voted two-to-one for Reagan in the 1984 presidential election." A new ad campaign was launched for the magazine, playing up the yippie-to-yuppie theme. Ads would show a marijuana roach clip with the word "Perception," then a picture of a dollar bill, with the word "Reality."[49]

All this suggests why Wenner wanted nothing to do with punk. To him, it was all just underground sputters that rejected his nostalgic memories of his hippie past. When the Sex Pistols came to America, Charles M. Young insisted that he put Johnny Rotten on the magazine's cover. Wenner quickly noted that sales of that issue tanked.[50]

But things started to change at *Rolling Stone* in 1985. First was a positive review of *Zen Arcade* and *Double Nickels on the Dime* in the February 14, 1985, issue (nearly eight months after both double albums were released, showing off just how in the know the magazine really wasn't). Then, in the July 18–August 1 issue of *Rolling Stone*, the headline blared "Punk Lives." It was Bill Brown's worst nightmare come true, where stars were picked off from a movement for media treatment. It probably wouldn't have happened if Black Flag's transformation from 1984 to 1985 hadn't occurred. As Greg Ginn started to admit that his long guitar solos were indebted to the Grateful Dead—the quintessential dinosaur band from the Haight-Ashbury scene of the 1960s—*Rolling Stone* pounced. The kids had done what they had to in order to get into the magazine's pages: genuflect to the baby boomer and hippie bands of the past. "Primal punk is passe," wrote Michael Goldberg in the article. He elaborated in condescending tones:

> The best of the American punk rockers have moved on. They have learned how to play their instruments. They have discovered melody, guitar solos and lyrics that are more than shouted political slogans. *Some of them have even discovered the Grateful Dead.*

This preceded a portrait of "the new punk rock, 1985," the sort that channeled the old rock 'n' roll of the past, including the psychedelic scene *Rolling Stone* held close to its heart. Black Flag sat at the helm of the story, along with the Minutemen, the Meat Puppets, and Husker Du (plus a portrait of the independent label SST, which released these bands' records).

Maybe, the story suggested, the underground was becoming overground. The question lingered though: Would any one of these bands make it onto a major corporate label? Asked directly, Bob Mould of Husker Du responded, "When you tie yourself down to a major label, you give up all your individual control over things. You become part of a machine." Bill Stevenson, who was playing drums for Black Flag at the time, said, "I won't sell my art for money. . . . I'd rather kill myself." If Jann Wenner had read these final lines of the story, he must have rolled his eyes or at least smirked and thought to himself: *those kids still don't know what they're talking about.*[51]

* * *

Another unspoken reason for the *Rolling Stone* story was the competition the magazine faced by the spring of 1985. A new music publication had emerged called *Spin*, a slick publication that followed *Rolling Stone* in putting celebrity visages on its covers. But *Spin* aimed to discuss "underground" music that *Rolling Stone* wouldn't (it was joined by *Option* magazine, similar to but not as slick as *Spin*). Reading *Spin* was like watching MTV, with short stories about bands whizzing by one after the other (next to loads of advertisements). The July 1985 issue, for instance, included stories on the Beastie Boys (following their tour with Madonna), as well as REM, Naked Raygun (from Chicago), Flipper (the sludgy San Francisco band who had refused Penelope Spheeris their music), and Asbestos Rockpyle (an industrial and political band). All of these stories sat next to one about the Eurythmics. Henry Rollins contributed a piece that took down Bruce Springsteen. And on the cover was a bare-chested Sting, the leader of the band the Police and now a British, new wave sex symbol of the moment. The jumble was the message: This was not *Rolling Stone*, lost in its boomer nostalgia and its tradition of long-form journalism, this was more like MTV. The magazine wanted to pull what was underground overground and create more choice in the marketplace of rock journalism, while helping build the celebrity culture it necessarily had to nurture.[52]

XXX

"Cyberpunk" Becomes a Thing . . . *to Walk Out On*

> I don't want to belong to any club that will accept me as a member.
> —Groucho Marx

In late August, the North American Science Fiction Convention (NASFiC) convened in Austin, Texas, and offered numerous panels, including one on "Cyberpunk." That term had been used back in 1983 by the novelist Bruce Bethke and then emerged in a late 1984 treatment in the *Washington Post*.

Now it was being proclaimed a "movement" that demanded attention, at least according to Bruce Sterling. If the size of the Texas panel was any indicator, the movement was growing. The plan was to have Lewis Shiner (the author of *Frontera*, a book unfairly overlooked when released the same year as *Neuromancer*) moderate a panel that included Sterling, John Shirley, Rudy Rucker, Pat Cadigan (the rare female participant), and Greg Bear (author recently of *Blood Music*). There was a notable absence here—the "star" artist at the time, William Gibson (*Neuromancer* had moved front and center in any discussion about "cyberpunk"). When the audience discovered that Gibson wasn't appearing, there were murmurs of disappointment that foreshadowed trouble.[53]

Things went off the rails quickly. First, Lewis Shiner faced off against the science fiction and comic book writer Ric Meyers, who suddenly claimed he was the moderator and started to berate the remaining panelists. Meyers, even though the same age as Sterling and Shirley, played the role of young upstart holding court, chastising what he saw as a bunch of oldsters proclaiming themselves leaders of a movement that existed only in their imagination. People on the floor started screaming how the whole thing wasn't about cyberpunk at all, just self-promotion for the panelists. Others on the floor demanded they be recognized as cyberpunks—thus, it started to sound like self-promotion all around. Chaos mounted, and Rudy Rucker, who stood his ground, felt he faced a "lynch mob." And then Sterling and Shirley—both boiling with anger—walked out with Shiner. Those who remained behind continued to shout down what they perceived less as a movement and more an initiative of hype and promotion. Sterling appeared to betray that point when asked about the panel's meltdown six months afterward. He called it a "big cause celebre" and a "neat publicity stunt." Perhaps one that he could capitalize on with his forthcoming compilation, *Mirrorshades: The Cyberpunk Anthology*.[54]

The incident said something about the state of "cyberpunk." At times, Sterling argued that the movement was "relentlessly intellectual." For it wanted to tackle "serious issues and serious problems" via futuristic writing. Especially one big idea: "You can't just continue to import technological innovation into society without having all sorts of bizarre after-effects that spread throughout the whole body of society." Sterling himself had explored this theme in his recently published *Schismatrix* (1985). A complicated story that spanned over a long time-frame, Sterling's novel depicted a future in which society had colonized space, escaping earth, which now suffered from wars and melted ice caps (the ecological ruin of what today would be called global warming). Looking back on his long life, the central character Abelard Lindsay "mourned mankind, and the blindness of men, who thought that the Kosmos had rules and limits that would shelter them from their own freedom. There were no shelters." The novel—like the work of John Shirley—provided a warning about where society was heading, poignant considering that, at this same time, the Reagan administration was touting its plans for the Strategic Defense Initiative (SDS, aka "Star Wars"), which found support from conservative science fiction writers like Jerry Pournelle. Sterling described Pournelle and his followers as "naïve space enthusiasts" who banked on the "Pentagon payroll." From this perspective, cyberpunk constituted a dystopian form of social and political criticism in a world overbrimming with confidence and optimism.[55]

But this sort of feisty intellectualism rubbed up against Sterling's self-pronounced desire to become a celebrity. He gushed in admiration for William Gibson, especially for what he called the writer's "pop star cool." Sterling explained, "I . . . think of myself as a pop star, rather than a writer with a capital W." All the more reason why some at the Texas panel believed that any and all talk about "cyberpunk" was merely branding and marketing, nothing more than an advertising stunt with a catchy name. And when Sterling published his edited anthology of "cyberpunk" a year after the panel had turned to mayhem, he would admit that "the movement" was "paralleled throughout Eighties pop culture," including the central institution of the "rock video." At the same time, it drew on "the subversive potential of the home printer and the photocopier," a tip of his hat to his own independent zine, *Cheap Truth.* Somehow these two very different things—one representing corporate culture, the other an initiative of DIY—constituted a movement within the "Eighties," a decade that Sterling now labeled an "era of . . . integration." A better term here might have been "absorption."[56]

XXX

More Turning Back(s)

The essence of being human is that one does not seek perfection, that one is sometimes willing to commit sins . . . and that one is prepared in the

end to be defeated and broken up by life, which is the inevitable price of
fastening one's love upon other human individuals.

—George Orwell[57]

Backs turned on the movement elsewhere. Jeff Bale turned his on *MRR*
so he could attend graduate school (he would eventually earn a PhD in
history). His departure grew out of rethinking his political views and the
work he had done while at *MRR*. If Ian MacKaye offered nostalgia, Bale
had little more than despair. He was emphasizing punk's noirish tendencies
and confessing a sense of futility.[58]

Pessimism wasn't new to Bale's thinking. His dark views on human nature always clashed with his hope for some sort of anarcho-social democratic form of politics. That tension mounted until it snapped in 1985. Two
years after leaving *MRR*, he would cite his sense of despair as a reason to
quit: "Most people are short-sighted and self-centered." Here was a growing
refrain that Jello Biafra had charted when he doubted the possibility of anarchism (Bale and Biafra had numerous discussions throughout the years).
Bale felt "very pessimistic about the possibilities of accomplishing anything."
He also worried about an authoritarian streak on the left—including what
he saw as Tim Yo's certainty about his ideas. Those things kept bothering
him during his years at *MRR*—a sense that things were more complex than
the zine let on. Much of his increasing doubt sprang from the sheer fact that
he was growing older and finding it a struggle to know "how you're going
to pay the rent and how you're going to eat." He found himself developing
more slack for others, while noting a puritanical streak among some punks.
Bale had started to question the notorious punk principle to never "sell
out." Like George Orwell, he rejected those who thought of themselves
as purified from society's pressures (in writing on Ghandi, for instance,
Orwell explained that "sainthood is . . . a living thing . . . human beings must
avoid"). As bands received treatment in *Rolling Stone* and *Spin*, he couldn't
begrudge them. "I don't really give a shit," Bale explained, "if a band makes
music that isn't as underground as it once was, as long as it's still good. If
it's still got some power and some guts." This was effrontery for Tim Yo's
DIY ethic. For Bale, everyone had to make a living, even if they dreamed
of a more just society sometime in the future. As he put it to Tim Yo: "life
doesn't get any easier, it gets harder and harder, you're faced with less and
less options; it just becomes very difficult to find anything you can do to

make life satisfying or bearable." This conclusion pushed Bale to jump ship and seek out another way to stoke his intellectual curiosities.[59]

Bale's departure upset Tim Yo, who saw it as a big loss. There would no longer be those articles with twenty-book bibliographies. There were to be no more long-winded, late-evening discussions about politics and ethics between two men who could hold their ground. The bright side for Tim Yo was that Bale's departure coincided with the recruitment of Martin Sprouse, a young editor of the zine *Leading Edge*, who moved from San Diego to the *MRR* office in Oakland just as Bale left. But Sprouse's decision to make the move provided mixed messages. His last issue of *Leading Edge* in 1985 spent a great deal of time discussing the difficulties of DIY culture. One organizer of shows confessed to Sprouse the tribulations of renting a hall, putting down a security deposit, getting insurance, dealing with city ordinances, and taking care of security. Sprouse himself documented the challenges of a harried editor trying to publish a zine on his own. He was attracted to the more stable and established structure he'd find at *MRR*. But a reader of the news couldn't help wonder about those zines that couldn't sustain their DIY ethic, including the now defunct *Leading Edge*.[60]

XXX

Celebrity Politicians

> We care a lot about the welfare of all the boys and girls
> We care a lot about you people 'cause we're out to save the world, yeah!
> —Faith No More (1985)

The month of September 1985 witnessed more celebrity activism, following in the footsteps of "We Are the World." This time Farm Aid. Willie Nelson, John Mellencamp, and Neil Young were chief organizers, egged on by Bob Dylan, who at Live Aid (a British concert held to raise funds for world famine and featuring Madonna) argued that musicians should do something for the sake of people in their own backyard rather than around the world. Eighty thousand people showed up for a concert in Champaign, Illinois; the list of performers seemed to go on for pages. Farm Aid, though, was not just a show about the plight of family farms in an era of agribusiness and rising mortgages. Willie Nelson saw it as more of a political thing, and he followed up by bringing small farmers to testify before Congress and push for legislation. Unlike Michael Jackson's "We Are the World," Farm Aid became a political act, although facilitated by celebrities in the music industry.

Willie Nelson, though, had nothing on First Lady Nancy Reagan, who was perfecting the art of turning celebrities into moral leaders. Her cause, as always, was stopping drug abuse, especially among young people. Her "Just Say No" slogan was first heard in 1983, when she cameoed in a television series, *Different Strokes*. She was looking for more ways to spread the message. She knew enough about how culture worked, that only a video could win the hearts and minds of a generation swimming in the images and sounds of MTV. And so she got to work on "Stop the Madness," a music video, qua public service announcement, that started to be filmed in September 1985 (it received circulation later in the year).

The video started with images of cocaine being cut with a razorblade and then an arrest and then two kids about to shoot heroin. . . . It was even more hyperkinetic than most fare on MTV. The music built as the video started to mimic "We Are the World," with one celebrity after another singing a different line of "Stop the Madness" (this included a young Whitney Houston and La Toya Jackson, Michael's sister). The lyrics to the song were even more perfunctory than expected: "Drugs are causing pain and everyone's a loser in this deadly game." The best scene follows a young woman who gets up from a chair in her living room and shuts off the television, walks to a closet door, and opens it only to find a dealer with a big suitcase full of drugs. She hands the dealer money, and then a poster on her closet door comes alive. It's David Hasselhoff, star of the television show *Knight Rider*, who lip-synchs, "Stop the Madness." She freaks out and turns away, and viewers can only wonder what's scarier for her, having David Hasselhoff come alive in her bedroom or the drugs she purchased. Our poor protagonist gets freaked again by spotting Stacy Keach peering out of her refrigerator and repeating Hasselhoff's line (especially funny considering Keach had been busted for cocaine possession the previous year). And after the celebrities have been rolled out, Nancy Reagan enters the picture, lip synching the three words "Stop the Madness." And then there she is again in the White House with a bunch of boys and girls at her side. The video ends with kids dancing on urban streets, conjuring visual memories of

Michael Jackson's Pepsi commercial. Kids and adults then swarm together and point to the Goodyear blimp that hovers above them and offers the words "Stop the Madness." It felt like blockbuster culture—wherever people turned, they faced the song's pounding message—or, better yet, like Big Brother.

Nancy Reagan exclaimed as she shot her scenes for the video, "I may have a career as a rock star." The problem was the whole thing was ham-fisted, knock you over the head, finger wagging at its essence. It foreshadowed the "War on Drugs" that Reagan would later spell out more forthrightly, which would center less on educational initiatives, like the First Lady's video, and more on empowering the Drug Enforcement Administration (DEA) to crack down on and incarcerate dealers (filling prisons up). Still, Nancy Reagan's video symbolized a key feature of Reaganism—to govern via entertainment. It had a simplicity to it: Addiction cured via three simple words pronounced over and over again, playing amid an ocean of images.[61]

* * *

As production of "Stop the Madness" chugged along, Ronald Reagan welcomed Singapore's prime minister, Lee Kuan Yew, to the White House on October 8. But diplomacy didn't seem the essence of the dinner. In the words of the *Washington Post*: "As seems to be the custom these days at the Reagan White House, celebrity guests took much of the focus off any serious problems confronting the administration." This evening, it was especially a visit from Michael J. Fox and, more formidably, Sylvester Stallone.[62]

Reagan had always admired Michael J. Fox as Alex Keaton on the long-running television show *Family Ties*, where he played the preppy who clashed with his hippie parents (the show coincided with his performance in the awful movie *Class of 1984*). But there was also his hit 1985 summer movie, *Back to the Future*, where Fox played Marty McFly, who, with the help of "Doc Brown," a nutty scientist exploring time travel, launches himself from the present back to the year 1955. McFly wants to arrange that his (then future) father hooks up with his mother so that his present life will unfold as it has. Reagan watched the movie at Camp David while convalescing from a colon operation. Mark Weinberg, a speechwriter for the president, remembered that there was a point of awkwardness when a young Doc tests out McFly's claim to live in the future. He asks McFly who the president was in 1985. McFly says Ronald Reagan, to which Doc goes off on a tirade of laughter: "Then who's vice president, Jerry Lewis? I suppose Jane Wyman [a Hollywood actress and Reagan's first wife] is the First Lady? . . . Jack Benny is secretary of the Treasury!" But Reagan ignored that quip and focused on the optimistic conservatism the film carried (when at the White House, Fox apologized to the First Lady about the embarrassing scene). Weinberg recounts that, "The president commented on . . . how this was the type of movie that Hollywood should be making as opposed to some of the more controversial, violent, or adult themed films." The line that he zeroed in on came out of the mouth of Doc when everyone is safely back in the present. As Doc gets into his time travel car for the last scene in the movie, he turns to McFly and says, "Where we're going, we don't need roads." Reagan loved that line and incorporated it into his State of the Union Address the next year, when he celebrated the present as "a time of rousing wonder and heroic achievement."[63]

If Reagan had to edit *Back to the Future* to make it fit his dreamland, he didn't need to with Sylvester Stallone's work. This was pure red meat for Reagan—Stallone serving as the perfect substitute for the now deceased John Wayne. The actor projected an overt anti-intellectualism fused to Cold War patriotism. John Rambo, for instance, could barely mumble complete sentences. Reagan had already endorsed Rambo's version of solving foreign policy issues—brute force and covert operations. And it's possible that Stallone was chafing a bit, wishing the dinner at the White House could be postponed to the end of November. By then his ultimate work of Reaganism—*Rocky IV*—would be playing in theaters. He knew the president would love it.

Rocky IV would perfect the Reagan aesthetic. It told the story of Rocky taking on the machine-like Soviet boxer Ivan Drago, after Drago has beaten and killed Apollo Creed (once Rocky's foe, now his deceased friend). Rocky travels to the USSR to set up his training camp in what looks like America's western frontier (it was filmed in Wyoming), where big mountains hover over snowy plains. He preps by lifting logs and pulling a loaded dogsled (again, the hearty pioneering American). Drago, to hammer home the contrast, uses a computer to prime his body, along with steroids that help forge a "perfectly bred athlete." And then, as with every *Rocky* movie made, the audience watches a long, drawn-out fight. At first, Drago's machine-like execution throttles Rocky, but then Rocky lands a lucky punch and cuts

Drago's eye. Some in the Russian crowd start rooting for Rocky, who winds up knocking the Soviet machine out in the final round. Rocky is wrapped in the American flag. The crowds roar. It was like an echo of the summer Olympics, "USA! USA!" This was the emotional patriotism that Reagan loved, the sort that made his eyes tear up. America as the underdog capable of anything.

When the film was released in November 1985 (Reagan wouldn't watch it until January), Stallone cooked up a plan to visit the White House again. He'd bring with him the very pair of boxing gloves he wore when he played Rocky. It would be presidential politics and Hollywood fused perfectly. The problem was that the idea jumpstarted what Michael Jackson's earlier appearance at the White house had. The lawyers went berserk. Future Supreme Court Chief Justice John Roberts jumped into the fray again to kibosh the whole idea. Roberts scolded, "*Rocky IV* is a current Christmas season release, and [United Artists studio head Jerry] Weintraub's offer seems a rather transparent publicity stunt to promote the film. With the Rambo comments and White House dinner invitation, the president has already given Stallone more than his fair share of free publicity." Reagan took the advice, but he probably didn't like hearing Roberts's language about limits—the sort that got in the way of blending entertainment with governance and giving voice to dreams.[64]

XXX

Hearts, Not Minds

> Spies, moving delicately among the enemy, the younger sons, the fools . . .
> Ambiguously signal, baffle, the eluded sentinel.
>   —James Agee, *Let Us Now Praise Famous Men*[65]

In November 1985, the Intercollegiate Broadcasting System (IBS) held its West Coast Conference. Major labels—Warner Bros., RCA, Polygram— sent their representatives, hoping to find ways to crash the world of college radio, those down-the-dial stations where there was, by law, no corporate pressure to play certain records (college radio was supposed to have an educational not a commercial function). College radio was once described as "the last bastion of the 1960s progressive-free-format FM," in which a deejay could decide for him or herself what to play during the course of the day. The Federal Communications Commission (FCC), as one zine pointed out back in the early 1980s, "prohibits college radio stations from receiving money through advertising," making it independent from the entertainment industry (and often helping out local punk scenes).[66]

David Ciaffardini, who edited a zine called *Sound Choice*, entered the IBS convention with a sense of unease. He armed himself with a stack of flyers that rang out: "Protest the Corruption of Non-Commercial Radio. DON'T BROADCAST MAJOR LABEL RECORDINGS." He knew this protest stood on shaky grounds. Major corporate labels had all the power, especially as the industry rebounded from its slump and witnessed more consolidation. Ciaffardini glumly confessed, "Your average punk band with a record out on their own label will never be able to compete with the large companies who can afford to be on the phone to college station personnel, offering them dozens of free records and concert tickets and subtle hints about possible jobs awaiting them after graduation." A shift occurred over the course of the last few years, Ciaffardini reasoned, from thinking of college radio as marginalized to "record companies realiz[ing] what a profitable bonanza college radio can be." He bemoaned how college students running the stations could get snowed by being given the chance to interview stars. And with the advent of the compact disc (CD), major labels would coax airplay by shipping the station a free CD player (rather expensive at the time), plus recent releases of their own CDs. "Another important, very effective method of manipulation is demanding," Ciaffardini explained, "that in order to receive promotional records, stations must subscribe and 'report' to at least one of several college radio journals, such as *CMJ* (*College Media Journal*), *Rockpool*, or the *Gavin Report*. These journals charge huge sums of money for subscriptions and are filled with page after page of record company advertisements (from companies that can afford the extremely expensive ad rates)." Most shocking of all to Ciaffardini was how the University of Florida (Gainesville) had dropped its noncommercial radio license entirely and turned itself it into a for-profit station, run not by students but "professionals." The future of nonprofit radio and DIY labels looked bleak from his perspective.[67]

* * *

Around the same time as the IBS conference, a young man named Jack Rabid assumed the position of "Alternative Section Editor" for *Rockpool* magazine, one of those industry publications Ciaffardini had cited (prior to Rabid, the editorial position was held by the writer Terry Tolkin, who, by some accounts, *created* the term "alternative"). *Rockpool* was often associated with the New Music Seminar, the organization that had hosted Madonna a year before. The magazine was started in 1979–1980 by Mark Josephson, who had previously worked at RCA as a College Radio Promotion agent. *Rockpool* set out, according to a story in the *Village Voice*, to "service club and college-radio deejays with imported and independent records; it soon became the principal organ of communication for new music, tabulating a dance club chart, based on the playlist of member deejays." *Rockpool* published "charts" that "reflected retail sales and college radio play." This helped "quantify" for bigger companies what was happening in the upper echelons of the American underground. The publication had reports written in classic American sales language. Take this 1983 *Rockpool* swarm of words as an example, "Once again the DKs are savaging retail, entering the national chart at number 2, and coming in top 5 in all our regions. No radio or club play to speak of, but you can expect college radio to play the record when they return from their vacations. The Dead Kennedys phenomenon remains intact." You could almost hear the baritone voice of confidence. It wasn't music talk, it was business and advertisement talk.[68]

Rabid was quite a snare for *Rockpool*. He had serious bona fides. Having grown up in the suburbs of Jersey, he moved to the East Village of New York City to earn a BA from New York University (which he completed in 1985). While there, he dove into the city's punk and hardcore scene, the one that gave rise to the Beastie Boys, among others. He played drums in Even Worse, a band whose name reflected a good sense of humor. He quickly soured on the scene and dropped out by 1982, bored with thrash music and tired of getting hurt when slamdancing erupted. He still had his own zine, *The Big Takeover* (the name of a Bad Brains' song), that he had started in 1981. Rabid would type it up and distribute it himself—early issues often ran as a single sheet. By late 1982, he started to charge for the magazine and upped his circulation to 7,000 (each issue seemed larger than the last). He would editorialize against slamdancing and too many anti-Reagan songs. In 1983, for a brief stretch, he started to write a column for *MRR*, giving him more national notoriety. What really bugged him about the stale category of "hardcore" was how it got dumped onto who played more interesting fare than formulaic thrash music. He pointed to the Minutemen, No Trend (a band from the D.C. area outside Dischord circles), D.O.A., Sonic Youth, and Savage Republic. All of those bands had their own style and persona, and he celebrated their diversity. By the summer of 1984, he was glorying in the fact that the Georgia-based band REM had hit the American Top Twenty. The underground music was starting to bust through, he thought, and he hoped to push it in that direction. In February 1985, he lashed out at critics—like those at *Rockpool* and the New Music Seminar—who thought they were discovering something that never existed before. Once the Replacements, a sloppy drunk band from Minneapolis, signed with a major (Sire), Rabid couldn't help but wonder where this attention had been when bands like Minor Threat and TSOL were sweating it out.[69]

The invitation from *Rockpool* must have felt a bit like, *OK, here's your chance to avenge the past. Tell the industry who we should pay attention to.* Some things stayed the same and some things changed in what Rabid would write about while perched at *Rockpool*. He'd continue to support the usual suspects, Husker Du, the Minutemen, Black Flag, the Meat Puppets, and the like. But now he wasn't a fan so much as a sifter, discerning quality and possibilities of breaking through. Non-industry-based fanzines could pillory bands they thought deserved it (a negative take on Black Flag was becoming a chorus in zines during this time), but that was not *Rockpool's* role. The purpose was to deem a band's worthiness of being considered for a higher level of promotion that major labels promised. No longer did the independence of the production and distribution of music, in the strictest sense, matter for Rabid; there were now new criteria. From 1985 into 1986, his criteria included music that felt "sincere" or was made from the "heart." Tricky business. While most fanzines focused on releases coming from noncorporate, independent, and DIY labels (an objective fact unlike the wavery term "sincere"), Rabid now saw his role as promoting "alternative" bands so they could get the chance to sign with a major. What was "sincere" and made from the "heart" sounded rather vague. It suggested "hipness," or being in the know about the product. DIY's democratic base of distinction—that anyone could create their own culture—now turned into subjective claims of authenticity. Rabid believed in a leverage of choice that could work in a consumer culture dominated by large corporations. He explained, "Not having sufficiently thought about possible alternatives, individuals often are unaware that they do have a better choice." Here was the philosophy of "alternative" culture—certainly no longer a "counter" culture. It was more like Pettibon's tongue in cheek statement: "Our system of healthy competition lets you decide."[70]

* * *

Rabid's interest in promoting independent music as "alternative" synched to a change in the world of independent record labels. By 1985, numerous independents stood strong: Alternative Tentacles, Dischord, Homestead, Touch and Go, and Toxic Shock, among others. The latter expressed its ethic this way: "We look at Toxic Shock as a service not as a capitalistic enterprise. After we meet our expenses any profits are put back into our operations." In addition, there were independent distribution networks created by the likes of Mordam Records (started in 1983 by Ruth Schwartz from *MRR*) and the older British company Rough Trade, which was showing some signs of wear and tear (its San Francisco record store witnessed a walkout of the collective's employees in 1984). Like Toxic Shock, Rough Trade saw itself as an independent "service," a collective, not a capitalist effort. Or consider Husker Du explaining how they ran their label, Reflex, in 1983: It was run "out of Mould's spare room" but managed "to secure national and international distribution for all their releases." Mould explained: "We've got a checkbook, a telephone, a desk, and a typewriter. I have a file cabinet and Greg does all the artwork. That's it." And that seemed the sort of typical DIY feel behind independent labels and distributors.[71]

By 1985, though, some independents were reconceiving their role. Lisa Fancher at Frontier Records, a label she organized out of her house (and that had released the likes of the Circle Jerks, TSOL, and the Adolescents) had refused to sell her label to a major. But she did sign "acts to one album deals so they could use the label as a stepping stone to a major record label." The term "stepping stone" sounded a lot like farming ground, like those East Village art galleries that pronounced what was hip for wealthy patrons to consider for purchase. Fancher also noted a trend where major labels set "up distribution and production alignments" (what had originally screwed over Black Flag with its *Damaged* album). Sometime before July 1985, Fancher signed "a distribution deal with Island Records, a major label." The major label could follow how much product was moving and thus identify bands worthy of *full* major support. Underground acts could be sized and fitted.[72]

So, in 1985, the punk rock world was being watched more and more closely. Not because it was a threat, not because of the violence that was seeping into numerous scenes by lunkheaded skinheads, but because it might provide an "alternative" to what the music industry had offered to date. The spies from outside (or *once* outside) were starting to take notes, reading the pages of *Rockpool* and forging alliances with independent labels. They hoped to reach new markets by crashing their way into college radio stations. The ethic here was not to nurture culture from below but to widen and diversify the multitude of choices given from above—from the skyscraper offices of major music industry outlets. MTV had already made youth culture into a perpetual choice of image after image, or what was really advertisement after advertisement, flattening out everything into a blurred stream (in October 1985, the Dead Kennedys released the album *Frankenchrist*, which included the blistering song "MTV Get Off the Air," with its line that video DJs' "job is to help destroy what's left of your imagination"). MTV created a world where, Greil Marcus suggested, there was no room for negation—for rejecting the corporate structure itself. Instead, it heaped more categories onto the corporate plate. The British critics Simon Frith and Howard Horne would observe two years later, "In the end, the very smoothness of new pop consumption implied that all cultural goods and consumers are equal, that none of them could be subversive."[73]

XXX

"After the First Death, There Is No Other"[74]

> Another movement, it's just another fad. Like a cry for help in a world gone mad.
>
> —Agent Orange

Three days before Christmas, D. Boon of the Minutemen died. He was sleeping in the band's van when his girlfriend fell asleep at the wheel and lost control. Boon was thrown out of the vehicle and instantly broke his neck. When the story spread, the phones at Black Flag's practice space and SST rang off the hook, with people trying to find out what had happened. Henry Rollins started to answer the phone by saying, "Hello, D. Boon hotline." One time, it wasn't a random caller but Mike Watt. And Rollins remembers Watt, shaken and sad, saying, "No more Minutemen. It's all over."[75]

It wasn't hard to read symbolism into the death, even if that seemed slightly overblown. Boone didn't just symbolize youthful hope (he was twenty-seven at the time of his death), he collaged together all the different elements that constituted the "punk rock world" of the 1980s. Not only did he front the Minutemen, a band who toured "econo" and thus helped carve out the DIY network that spread throughout the country, but he also called for a "band on every block." Barbara Rice at *Truly Needy* in D.C., in announcing Boon's death, called him a "practicing populist." He was known now for handing out "U.S. Out of Central America" leaflets at shows, protesting Reagan's foreign policy (as it turned toward secrecy and covert operations). He used his artwork on the Minutemen's record covers, when the job hadn't been given to Raymond Pettibon. He wrote, edited, and distributed his own zine, *Prole*. He balanced seriousness in lyric matter with humor. He hoped to provoke thought through his art rather than impose his own political views. Right before his death, he was preparing to work with Richard Meltzer, the oldster rock journalist who had emceed the Sex Pistols show in San Francisco in 1978, on an album (Boon always liked having others write songs for the band, since that accentuated the communal feel he had found in the "punk rock world"). The Meltzer project was one of many things that Boon never got to realize.[76]

* * *

Slightly before *Rolling Stone* got around to reviewing *Zen Arcade* (showing off the publication's slowness in discovering 1980s punk), Husker Du released the album *New Day Rising* on SST. Many critics praised it for synthesizing a slower pop feel together with the band's notorious distortion and angular sound, screaming still but with melody. *Spin* had praised the album for being "loud" and "angry" (there was plenty of torn vocal chord sound to it) but at the same time "accessible" and not as "overreaching" as *Zen Arcade*. The band seemed to be—or so it was hinted—at something of a breakthrough.[77]

When the *Rolling Stone* story about the band appeared in the summer, Husker Du was topping the college radio listening charts (the sort that *Rockpool* published) with their summer single "Makes No Sense at All" (the B-side was a cover of the theme song for *The Mary Tyler Moore* television show). They even found some commercial radio play. "Makes No Sense at All" was slowed down in tempo from previous songs, becoming much more "pop" with a slight distort on the guitar. The song was melodic and jangly, not frenetic or edgy. Its lyrics suggested almost a conservative tone: "Is it important?" Mould asks, "You're yelling so loud—makes no sense at all." And this clincher: "Makes no difference at all." It sounded like a rejection of those spastic, shouted protest songs against the military-industrial complex that populated *Land Speed Record*, released more than three years earlier. The video for "Makes No Sense at All" showed the band smiling and goofing off and shots of downtown Minneapolis. The video of the *Mary Tyler Moore* theme song showed the band taking a department store escalator together. Both got a good amount of play on VH1 (short for Video Hits One), which had emerged in 1985 in competition with MTV (and was hosted by Warner Communications). The song sat at the top of the charts for an extended period at *College Music Journal* (*CMJ*).[78]

Though some liked the single (obviously), the zine world often shuddered at "Makes No Sense at All" and the band's appearance in *Rolling Stone* and *Spin*. One zine out of Medford, Massachusetts, called *Bang* (among its writers was Al Quint, who was editor of *Suburban Voice*) felt "cynicism" when listening to "Makes No Sense at All." "Because the rage that has been a key element to their sound, no matter how subtly it existed, seems subdued." Barbara Rice, the perceptive editor at *Truly Needy* in D.C., worried, "My sincere hope is that they don't lapse into slightly more charged REM-like fade-into-the-wallpaper pop." Little did these critics know what lay around the corner.[79]

Like their counterparts, the Minutemen, Husker Du was growing discontented with Black Flag. In an interview with the zine *Uncle Fester*, Mould complained about the "whole power trip" Black Flag was on. Perhaps that "power trip" was best dissected in a letter to *MRR*, in November 1985, that recounted a recent Black Flag show in Walla Walla, Washington. Though opening bands Tom Troccoli's Dog and SWA allowed the audience to share the stage with the performers, when it came to Black Flag, huge bouncers suddenly appeared and pushed kids off the stage. The letter writer complained about "Holy Henry hitting me in the face with his microphone," and a paralysis among the fans at the show, "brainwashed by their rock stardom." To add insult to injury, MRR printed a flyer that announced Henry Rollins would "sign autographs" at Bleecker Bob's Record Store in Manhattan (the same man who couldn't comprehend why anyone would want his autograph). Add to this a mock-up of a Black Flag gig circa late 1985:

You're in the auditorium. Expectations are high, spirits soaring. Suddenly the band launches into their first song. It's an instrumental, heavy metal thunder, and its [sic] 20 MINUTES LONG. Fist [sic] fly up, bics dot the darkness.... Then ... out dances the singer. He's tight pants, no shirt, a perfect bod. . . . And who is this band? Journey? Van Halen? Molly Hatchback? Why no, you little tinkertoys, it's Black Flag.

That description might explain what Mould meant when he complained about the band's power trip.[80]

At the same time, Husker Du was growing increasingly frustrated by Black Flag's label, SST. They would release the Flip Your Wig album in September on the label, and though it offered more jangly tunes that seemed sure college radio hits (the album contained the single "Makes No Sense at All"), SST didn't promote the album sufficiently for the band. Though they had dissed major labels since the Clash had sold out to CBS eight years earlier, Husker Du followed in the footsteps of the drunk punk band, the Replacements, and signed with a major label, Warner Bros. The A&R recruitment of Karin Berg worked its magic here. She headed up what Warner Bros. called its "Alternative Marketing Department," which sounded like the position Rockpool editor Mark Josephson had as a "College Radio Promotion Agent" at RCA earlier. The decision was quite a leap into the belly of a corporate behemoth, into what Op had once called "a communications and entertainment conglomerate with nonmusic operations in television, motion pictures, cable TV, publishing, toys, electronic games (Atari) and sports (Cosmos Soccer Club)." Husker Du had signed not just to a major label but a "megagiant."[81]

And they didn't do so with a good deal of grace. When a fanzine asked why the band had gotten so much recognition of late, Mould explained, "We're probably the only thing that's worth talking about this year. . . . I just like to think that we're better than all the other bands." In the December 1985 issue of *The Rocket* (Seattle), Grant Hart, the band's drummer, noted, "I wouldn't be bursting any bubbles by telling you that a lot of the stuff on SST is of inferior quality." Still, they were defensive about the whole thing, telling Jack Rabid—who wrote a story about punk for none other than Andy Warhol's *Interview* in 1986—that the band "may have just signed to Warner Brothers," but they were "still self-managed, self-produced." Whatever the case, they were clearly turning their backs on the independent labels and the DIY culture that helped shape and form who they were (and the scene they helped build in Minneapolis). They now stood above the communal networks punk had built, both locally and nationally. They were now "stars," picked off by big business, the sort that Bill Brown had warned about. Husker Du was now *corporate* material. And soon the band learned what that meant. Karin Berg started to press them to "shine it up" and hire a "'real' booking agent" and "real manager." The band's hope of retaining control was slipping out of their hands, as they faced what they should have expected.[82]

* * *

There's an artifact of this moment, namely the December 1985 issue of *Spin* magazine. On the cover, Bob Dylan's face gazes out at a reader (so much for "new music"); within there are a slew of advertisements for alcohol, cigarettes, and Casio recorders. There's also a "long" story and interview with Husker Du. It spazzes out with the over-the-top language *Spin* was known for—the language of hype. Husker Du becomes a bunch of "bo-hunks" who constitute "the second or third greatest group of rock 'n' roll superheroes in the world." During the interview, Mould talks about how the Huskers constitute "a diamond in the rough," suggesting again that the band stood above those still mired in the DIY world. He called the band the "ultimate pop band" and rejected the politicization of punk he recently witnessed (and that he partially helped originate on *Land Speed Record*). "I don't want to influence anybody's political thinking," he explained (that might be the same logic behind the lyrics, "makes no difference at all").

Now with the band on a major label—a megagiant at that—it felt that a chapter in punk had passed.[83]

Sadder, that same issue of *Spin* also included a piece that Byron Coley wrote about the Minutemen. In retrospect, it read like a love letter to the deceased, having been sent to press before Boon had died. Coley gushed about the band's humorous and sophisticated lyrics that "thrust a naked, pimply rump in the face of that New America taking shape under Reagan's malignant tutelage." He noted the band's recent attempt to go "mersh." Coley placed tongue in cheek and wrote, "Canny capitalists that they are, the Minutemen's drive to snare a buck included such sure-to-please titles as 'Futurism Restated,' 'Mutiny in Jonestown,' and 'Dreams are Free, Motherfucker.'" Even the band's video for "King of the Hill"—another attempt to go mersh—wouldn't find play on MTV, Coley suggested. "Its message is potent, direct, and far too radical for these namby pamby times." Which made D. Boon's death feel that much worse. An end of sorts.[84]

EPILOGUE

PUNK BREAKS AGAIN . . .

In the mid-80's something was fuckin' happening; no one was saying anything about it, and it died and it went away. But it did happen, and it was much bigger than the hippie movement. . . .

—Glenn Branca[1]

A straight line can be drawn from the signing of Husker Du to Warner Bros. to where this book started—in the blockbuster success of Nirvana in the early 1990s. Having formed in 1987, Nirvana released their first album, *Bleach*, in 1989, with Sub Pop, the very same *Sub Pop* that in 1980 was a small zine that championed anarcho-communalism and screamed with derision against the "CORPORATE MANIPULATION OF OUR CULTURE." By 1989, Sub Pop had transformed itself into an independent record company ready to hype Seattle's "cross-over" punk-metal bands. Sub Pop became, in the process (much like Frontier earlier), the farming ground for the big leagues—in this case for Geffen, who had allied recently with MCA to become a huge player in the music industry, 100 percent corporate. Nirvana signed with Geffen for their second album (*Nevermind*), but not before Sub Pop secured royalties from *Bleach* (which, of course, would balloon after the band hit number one, making the independent label rich, at least briefly). Indeed, the founder of Sub Pop, Bruce Pavitt, would recognize history at work when he commented that *Candy Apple Grey*—Husker Du's first release on Warner Bros. in 1986—"with its huge production . . . was an obvious predecessor to *Nevermind*."[2]

First time as tragedy, second time as farce . . . "Stars" had been picked from the underground, turned into overground acts, expected to become hit factories (in the case of Nirvana that happened, at least for a few years; in the case of Husker Du, it didn't pan out so well). Here was the recipe for "alternative rock" that would dominate the 1990s but whose roots could be gleaned in the mid-1980s workings of the New Music Seminar, the "alternative" chart reporting in *Rockpool* magazine, and the pep talks provided by Jack Rabid and *Spin* about music with "heart." Independently made music was no longer a threat to the corporate music industry; it was now a supplement, a "choice," as the term was used in Raymond Pettibon's humorous 1985 drawing. DIY's ethic of producerism shifted to DIY as a space where bands learned their chops (how to play their instruments, the saying went) and tested the waters before making it where they all wanted to go—big corporate record labels.

Pondering his rock star success, Kurt Cobain, Nirvana's lead singer, hoped new fans who were flocking the band's way would be "exposed to the underground by reading interviews with us. Knowing that we do come from a punk rock world, maybe they'll look into that and change their ways a bit." Nice try. Why would anyone "look" or "expose" themselves to the "punk rock world"? It was being handed to them on a corporate platter, broadcast on MTV. And a platter that filled up fast, as major labels started signing other Seattle bands left and right. When Seattle had been sucked dry, it was onto California for the "'East Bay' pop punk" of Green Day and a whole host of other bands who had been connected, once, to a DIY experiment known as the Gilman Street Project in Berkeley, started in 1986 by none other than Tim Yo of *MRR*.[3]

Ironically, the way Michael Jackson saved the music industry from its doldrums of the early 1980s, Nirvana offered a "blockbuster" version of punk that helped line the wallets of CEOs and marketers in the corporate record industry.

* * *

But to end on "stars" would be to miss the point. The story told here is about the "punk rock world" that Bob Mould helped develop and where Cobain discovered "ethics." Though the mainstream press overlooked them, there were ideas informing this world. First and foremost DIY, the vision of kids building their "own culture," resisting arena rock and the music industry. It included a vast array of self-produced zines—themselves brimming with ideas—traded with others through the postal system (direct barter reflected Kropotkin's idea of "mutual aid" and what Reagan condemned as an "underground economy"). There were those tour networks rooted in local scenes building themselves from the bottom up (and that demanded bands "jam econo," in the words of the Minutemen). Low-budget movies showed those producing their own culture to fellow producers (*Debt Begins at Twenty* especially, and to a lesser extent *Decline of Western Civilization*). Punk's spirit moved into literature, including the dark poetry of Dennis Cooper and the noir fiction of John Shirley, William Gibson, and Bruce Sterling—what became "cyberpunk" with its sci-fi warnings about a dystopian future. In Raymond Pettibon's and Winston Smith's artwork, provocation demanded thoughtful excavation on the part of the viewer, unlike the undemanding viewing of television (often called the "boob tube"), especially MTV. Most importantly, 1980s punk nurtured a discussion among participants, those Matt Groening called "the smartest kids in the history of adolescence" who would "debate the throes and cons of punkish behavior." Punk in the 1980s might best be described as a consciousness or vision as much as a movement, fueled by discussions of personal ethics (straight edge, for instance), existentialism, anarchism, and the art of dissent. We ignore the extent of all this because we see the 1980s as the decade of the preppy, yuppie, or the "MTV generation" who genuflected to corporate acts like Michael Jackson or Madonna and who became "Fritzbusters" when the 1984 presidential campaign heated up.

From 1981 to 1985, a moment opened when making your "own culture" took aim not just at a fledgling entertainment industry but also at a president who synched himself to that entertainment industry. Ronald Reagan loved all things that were corporate blockbuster, as witnessed in his fawning over Michael Jackson's stellar success (and his earlier celebration of Steven Spielberg's movie *E.T.*). He governed as an actor, through the wink and the nod and the entertaining quip. He consistently led with a soundtrack and movie in mind. He drew from the simplicity of Hollywood films, cheering on Sylvester Stallone, who single-handedly rescued POWs from the jungle and pummeled a Soviet boxer to imagined chants of "USA! USA!" Movies—like *Back to the Future* and *Ghostbusters*—helped him dream dreams. As the cultural critic Neal Gabler put it, "Reagan had so thoroughly internalized the cosmology of the movies that he . . . lived entirely within it."[4]

But behind the screen and the smiley-face persona there lurked a meanness that fell largely on young people. An obvious case in point: How Reagan's 1981 tax cut for the wealthy necessitated a cut in school lunch programs. Reagan started his presidency by flip-flopping into supporting the Selective Service Act, promising to crack down on those who failed to register (cutting off financial aid for higher education for nonregistrants and threatening "criminal proceedings"). Young people constituted for him the future warriors for Cold War 2. When he looked at a twelve-year-old boy playing the video game "Space Invaders," he saw a future fighter pilot. Though often thought of as a great communicator, Reagan's real skill (though it ultimately failed him) was in hiding secrets, especially covert operations in Central America. Any dissent against his policies were, for him, traitorous. The polite protesters demanding a nuclear freeze were simply dupes of the Soviet Union who had no capacity to understand "evil" (making the televangelist Jerry Falwell break into a wide grin as he thought about the Rapture). The president spoke of end days and made jokes about "bombing" the Soviet Union while plotting out creepy civil defense scenarios. All of this in his smiling, ah-shucks style. The zine *Third Rail* summed it up: "Who could be easier to hate as president? Reagan presented the perfect picture of an idiotic, argumentative, disgruntled, reactionary, doddering old uncle who was nonetheless charming enough to be unbelievably irritating." But, of course, many historians and conservatives ignore this impression of the president, because Reagan "invented the eighties" with a "sparkle in his eyes" (Gil Troy) and projected a soulful "character and vision" (John Patrick Diggins), making him, for some on the right, nearly a saint.[5]

By 1985, Reaganism seemed all-powerful. The president's second term was won in a landslide, just as "the friends of President Reagan" watched as the music industry and Hollywood bounced back, in part thanks to MTV (and "synergy" within the industry as a whole). It felt like a moment passed,

which explains why this book ends in 1985. Punk didn't die in 1985—
as preposterous an idea as saying that punk died in 1979. After all, *MRR*
continued to publish and created the Gilman Street Project in 1986. DIY
shows continue up into our own time, as Daniel Makagon has documented,
often going more underground (into basements of homes, for instance).
Debates and discussions about punk ethics—the sort that Matt Groening
documented—erupted again with the rise of "riot girl" in the late eighties,
reviving the critique of macho found in the complaints of Jello Biafra but
going further in its call for sexual equality and rooting out sexism from
within the ranks of punks. And the organization Positive Force (at least
the one in Washington, D.C.) continues to this day, although different from
what it was in 1985. And the band Fugazi—which Ian MacKaye started up
around two years after Positive Force had formed—remained anti-corporate
and committed to DIY principles for some time to come.[6]

If punk didn't die, something still changed in 1985. During the early
years of the 1980s, the mainstream media treated punk as stupid but also
as a threat and menace to society—witnessed in popular television shows
like *Quincy* and *CHiPs*, movies like the *Class of 1984*, and the ravings of the
tele-pundit psychologist and founder of "Parents of Punkers," Serena Dank.
In Los Angeles, the police force went to war against punk. Shows were shut
down, venues shuttered. The FBI sent an agent to intimidate the editors of
Destroy L.A. zine. Television documentaries suggested that punk was destroying ordinary families (just after Black Flag's first album was decried as
"anti-parent"). Even Penelope Spheeris, who seemed at first sympathetic to
the movement, showed punks in *Suburbia* as moronic rapists.

But the real (versus the perceived) threat came to those sitting in skyscrapers that housed the entertainment industry and trade groups like
the Recording Industry Association of America. It was announced on
the Dead Kennedys cassette tape version of "We've Got Bigger Problems
Now," which on its B-side had a drawing of a pirate and the words: "Home
taping is killing record industry profits! We left this side blank so you can
help out." Every time a cassette compilation tape and a zine (both often
made at home) were dropped into the mailboxes of suburban houses, kids
conceived of themselves as producers of their own culture and aimed their
sight at the recording industry, which seemed out of touch while fretting
about future sales.

But by 1985, *Rolling Stone*—practically an appendage of the music industry—declared a "new punk rock." It was a safer form of punk and could be found in the pages of *Spin* magazine, the videos of MTV, and *Rockpool's* alternative charts. It was confirmed when Karin Berg signed Husker Du to Warner Bros. The celebrity-cluttered *People* magazine spotted it in their story about Jennifer Cunningham shutting down the punk venue C.A.S.H. and turning it into a Hollywood agency that scored cameos for young punks, especially those with purple hair and other easy-to-identify symbols. In 1985, Cunningham told *People*, punk was "marketable in the mainstream." As the critic George Melly would put it, punk had turned from revolt into style, ideas whittled down to visual cues on screens. By 1985, punk was no longer a threat to the entertainment industry—it was more like a side dish supplement or a look and a style.

So some might say, by way of conclusion, that Reagan won the culture war of the 1980s. For sure, we live under his shadow. Who would deny the blaring fact that the wall between entertainment and politics is even more porous today than under Reagan, with so many of us getting our news from late-night talk shows and having elected a president indebted to "reality television"? Reagan set the mark when he turned governing into acting. His ethic of entertainment drove his tendency to eschew reality and make things up to suit his views of the world—the idea that if he said one thing more than five times, it was considered truth, as a White House spokesman once explained. Reagan helped elevate a culture of celebrity— especially the success of Michael Jackson in 1984—that turned idols into spectacular beings but also moral leaders ("We Are the World"). That too is our inheritance today. And many of those who study the "blockbuster" culture Reagan championed believe that the big, hit movies and mega-star music acts made with gargantuan budgets are around to stay (even with the Internet's pluralism of choice). It goes without saying that large culture trust entities like Warner Bros. still hold more power than kids promoting their own music and playing shows in suburban basements.[7]

But this just makes understanding punk in the 1980s all the more important. We can remember it for its creativity, found today in the shards it left behind. But it should also be understood as a moment when kids saw themselves as creating their own culture, prompting them to think about the world differently. At its core lurked a visceral hatred of corporate culture—whether it be corporations marketing entertainment or those making weapons of mass destruction—and the entertainer-in-chief sitting in the White House. In the words of the cartoonist John Crawford, "Punk is an anathema to the corporate greedheads." Such a statement reminds us both of punk's promise and its overburdened challenge. After all, we have to ask how a bunch of scroungy kids could overthrow the entertainment industry. As much as discussions about "mutual aid" fueled punk in the 1980s, there were just as many reports about the burn-out factor and fragility of DIY practices as well as the impossibilities of anarchism. It was just too damned difficult to imagine how kids with little power were going to overturn those with all the power—the juggernauts of the entertainment industry, like the corporate behemoth Warner Bros. But, for a moment, they tried, while often consoling themselves with dark humor. A "punk rock world" had been built, and though it was fragile, it expressed a hope for a world different from the decadence that Reagan and the corporate entertainment industry stood for. We should remember it precisely for that.

ACKNOWLEDGMENTS

My first acknowledgment is for the title of the book. It comes from the journals of Henry Rollins, *Get in the Van* (the second edition, 1995, Los Angeles: 2.13.61, page 88). I also rely upon previous treatments of American punk rock in the 1980s. My thanks here go out to numerous authors: George Hurchalla, Steven Blush, Tony Rettman, Mark Andersen, Mark Jenkins, Bradford Martin, Dewar MacLeod, David Ensminger, Gina Arnold, and Michael Azerrad. My apologies to those I left out. A very big thanks to those who participated in this movement (or earlier renditions of punk) and who have made their archives open for research at various libraries (versus selling them to private bidders). Having access to these archives was crucial, and so I'd like to thank Mark Andersen, Aaron Cometbus, Dennis Cooper, Richard Hell, John Holmstrom, Johan Kugelberg, Jon Savage, Rebecca Solnit, and Matt Wobensmith. And thanks to those archivists who helped me make it through the zines and artwork that I write about here. A special thanks to Penelope Houston at the San Francisco Public Library, Michele Castro at the D.C. Public Library, Jennie Thomas at the Rock and Roll Hall of Fame Archives, and Timothy Young at Yale University. Two readers at Oxford University Press provided excellent commentary and tips on how to revise. Thanks especially to the wonderful Zack Furness. Michael Stewart Foley put together a great panel for the Organization of American Historians (OAH), which helped sharpen my arguments. Not only that but Michael shared his research findings with me, predominantly about San Francisco based punk (when that book is written, it's going to be awesome). Two graduate students helped immensely with the research for this book. It's a pleasure finally to give kudos to Jasper Verschoor and Shalon van Tine. Both were meticulous (way more actually). I want to thank Patricia Connor Study for financing a chair in her name at Ohio University (OU); holding that chair has made researching this book much more feasible. I am grateful for a year of faculty leave at OU, during which I researched and wrote a great deal of this book. I also thank my colleagues in the History Department. They have been kind enough to host a presentation where I could test out my ideas. I'm lucky to have wound up working with Oxford University Press, especially with my superb editor. Dave McBride did so much for this book: he helped me sharpen my arguments, corrected mistakes, and at times seemed to know more about 1980s punk rock than I did. He's a truly great editor and co-conspirator. Thanks also to Holly Mitchell for shepherding this book through to completion. She had a certain grace in bugging me when necessary and was always helpful. Two readers really saved me from my mistakes—Mark Arm and Sharon Cheslow, both of them very, very, very active in the movement discussed here. Thanks also to Liz Davey at Newgen KnowledgeWorks who moved this book through its production process. My agent Heather Schroder helped locate me the right publisher and has offered so much helpful advice (I remember smiling and laughing during our numerous phone calls). Last but not least, a heartfelt thanks to my family. My son Jay put up with a father whose head swirled with the music of the Minutemen and the presidency of Ronald Reagan and who seemed, at times I'm sure, scattered. He helped me in ways he might not realize. Finally, my wife Vicky has made my life so much the better. It's been twenty-five years for us together, and she has supported me through both wonderful and difficult times. She knows what I'm talking about.

BIBLIOGRAPHY

What follows are a list of my sources and explanations of many of them. This is intended to help a reader understand the endnotes that come next.

INTERVIEWS

Anstaett, Tim. Email. September 23, 2018.
Bale, Jeff. Email. April 19, 2017.
Belsito, Peter. Phone. February 28, 2018.
Brown, Bill. Email. July 28, 1917.
Coley, Byron. Email. September 9, 2018.
Fleming, Lorry. Email. March 14, 2018.
Kester, Marian. Email. March 4, 2018.
Miro, Michael. Email. March 13, 2018.
Shirley, John. Email. August 9, 2017.
Skelley, Jack. Phone. May 13, 2017.
Stern, Shawn. Email. February 10, 2018.
Titus, Peter. Email. April 4, 2018.
Wilson, Verna. Email. August 14, 2017.

ARCHIVES/LIBRARY HOLDINGS

(Note the abbreviations I provide here; these are intended to provide readers with the location of zines that are cited throughout the endnotes.)

Bancroft Library (Berkeley, California):
   Craig Stockfleth Zine Collection (Stockfleth).
   Rebecca Solnit Papers (Solnit).
   Matt Wobensmith Collection (Wobensmith).
Bowling Green University (Bowling Green, Ohio):
   Zine Collection, Music Library (BGSU).
Cornell University:
   Aaron Cometbus Punk and Underground Press Collection (Cometbus).
   Johan Kugelberg Punk Collection (JK).
   Los Angeles Punk Collection (LAP).

Kent State University:
  Progressive Student Alliance/Network Papers.
Mills College:
  Patti Smith Collection.
New York University, Fales Library (NYU):
  Richard Hell Papers.
  Dennis Cooper Papers.
Rock & Roll Hall of Fame Library and Archives, Cleveland, Ohio (RHOF).
San Francisco Public Library:
  Small Magazine Collection (SFPL).
State Archive of New York (Albany):
  Factsheet Five Collection (FSF).
University of Maryland:
  Zine Collection (UMD).
Washington D.C. Public Library:
  Mark Andersen Papers (DCPLMA).
  Mike Ross Collection (DCPLMAMR).
Yale University:
  John Holmstrom Papers, Yale University (Holmstrom).
  Raymond Pettibon Publications, Yale University.
  Danny Fields's Papers, Yale University.

PUBLICATIONS

Newspapers and Magazines

This a list of magazines and newspapers consulted for this study and usually cited within by simply the date or number of the issue (and page numbers if possible). If I think that they are most likely only to be located within an archival collection, I have listed that out after the title. Someties I will provide an online web address for articles within these publications.

ArtForum
Atlantic
Bay Area Music (BAM): SFPL
Billboard
Bomb
Chicago Tribune
East Village Eye
The Face: RHOF
High Times
In These Times
Interview
L.A. Reader
L.A. Times
L.A. Weekly

Mother Jones
The Nation
New Music Express (NME): RHOF
New Republic
New West
New York
New York Rocker
New York Times
Newsweek
Nuclear Times
October
Overthrow
People
Radical America
The Rocket
Rockpool: RHOF
Rolling Stone
San Francisco Bay Guardian
San Francisco Chronicle
San Francisco Examiner
Semiotext(e) (I consulted holdings at Miami University)
Southern California Art Journal
Time
Trouser Press
Village Voice
Washington Post
Wet

ZINES

The following titles are fanzines now turned into or incorporated into a book:

Bullshit Detector: Kanger-Born, Marie. *Confessions of a Chicago Punk Bystander*. Morrisville: Lulu, 2010.
Desperate Times: Masco, Maire M. *Desperate Times: The Summer of 1981*. Tacoma: Fluke, 2015.
Search and Destroy: Vale, V. *Search and Destroy: The Complete Reprint, 1–6*. San Francisco: V/Search, 1996. Vale, V. *Search and Destroy: The Complete Reprint, 7–11*. San Francisco: V/Search, 1997.
Slash: Roettinger, Brian, and J. C. Gabel, eds. *Slash: A Punk Magazine from Los Angeles, 1977–1980*. Los Angeles: Hart and Beard Press, 2016.
Sub Pop: Pavitt, Bruce. *Sub Pop USA: The Subterranean Pop Music Anthology, 1980–1988*. Brooklyn: Bazillion Points, 2014.
Touch and Go: Vee, Tesco, and Dave Stimson. *Touch and Go: The Complete Hardcore Punk Zine, '79–'83*. Edited by Steve Miller. Brooklyn: Bazillion Points, 2010.

We Got Power!: Markey, David, and Jordan Schwartz. *We Got Power! Hardcore Punk Scenes from 1980s Southern California*. Brooklyn: Bazillion Points, 2012.

xXx: Gitter, Mike. *xXx Fanzine (1983–1988)*. Edited by Chris Wrenn. Boston: Bridge Nine Press, 2017.

ZINES/SMALL PUBLICATIONS

The following zines or small-print publications were all consulted. Their archival locations are listed (those can be figured out from the earlier archive list). Almost all of these were published between 1980 and 1985. A great number of them are unpaginated; when page numbers exist, I include those in the endnotes. Otherwise I simply use a date or an issue number (when those exist). In certain cases I will give my own estimate of what year a publication was likely printed. Those come in parentheses and a question mark.

Absolutely No Corporations: Solnit.

Age Home: Stockfleth.

AKA: DCPLMA.

All the Drugs You Can Eat: JK.

Altered Statements: BGSU.

Alternative America: BGSU.

Another Opening: Cometbus.

Another Room: SFPL, Cometbus.

Another Unslanted Opinion: UMD.

Antagonist: BGSU.

Antimedia: FSF.

Antiseptic: Cometbus, Solnit.

Appeal to Reason: Cometbus.

The Attack: BGSU.

Backdoor Man: JK, RHOF.

Bad Meat: Cometbus, Stockfleth.

Bad News: FSF.

Bang: FSF, BGSU.

Be My Best Friend: Cometbus.

Bean-O: Stockfleth.

Behind the Zion Curtain: Cometbus.

Big City: DCPLMA.

The Big Takeover: RHOF, BGSU, Stockfleth, DCPLMA.

Blind Obedience: Cometbus.

Blatch: Stockfleth.

Blitz: BGSU.

Bloody Mess: Stockfleth.

Blow It Off: FSF, BGSU.

Blur: BGSU.

Boredom: BGSU.

Boston Rock: LAC Collection Cornell, DCPL.

Bound Together Newsletter: SFPL, FSF.

Bornage: Cometbus.
Boulevards: SFPL.
Brouhaha: FSF.
Brand New Age: DCPLMAMR.
BravEar: SFPL, Stockfleth, BGSU, and some in possession of Michael Miro.
Breakfast without Meat: Cometbus, Stockfleth.
Buff@lo: Stockfleth.
Bullet: BGSU.
Capitol Crisis: UMD.
Cerebral Discourse: Solnit.
Cheap Truth: Online.
Chow Chow Times: UMD.
Cigarette Philosophy: Cometbus.
Circle A: FSF.
Conflict: FSF.
Contempo Culture: Held at University of Texas, Austin, sent to me via Interlibrary Loan.
A Contradiction of Terms: Stockfleth.
Coolest Retard: BGSU.
Cranial Crap: BGSU.
Creep: SFPL.
Cretin Bull: Cometbus.
The Daily Battle: Cometbus, Stockfleth.
Daily Impulse: FSF, SFPL.
Damage: SFPL, Online.
Damaged Goods: BGSU, DCPLMA.
Dangerous Rhythms: BGSU.
DeScenes: DCPLMA.
Desperate Times: BGSU but also now a book (see earlier list).
Destroy L.A.: LAP.
Discords: BGSU, DCPLMA.
Disposable Press: BGSU.
D.O.V.E.: Stockfleth.
Dry: Online.
Dry Heave: Stockfleth.
Earwax: FSF.
Ego: Cometbus, Stockfleth.
Emancipation: FSF.
End Times: UMD.
Entertainment Revue: Solnit.
Existential Rage: Cometbus.
Fallout: Solnit, Cometbus.
Famous Dicks: BGSU.
Famous Hardcore of Punkland: DCPLMA.
FFanzeen: BGSU.
Fight for Freedom: Cometbus.
Flesh and Bones: BGSU, Cometbus, JK.

Film Threat: BGSU.
Flipside: Kugelberg, RHOF, BGSU, LAP, FSF, JK.
Forced Exposure: BGSU, FSF.
Forget It!: Cometbus
Frank: Stockfleth.
Free Beer Press: Online.
Free Venus Beachhead: Online.
The Fringe: Stockfleth.
Frisco: Stockfleth.
Going Under: FSF.
Guillotine: DCPLMA.
Hard Times: LAP.
Idle Time: BGSU.
If This Goes On: DCPL.
Independent America: BGSU.
Infiltrator: DCPLMA, UMD.
Ink Disease: BGSU, LAP, DCPLMA.
Innervoid: BGSU.
In the Ditch: JK.
I Wanna: BGSU.
Impending Doom: Cometbus.
Jersey Beat: BGSU.
KOA: DCPLMA.
Last Rites: Cometbus, DCPLMA.
Leading Edge: Cometbus, Stockfleth.
Little Caesar: NYU.
Little Friend: Stockfleth.
Magazine X: JK.
Malice: BGSU.
Matter: BGSU.
MAXIMUMROCKNROLL (MRR): BGSU, Stockfleth, FSF.
Modern Muzik: BGSU.
Mutual Oblivion: BGSU.
Nart: Cometbus.
Nashville Intelligence Reporter: Online.
New Magazine: RHOF.
Negative Army: DCPLMA.
Negative Print: BGSU, Stockfleth, LAP.
New Dachau: BGSU.
New Magazine: JK.
New Magazine (Pittsburgh): BGSU.
Newsreel: BGSU.
New Wave: JK.
Night Voices: LAP, BGSU.
NME: RHOF.
No Cause for Concern: DCPLMA.

The Noise (Boston): BGSU.
Noise (Xenia, Ohio): BGSU.
No Loitering: BGSU.
No Magazine: RHOF, Online.
No Middle Ground: Stockfleth. *Non LP B Side*: BGSU
NO S.H.I.T.: BGSU.
Now God: Stockfleth.
NPC: Stockfleth.
O.C. Shitz: DCPLMA.
The Offense: BGSU.
Onslaught: Cometbus.
Ooops!: BGSU.
Op: BGSU.
Out: Cometbus, Stockfleth
Outcry: BGSU, DCPLMA.
Own the Whole World: BGSU.
Patio X Table: JK.
The Peace Alternative: FSF.
Plan 9: BGSU.
Point Drawn: Holmstrom Papers.
Pollution Control: BGSU.
Postwar: FSF.
Processed World: FSF, Online.
Protest and Survive: Cometbus.
Puddles of Blood: Cometbus.
Puncture: Cometbus, FSF.
Punk Globe: Stockfleth.
Punk Lives: BGSU.
Punk Lust: BGSU, JK.
Rabies: SFPL.
RAD: FSF, BGSU, SFPL.
Rats in the Streets: Cometbus.
Reagan Death: LAP.
Real Fun: Cometbus.
Reasons for Living: BGSU.
Re/Search: SFPL, RHOF, BGSU.
Revealin Da Lies: Cometbus.
Revenge against Boredom: Cometbus.
Revolutionary Wanker: SFPL.
Riding the Blinds: BGSU, JK.
RIP: LAP.
Ripper: SFPL, Stockfleth, BGSU.
Rude, Crude, and Socially Unacceptable: BGSU.
Saboteur: Cometbus.
Self Destruct: BGSU.
Sense of Purpose: BGSU.

Shoot: Cometbus.
Sick Teen: Cometbus.
Silence: BGSU.
Sixty Miles North: LAP.
Skank: LAP.
Skatepunk: JK.
Skeeno Scope: DCPLMA.
Skid: BGSU.
Skin Effect: DCPLMA.
Sleeping Dogs: Cometbus.
Sluggo: Stockfleth.
Smash Apathy: FSF.
Smegma Journal: DCPLMA, JK.
Sound Choice: Stockfleth.
Spastic Culture: Stockfleth.
S.P.E.W.: DCPLMA, FSF.
Squat for Life: Solnit.
The Steel Press: BGSU.
Stellazine: SFPL, BGSU.
Still Too Small: Cometbus.
Storms of Youth: Solnit.
Strikes Again: DCPLMA.
Sub Cin: Cometbus.
Sub Pop: BGSU, JK.
Suburban Outcast: DCPLMA.
Suburban Relapse: BGSU, DCPLMA.
Suburban Voice: BGSU, DCPLMA.
Take It!: JK, BGSU.
Talk Talk: BGSU.
Terminal: BGSU.
Third Rail: FSF.
This Magazine: Stockfleth.
Thrillseeker: BGSU, UMD.
Time's Up: BGSU.
Town without Pity: Stockfleth.
Tripping Corpse: Yale University.
Tropical Depression: BGSU.
Troubled Times: FSF.
Truly Needy: DCPLMA, UMD.
Twisted Image: Cometbus.
Uncle Fester: Stockfleth.
Underdog Fun Book: Stockfleth.
Unsound: BGSU, Cometbus, SFPL, Stockfleth.
Useless Knowledge: BGSU.
Vacation: SFPL.
Vintage Violence: UMD.

Voice of the Rat: DCPLMA.
Vomit Landscapes: Stockfleth.
Vortex: SFPL.
The War Hawks: Stockfleth.
Warning: BGSU, Cometbus, DCPLMA.
Wave Sector: Cometbus.
WDC Period: UMD, FSF
White Noise: DCPLMA.
Wild Dog: BGSU, JK.
Wiring Department: Stockfleth.
Xerox Mouth: Cometbus.
Xiphoid Press: JK.
Your Flesh: Cometbus.
Zat: Stockfleth.
Zone V: UMD, DCPLMA.

DISSERTATIONS AND THESES

Kirwin, Elizabeth Seton. "It's All True: Imagining New York's East Village Art Scene of the 1980s." PhD diss., University of Maryland, 1999.
Little, David. "Collaborative Projects, Inc. A History of an American Artists' Collective, 1977–1983." PhD diss., Duke University, 2001.
Ruggles, Brock J. "Not So Quiet on the Western Front: Punk Politics during the Conservative Ascendancy in the United States, 1980–2000." PhD diss., Arizona State University, 2008.
Traulsen, Andrew M. "More Than Music: American Punk Rock, 1980–1985." MA Thesis, California State University, Chico, 2009.
Williams, Johnathan Kyle. "'Rock against Reagan': The Punk Movement, Cultural Hegemony, and Reaganism in the Eighties." MA Thesis, University of Northern Iowa, 2016.
Wolf, Mary Montgomery. "'We Accept You, One of Us?': Punk Rock, Community, and Individualism in an Uncertain Era, 1974–1985." PhD diss., University of North Carolina, 2007.

KEY SPEECHES OF RONALD REAGAN

These are not the only speeches consulted but are the most important in terms of this book.
"Address before a Joint Session of the Congress on the State Station of the Union." January 25, 1983. Online.
"Inaugural Address." January 20, 1981. Online.
"Radio Address to the Nation on Taxes, Tuition Tax Credit, and Interest Rates." April 24, 1982. Online.
"Remarks at the Annual Convention of the National Association of Evangelicals in Orlando, Florida." March 8, 1983. Online.

"Remarks in Chicago, Illinois, at the Citizens for Thompson Fundraising Dinner for Governor James T. Thompson." July 7, 1981. Online.

"Remarks on the Program for Economic Recovery at a White House Luncheon for Editors and Broadcasters from Southeastern States." April 16, 1982. Online.

"Second Inaugural Address." January 21, 1985.

ARTICLES

Arthur, Paul. "The Last of the Last Machine: Avant-Garde Film since 1966." *Millennium Film Journal*, no. 16. (1986–7): 69–93.

Aufderheide, Pat. "Music Videos: The Look of the Sound." *Journal of Communication* 36, no. 1 (1986): 57–78.

Barnes, Hugh. "Young Ones." *London Review of Books*, June 1986. 22.

Barrett, Dawson. "DIY Democracy: The Direct Action Politics of U.S. Punk Collectives." *American Studies* 52, no. 2 (2013): 23–42.

Barron, John. "The KGB's Magic War for Peace." *Reader's Digest*, October 1982. 206–259.

Black, Bob. "Mailing Their Way to Anarchy." *Boston Review*, August 1986. Online.

Bradley, Barbara. "Record Industry Out to Fight Home Taping." *Christian Science Monitor*, October 6, 1982. Online.

Brown, Jayna, Patrick Deer, and Tavia Nyong'o. "Punk and Its Afterlives." *Social Text* 31, no. 3 (2013): 1–11.

Buchsbaum, Jonathan. "A La Recherche des Punks Perdus." *Film Comment* 17, no. 3 (1981): 43–46.

Dale, Pete. "It Was Easy, It Was Cheap, So What? Reconsidering the DIY Principle of Punk and Indie Music." *Popular Music History* 3, no. 2 (2009): 171–193.

Dancis, Bruce. "Goodbye Punk Rock." *San Francisco Bay Guardian*, August 26, 1981. 20.

Domowitz, Janet. "Vermont Youths Declare War on Nuclear Weapons." *Christian Science Monitor*, March 18, 1982. Online.

Dunn, Kevin. "Anarcho-Punk and Resistance in Everyday Life." *Punk & Post-Punk* 1, no. 2 (2012): 201–218.

Easterbrook, Neil. "The Arc of Our Destruction: Reversal and Erasure in Cyberpunk." *Science Fiction Studies* 19, no. 3 (1992): 378–394.

Erickson, Holly. "The Birth and Death of Punk in North Beach." *North Beach Magazine*, September 1985. 13–15.

Friedman, Michael. "Finding Home with Jesse Malin." *Psychology Today*, April 15, 2015. Online.

Goldthorpe, Jeff. "Intoxicated Culture." *Socialist Review* 1, no. 22 (1992): 36–60.

Grand, Glenn. "Transcendence through Detournement in William Gibson's Neuromancer." *Science Fiction Studies* 17, no. 1 (1990): 41–49.

Harsch, Jonathan. "Reagan Cuts Eat into School Lunches." *Christian Science Monitor*, September 17, 1981. Online.

Heller, Karen. "A Trendy Gotham Trek with Mr. Musto." *Chicago Tribune*, July 20, 1986. Online.

Hsu, Hua. "The Branding of the Olympics." *Grantland*, February 11, 2014. Online.

Keenan, Allan. "Angry Young Men." *The Washington Tribune*, October 8, 1982. 1, 12–15.

Kellner, Douglas. "From 1984 to One-Dimensional Man: Critical Reflections on Orwell and Marcuse." *Current Perspectives in Social Theory* 10, no. 1 (1990): 223–252.

Klein, Norman. "Building Blade Runner." *Social Text* 28, no. 1 (1991): 147–152.

Lamy, Philip, and Jack Levin. "Punk and Middle-Class Values." *Youth and Society* 17, no. 2 (1985): 157–170.

Larsen, Al. "Fast, Cheap, and Out of Control: The Graphic Symbol in Hardcore Punk." *Punk & Post-Punk* 2, no. 1 (2014): 91–105.

Lippard, Lucy. "Real Estate and Real Art." *Seven Days*, April 1980. 32–34.

Lyons, Paul. "Yuppies." *Socialist Review*, March 1989. 163–180.

Maddox, Tom. "Cobra, She Said." *Fantasy Review*, April 1986. 46–48.

Martin, Bradford. "'And You Voted for That Guy': 1980s Post-Punk and Oppositional Politics." *Journal of Popular Music Studies* 16, no. 2 (2004): 142–174.

Martin, William. "Waiting for the End." *The Atlantic*, June 1982. Online.

Maskell, Shayna. "Performing Punk: Bad Brains and the Construction of Identity." *Journal of Popular Music Studies* 21, no. 4 (2009): 411–426.

McCarthy, Todd. "Hard Alex." *Film Comment* 22, no. 5 (1986): 36–39.

Moore, Ryan. "Postmodernism and Punk Subculture: Cultures of Authenticity and Deconstruction." *The Communication Review* 7, no. 3 (2004): 305–327.

Nehring, Neil. "The Situationist International in American Hardcore Punk, 1982–2002." *Popular Music and Society* 29, no. 5 (2006): 519–530.

Newitz, Annalee. "Madonna's Revenge." *Bad Subjects*, November 1993. Online.

O'Connor, Colleen. "Good Punks, Tough Life." *Washington Weekly*, June 7, 1985. 8–9.

O'Connor, John. "An Interview with Raymond Pettibon." *The Believer*, January 1, 2005. Online.

Owens, Craig. "Commentary: The Problem with Puerilism." *Art in America*, June 1984. 162–163.

Palmer, Cara E. "'Our Silence Buys the Battles': The Role of Protest Music in the U.S.–Central American Peace and Solidarity Movement." *Music & Politics* 11, no. 2 (2017): 1–15.

Parenti, Christian, and Peter Plate. "Writing the Left Coast." *The Brooklyn Rail*, January 1, 2002. Online.

Robinson, Walter, and Carlo McCormick. "Report from the East Village: Slouching toward Avenue D." *Art in America*, June 1984. 136–161.

Rossen, Jake. "How Jane Fonda's Workout Conquered the World." *Mental Floss*, June 19, 2015. Online.

Stevenson, John. "Rads." *Chicago Reader*, January 31, 1986. 14–35.

Sudo, Philip. "What's There to Fear about Husker Du?" *Mac Weekly*, March 5, 1982. 4A–5A.

Tatsumi, Takayuki. "Eye to Eye: An Interview with Bruce Sterling." *Science Fiction Eye*, January 1987. 27–42.

Timms, Ed. "Abbie Hoffman's Plaint: These Kids Today." *Chicago Tribune*, September 13, 1984. Online.

Wilson, Elizabeth. "The Bohemianization of Mass Culture." *International Journal of Cultural Studies* 2, no. 1 (1999): 11–32.

Worley, Matthew. "One Nation under the Bomb: The Cold War and British Punk to 1984." *Journal for the Study of Radicalism* 5, no. 2 (2011): 65–84.

Young, Charles M. "Skank or Die." *Playboy*, June 1984. 97–196.

BOOKS

Abu-Lughod, Janet L. *From Urban Village to East Village: The Battle for New York's Lower East Side*. Cambridge: Blackwell, 1994.

Acker, Christian. *Flip the Script*. Berkeley: Gingko Press, 2013.

Acker, Kathy. *Blood and Guts in High School*. New York: Grove Press, 1978.

Acker, Kathy. *Great Expectations*. New York: Grove Press, 1982.

Acker, Kathy. *Hannibal Lecter, My Father*. New York: Semiotext(e), 1991.

Adler, Warren. *The War of the Roses*. New York: Warner Books, 1981.

Alberro, Alexander, and Blake Stimson, eds. *Conceptual Art: A Critical Anthology*. Cambridge: MIT Press, 1999.

Allison, Aimee, and David Solnit. *Army of None: Strategies to Counter Military Recruitment, End War, and Build a Better World*. New York: Seven Stories Press, 2007.

Altschuler, Glenn C. *All Shook Up: How Rock 'n' Roll Changed America*. New York: Oxford University Press, 2003.

Amis, Martin. *Invasion of the Space Invaders*. London: Hutchinson, 1982.

Amis, Martin. *Money*. New York: Penguin, 1984.

Andersen, Mark, and Mark Jenkins. *Dance of Days: Two Decades of Punk in the Nation's Capital*. New York: Soft Skull Press, 2003.

Anker, Steve, Kathy Geritz, and Steve Seid, eds. *Radical Light: Alternative Film and Video in the San Francisco Bay Area, 1945–2000*. Berkeley: University of California Press, 2010.

Arnold, Gina. *Kiss This: Punk in the Present Tense*. New York: St. Martin's Press, 1997.

Arnold, Gina. *Route 666: On the Road to Nirvana*. New York: St. Martin's Press, 1993.

Ashby, LeRoy. *With Amusement for All: A History of American Popular Culture since 1830*. Lexington: University Press of Kentucky, 2006.

Ashley, Mike. *Science Fiction Rebels: The Story of the Science-Fiction Magazines from 1981 to 1990*. Liverpool: Liverpool University Press, 2016.

Astor, Pete. *Blank Generation*. New York: Bloomsbury, 2014.

Auchincloss, Louis. *Diary of a Yuppie*. Boston: Houghton Mifflin, 1986.

Austin, Joe. *Taking the Train: How Graffiti Art Became an Urban Crisis in New York City*. New York: Columbia University Press, 2001.

Austin, Joe, and Michael Nevin Willard, eds. *Generations of Youth: Youth Cultures and History in Twentieth-Century America*. New York: New York University Press, 1998.

Avrich, Paul. *Anarchist Portraits*. Princeton: Princeton University Press, 1988.

Azerrad, Michael. *Come as You Are: The Story of Nirvana*. New York: Doubleday, 1994.

Azerrad, Michael. *Our Band Could Be Your Life: Scenes from the American Indie Underground 1981–1991*. Boston: Little, Brown, 2001.

Bag, Alice. *Violence Girl: East L.A. Rage to Hollywood Stage, a Chicana Punk Story*. Port Townsend: Feral House, 2011.

Bai, Matt. *All the Truth Is Out: The Week Politics Went Tabloid*. New York: Vintage Books, 2014.

Bailey, Beth, and David Farber, eds. *America in the Seventies*. Lawrence: University Press of Kansas, 2004.

Bailey, Thomas Bey William. *Unofficial Release: Self-Released and Handmade Audio in Post-Industrial Society*. No Place: Belsona Books, 2012.

Balko, Radley. *Rise of the Warrior Cop: The Militarization of America's Police Forces*. New York: Public Affairs, 2014.

Ballard, J. G. *Crash*. London: Jonathan Cape, 1973.

Ballard, J. G. *High Rise*. London: Jonathan Cape, 1975.

Ballard, J. G. *Love and Napalm: Export U.S.A.* New York: Grove Press, 1972.

Ballard, J. G. *The Unlimited Dream Company*. New York: Holt, Rinehart, and Winston, 1979.

Ballard, J. G. *A User's Guide to the Millennium: Essays and Reviews*. New York: HarperCollins, 1996.

Bangs, Lester. *Main Lines, Blood Feasts, and Bad Taste: A Lester Bangs Reader*. Edited by John Morthland. New York: Anchor Books, 2003.

Bangs, Lester. *Psychotic Reactions and Carburetor Dung*. Edited by Greil Marcus. New York: Vintage, 1987.

Barber, Chris, and Jack Sargeant. *No Focus: Punk on Film*. London: Headpress, 2006.

Baritz, Loren. *Backfire: A History of How American Culture Led Us into Vietnam and Made Us Fight the Way We Did*. New York: William Morrow, 1985.

Barnett, Anthony, and John Pilger. *Aftermath: The Struggle of Cambodia and Vietnam*. Manchester: Manchester Free Press, 1982.

Barrett, Lawrence. *Gambling with History: Reagan in the White House*. New York: Doubleday, 1983.

Batchelor, Bob, and Scott Stoddart. *The 1980s*. Westport: Greenwood, 2007.

Baudrillard, Jean. *America*. New York: Verso, 1988.

Baudrillard, Jean. *In the Shadow of the Silent Majorities*. Los Angeles: Semiotext(e), 1983.

Baudrillard, Jean. *Simulations*. Los Angeles: Semiotext(e), 1983.

Baudrillard, Jean. *Symbolic Exchange and Death*. London: SAGE, 1993.

Baumgarten, Mark. *Love Rock Revolution: K Records and the Rise of Independent Music*. Seattle: Sasquatch, 2012.

Baumgartner, Jody, and Jonathan S. Morris, eds. *Laughing Matters: Humor and American Politics in the Media Age*. New York: Routledge, 2008.

Baxter, Jeanette. *J. G. Ballard's Surrealist Imagination: Spectacular Authorship*. New York: Routledge, 2009.

Baxter, John. *Buñuel*. New York: Carroll & Graff Publishers, 1994.

Beauchamp, Monte. *Masterful Marks: Cartoonists Who Changed the World*. New York: Simon & Schuster, 2014.

Beeber, Steven Lee. *The Heebie-Jeebies at CBGB's: A Secret History of Jewish Punk*. Chicago: Chicago Review Press, 2006.

Belsito, Peter, and Bob Davis. *Hardcore California: A History of Punk and New Wave*. San Francisco: Last Gasp, 1983.

Belsito, Peter. *Notes from the Pop Underground*. San Francisco: Last Gasp, 1985.

Belsito, Peter. *Street Art: Punk Poster in San Francisco*. San Francisco: Last Gasp, 1981.

Bennett, Andy, and Richard A. Peterson, eds. *Music Scenes: Local, Translocal, and Virtual*. Nashville: Vanderbilt University Press, 2004.

Benson, Richard, ed. *Night Fever: Club Writing in the Face, 1980–1997.* London: Boxtree, 1997.

Berger, George. *The Story of Crass.* Oakland: PM Press, 2009.

Berger, Thomas. *Neighbors.* New York: Delacorte, 1980.

Berkowitz, Edward D. *Something Happened: A Political and Cultural Overview of the Seventies.* New York: Columbia University Press, 2007.

Bernière, Vincent, and Mariel Primois, eds. *Punk Press: Rebel Rock in the Underground Press, 1968–1980.* New York: Abrams, 2012.

Bessy, Claude, et al. *Forming: The Early Days of L.A. Punk.* Santa Monica: Smart Art Press, 1999.

Best Comics of the Decade: Volume 1. Seattle: Fantagraphics Books, 1980.

Bestley, Russ, and Alex Ogg. *The Art of Punk: The Illustrated History of Punk Rock Design.* Minneapolis: Voyageur Press, 2012.

Bethke, Bruce. *Cyberpunk.* New York: Experimenter Publishing, 1983.

Beuys, Joseph. *Joseph Beuys: The Reader.* Edited by Clauda Mesch and Viola Michely. Cambridge: MIT Press, 2007.

Birnbach, Lisa. *The Official Preppy Handbook.* New York: Workman Publishing, 1980.

Biskind, Peter. *Easy Riders, Raging Bulls: How the Sex-Drugs-and-Rock 'n' Roll Generation Saved Hollywood.* New York: Simon & Schuster, 1999.

Black, Bob. *The Abolition of Work and Other Essays.* Port Townsend: Loompanics, 1986.

Black, Bob, and Adam Parfrey, eds. *Rants and Incendiary Tracts: Voices of Desperate Illuminations, 1558–Present.* New York: Amok Press, 1989.

Blashill, Pat. *Noise from the Underground: A Secret History of Alternative Rock.* New York: Fireside, 1996.

Blauvelt, Andrew, ed. *Hippie Modernism: The Struggle for Utopia.* Minneapolis: Walker Art Center, 2015.

Blumenthal, Sidney, and Thomas Bryne Edsall, eds. *The Reagan Legacy.* New York: Pantheon, 1988.

Blush, Steven. *American Hardcore: A Tribal History.* Port Townsend: Feral House, 2001.

Board, Mykel. *I A, Me-Ist or the Portable Board.* Chicago: Hope and Nonthings, 2005.

Bockris, Victor. *Beat Punks: New York's Underground Culture from the Beat Generation to the Punk Explosion.* Boston: Da Capo Press, 1998.

Bockris, Victor. *Patti Smith: An Unauthorized Biography.* New York: Simon & Schuster, 1999.

Bolton, Andrew. *Punk: Chaos to Couture.* New York: Metropolitan, 2013.

Bookchin, Murray. *Post-Scarcity Anarchism.* Chico: AK Press, 2004.

Borden, Iain. *Skateboarding, Space and the City: Architecture and the Body.* New York: Oxford University Press, 2001.

Borgmann, Albert. *Crossing the Postmodern Divide.* Chicago: University of Chicago Press, 1992.

Boulware, Jack, and Silke Tudor. *Gimme Something Better: The Profound, Progressive, and Occasionally Pointless History of Bay Area Punk from Dead Kennedys to Green Day.* New York: Penguin Books, 2009.

Boyer, Paul. *When Time Shall Be No More: Prophecy Belief in Modern American Culture.* 1992; Cambridge: Belknap Press, 1999.

Brake, Mike. *The Sociology of Youth Culture and Youth Subcultures: Sex and Drugs and Rock 'n' Roll.* London: Routledge, 1980.

Bronsteen, Ruth. *The Hippy's Handbook.* New York: Canyon Books, 1967.

Bravin, Jess. *Squeaky: The Life and Times of Lynette Alice Fromme.* New York: Buzz Books, 1997.

Brenner, Joël Glenn. *The Emperors of Chocolate: Inside the Secret World of Hershey and Mars.* New York: Random House, 1999.

Bretall, Robert, ed. *A Kierkegaard Anthology.* New York: Modern Library, 1946.

Breton, Andre, ed. *Anthology of Black Humor.* San Francisco: City Lights Publishers, 1997.

Bromberg, Craig. *The Wicked Ways of Malcolm McLaren.* New York: HarperCollins, 1989.

Brotchie, Alastair. *Alfred Jarry: A Pataphysical Life.* Cambridge: MIT Press, 2015.

Brown, Bill. *Not Bored!: Anthology, 1983–2010.* Cincinnati: Colossal Books, 2011.

Brown, Bill. *You Should've Heard Just What I Seen: Collected Newspaper Articles, 1981–1984.* Cincinnati: Colossal Books, 2010.

Browne, David. *Goodbye 20th Century: A Biography of Sonic Youth.* Boston: Da Capo Press, 2008.

Bruegmann, Robert. *Sprawl: A Compact History.* Chicago: University of Chicago Press, 2005.

Buchmuller, Eva, and Anna Koos. *Squat Theater.* New York: Artists Space, 1996.

Buckley, William F. *Overdrive: A Personal Documentary.* New York: Doubleday, 1984.

Bull, Gregory, and Mark Dines, eds. *Tales from the Punkside.* Scotts Valley: CreateSpace Independent Publishing, 2014.

Bunyan, John. *The Pilgrim's Progress.* New York: Penguin Books, 1987.

Burchill, Julie. *Love It or Shove It.* London: Century, 1985.

Burden, Chris. *Chris Burden: A Twenty-Year Survey.* Newport: Harbor Art Museum, 1988.

Burger, Peter. *Theory of the Avant-Garde.* Minneapolis: University of Minnesota, 1984.

Burgess, Anthony. *A Clockwork Orange.* New York: Norton, 1962.

Burns, James. *Let's Go to Hell: Scattered Memories of the Butthole Surfers.* No place: Cheap Drugs, 2015.

Burroughs, William S. *Junky.* New York: Grove Press, 1953.

Burroughs, William S. *Naked Lunch.* New York: Grove Press, 1959.

Burroughs, William S. *The Place of Dead Roads.* New York: Grove Press, 1983.

Burroughs, William S. *The Wild Boys.* New York: Grove Press, 1971.

Busch, Andrew. *Reagan's Victory: The Presidential Election of 1980 and the Rise of the Right.* Lawrence: University Press of Kansas, 2005.

Butt, Gavin, Kodwo Eshun, and Mark Fisher, eds. *Post-Punk Then and Now.* London: Repeater Books, 2014.

Butz, Konstantin. *Grinding California: Culture and Corporeality in American Skate Punk.* London: Transcript-Verlag, 2012.

Byrne, Malcolm. *Iran-Contra: Reagan's Scandal and the Unchecked Abuse of Presidential Power.* Lawrence: University Press of Kansas, 2014.

Cabut, Richard, and Andrew Gallix. *Punk is Dead.* Croydon: Zero, 2017.

Caen, Bruce. *Sub-Hollywood: A Novel.* Westerville: Yes Press, 2005.

Caldicott, Helen. *Missile Envy: The Arms Race and Nuclear War.* New York: Bantam Books, 1984.

Caldicott, Helen. *Nuclear Madness: What You Can Do.* New York: Norton, 1979.

Callenbach, Ernest. *Ecotopia.* Berkeley: Banyan Tree, 1975.

Callenbach, Ernest. *Ecotopia Emerging.* Berkeley: Banyan Tree, 1981.

Cameron, Dan, et al. *East Village USA.* New York: New Museum, 2007.

Cameron, Keith. *Mudhoney: The Sound and the Fury from Seattle*. Minneapolis: Voyageur Press, 2013.

Camus, Albert. *The Rebel*. New York: Vintage Books, 1956.

Camus, Albert. *The Stranger*. New York: Random House, 1946.

Campbell, Lisa D. *Michael Jackson: The King of Pop*. Boston: Branden Books, 1993.

Carducci, Joe. *Enter Naomi: SST, L.A. and All That*. Laramie: Redoubt Press, 2007.

Carducci, Joe. *Life against Dementia: Essays, Reviews, Interviews*. Laramie: Redoubt Press, 2012.

Carducci, Joe. *Rock and the Pop Narcotic: Testament for the Electric Church*. Centennial: Redoubt Press, 1994.

Carlson, Zack, and Bryan Connolly, eds. *Destroy All Movies!!! The Complete Guide to Punks on Film*. Seattle: Fantagraphics, 2010.

Cannon, Lou. *President Reagan: The Role of a Lifetime*. New York: Public Affairs, 2000.

Carr, Cynthia. *Fire in the Belly: The Life and Times of David Wojnarowicz*. New York: Bloomsbury, 2012.

Carr, Gordon. *The Angry Brigade: A History of Britain's First Urban Guerilla Group*. East Sussex: Christie Books, 2003.

Carroll, Linda. *Her Mother's Daughter: A Memoir of the Mother I Never Knew and of My Daughter, Courtney Love*. New York: Broadway Books, 2005.

Carroll, Peter N. *It Seemed Like Nothing Happened: America in the 1970s*. New Brunswick: Rutgers University Press, 2000.

Carson, David A. *Grit, Noise, and Revolution: The Birth of Detroit Rock 'n' Roll*. Ann Arbor: University of Michigan Press, 2006.

Carter, Jimmy. *Keeping Faith: Memoirs of a President*. Fayetteville: University of Arkansas Press, 1995.

Cateforis, Theo. *Are We Not New Wave? Modern Pop at the Turn of the 1980s*. Ann Arbor: Michigan, 2011.

Cateforis, Theo, ed. *The Rock History Reader*. New York: Routledge, 2007.

Cavallaro, Dani. *Cyberpunk and Cyberculture: Science Fiction and the Work of William Gibson*. London: Athlone Press, 2000.

Céline, Louis-Ferdinand. *Death on the Installment Plan*. New York: New Directions, 1966.

Chandler, Raymond. *Later Novels and Other Writings*. New York: Library of America, 1995.

Chapple, Steve, and Reebee Garofalo. *Rock 'n' Roll Is Here to Pay: The History and Politics of the Music Industry*. Chicago: Nelson Hall, 1977.

Che, Cathay. *Deborah Harry: The Biography*. New York: Fromm International, 2000.

Chick, Stevie. *Spray Paint the Walls: The Story of Black Flag*. London: Omnibus, 2009.

Christe, Ian. *Sound of the Beast: The Complete Headbanging History of Heavy Metal*. New York: HarperCollins, 2003

Christgau, Robert. *Going into the City: Portrait of a Critic as a Young Man*. New York: HarperCollins, 2015.

Chrome, Cheetah. *A Dead Boy's Tale from the Front Lines of Punk Rock*. Minneapolis: Voyageur Press, 2010.

Clark, Al, ed. *The Rock Yearbook*. London: Virgin Books, 1983.

Clay, Steven, and Rodney Phillips. *A Secret Location on the Lower East Side: Adventures in Writing, 1960–1980*. New York: Granary Books, 1998.

Cloonan, Martin, and Reebee Garofalo, eds. *Policing Pop*. Philadelphia: Temple University Press, 2003.

Cogan, Brian, ed. *The Encyclopedia of Punk*. New York: Sterling, 2008.

Cohen, Lizabeth. *A Consumers' Republic: The Politics of Mass Consumption in Postwar America*. New York: Vintage Books, 2003.

Colacello, Bob. *Holy Terror: Andy Warhol Close Up*. New York: Vintage Books, 1990.

Colegrave, Stephen, and Chris Sullivan. *Punk: The Definitive Record of a Revolution*. New York: Thunder's Mouth Press, 2001.

Coles, Robert. *The Moral Life of Children*. New York: Grove Press, 1986.

Coley, Byron. *Chuck Norris*. New York: St. Martin's Press, 1986.

Coley, Byron. *C'est La Guerre: Early Writings, 1978–1983*. Montreal: L'Oie de Cravan, 2011.

Collins, Cyn. *Complicated Fun: The Birth of Minneapolis Punk and Indie Rock*. St. Paul: Minnesota Historical Society Press, 2017,

Collins, Robert M. *More: The Politics of Economic Growth in Postwar America*. New York: Oxford University Press, 2000.

Collins, Robert M. *Transforming America: Politics and Culture during the Reagan Years*. New York: Columbia University Press, 2007.

Colver, Edward. *Blight at the End of the Funnel*. San Francisco: Last Gasp, 2006.

Combs, James. *The Reagan Range: The Nostalgic Myth in American Politics*. Madison: Popular Press, 1993.

Cometbus, Aaron. *Add Toner: A Cometbus Collection*. San Francisco: Last Gasp, 2011.

Cometbus, Aaron. *Despite Everything: A Cometbus Omnibus*. San Francisco: Last Gasp, 2002.

Compost, Terri, ed. *People's Park: Still Blooming*. Berkeley: Slingshot Collective, 2009.

Conard, Mark T., ed. *The Philosophy of Neo-Noir*. Lexington: University Press of Kentucky, 2007.

Conner, Bruce. *Mabuhay Gardens*. Dusseldorf: NRW-Forum, 2006.

Connolly, Cynthia, et al. *Banned in D.C.: Photos and Anecdotes from the DC Punk Underground (79–85)*. Madison: Sun Dog, 1992.

Conrad, Joseph. *Heart of Darkness*. New York: Penguin, 1983.

Conrad, Joseph. *The Secret Agent*. Hertfordshire: Wordsworth, 1993.

Cooper, Aimee. *Coloring Outside the Lines: A Memoir*. Elgin: Rowdy's Press, 2003.

Cooper, Dennis. *All Ears: Cultural Criticism, Essays and Obituaries*. Brooklyn: Soft Skull Press, 1999.

Cooper, Dennis, ed. *Coming Attractions: An Anthology of American Poets in Their Twenties*. Los Angeles: Little Caesar Press, 1980.

Cooper, Dennis. *Idols*. New York: SeaHorse Press, 1979.

Cooper, Dennis. *The Missing Men*. Eden: Am Here Books, 1981.

Cooper, Dennis. *The Tenderness of Wolves*. Trumansburg: Crossing Press, 1982.

Cooper, Dennis. *The Terror of Earrings*. Arcadia: Dennis Cooper, 1973.

Cooper, Dennis. *Tiger Beat*. Los Angeles: Little Caesar Press, 1978.

Corbisier, Isabelle. *Music for Vagabonds: The Tuxedo Moon Chronicles*. Berlin: OpenMute Press, 2008.

Cotkin, George. *Existential America*. Baltimore: Johns Hopkins University Press, 2003.

Cotkin, George. *Feast of Excess: A Cultural History of the New Sensibility*. New York: Oxford University Press, 2016.

Cox, Alex. *X Films: True Confessions of a Radical Filmmaker.* Berkeley: Soft Skull Press, 2008.

Craig, Stephen C., and Stephen Earl Bennett. *After the Boom: The Politics of Generation X.* Lanham: Rowman & Littlefield Publishers, 1997.

Crane, Michael, and Mary Stofflet, eds. *Correspondence Art: Source Book for the Network of International Postal Art Activity.* San Francisco: Contemporary Arts Press, 1984.

Crawford, John. *Baboon Dooley Rock Critic! Baboon Gets Ahead in Life.* Ann Arbor: Popular Reality, 1988.

Cross, Charles R. *Heavier Than Heaven: A Biography of Kurt Cobain.* New York: Hachette Books, 2001.

Coupland, Douglas. *Generation X: Tales for an Accelerated Culture.* New York: St. Martin's Press, 1991.

D'Agati, Philip. *The Cold War and the 1984 Olympic Games: A Soviet-American Surrogate War.* New York: Palgrave Macmillan, 2013.

Dannen, Fredric. *Hit Men: Power Brokers and Fast Money inside the Music Business.* New York: Vintage Books, 1991.

Davis, Mike. *City of Quartz: Excavating the Future in Los Angeles.* New York: Verso, 1990.

Davis, Mike, and Michael Sprinker, eds. *Reshaping the US Left: Popular Struggles in the 1980s.* New York: Verso, 1988.

Davis, Stephen. *Hammer of the Gods: The Led Zeppelin Saga.* New York: It Books, 1985.

Debies-Carl, Jeffrey S. *Punk Rock and the Politics of Place: Building a Better Tomorrow.* New York: Routledge, 2014.

Debord, Guy. *Society of the Spectacle.* Detroit: Black & Red, 1970.

Dellinger, Jade, and David Giffels. *Are We Not Men? We Are Devo!* London: SAF Publishing, 2003.

Dellio, Phil, and Scott Woods. *I Wanna Be Sedated: Pop Music in the Seventies.* Toronto: Sound and Vision, 1993.

Denselow, Robin. *When the Music's Over: The Story of Political Pop.* London: Faber and Faber, 1990.

Denisoff, R. Serge, and William Romanowski. *Risky Business: Rock in Film.* New Brunswick: Transaction, 2016.

DeRogatis, Jim. *Let It Blurt: The Life and Times of Lester Bangs.* New York: Broadway Books, 2000.

Dick, Philip K. *The Dark Haired Girl.* Shingletown: Ziesing Books, 1988.

Dick, Philip K. *Philip K. Dick: Four Novels of the 1960s.* New York: Library of America, 2007.

Dick, Philip K. *A Scanner Darkly.* New York: Doubleday, 1977.

Dick, Philip K. *VALIS and Later Novels.* New Yok: Library of America, 2009.

Dickstein, Morris. *Leopards in the Temple: The Transformation of American Fiction, 1945–1970.* Cambridge: Harvard University Press, 2002.

Dictor, Dave. *MDC: Memoir from a Damaged Civilization.* San Francisco: Manic D Press, 2016.

Didion, Joan. *After Henry.* New York: Vintage Books, 1993.

Diehl, Matt. *My So-Called Punk: Green Day, Fall Out Boy, The Distillers, Bad Religion—How Neo-Punk Stage-Dived into the Mainstream.* New York: St. Martin's Press, 2007.

Diggins, John Patrick. *Ronald Reagan: Fate, Freedom, and the Making of History.* New York: Norton, 2007.

Dika, Vera. *The (Moving) Pictures Generation: The Cinematic Impulse in Downtown New York Art and Film.* New York: Palgrave Macmillan, 2012.

Dines, Mike, and Matthew Worley. *The Aesthetic of Our Anger: Anarcho-Punk, Politics and Music.* London: Minor Compositions, 2016.

Doe, John. *Under the Big Black Sun: A Personal History of L.A. Punk.* Boston: Da Capo Press, 2016.

Doggett, Peter. *There's a Riot Going On: Revolutionaries, Rock Stars, and the Rise and Fall of the '60s.* Edinburgh: Canongate Books, 2007.

Domanick, Joe. *To Protect and to Serve: The LAPD's Century of War in the City of Dreams.* Los Angeles: Figueroa Press, 1994.

Draper, Robert. *Rolling Stone Magazine: The Uncensored History.* New York: Doubleday, 1990.

Dugger, Ronnie. *On Reagan: The Man and His Presidency.* New York: McGraw-Hill, 1983.

Duncan, Chris, ed. *My First Time: A Collection of First Punk Show Stories.* Oakland: AK Press, 2007.

Duncombe, Stephen. *Notes from Underground: Zines and the Politics of Alternative Culture.* New York: Verso, 1997.

Duncombe, Stephen, and Maxwell Tremblay, eds. *White Riot: Punk Rock and the Politics of Race.* New York: Verso, 2011.

Earles, Andrew. *Husker Du: The Story of the Noise-Pop Pioneers Who Launched Modern Rock.* Minneapolis: Voyager Press, 2010.

Ebersole, Stewart Dean. *Barred for Life: How Black Flag's Iconic Logo Became Punk Rock's Secret Handshake.* Oakland: Renegade Art Front, 2013.

Echols, Alice. *Hot Stuff: Disco and the Remaking of American Culture.* New York: Norton, 2010.

Edison, Mike. *I Have Fun Everywhere I Go: Savage Tales of Pot, Porn, Punk Rock, Pro Wrestling, Talking Apes, Evil Bosses, Dirty Blues, American Heroes, and the Most Notorious Magazines in the World.* New York: Faber and Faber, 2008.

Eklund, Douglas. *The Pictures Generation, 1974–1984.* New Haven: Yale University Press, 2009.

Elberse, Anita. *Blockbusters: Why Big Hits and Big Risks Are the Future of the Entertainment Business.* New York: Henry Holt, 2013.

Eliot, Marc. *Rockonomics: The Money Behind the Music.* New York: Franklin Watts, 1989.

Elkind, David. *All Grown Up and No Place to Go: Teenagers in Crisis.* Boston: Da Capo Press, 1984.

Enrico, Roger. *The Other Guy Blinked: How Pepsi Won the Cola Wars.* New York: Bantam Press, 1986.

Ellison, Harlan. *The Essential Ellison: A 50 Year Retrospective.* Beverly Hills: Morpheus International, 1991.

Ensminger, David. *Left of the Dial: Conversations with Punk Icons.* Oakland: PM Press, 2013.

Ensminger, David. *Visual Vitriol: The Street Art and Subcultures of the Punk and Hardcore Generation.* Jackson: University Press of Mississippi, 2011.

Epstein, Barbara. *Political Protest and Cultural Revolution: Nonviolent Direct Action in the 1970s and 1980s*. Berkeley: University of California Press, 1993.

Epstein, Jonathan, ed. *Adolescents and Their Music*. New York: Routledge, 1995.

Evans, Thomas W. *The Education of Ronald Reagan: The General Electric Years and the Untold Story of His Conversion to Conservatism*. New York: Columbia University Press, 2006.

Farber, David. *Taken Hostage: The Iran Hostage Crisis and America's First Encounter with Radical Islam*. Princeton: Princeton University Press, 2005.

Fensterstock, Ann. *Art on the Block: Tracking the New York Art World from SoHo to the Bowery, Bushwick and Beyond*. New York: Palgrave Macmillan, 2013.

Felder, Rachel. *Manic, Pop, Thrill*. New York: Ecco Press, 1993.

Felton, David. *Mindfuckers: A Source Book on the Rise of Acid Fascism in America*. San Francisco: Straight Arrow, 1972.

Ferguson, Russell, et al., eds. *Discourses: Conversations about Postmodern Culture*. Cambridge: MIT Press, 1990.

Fiedler, Leslie. *The Collected Essays, Vol. II*. New York: Stein and Day, 1971.

Fiedler, Leslie. *Love and Death in the American Novel*. New York: Stein and Day, 1966.

Fine, Jon. *Your Band Sucks: What I Saw at Indie Rock's Failed Revolution (But Can No Longer Hear)*. New York: Penguin Books, 2016.

Fitzgerald, Frances. *Way Out There in the Blue*. New York: Simon & Schuster, 2000.

Fitzgerald, f-Stop. *Weird Angle*. San Francisco: Last Gasp, 1982.

Flanagan, Harley. *Hard-Core: Life of My Own*. Port Townsend: Feral House, 2016.

Fleming, Jim, and Peter Lamborn Wilson, eds. *Semiotext(e) USA*. New York: Semiotext(e), 1987.

Floyd, Gary. *Please Bee Nice: My Life Up 'Til Now*. Lexington: Left of the Dial, 2014.

Foege, Alec. *Confusion Is Next: The Sonic Youth Story*. New York: St. Martin's Press, 1994.

Foley, Michael Stewart. *Dead Kennedys' Fresh Fruit for Rotting Vegetables*. New York: Bloomsbury Academic, 2015.

Foley, Michael Stewart. *Front Porch Politics: The Forgotten Heyday of American Activism in the 1970s and 1980s*. New York: Hill and Wang, 2013.

Ford, Simon. *The Situationist International: A User's Guide*. London: Black Dog Publishing, 2005.

Foster, Hal, ed. *The Anti-Aesthetic: Essays on Postmodern Culture*. New York: The New Press, 2002.

Foster, Hal. *Recodings: Art, Spectacle, Cultural Politics*. Port Townsend: Bay Press, 1985.

Foucault, Michel. *Discipline and Punish: The Birth of the Prison*. New York: Vintage Books, 1995.

Foucault, Michel. *This Is Not a Pipe*. Oakland: University of California Press, 1982.

Fournier, Michael T. *The Minutemen's Double Nickels on the Dime*. New York: Bloomsbury Academic, 2007.

Fowley, Kim. *Lord of Garbage*. New York: Kicks Books, 2012.

Frank, Josh, and Charlie Buckholtz. *In Heaven Everything Is Fine: The Unsolved Life of Peter Ivers and the Lost History of New Wave Theatre*. New York: Free Press, 2008.

Fraser, Steve. *The Age of Acquiescence: The Life and Death of American Resistance to Organized Wealth and Power*. New York: Little, Brown, 2015.

Fretz, Eric. *Jean-Michel Basquiat: A Biography*. Westport: Greenwood, 2010.

Friedenberg, Edgar Z. *Coming of Age in America: Growth and Acquiescence.* New York: Random House, 1965.

Friedlander, Paul. *Rock & Roll: A Social History.* Boulder: Westview Press, 1996.

Friedman, R. Seth, ed. *The Factsheet Five Zine Reader: The Best Writing from the Underground World of Zines.* New York: Three Rivers, 1997.

Frith, Simon. *Sound Effects.* New York: Pantheon, 1981.

Frith, Simon, and Andrew Goodwin, eds. *On Record: Rock, Pop, and the Written Word.* New York: Pantheon, 1990.

Frith, Simon, and Howard Horne. *Art into Pop.* London: Methuen, 1987.

Fuller, John G. *Are the Kids All Right? The Rock Generation and Its Hidden Death Wish.* New York: Times Books, 1981.

Furek, Maxim W. *The Death Proclamation of Generation X: A Self-Fulfilling Prophesy of Goth, Grunge and Heroin.* Bloomington: iUniverse, 2008.

Furness, Zack, ed. *Punkademics: The Basement Show in the Ivory Tower.* Brooklyn: Autonomedia, 2012.

Gabler, Neal. *Life: The Movie: How Entertainment Conquered Reality.* New York: Vintage Books, 1998.

Gaines, Donna. *Teenage Wasteland.* New York: Pantheon, 1991.

Gamson, Joshua. *Claims to Fame: Celebrity in Contemporary America.* Berkeley: University of California Press, 1994.

Garreau, Joel. *Edge City: Life on the New Frontier.* New York: Doubleday, 1991.

Gehman, Pleasant. *Showgirl Confidential: My Life Onstage, Backstage, and on the Road.* Hollywood: Punk Hostage Press, 2013.

Gendron, Bernard. *Between Montmartre and the Mudd Club: Popular Music and the Avant-Garde.* Chicago: University of Chicago Press, 2002.

George, Wally. *Wally George: The Father of Combat TV.* Santa Ana: Seven Locks Press, 1999.

Germond, Jack W., and Jules Witcover. *Blue Smoke and Mirrors: How Reagan Won and Why Carter Lost the Election of 1980.* New York: Viking Press, 1981.

Ghez, Susanne, et al., eds. *Raymond Pettibon: A Reader.* Philadelphia: Philadelphia Museum of Art, 1998.

Gibbs, Alvin. *Destroy: The Definitive History of Punk.* Bridgend: Britannia, 1996.

Gibson, William. *Burning Chrome.* New York: Arbor, 1986.

Gibson, William. *Neuromancer.* New York: Ace, 1984.

Gilmore, Mikal. *Night Beat: A Shadow of Rock & Roll.* New York: Anchor Books, 1998.

Gimarc, George. *Punk Diary: The Ultimate Trainspotter's Guide to Underground Rock, 1970–1982.* San Francisco: Backbeat, 2005.

Glasper, Ian. *The Day the Country Died: A History of Anarcho-Punk, 1980–1984.* London: Cherry Red Books, 2006.

Glatt, John. *Rage & Roll: Bill Graham and the Selling of Rock.* New York: Birch Lane Press, 1993.

Godfrey, Tony. *Conceptual Art.* London: Phaidon Press, 1988.

Goldberg, Robert. *Enemies Within: The Culture of Conspiracy in Modern America.* New Haven: Yale University Press, 2001.

Goodman, Andrew. *Dancing in the Distraction Factory: Music Television and Popular Culture.* Minneapolis: University of Minnesota Press, 1992.

Gora, Susannah. *You Couldn't Ignore Me If You Tried: The Brat Pack, John Hughes, and Their Impact on a Generation.* New York: Three Rivers Press, 2010.

Gordon, Kim. *Girl in a Band: A Memoir.* New York: Dey Street Books, 2015.

Gordon, Kim. *Is It My Body? Selected Texts.* Frankfurt: Sternberg Press, 2014.

Graeber, David. *Direct Action: An Ethnography.* Oakland: AK Press, 2009.

Graham, Bill, and Robert Greenfield. *Bill Graham Presents: My Life inside Rock and Out.* New York: Delta, 1992.

Graham, Dan. *Rock/Music Writings.* Brooklyn: Primary Information, 2009.

Graham, Dan. *Rock My Religion: Writings and Art Projects 1965–1990.* Cambridge: MIT Press, 1993.

Graham, Dan. *Two-Way Mirror Power: Selected Writings by Dan Graham on His Art.* Cambridge: MIT Press, 1999.

Gray, Christopher, ed. *Leaving the 20th Century: The Incomplete Work of the Situationist International.* London: Rebel Press, 1974.

Greenberg, Arielle. *Youth Subcultures: Exploring Underground America.* New York: Longman, 2007.

Greenberg, Miriam. *Branding New York: How a City in Crisis Was Sold to the World.* New York: Routledge, 2008.

Greene, James. *This Music Leaves Stains: The Complete Story of the Misfits.* Lanham: Scarecrow, 2013.

Greenwald, Andy. *Nothing Feels Good: Punk Rock, Teenagers, and EMO.* New York: St. Martin's Press, 2003.

Grisham, Jack. *An American Demon: A Memoir.* Toronto: ECW Press, 2011.

Grogan, Emmett. *Ringolevio: A Life Played for Keeps.* New York: Citadel, 1990.

Gross, Bertram. *Friendly Fascism: The New Face of Power in America.* New York: M. Evans and Company, 1980.

Gross, Michael. *My Generation: Fifty Years of Sex, Drugs, Rock, Revolution, Glamour, Greed, Valor, Faith, and Silicon Chips.* New York: Cliff Street Books, 2000.

Gudis, Catherine, ed. *Helter Skelter: L.A. Art in the 1990s.* Los Angeles: Museum of Contemporary Art, 1992.

Guérin, Daniel. *Anarchism: From Theory to Practice.* New York: Monthly Review Press, 1970.

Gusterson, Hugh. *Nuclear Rites: A Weapons Laboratory at the End of the Cold War.* Berkeley: University of California Press, 1996.

Hackett, Pat, ed. *The Andy Warhol Diaries.* New York: Warner Books, 1989.

Haden-Guest, Anthony. *The Last Party: Studio 54, Disco, and the Culture of the Night.* New York: Willian Morrow, 1997.

Hagan, Joe. *Sticky Fingers: The Life and Times of Jann Wenner and Rolling Stone Magazine.* New York: Knopf, 2017.

Hager, Steven. *Adventures in the Counterculture: From Hip Hop to High Times.* Berkeley: High Times, 2002.

Hager, Steven. *Art after Midnight: The East Village Scene.* New York: St. Martin's Press, 1986.

Halasz, Judith R. *The Bohemian Ethos: Questioning Work and Making a Scene on the Lower East Side.* New York: Routledge, 2015.

Haring, Keith. *Art in Transit: Subway Drawings.* New York: Harmony, 1984.

Hartman, Andrew. *A War for the Soul of America: A History of the Culture Wars.* Chicago: University of Chicago Press, 2015.

Harvey, Lyle. *American Anti-Nuclear Activism, 1975–1990.* New York: Palgrave, 2014.

Harvey, Tom. *The Eighties: A Bitchen Time to Be a Teenager.* Kirkland: Just Load the Wagon Publishing, 2012.

Hauser, Luke. *Direct Action.* San Francisco: Groundwork, 2003.

Hebdige, Dick. *Subculture: The Meaning of Style.* London: Methuen, 1979.

Hegarty, Paul, and Danny Kennedy, eds. *Dennis Cooper: Writing at the Edge.* Chicago: Sussex Academic Press, 2008.

Hell, Richard. *I Dreamed I Was a Very Clean Tramp: An Autobiography.* New York: Ecco Press, 2014.

Heller, Joseph. *Catch-22.* New York: Simon & Schuster, 1961.

Henry, Tricia. *Break All Rules! Punk Rock and the Making of a Style.* Ann Arbor: UMI Research Press, 1989.

Herf, Jeffrey. *War by Other Means: Soviet Power, West German Resistance, and the Battle of the Euromissiles.* New York: Free Press, 1991.

Hermes, Will. *Love Goes to Buildings on Fire: Five Years in New York That Changed Music Forever.* New York: Faber and Faber, 2011.

Heuser, Sabine. *Virtual Geographies: Cyberpunk at the Intersection of the Postmodern and Science Fiction.* Amsterdam: Rodopi, 2003.

Heylin, Clinton. *From the Velvets to the Voidoids: A Pre-Punk History for a Post-Punk World.* New York: Penguin Books, 1993.

Heylin, Clinton, ed. *The Da Capo Press Book of Rock & Roll Writing.* Boston: Da Capo Press, 1992.

Heylin, Clinton, ed. *The Penguin Book of Rock & Roll Writing.* New York: Viking Press, 1992.

Hibbard, Don, and Carol Kaleialoha. *The Role of Rock.* Englewood Cliffs: Prentice-Hall, 1983.

Hill, Christopher R. *Olympic Politics: Athens to Atlanta, 1896–1996.* Manchester: Manchester University Press, 1996.

Hill, Doug, and Jeff Weingrad. *Saturday Night: A Backstage History of Saturday Night Live.* New York: Beach Tree Books, 1986.

Himelstein, Abram Shalom, and Jamie Schweser. *Tales of a Punk Rock Nothing.* New Orleans: New Mouth from the Dirty South, 1998.

Hirsch, Foster. *Detours and Lost Highways: A Map of Neo-Noir.* New York: Limelight, 1995.

Hobbs, Stuart D. *The End of the American Avant Garde.* New York: New York University Press, 1997.

Hoeveler, J. David. *The Postmodernist Turn: American Thought and Culture in the 1970s.* New York: Twayne Publishers, 1996.

Hoffman, Abbie. *Revolution for the Hell of It.* New York: Thunder's Mouth Press, 1968.

Hogan, J. Michael. *The Nuclear Freeze Campaign: Rhetoric and Foreign Policy in the Telepolitical Age.* Lansing: Michigan State University Press, 1994.

Holtz, Geoffrey T. *Welcome to the Jungle: The Why behind "Generation X."* New York: St. Martin's Press, 1995.

Holzer, Jenny, and Peter Nadin. *Eating through Living.* New York: Tanam Press, 1981.

Home, Stewart. *The Assault on Culture: Utopian Currents from Lettrisme to Class War.* Oakland: AK Press, 1991.

Home, Stewart. *Cranked Up Really High: Genre Theory and Punk Rock.* New York: Codex Books, 1995.

Home, Stewart, ed. *What Is Situationism? A Reader.* Oakland: AK Press, 1996.

Hoopes, James. *Corporate Dreams.* New Brunswick: Rutgers University Press, 2011.

Hoskyns, Barney. *The Sound and the Fury: 40 Years of Classic Rock Journalism.* New York: Bloomsbury, 2003.

Hoskyns, Barney. *Waiting for the Sun: A Rock 'n' Roll History of Los Angeles.* New York: Viking Press, 1996.

Humphrey, Clark. *Loser: The Real Seattle Music Story.* Seattle: MISCmedia, 1995.

Hunt, John Dixon, David Lomas, and Michael Corris, eds. *Art, Word and Image: 2,000 Years of Visual/Textual Interaction.* London: Reaktion Books, 2010.

Hurchalla, George. *Going Underground: American Punk 1979–1989.* Oakland: PM Press, 2016.

Hussey, Andrew. *The Game of War: The Life and Death of Guy Debord.* London: Pimlico, 2002.

Huxley, Aldous. *Brave New World.* New York: Harper & Brothers, 1932.

Ibarra, Craig. *A Wailing of a Town: An Oral History of Early San Pedro Punk and More 1977–1985.* San Pedro: END FWY Press, 2015.

Isaacs, Arnold. *Without Honor: Defeat in Vietnam and Cambodia.* Baltimore: Johns Hopkins University Press, 1983.

Jackson, Kenneth T. *Crabgrass Frontier: The Suburbanization of the United States.* New York: Oxford University Press, 1995.

Jaffe, Harry, and Tom Sherwood. *Dream City: Race, Power, and the Decline of Washington D.C.* Brooklyn: Dream City Books, 1994.

Jamieson, Kathleen Hall. *Eloquence in an Electronic Age: The Transformation of Political Speechmaking.* New York: Oxford University Press, 1988.

James, Robin, ed. *Cassette Mythos.* Brooklyn: Autonomedia, 1992.

Janowitz, Tama. *American Dad.* New York: G. P. Putnam's Sons, 1981.

Janowitz, Tama. *Slaves of New York.* New York: Crown Publishing Group, 1986.

Jeffries, Stuart. *Grand Hotel Abyss: The Lives of the Frankfurt School.* New York: Verso, 2016.

Jenkins, Philip. *Decade of Nightmares: The End of the Sixties and the Making of Eighties America.* New York: Oxford, 2006.

Jeter, K. W. *Dr. Adder.* New York: Bluejay Books, 1984.

Jeter, K. W. *Soul Eater.* New York: Tom Doherty, 1983.

Jezer, Marty. *Abbie Hoffman: American Rebel.* New Brunswick: Rutgers University Press, 1992.

Johnson, Haynes. *In the Absence of Power: Governing America.* New York: Viking Press, 1980.

Johnson, Haynes. *Sleepwalking through History: America in the Reagan Years.* New York: Norton, 1991.

Joseph, John. *The Evolution of a Cro-Magnon.* Brooklyn: Punkhouse, 2007.

Joselit, David. *American Art since 1945.* London: Thomas and Hudson, 2003.

Joyce, James. *Ulysses.* New York: Random House, 1986.

Kahn, Ashley, et al., eds. *Rolling Stone: The '70s.* Boston: Little, Brown, 1998.

Kane, Daniel. *All Poets Welcome: The Lower East Side Poetry Scene in the 1960s.* Berkeley: University of California, 2003.

Kane, Daniel. *"Do You Have a Band?": Poetry and Punk Rock in New York City.* New York: Columbia University Press, 2017.

Kaplan, E. Ann. *Rocking around the Clock: Music Television, Postmodernism, and Consumer Culture.* New York: Routledge, 1987.

Kardon, Janet, ed. *The East Village Scene.* Philadelphia: University of Pennsylvania Press, 1984.

Katzeff, Miriam, et al., eds. *Real Life Magazine: Selected Writings and Projects 1979–1994.* Brooklyn: Primary Information, 2007.

Kauffman, Linda S. *Bad Girls and Sick Boys: Fantasies in Contemporary Art and Culture.* Berkeley: University of California Press, 1998.

Kaufmann, Walter, ed. *Existentialism: From Dostoevsky to Sartre.* New York: Penguin Group, 1956.

Keithley, Joey. *I, Shithead: A Life in Punk.* Vancouver: Arsenal, 2003.

Kennedy, Edward M., and Mark O. Hatfield. *Freeze! How You Can Prevent Nuclear War.* New York: Bantam Books, 1982.

Kennedy, Pagan. *Platforms: A Microwaved Cultural Chronicle of the 1970s.* New York: St. Martin's Press, 1994.

Kester, Marian. *Dead Kennedys.* San Francisco: Last Gasp, 1983.

Kiedis, Anthony. *Scar Tissue.* New York: Hachette Books, 2004.

Kleinknecht, William. *The Man Who Sold the World: Ronald Reagan and the Betrayal of Main Street America.* New York: Nation Books, 2009.

Knabb, Kenneth. *Public Secrets.* Berkeley: Bureau of Public Secrets, 1997.

Knabb, Kenneth, ed. *The Situationist International Anthology.* Berkeley: Bureau of Public Secrets, 1981.

Knelman, Fred H. *Reagan, God and the Bomb: From Myth to Policy in the Nuclear Arms Race.* Buffalo: Prometheus Books, 1985.

Knoblauch, William M. *Nuclear Freeze in a Cold War: The Reagan Administration, Cultural Activism, and the End of the Arms Race.* Amherst: University of Massachusetts Press, 2017.

Knopper, Steve. *Appetite for Self-Destruction: The Spectacular Crash of the Record Industry in the Digital Age.* New York: Free Press, 2010.

Konstantinou, Lee. *Cool Character: Irony and American Fiction.* Cambridge: Harvard University Press, 2016.

Kopkind, Andrew. *The Thirty Years' War: Dispatches and Diversions of a Radical Journalist, 1965–1994.* New York: Verso, 1995.

Koren, Leonard. *Making WET: The Magazine of Gourmet Bathing.* Point Reyes: Imperfect Publishing, 2012.

Kostelanetz, Richard. *The End of Intelligent Writing: Literary Politics in America.* New York: Sheed and Ward, 1974.

Kugelberg, Johan. *Brad Pitt's Dog: Essays on Fame, Death, Punk.* Alresford: Zero Books, 2012.

Kugelberg, Johan, and Jon Savage, eds. *Punk: An Aesthetic.* New York: Rizzoli, 2012.

Kozak, Roman. *This Ain't No Disco: The Story of CBGB.* Boston: Faber and Faber, 1988.

Kropotkin, Peter. *Kropotkin's Revolutionary Pamphlets*. New York: Dover Publications, 1970.

Kuhn, Gabriel, ed. *Sober Living for the Revolution: Hardcore Punk, Straight Edge, and Radical Politics*. Oakland: PM Press, 2009.

Kuper, Peter, and Seth Tobocman, eds. *World War 3 Illustrated*. Oakland: PM Press, 2014.

Ladd, Jim. *Radio Waves: Life and Revolution on the FM Dial*. New York: St. Martin's Press, 1991.

La Farge, Phyllis. *The Strangelove Legacy: Children, Parents and Teachers in the Nuclear Age*. New York: HarperCollins, 1987.

Laing, Dave. *One Chord Wonders: Power and Meaning in Punk Rock*. Oakland: PM Press, 2015.

Lake, Bambi. *The Unsinkable Bambi Lake*. San Francisco: Manic D Press, 1996.

Larkin, Ralph W. *Suburban Youth in Cultural Crisis*. New York: Oxford University Press, 1979.

Lasch, Christopher. *The Culture of Narcissism: American Life in an Age of Diminishing Expectations*. New York: Warner, 1979.

Lasch, Christopher. *The Minimal Self: Psychic Survival in Troubled Times*. New York: Norton, 1984.

Lawrence, Tim. *Hold On to Your Dreams: Arthur Russell and the Downtown Music Scene, 1973–1992*. Durham: Duke University Press, 2009.

Lawrence, Tim. *Love Saves the Day: A History of American Dance Music Culture, 1970–1979*. Durham: Duke University Press, 2003.

Le Guin, Ursula. *The Dispossessed*. New York: Avon, 1975.

Lehman, David. *The Last Avant-Garde: The Making of the New York School of Poets*. New York: Doubleday, 1998.

Leland. John. *Hip: The History*. New York: Harper Perennial, 2004.

Lenburg, Jeff. *Matt Groening: From Spitballs to Springfield*. New York: Chelsea House, 2011.

Lens, Jenny. *Punk Pioneers: When Punk Was Fun*. New York: Universe, 2008.

Lester, Paul. *Gang of Four: Damaged Goods*. London: Omnibus, 2008.

Lev, Leora. *Enter at Your Own Risk: The Dangerous Art of Dennis Cooper*. Madison: Farleigh Dickinson Press, 2006.

Levine, Cary. *Pay for Your Pleasures: Mike Kelley, Paul McCarthy, Raymond Pettibon*. Chicago: University of Chicago Press, 2013.

Leyden, T. J. *Skinhead Confessions: From Hate to Hope*. Springville: Sweetwater, 2008.

Lindlof, Thomas R., ed. *Natural Audiences*. Westport: Praeger, 1987.

Linenthal, Edward. *Symbolic Defense: The Cultural Significance of the Strategic Defense Initiative*. Chicago: University of Illinois Press, 1989.

Listfield, Emily. *It Was Gonna Be Like Paris*. New York: Dial Press, 1984.

Livermore, Lawrence. *Spy Rock Memories*. Brooklyn: Don Giovanni, 2013.

Livingston, James. *The World Turned Inside Out: American Thought and Culture at the End of the 20th Century*. Lanham: Rowman & Littlefield Publishers, 2010.

Loock, Ulrich, and Harald Falckenberg, eds. *Raymond Pettibon: Homo Americanus*. Hamburg: David Zwirner Books, 2016.

Lovecraft, H. P. *H. P. Lovecraft: Selected Stories*. New York: HarperCollins, 2018.

Ludlow, Peter, ed. *Crypto Anarchy, Cyberstates, and Pirate Utopias*. Cambridge: MIT Press, 2001.

Lynskey, Dorian. *The Ministry of Truth: The Biography of George Orwell's 1984*. New York: Doubleday, 2019.

Lynskey, Dorian. *33 Revolutions per Minute: A History of Protest Songs, from Billie Holiday to Green Day*. New York: HarperCollins, 2011.

MacDonald, Scott. *A Critical Cinema: Interviews with Independent Filmmakers*. Berkeley: University of California Press, 1988.

MacLeod, Dewar. *Kids of the Black Hole: Punk Rock Postsuburban California*. Norman: University of Oklahoma Press, 2010.

MacShane, Frank. *The Life of Raymond Chandler*. New York: E. P. Dutton, 1976.

Madden, David. *Critical Essays on Thomas Burger*. New York: Twayne Publishers, 1995.

Mahler, Jonathan. *Ladies and Gentlemen, the Bronx Is Burning: 1977, Baseball, Politics, and the Battle for the Soul of a City*. New York: Picador, 2005.

Mailer, Norman. *The Faith of Graffiti*. New York: Praeger, 1974.

Makagon, Daniel. *Underground: The Subterranean World of DIY Punk Shows*. Portland: Microcosm, 2015.

Marcus, Greil. *In the Fascist Bathroom: Punk in Pop Music, 1977–1992*. Cambridge: Harvard University Press, 1999.

Marcus, Greil. *Mystery Train: Images of America in Rock 'n' Roll Music*. New York: E. P. Dutton, 1975.

Marcuse, Herbert. *One-Dimensional Man: Studies in the Ideology of Advanced Industrial Society*. Boston: Beacon Press, 1964.

Mark, Lisa Gabrielle, and Paul Schimmel, et al., eds. *Under the Big Black Sun: California Art, 1974–1981*. Los Angeles: Museum of Contemporary Art, 2011.

Marshall, Richard, ed. *Jean-Michel Basquiat*. New York: Whitney, 1992.

Martin, Andy. *The Boxer and the Goalkeeper: Sartre vs. Camus*. New York: Simon & Schuster, 2012.

Martin, Bill. *Avant Rock: Experimental Music from the Beatles to Bjork*. Chicago: Open Court, 2002.

Martin, Bradford. *The Other Eighties: A Secret History of America in the Age of Reagan*. New York: Hill and Wang, 2011.

Martin, Jim. *1984: The Summer of Hate*. Fort Bragg: Flatland, 1989.

Marty, Myron A. *Daily Life in the United States, 1960–1990*. Westport: Greenwood, 1997.

Masters, Marc. *No Wave*. London: Black Dog Publishing, 2007.

Mathijs, Ernest, and Xavier Mendik. *100 Cult Films*. New York: Palgrave Macmillan, 2011.

McCaffery, Larry, ed. *Storming the Reality Studio: A Casebook of Cyberpunk and Postmodern Science Fiction*. Durham: Duke University Press, 1991.

McDonnell, Evelyn, and Ann Powers, eds. *Rock She Wrote: Women Write about Rock, Pop, and Rap*. New York: Delta Press, 1995.

McGirr, Lisa. *Suburban Warriors: The Origins of the New American Right*. Princeton: Princeton University Press, 2001.

McInnes, Gavin. *How to Piss in Public: From Teenage Rebellion to the Hangover of Adulthood*. New York: Scribner, 2012.

McKenna, Kristine, and David Hollander. *Notes from a Revolution: Com/Co, the Diggers, and the Haight*. No Place: Foggy Notion Books, 2012.

McMahon, Tyler. *How the Mistakes Were Made*. New York: St. Martin's Press, 2011.

McMillian, John. *Beatles vs. Stones*. New York: Simon & Schuster, 2013.

McMurray, Jacob. *Taking Punk to the Masses: From Nowhere to Nevermind*. Seattle: Fantagraphics Books, 2011.

McNeil, Legs, and Gillian McCain. *Please Kill Me: The Uncensored Oral History of Punk*. New York: Grove Press, 1996.

McRobbie, Angela, ed. *Zoot Suits and Second-Hand Dresses: An Anthology of Fashion and Music*. New York: Routledge, 1989.

Meisel, Perry. *Myth of Popular Culture: From Dante to Dylan*. West Sussex: Wiley, 2010.

Mele, Christopher. *Selling the Lower East Side: Culture, Real Estate, and Resistance in New York City*. Minneapolis: University of Minnesota, 2000.

Melly, George. *Revolt into Style: The Pop Arts in Britain*. London: Allan Lane, 1970.

Meltzer, Richard. *L.A. Is the Capital of Kansas: Painful Lessons in Post-New York Living*. New York: Harmony, 1988.

Meltzer, Richard. *A Whore Just Like the Rest*. New York: Da Capo Press, 2000.

Meyers, Jeffrey. *Joseph Conrad: A Biography*. New York: First Cooper Square Press, 1991.

Middles, Mike, and Mark E. Smith. *The Fall*. London: Omnibus, 2008.

Miessgang, Thomas. *Punk: No One Is Innocent*. Nuremburg: Verlag für Moderne Kunst, 2008.

Miller, Henry. *The Air-Conditioned Nightmare*. New York: New Directions, 1945.

Miller, Henry. *Tropic of Cancer*. Paris: Obelisk Press, 1934.

Miller, Henry. *Tropic of Capricorn*. New York: Grove Press, 1961.

Miller, Ivor L. *Aerosol Kingdom: Subway Painters of New York City*. Jackson: University of Mississippi, 2002.

Miller, James. *Flowers in the Dustbin: The Rise of Rock and Roll, 1947–1977*. New York: Fireside, 1999.

Miller, Mark Crispin. *Boxed In: The Culture of TV*. Evanston: Northwestern University Press, 1988.

Mills, Nicolaus, ed. *Culture in an Age of Money*. Chicago: I. R. Dee, 1990.

Milner, Greg. *Perfecting Sound Forever: An Aural History of Recorded Music*. New York: Farrar, Straus and Giroux, 2009.

Mitchell, Tim. *Sonic Transmission: Television, Tom Verlaine, Richard Hell*. London: Glitter Books, 2006.

Molesworth, Helen, ed. *This Will Have Been: Art, Love, and Politics in the 1980s*. New Haven: Yale University Press, 2012.

Molon, Dominic. *Sympathy for the Devil: Art and Rock and Roll since 1967*. New Haven: Yale University Press, 2007.

Monk, Noel E., and Jimmy Guterman. *12 Days on the Road: The Sex Pistols in America*. New York: Willian Morrow, 1990.

Moore, Alan W. *Art Gangs: Protest and Counterculture in New York City*. Brooklyn: Autonomedia, 2011.

Moore, Alan W. *Occupation Culture: Art and Squatting in the City from Below*. London: Minor Compositions, 2015.

Moore, Alan, and Marc Miller. *ABC No Rio Dinero: The Story of a Lower East Side Art Gallery*. New York: ABC No Rio, 1985.

Moore, Jack B. *Skinheads Shaved for Battle: A Cultural History of American Skinheads*. Madison: Popular Press, 1993.

Moore, Ryan. *Sells Like Teen Spirit: Music, Youth Culture, and Social Crisis*. New York: New York University Press, 2010.

Moore, Thurston, ed. *Mix Tape: The Art of Cassette Culture*. New York: Universe, 2004.

Moore, Thurston, and Byron Coley. *No Wave: Post-Punk Underground New York, 1976–1980*. New York: Abrams Image, 2007.

Moran, Joe. *Star Authors: Literary Celebrity in America*. London: Pluto Press, 2000.

Morris, Chris, and f-Stop Fitzgerald. *Beyond and Back: The Story of X*. San Francisco: Last Gasp, 1983.

Mould, Bob, and Michael Azerrad. *See a Little Light*. New York: Little, Brown, 2011.

Mueller, Cookie. *Ask Dr. Mueller: The Writings of Cookie Mueller*. Edited by Amy Scholder. New York: High Risk Books, 1997.

Muggleton, David. *Inside Subculture: The Postmodern Meaning of Style*. Oxford: Berg, 2000.

Muggleton, David, and Rupert Weinzierl, eds. *The Post-Subcultures Reader*. Oxford: Berg, 2003.

Mullen, Brendan. *Live at the Masque: Nightmare in Punk Alley*. Santa Rosa: Gingko Press, 2007.

Mullen, Brendan, Don Bolles, and Adam Parfrey. *Lexicon Devil: The Fast Times and Short Life of Darby Crash and the Germs*. Los Angeles: Feral House, 2002.

Muller, Eddie. *Dark City: The Lost World of Film Noir*. New York: St. Martin's Press, 1998.

Mulvihill, Robert, ed. *Reflections on America, 1984: An Orwell Symposium*. Athens: University of Georgia Press, 1986.

Murphy, Gareth. *Cowboys and Indies: The Epic History of the Record Industry*. New York: St. Martin's Press, 2014.

Murray, Charles Shaar. *Shots from the Hip: Notes on the Counterculture*. London: Penguin Books, 1991.

Murray, Nicholas. *Aldous Huxley: An English Intellectual*. New York: Time Warner Books, 2003.

Murphy, Graham J., and Sherryl Vint, eds. *Beyond Cyberpunk: New Critical Perspectives*. New York: Routledge, 2010.

Musto, Michael. *Downtown*. New York: Vintage Books, 1986.

Myers, Ben. *American Heretics: Rebel Voices in Music*. New York: Codex Books, 2002.

Nadel, Alan. *Flatlining in the Field of Dreams: Cultural Narratives in the Films of President Reagan's America*. New Brunswick: Rutgers University Press, 1997.

Nadel, Dan, ed. *Gary Panter*. Toronto: Picture Box, 2008.

Nedorostek, Nathan, and Anthony Pappalardo. *Radio Silence: A Selected Visual History of American Hardcore Music*. New York: MTV Press, 2008.

Neer, Richard. *FM: The Rise and Fall of Rock Radio*. New York: Villard Books, 2001.

Neuwirth, Robert. *Shadow Cities: A Billion Squatters, a New Urban World*. New York: Routledge, 2005.

New Yippie Book Collective. *Blacklisted News: Secret History from Chicago '68 to 1984*. New York: Bleecker Publishing, 1983.

Nicholl, Charles. *Somebody Else: Arthur Rimbaud in Africa, 1880–91*. Chicago: University of Chicago Press, 1997.

Nobakht, David. *Suicide: No Compromise*. London: SAF Publishing, 2005.

Noonan, Peggy. *What I Saw at the Revolution: A Political Life in the Reagan Era*. New York: Random House, 1990.

Norko, Damon. *Alias Art Mann*. Cherry Valley: Beach and Company, 1985.

Novoselic, Krist. *Of Grunge and Government: Let's Fix This Broken Democracy!* New York: RDV Books, 2004.

Nuttall, Jeff. *Bomb Culture*. New York: Delacorte, 1968.

Oates, Joyce Carol, ed. *Tales of H.P. Lovecraft*. New York: Ecco Press, 1996.

O'Brien, Geoffrey. *Hardboiled America*. New York: Da Capo Press, 1997.

O'Connor, Alan. *Punk Record Labels and the Struggle for Autonomy*. Lanham: Lexington, 2008.

O'Dair, Barbara, ed. *Trouble Girls: The Rolling Stone Book of Women in Rock*. New York: Random House, 1997.

Ogg, Alex. *Dead Kennedys Fresh Fruit for Rotting Vegetables, the Early Years*. Oakland: PM, 2014.

Ogg, Alex. *No More Heroes*. London: Cherry Red Books, 2006.

Oglesby, Carl. *The Yankee and Cowboy War*. New York: Berkeley, 1976.

O'Hara, Craig. *The Philosophy of Punk: More Than Noise!!* San Francisco: AK Press, 1995.

Ortved, John. *The Simpsons*. New York: Faber and Faber, 2009.

Orwell, George. *A Collection of Essays*. New York: HBJ, 1981.

Orwell, George. *1984*. New York: Signet Classics, 1984.

Osborne, John. *Look Back in Anger*. New York: Criterion, 1957.

Palmer, Myles. *New Wave Explosion: How Punk Became New Wave Became the 80's*. London: Proteus, 1981.

Panter, Gary. *Invasion of the Elvis Zombies*. New York: Raw, 1984.

Panter, Gary. *Jimbo*. New York: Pantheon, 1988.

Parfrey, Adam, ed. *Apocalypse Culture*. New York: Amok, 1987.

Parker, James. *Turned On: A Biography of Henry Rollins*. New York: Cooper Square, 1998.

Patterson, Clayton, ed. *Captured: A Film/Video History of the Lower East Side*. New York: Seven Stories Press, 2005.

Patterson, Clayton. *Resistance*. New York: Seven Stories Press, 2007.

Patterson, James. *Restless Giant: The United States from Watergate to Bush v. Gore*. New York: Oxford, 2005.

Pearlman, Alison. *Unpackaging Art of the 1980s*. Chicago: University of Chicago, 2003.

Perelman, Bob. *The Marginalization of Poetry: Language Writing and Literary History*. Princeton: Princeton University Press, 1996.

Perlstein, Rick. *The Invisible Bridge: The Fall of Nixon and the Rise of Reagan*. New York: Scribner, 2014.

Phillips, Kevin. *The Politics of Rich and Poor*. New York: Random House, 1990.

Picciolini, Christian. *White American Youth: My Descent into America's Most Violent Hate Movement and How I Got Out*. New York: Hachette, 2017.

Pierce, Jeffrey Lee. *Go Tell the Mountain: The Stories and Lyrics of Jeffrey Lee Pierce*. Los Angeles: 2.13.61 Publications, 1998.

Piesman, Marissa, and Marilee Hartley. *The Yuppie Handbook*. New York: Pocket, 1984.

Polizzotti, Mark. *Revolution of the Mind: The Life of Andre Breton*. New York: FSG, 1995.

Porter, Dick, and Kris Needs. *Blondie: Parallel Lives*. London: Omnibus, 2012.

Postman, Neil. *Amusing Ourselves to Death: Public Discourse in the Age of Show Business*. New York: Penguin, 1985.

Postman, Neil. *The Disappearance of Childhood*. New York: Delacorte, 1982.

Powers, Ann. *Weird Like Us: My Bohemian America*. New York: Simon & Schuster, 2000.

Prato, Greg. *Grunge Is Dead: The Oral History of Seattle Rock Music*. Toronto: ECW, 2009.

Prato, Greg. *MTV Ruled the World: The Early Years of Music Video*. Morrisville: Lulu, 2010.

Prato, Greg. *Too High to Die: Meet the Meat Puppets*. New York: Prato, 2012.

Prested, Kevin. *Punk USA*. Portland: Microcosm, 2014.

Prince, Stephen, ed. *American Cinema of the 1980s*. New Brunswick: Rutgers University Press, 2007.

Prince, Stephen. *A New Pot of Gold*. New York: Scribner's, 2000.

Pynchon, Thomas. *The Crying of Lot 49*. New York: Lippincott, 1965.

Pynchon, Thomas. *Gravity's Rainbow*. New York: Penguin, 1973.

Rachel, Daniel. *Walls Come Tumbling Down*. London: Picador, 2016.

RAND. *Trends in Anti-Nuclear Protests in the United States, 1984–1987*. Santa Monica: RAND, 1989.

Raskin, Jonah. *For the Hell of It: The Life and Times of Abbie Hoffman*. Berkeley: University of California Press, 1996.

Reagan, Ronald. *The Reagan Diaries*. New York: HarperCollins, 2007.

Reeves, Richard. *The Reagan Detour*. New York: Simon & Schuster, 1985.

Reich, Wilhelm. *The Mass Psychology of Fascism*. New York: FSG, 1970.

Reith, Gerry. *Neutron Gun*. Ann Arbor: Neither/Nor, 1985.

Ressler, Judy. *Inside People*. New York: Villard, 1994.

Rettenmund, Matthew. *Totally Awesome 80s*. New York: St. Martin's Press, 1996.

Rettman, Tony. *NYHC: New York Hardcore 1980–1990*. Brooklyn: Bazillion, 2014.

Rettman, Tony. *Straight Edge: A Clear-Headed Hardcore Punk History*. Brooklyn: Bazillion, 2017.

Rettman, Tony. *Why Be Something That You're Not: Detroit Hardcore, 1979–1985*. Huntington Beach: Revelation Records, 2010.

Reynolds, Simon. *Bring the Noise: 20 Years of Writing about Hip Rock and Hip Hop*. London: Faber and Faber, 2007.

Reynolds, Simon. *Rip It Up and Start Again*. Faber and Faber, 2005.

Reynolds, Simon. *Totally Wired: Post Punk Interviews and Overviews*. New York: Soft Skull, 2009.

Reynolds, Simon, and Joy Press. *The Sex Revolts*. Cambridge: Harvard, 1995.

Rifkin, Jeremy. *Entropy*. New York: Viking, 1980.

Rimbaud, Penny. *Shibboleth*. Edinburgh: AK Press, 1998.

Rimmer, Dave. *Like Punk Never Happened: Culture Club and the New Pop*. London: Faber and Faber, 1985.

Roberts, Jerry. *Diane Feinstein*. San Francisco: HarperCollins West, 1994.

Rocco, John. *The Nirvana Companion*. New York: Schirmer, 1998.

Roderick, Kevin. *The San Fernando Valley: America's Suburb*. Los Angeles: Los Angeles Times Books, 2001.

Rogin, Michael. *Ronald Reagan: The Movie*. Berkeley: University of California, 1987.

Rollins, Henry. *Get in the Van*. Los Angeles: 2.13.61 Publishing, 1994.

Rollins, Henry. *Henry Rollins Reader*. New York: Villard, 1997.

Rombes, Nicholas. *A Cultural Dictionary of Punk*. New York: Continuum, 2009.

Rombes, Nicholas, ed. *New Punk Cinema*. Edinburgh University Press, 2005.

Rombes, Nicholas. *Ramones*. New York: Continuum, 2006.

Rorabaugh, W. J. *American Hippies*. New York: Cambridge University Press, 2015.

Rose, Joel. *Kill the Poor*. New York: Atlantic Monthly Press, 1988.

Rossinow, Doug. *The Reagan Era: A History of the 1980s*. New York: Columbia University Press, 2015.

Rowse, Arthur. *One Sweet Guy*. Washington, D.C.: Consumer News, 1981.

Rucker, Rudy. *Nested Scrolls*. New York: TOR, 2011.

Rucker, Rudy. *Software*. New York: Ace, 1982.

Rucker, Rudy. *White Light*. New York: Ace, 1980.

Russo, Stacy. *We Were Going to Change the World: Interviews with Women from the 1970s and 1980s Southern California Punk Rock Scene*. Solana Beach: Santa Monica Press, 2017.

Sabin, Roger, ed. *Punk Rock: So What? The Cultural Legacy of Punk*. London: Routledge, 1999.

Sammon, Paul. *Future Noir: The Making of Blade Runner*. New York: HarperCollins, 1996.

Sandford, Christopher. *Kurt Cobain*. New York: Carroll and Graf, 1996.

Sargeant, Jack. *Deathtripping*. New York: Creation Books, 1999.

Sartre, Jean Paul. *Nausea*. New York: New Directions, 1964.

Savage, Jon. *England's Dreaming: Sex Pistols and Punk Rock*. London: Faber and Faber, 1991.

Savage, Jon. *The England's Dreaming Tapes*. Minneapolis: University of Minnesota, 2010.

Savage, Jon. *Time Travel*. London: Vintage, 1997.

Scheer, Robert. *With Enough Shovels*. New York: Random House, 1982.

Schrank, Jeffrey, *Snap, Crackle, and Popular Taste*. New York: Delta, 1977.

Schreck, Nikolas. *The Manson File*. New York: Amok, 1988.

Schulman, Bruce. *The Seventies: The Great Shift in American Culture, Society, and Politics*. New York: Free Press, 2001.

Schulman, Robert, and Julian Zelzer, eds. *Rightward Bound: Making America Conservative in the 1970s*. Cambridge: Harvard University Press, 2008.

Schwartzman, Allan. *Street Art*. Garden City: Dial, 1985.

Seno, Ethel, ed. *Trespass: A History of Uncommissioned Urban Art*. Koln, Germany: Taschen, 2010.

Scott, James C. *Two Cheers for Anarchism: Six Easy Pieces on Autonomy, Dignity, and Meaningful Work and Play*. Princeton: Princeton University Press, 2004.

Seed, David, ed. *A Companion to Science Fiction*. Malden: Blackwell, 2005.

Selvin, Joel. *Altamont: The Rolling Stones, the Hells Angels, and the Inside Story of Rock's Darkest Day*. New York: Dey Street Books, 2016.

Sewall, Gilbert, ed. *The Eighties: A Reader*. Reading: Addison-Wesley, 1997.

Shane, Tom. *Blockbuster*. New York: Free Press, 2004.

Shank, Barry. *Dissonant Identities*. Hanover: Wesleyan University Press, 1994.

Shank, Barry. *The Political Force of Musical Beauty*. Durham: Duke University Press, 2014.

Shapiro, Peter. *Turn the Beat Around: The Secret History of Disco.* New York: FSG, 2005.

Shattuck, Roger. *The Banquet Years: The Origins of the Avant-Garde in France, 1885 to World War I.* Garden City: Anchor, 1961.

Shattuck, Roger, and Simon Watson Taylor, eds. *Selected Works of Alfred Jarry.* New York: Grove Press, 1965.

Shaw, Philip. *Horses.* New York: Continuum, 2008.

Shelden, Michael. *Orwell.* New York: HarperCollins, 1991.

Shelton, Syd. *Rock against Racism.* London: Autograph, 2015.

Shiner, Lewis. *Frontera.* New York: Baen,1984.

Shirley, John. *Cellars.* New York: Avon, 1982.

Shirley, John. *City Come A-Walkin.* New York: Dell, 1980.

Shirley, John. *Dracula in Love.* New York: Kensington, 1979.

Shirley, John. *Three Ring Psychus.* New York: Zebra, 1980.

Shirley, John. *Transmaniacon.* New York: Zebra, 1979.

Siegle, Robert. *Suburban Ambush: Downtown Writing and the Fiction of Insurgency.* Baltimore: Johns Hopkins University Press, 1989.

Silliman, Ron, ed. *In the American Tree: Language, Realism, Poetry.* Orono: University of Maine, 1986.

Simmons, Matty. *Fat, Drunk, and Stupid: The Inside Story behind the Making of Animal House.* New York: St. Martin's Press, 2012.

Simpson, Kim. *Early '70s Radio: The American Format Revolution.* New York: Continuum, 2011.

Sinker, Daniel, ed. *We Owe You Nothing.* New York: Akashic, 2001.

Sirota, David. *Back to Our Future: How the 1980s Explains the World We Live in Now.* New York: Ballantine, 2011.

Skelley, Jack. *From Fear of Kathy Acker.* Los Angeles: Illuminati, 1984.

Skelley, Jack. *Monsters.* Los Angeles: Little Caesar, 1982.

Sladen, Mark, and Ariella Yedgar. *Panic Attack! Art in the Punk Years.* London: Merrell, 2007.

Slansky, Paul. *The Clothes Have No Emperor: A Chronicle of the America '80s.* New York: Simon & Schuster, 1989.

Slusser, George, and Tom Shippey, eds. *Fiction 2000: Cyberpunk and the Future of Narrative.* Athens: University of Georgia Press, 1992.

Smith, Christian. *Resisting Reagan: The U.S. Central America Peace Movement.* Chicago: University of Chicago Press, 1996.

Smith, Patti. *Early Work.* New York: Norton, 1994.

Smith, Patti. *Just Kids.* New York: Ecco Press, 2010.

Smith, Winston. *Act Like Nothing's Wrong: The Montage Art of Winston Smith.* San Francisco: Last Gasp, 1994.

Smokler, Kevin. *Brat Pack America: A Love Letter to '80s Teen Movies.* Los Angeles: Rare Bird, 2016.

Snowden, Don, ed. *Make the Music Go Bang! The Early L.A. Punk Scene.* New York: St. Martin's Press, 1997.

Solnit, Rebecca. *Hollow City: The Siege of San Francisco and the Crisis of American Urbanism.* New York: Verso, 2000.

Solomon, Frederic, and Robert Marston, eds. *The Medical Implications of Nuclear War.* Washington, D.C.: National Academy Press, 1986

Sorel, Georges. *Reflections on Violence.* New York: Collier, 1974.

Sorkin, Michael, ed. *Variations on a Theme Park.* New York: Hill and Wang, 1992.

Spiegelman, Art, and Francoise Mouly, eds. *Read Yourself Raw.* New York: Pantheon, 1987.

Spitz, Marc, and Brendan Mullen. *We Got the Neutron Bomb: The Untold Story of L.A. Punk.* New York: Three Rivers Press, 2001.

Sprouse, Martin. *Threat by Example: A Documentation of Inspiration.* San Francisco: Pressure Drop Press, 1990.

Stark, James. *Punk 77: An Inside Look at the San Francisco Rock 'n' Roll Scene 1977.* San Francisco: RE/Search, 2006.

Stein, Ellin. *That's Not Funny, That's Sick: The National Lampoon and the Comedy Insurgents Who Captured the Mainstream.* New York: Norton, 2013.

Sten, Mark. *All Ages: The History of Portland Punk, 1977–1981.* Portland: Reptilion, 2015.

Sterling, Bruce. *The Artificial Kid.* New York: Harper & Row, 1980.

Sterling, Bruce, ed. *Mirrorshades: The Cyberpunk Anthology.* New York: Arbor, 1986.

Sterling, Bruce. *Schismatrix.* New York: Arbor, 1985.

Stevenson, Nils. *Vacant: A Diary of the Punk Years, 1976–1979.* Thames and Hudson, 1991.

Stimson, Blake, and Gregory Shollette, eds. *Collectivism after Modernism.* Minneapolis: University of Minnesota, 2007.

Stone, Robert. *Dog Soldiers.* Boston: Houghton Mifflin, 1974.

Storr, Peter. *Logics of Failed Revolt: French Theory after May '68.* Stanford: Stanford University Press, 1995.

Storr, Robert, et al. *Raymond Pettibon.* New York: Phaidon, 2001.

Stosuy, Brandon. *Up Is Up, But So Is Down: New York's Downtown Literary Scene, 1974–1992.* New York: New York University Press, 2006.

Stuessy, Joe. *Rock and Roll: Its History and Stylistic Development.* Englewood Cliffs: Prentice Hall, 1994.

Suarez, Juan. *Jim Jarmusch.* Urbana: University of Illinois Press, 2007.

Sukenik, Ronald. *Down and In: Life in the Underground.* New York: Willian Morrow, 1987.

Sussman, Elisabeth, ed. *On the Passage of a Few People through a Rather Brief Moment in Time.* Cambridge: MIT Press, 1989.

Sutin, Lawrence. *Divine Invasion: A Life of Philip K. Dick.* New York: Harmony, 1989.

Suven, Bob. *Crate Digger: An Obsession with Punk Records.* Portland: Microcosm, 2015.

Suvin, Darko. *Metamorphoses of Science Fiction: On the Poetics and History of a Literary Genre.* New Haven: Yale University Press, 1979.

Svenonius, Ian F. *Censorship Now!!* Brooklyn: Akashic, 2015.

Swanwick, Michael. *The Postmodern Archipelago: Two Essays on Science Fiction and Fantasy.* San Francisco: Tachyon, 1997.

Szatmary, David P. *Rockin' in Time.* Upper Saddle River: Prentice Hall, 1996.

Taraborrelli, J. Randy. *Madonna: An Intimate Biography.* New York: Simon & Schuster, 2001.

Taylor, Chris. *How Star Wars Conquered the Universe: The Past, Present, and Future of a Multibillion Dollar Franchise.* New York: Basic Books, 2014.

Taylor, Marvin, ed. *The Downtown Book: The New York Art Scene, 1974–1984*. Princeton: Princeton University Press, 2006.

Taylor, Todd. *Born to Rock: Heavy Drinkers and Thinkers*. Los Angeles: Gorsky Press, 2004.

Thomas, Pat. *Did It! From Yippie to Yuppie: Jerry Rubin, An American Revolutionary*. Seattle: Fantagraphics, 2017.

Thompson, Dave. *Alternative Rock*. San Francisco: Miller Freeman, 2000.

Thompson, E. P. *The Making of the English Working Class*. New York: Vintage, 1986.

Thompson, E. P. *Protest and Survive*. New York: Penguin, 1980.

Thompson, Graham. *American Culture in the 1980s*. Edinburgh: Edinburgh University Press, 2007.

Thompson, Hunter S. *Generation of Swine*. New York: Summit, 1988.

Thompson, Stacy. *Punk Productions*. Albany: SUNY Press, 2004.

Todd, Dan, and John Zerzan. eds. *Adventures in Subversion: Flyers and Posters, 1981–85*. San Francisco: Oh! Press, 1985.

Todd, Olivier. *Alert Camus: A Life*. New York: Norton, 1997.

Torgoff, Martin. *Can't Find My Way Home: America in the Great Stoned Age, 1945–2000*. New York: Simon & Schuster, 2004.

Tosches, Nick. *The Nick Tosches Reader*. New York: Da Capo Press, 2000.

Tow, Stephen. *The Strangest Tribe: How a Group of Seattle Rock Bands Invented Grunge*. Seattle: Sasquatch, 2011.

Townshend, Pete. *Who I Am*. New York: Harper, 2012.

Travis, Tiffini, and Perry Harden. *Skinheads*. Santa Barbara: Greenwood, 2012.

Triggs, Teal. *Fanzines: The DIY Revolution*. San Francisco: Chronicle, 2010.

Trinidad, David. *Pavane*. Chatsworth: Sherwood Press, 1981.

Troy, Gil. *Morning in America: How Ronald Reagan Invented the 1980s*. Princeton: Princeton University Press, 2005.

True, Everett. *Hey Ho Let's Go: The Story of the Ramones*. London: Omnibus, 2002.

Turcotte, Bryan Ray, ed. *Punk Is Dead, Punk Is Everything*. Corte Madera: Gingko, 2007.

Turcotte, Bryan Ray, and Christopher Miller. *Fucked Up and Photocopied: Instant Art of the Punk Rock Movement*. Corte Madera: Gingko, 1999.

Turow, Joseph. *Breaking Up America: Advertisers and the New Media World*. Chicago: University of Chicago Press, 1997.

Vale, V. *Real Conversations, No. 1*. San Francisco: RE/Search, 2011.

Vaneigem, Raoul. *The Revolution of Everyday Life*. Oakland: PM, 2012.

Vaucher, Gee. *Crass Art and Other Pre Post-Modernist Monsters*. San Francisco: AK Press, 1999.

Vermorel, Fred. *Vivienne Westwood: Fashion, Perversity, and the Sixties Laid Bare*. Woodstock: Overlook, 1996.

Vonnegut, Kurt. *Novels and Stories, 1963–1973*. New York: Library of America, 2011.

Waksman, Steve. *Instruments of Desire: The Electric Guitar and the Shaping of Musical Experience*. Cambridge: Harvard University Press, 1999.

Waksman, Steve. *This Ain't the Summer of Love: Conflict and Crossover in Heavy Metal and Punk*. Berkeley: California University Press, 2009.

Wallace, Amy, and Dick Manitoba, eds. *The Official Punk Rock Book of Lists*. New York: Backbeat, 2007.

Wallerstein, Judith S. *Surviving the Breakup: How Children and Parents Cope with Divorce*. New York: Basic Books, 1980.

Wallis, Brian, ed. *Art after Modernism: Rethinking Representation.* New York: New Museum of Contemporary Art, 1984.

Walker, Michael. *What You Want Is in the Limo.* New York: Spiegel and Grau, 2013.

Ward, Colin. *Anarchy in Action.* London: Allen and Unwin, 1973.

Wark, McKenzie. *The Beach Beneath the Street: The Everyday Life and Glorious Times of the Situationist International.* London: Verso, 2011.

Warner, Brad. *Hardcore Zen: Punk Rock, Monster Movies and the Truth about Reality.* Boston: Wisdom Publications, 2003.

Watt, Mike. *Spiels of a Minutemen.* Montreal: L'Oie de Craven, 2003.

Weinberg, Mark. *Movie Nights with the Reagans.* New York: Simon & Schuster, 2018.

Weisbard, Eric, ed. *Listen Again: A Momentary History of Pop Music.* Durham: Duke University Press, 2007.

Weisbard, Eric. *Top 40 Democracy: The Rival Mainstreams of American Music.* Chicago: University of Chicago Press, 2014.

Wheen, Francis. *Strange Days Indeed: The Golden Age of Paranoia.* London: Fourth Estate, 2009.

White, Theodore H. *America in Search of Itself: The Making of the President 1956–1980.* New York: Harper & Row, 1982.

Whiteside, Thomas. *The Blockbuster Complex: Conglomerates, Show Business, and Book Publishing.* Wesleyan University Press, 1981.

Wilde, Oscar. *Complete Works of Oscar Wilde: Stories, Plays, Poems and Essays.* New York: Perennial Library, 1989.

Wilentz, Sean. *The Age of Reagan: A History, 1974–2008.* New York: HarperCollins, 2008.

Wills, Garry. *John Wayne's America.* New York: Simon & Schuster, 1997.

Wills, Garry. *Reagan's America.* New York: Penguin, 1988.

Wilson, Colin. *The Angry Years: The Rise and Fall of the Angry Young Men.* London: Robson Books, 2007.

Wilson, Colin. *The Outsider.* Boston: Houghton Mifflin, 1956.

Winn, Marie. *Children without Childhood.* New York: Pantheon, 1983.

Wittgenstein, Ludwig. *On Certainty.* New York: Harper & Row, 1972.

Wittner, Lawrence. *Toward Nuclear Abolition: A History of the World Nuclear Disarmament Movement.* Stanford: Stanford University Press, 2003

Wolfe, Tom. *In Our Time.* New York: FSG, 1980.

Wolfe, Tom. *Mauve Gloves and Madmen.* New York: FSG, 1976.

Wolfe, Tom. *The Purple Decade.* New York: FSG, 1982.

Woodcock, George. *Anarchism: A History of Libertarian Ideas and Movements.* New York: New American, 1962.

Woodward, Bob. *Wired: The Short Life and Fast Times of John Belushi.* New York: Simon & Schuster, 1984.

Worley, Matthew. *No Future: Punk, Politics and British Youth Culture, 1976–1984.* Cambridge: Cambridge University Press, 2017.

Wuelfing, Amy Yates, and Steven DiCodorico. *No Slam Dancing, No Stage Dives, No Spikes.* Morrisville: Diwulf, 2014.

Yankelovich, Daniel. *New Rules, Searching for Self-Fulfillment in a World Turned Upside Down.* New York: Random House, 1981.

York, Peter. *Style Wars*. London: Sidgwick and Jackson, 1980.

Young, Elizabeth, and Graham Caveney, eds. *Shopping in Space: Essays on American "Blank Generation" Fiction*. London: Serpent's Tail, 1992.

Young, Rob. *Rough Trade*. London: Black Dog, 2006.

Zaretsky, Natasha. *No Direction Home: The American Family and the Fear of National Decline, 1968–1980*. Chapel Hill: North Carolina University Press, 2007.

Zedd, Nick. *Bleed Part One*. New York: Hanuman, 1992.

Zukin, Sharon. *Loft Living: Culture and Capital in Urban Change*. New Brunswick: Rutgers University Press, 1989.

MOVIES

The following movies were released during the years studied here (for the most part) and are sometimes interpreted throughout the text. Some are online, but I consulted DVDs usually.

After Hours (1985)
American Gigolo (1980)
Another State of Mind (1984)
Atomic Café (1981)
Back to the Future (1985)
The Big Chill (1983)
Blade Runner (1982)
Blank Generation (1976)
Born in Flames (1983)
The Boys Next Door (1985)
Breakfast Club (1985)
Class of 1984 (1982)
The Day After (1983)
Debt Begins at 20 (1980)
Decline of Western Civilization (1981)
Desperate Teenage Lovedolls (1984)
Desperately Seeking Susan (1985)
D.O.A. (1980)
Edge City (1980)
Emerald Cities (1983)
Endless Love (1981)
Escape from New York (1981)
E.T. (1982)
Fast Times at Ridgemont High (1982)
Flashdance (1983)
Footloose (1984)
Foxes (1980)
Get Crazy (1983)
The Great Rock 'n' Roll Swindle (1980)
Invasion USA (1985)

King of Comedy (1982)
Ladies and Gentlemen, the Fabulous Stains (1982)
Mad Max II (1981)
Max Headroom (1985)
My Dinner with Andre (1981)
Neighbors (1981)
Nightmares (1983)
Not a Love Story (1981)
Out of the Blue (1980)
The Outsiders (1983)
Perfect (1985)
Permanent Vacation (1980)
Poltergeist (1982)
Purple Rain (1984)
Raiders of the Lost Ark (1981)
Rambo: First Blood (1982)
Rambo: First Blood, Part II (1985)
Red Dawn (1984)
Repo Man (1984)
Revenge of the Nerds (1984)
The Right Stuff (1983)
Risky Business (1983)
Roadie (1980)
Rock 'n' Roll High School (1979)
Rocky IV (1985)
Rumblefish (1983)
Scanners (1981)
Shoot the Moon (1982)
Silkwood (1983)
Sixteen Candles (1984)
The Slog Movie (1982)
Smithereens (1982)
St. Elmo's Fire (1985)
Stranger Than Paradise (1984)
Suburbia (1983)
Tempest (1982)
Testament (1983)
That Was Then This Is Now (1985)
Times Square (1980)
Tron (1982)
Vacation (1983)
Valley Girl (1983)
Videodrome (1983)
Vision Quest (1985)
Vortex (1982)
Wargames (1983)
Wild Style (1983)

NOTES

PREFACE

1. As quoted in Charles Bowden, *Blood Orchid* (New York: Random House, 1995), xv.
2. Charles Cross, *Heavier Than Heaven: A Biography of Kurt Cobain* (New York: Hyperion, 2001), 45; a copy of Kurt Cobain's suicide note has been posted here: https://kurtcobainssuicidenote.com/kurt_cobains_suicide_note.html.
3. See here Tom Wolfe's classic essay, "The Me Decade and the Third Great Awakening," in *Mauve Gloves and Madmen, Clutter and Vine* (New York: Bantam, 1977).
4. Gil Troy, *Morning in America: How Ronald Reagan Invented the 1980s* (Princeton: Princeton University Press, 2005), 7; John Patrick Diggins, *Ronald Reagan: Fate, Freedom, and the Making of History* (New York: Norton, 2007), 13; see also here Sean Wilentz, *The Age of Reagan* (New York: Harper, 2008).
5. Ian MacKaye in MAXIMUMROCKNROLL (*MRR* from now on), #1, 1982. See the best of the exception to the rule: Bradford Martin, *The Other Eighties* (New York: Hill and Wang, 2011). I rely on Martin's work throughout this book.

PRELUDE

1. Quoted in Jon Savage, *Time Travel* (London: Vintage, 1997), 76.
2. *L.A. Weekly*, July 5, 1979, 29.
3. *Search and Destroy, #7–11: The Complete Reprint* (San Francisco: V/Search Publications, no date), 142. Jello Biafra of the Dead Kennedys argued there were three generations of bands in the San Francisco punk scene: the first consisting of Crime, The Nuns, and The Dils; the second generation as the Avengers, Mutants, Offs, Negative Trend, UXA; and the third including the Dead Kennedys, who survived past 1979, plus new bands from the suburbs of San Francisco. See *Search and Destroy, #1–6 Anthology* (San Francisco: V/Search, 1996), iii.
4. See here the *East Village Eye*, June 1980, 16; when I first started researching this project, I consulted a run of *Punk* magazine held at Washington University, St. Louis; I also relied on the John Holmstrom Papers, Yale University, Box A-11: "Art from the Unpublished Punk, #18." See also *Punk: The Original* (New York: High

Times, 1998) and John Holmstrom, *The Best of Punk Magazine* (New York: It Books, 2011).

5. Cortez to Holmstrom, no date, found in John Holmstrom Papers, Box 52, Folder Hi Times; *L.A. Times*, April 22, 1979, U86.

6. Bangs quoted in *Take It!*, Issue B, 1981: 25; Lester Bangs in *Village Voice*, January 10, 1977, 63; Lester Bangs, *Blondie* (New York: Fireside, 1980), no pagination in book; Andy Warhol, *The Philosophy of Andy Warhol* (New York: HBJ, 1975), 43–44; Lester Bangs, "On the Merits of Sexual Repression," in John Morthland, ed., *Mainlines, Blood Feasts, and Bad Taste: A Lester Bangs Reader* (New York: Anchor, 2003), 114.

7. Schrader interviewed in *Slash*, August 1979, 12; *L.A. Weekly*, February 15–21, 1980, 54.

8. Dick Porter and Kris Needs, *Blondie: Parallel Lives* (New York: Omnibus, 2017), 188; the song's lyrics can be found via a Google search; Georg Gimarc, *Punk Diary* (San Francisco: Backbeat, 2005), 314.

9. *Time* quoted in Geoffrey Holtz, *Welcome to the Jungle: The Why behind "Generation X"* (New York: St. Martin's, 1995), 22–23; Dick Porter and Kris Needs, *Blondie*, 189; see also the *New York Times*, February 13, 1981, C1; *Boulevards*, February 1981, 19. For Brooke Shields's advertisement, see Bob Batchelor and Scott Stoddard, *The 1980s* (Westport: Greenwood, 2007), 43; see also Emma McClendon, *Denim: Fashion's Frontier* (New Haven: Yale University Press, 2016), 128. The advertisement itself can be seen here: https://www.youtube.com/watch?v=BZTH8A4vwQ4.

10. George Melly, *Revolt into Style* (London: Allen Lane, 1970).

11. *New York Times*, August 26, 1979, online: https://www.nytimes.com/1979/08/26/archives/looking-past-the-popmusic-blues-beyond-the-popmusic-blues.html; Graham Thompson, *American Culture in the 1980s* (Edinburgh: Edinburgh University Press, 2007), 123; see also Fredric Dannen, *Hit Men* (New York: Times Books, 1990), 208; R. Serge Denisoff and William Romanowski, *Risky Business* (New Brunswick: Transaction, 1991), 313; Joe Carducci, *Life against Dementia* (Centennial: Redoubt, 2012), 174.

12. *New York*, March 26, 1979, 40.

13. Richard Neer, *FM: The Rise and Fall of Rock Radio* (New York: Villard, 2001), 270–271.

14. Joel Selvin, *Altamont* (New York: Dey St., 2016), 109; John Fuller, *Are the Kids Alright?* (New York: Times Books, 1981), 13.

15. *Rolling Stone*, January 24, 1980, online: https://www.rollingstone.com/music/music-news/after-the-whos-cincinnati-concert-disaster-a-promoter-under-fire-89528/; Jonathon Epstein, ed., *Adolescents and Their Music* (New York: Garland, 1994), 258; see also Fuller, *Are the Kids Alright?*, 24.

16. Pete Townshend, *Who I Am* (New York: Harper, 2012), 323; Dave Marsh, *Before I Get Old* (New York: St. Martin's, 1983), 514; *Rolling Stone*, January 4, 1980; Fuller, *Are the Kids Alright?*, 254.

17. Quoting Carter's speech, which can be found at: http://www.presidency.ucsb.edu/ws/?pid=7552; Garry Wills, *Reagan's America* (Garden City: Doubleday, 1987), 399.

18. Sean Wilentz, *The Age of Reagan*, 110; *Rolling Stone*, September 30, 1982, on-line: https://www.rollingstone.com/politics/politics-news/nothing-about-the-draft-makes-sense-87900/.

CHAPTER 1

1. Albert Camus, *The Rebel* (New York: Vintage, 1956), 14.
2. *L.A. Times*, June 29, 1980, Y3–Y4.
3. William Brown, *You Should Have Heard Just What I Seen: Collected Newspaper Articles, 1981–1984* (Cincinnati: Colossal, 2010), 267; *L.A. Times*, June 29, 1980, Calendar Section, 3–4; "Carrot Woman," in Stacy Russo, ed., *We Were Going to Change the World* (Solana Beach: Santa Monica Press, 2017), 277.
4. *Washington Post*, July 19, 1981, G1; *Truly Needy*, Vol. 1, No. 4, (1982?), 8; *The Attack*, #7, 1982, 24; *Washington Weekly*, June 7, 1985, 9; David Browne, *Goodbye 20th Century: A Biography of Sonic Youth* (New York: Da Capo, 2008), 97; Dan Graham, *Rock My Religion* (Cambridge: MIT Press, 1993), 85; Dan Graham, *Two-Way Mirror Power* (Cambridge: MIT Press, 1999), 125.
5. *Punk Lust*, September–October (1982?), 3; Dennis Cooper, *Idols* (New York: Seahorse, 1979), 55; Hannah Arendt, *The Origins of Totalitarianism* (New York: World Publishing, 1958), 323; *WDC Period*, January 1985, 13.
6. *Selected Works of Ralph Waldo Emerson*, ed. William Gilman (New York: Signet, 1965), 114.
7. Mary Montgomery Wolf, "'We Accept You as One of Us?': Punk Rock, Community, and Individualism in an Uncertain Era, 1974–1985" (PhD Dissertation, University of North Carolina Chapel Hill, 2007), 247.
8. *Thrillseeker*, #1, 27; *New York Rocker*, July–August, 1981, 20; *Search and Destroy*, #9, 1978, 63.
9. There are two recent books about *Fresh Fruit*. Alex Ogg in *Dead Kennedys Fresh Fruit for Rotting Vegetables (the Early Years)* (Oakland: PM Press, 2014) links Biafra's political criticism to Swift and specifically "A Modest Proposal," 108. But Michael Stewart Foley's *Fresh Fruit for Rotting Vegetables* (New York: Bloomsbury, 2015), asserts that Biafra claimed not to be influenced by Swift (at least not when writing "Kill the Poor"), 114. See also pp. 3–17 in Andre Breton, *Anthology of Black Humor* (1940; San Francisco: City Lights Books, 1997), where "A Modest Proposal" can be read, placed in the wider tradition of surrealism.
10. *New York Rocker*, July–August 1981, 19; *Wet*, November 1980, 36; Biafra state-ment found in Wobensmith, A Folder; *Boulevards*, May 1980, 14; Foley, *Fresh Fruit*, 98–103.
11. *Search and Destroy*, #9, 1978, 61; Brock Ruggles, "Not So Quiet on the Western Front: Punk Politics during the Conservative Ascendancy in the United States, 1980–2000" (PhD Dissertation, Arizona State University, 2008), 159–161; *Search and Destroy*, #9, 1978, 61–62; interview with Smith in *MRR*, January–February, 1984; *Wet*, November 1980, 36.
12. Ian MacKaye in *Gimme Something Better*, ed. Jack Boulware and Silke Tudor (New York: Penguin, 2009), 48.
13. William S. Burroughs, *The Wild Boys* (1971; New York: Grove, 1992), 165.

14. All song lyrics, unless otherwise noted, can be found with a Google search: The band's name and the song's title are the only things necessary to input.
15. Ted Kennedy and Mark Hatfield, *Freeze!* (New York: Bantam, 1982), 8; Frederic Solomon and Robert Marston, eds., *The Medical Implications of Nuclear War* (Washington, D.C.: National Academy Press, 1986), 423–431; Lawrence Wittner, *Toward Nuclear Abolition* (Stanford: Stanford University Press, 2003), 170; Robert Coles, *The Moral Life of Children* (Boston: Atlantic, 1986), 244–245. See also here Joel Kovel, *Against the State of Nuclear Terror* (Boston: South End, 1983).
16. *Thrillseeker*, #3, 1984, 26–27; *Damage*, #11, 1981, 11.
17. *Night Voices*, #4, April–June 1981, no pagination; Peter Belsito and Bob Davis, *Hardcore California* (San Francisco: Last Gasp, 1983), no pagination; *WDC*, #8, 7. For a nice memoir about Canterbury Apartments and the Masque scene, see Alice Bag, *Violence Girl* (Port Townsend: Feral House, 2011).
18. *Ripper*, #3, 1984, 16; Stevie Chick, *Spraypaint the Walls: The Story of Black Flag* (London: Omnibus, 2009), 62; Belsito and Davis, *Hardcore California*; *Discords*, May 1981, 10; *Outcry*, (1980?), 7; *Flipside*, #18, no pagination.
19. *Suburban Relapse*, August 1982, 10; for a fine story on the connection between antifashion and thrift stores, see the Pittsburgh zine, *New Magazine*, #2, (1978?), no pagination.
20. Mike Watt quoted in *Ink Disease*, #8 (1984?); *Thrillseeker*, #3, 1984, 30; *Forced Exposure*, #6, no pagination; *Truly Needy*, #10, 18, 19; *Your Flesh*, #5, 1982; *L.A. Weekly*, July 15–22, 1982, 22.
21. *No Mag*, 1983: no pagination. For records I have relied on the very helpful website known as *Discogs*.
22. *Creep*, #3, 1980, 4.
23. Mike Watt, *Spiels of a Minuteman* (Quebec: L'Oie de Cravan, 2003), 24; Michael Fournier, *Double Nickels on the Dime* (New York: Bloomsbury, 2007), 90.
24. Michel Foucault, *This Is Not a Pipe* (Berkeley: University of California Press, 1983), 41; *Forced Exposure*, #13, 62. *Raymond Pettibon: Homo Americanus*, ed. Ulrich Loock et al. (Hamburg: David Zwirner, 2016), 294. Peter Belsito argued that punks would "reject advertising by twisting its repressive Everyman imagery into a grotesque and blackly humorous caricature that belie the falsehoods upon which the masses are fed." Peter Belsito et al., eds., *Streetart* (San Francisco: Last Gasp, 1981), 8. You can see the rejection of the comic book format in Pettibon's 1978 magazine *Captive Chains*, reprinted in *Raymond Pettibon: Homo Americanus*.
25. Raymond Pettibon's *Tripping Corpse* (1981), Yale Collection; Pettibon in Dennis Cooper, "Between the Lines." This is cited in the following online article: https://www.huckmag.com/art-and-culture/raymond-pettibon-artist-punk/; J. Hoberman in Brian Wallis, ed., *Art after Modernism* (New York: Museum of Contemporary Art), 64. Susan Sontag, *A Susan Sontag Reader* (New York: Random House, 1982), 103. It's ironic to note that Allen Ginsberg was trying to reach out to punk poets at the time: see *L.A. Weekly*, August 3–9, 1979, 4.
26. *Los Angeles Reader*, February 27, 1981, 7 (from now on *L.A. Reader*), February 12, 1982, Section 2, 2; *L.A. Times*, March 3, 1981, G6; *L.A. Weekly*, November 12–18, 1982, 39; *Unsound*, September 1983, 7; *L.A. Reader*, July 9, 1982, 19, and August 28, 1981, 8, 9, 15.

27. *Coolest Retard*, February–March 1981; *My Dinner with Andre* quoted in Theodore Roszak, *The Making of a Counterculture* (1968; Berkeley: University of California Press, 1995), xi.

28. David Felton, *Mindfuckers* (San Francisco: Straight Arrow, 1972); and see also Ed Sanders, *The Family* (New York: Dutton, 1971); Kevin Roderick, *The San Fernando Valley: America's Suburb* (Los Angeles: L.A. Times Books, 2001), 163; *Forced Exposure*, #13, 61. The drawing can be found in *Raymond Pettibon: Homo Americanus*, 93.

29. Gibson quoted in Georges., *Fiction 2000* (Athens: University of Georgia Press, 1992), 21.

30. Most of this is gleaned from an email interview with Shirley.

31. *Sub Pop*, Spring 1981; *Subterranean Pop*, #2, 1980 (note that *Subterranean Pop* turned into *Sub Pop* at this time); Mark Sten, *All Ages* (Portland: Reptilicus, 2015), 221–223; on Biafra's love of Portland, see Dave Corboy's statement in Ogg, *Fresh Fruit*, 186.

32. *The Magazine X*, no pagination.

33. John Shirley to Holmstrom, April 29 (no year), Holmstrom Papers, Yale University, Box 54.

34. John Shirley, *City Come A-Walkin* (New York: Dell, 1980), 20, 177, 108, 134.

35. Shirley, *City Come A-Walkin*, 53, 75, 25, 8. In the summer of 1981, *Frisco* magazine ran a story of a sweep on Polk Street getting mostly gay prostitutes but also Ginger Coyote, who edited *Punk Globe*. *Frisco*, Vol. 1, No. 1, 1981, 7. It should be noted that there's similarity here with Philip Dick's writing. As one critic, George Sussler, has pointed out, Dick portrayed in his work "shadowy business conglomerates controlling the political structure, 'little' or disenfranchised men and woman as protagonists engaged in futile if not always violent acts." See Larry McCaffery, ed., *Storming the Reality Studio* (Durham: Duke University Press, 1991), 336.

36. Shirley, *City Come A-Walkin*, 74–75, 147.

37. Shirley, *City Come A-Walkin*, 120, 133, 199; Jean Paul Sartre, *Nausea* (New York: New Directions, 1964), 68.

38. Shirley, *City Come A-Walkin*, 204.

39. Anthony Burgess, *A Clockwork Orange* (1962; reprint New York: Norton, 1963), 105.

40. Stephanie Beroes interviewed in *Vice*: https://www.vice.com/en_us/article/avjxgj/debt-begins-at-20; Pittsburgh's scene is also documented in *Damage*, June 1981, 10. The movie is available at Vimeo.

41. Fredric Dannen, *Hit Men* (New York: Times Books, 1990), 174.

42. *L.A. Reader*, October 17, 1980, 2.

43. Guy Debord, *Society of the Spectacle* (Detroit: Black and Red, 1983), Thesis 12.

44. Ronald Reagan, *An American Life* (New York: Simon & Schuster, 1981), 205; the speech is reprinted in my *"What the Heck Are You Up To, Mr. President?"* (New York: Bloomsbury, 2009), 207–217; Thomas Evans, *The Education of Ronald Reagan* (New York: Columbia University Press, 2008), 84; Sean Wilentz, *The Age of Reagan* (New York: HarperCollins, 2008), 127; Sidney Blumenthal, *Our Long National Daydream* (New York: Harper & Row, 1988), 107. The comparison between Carter and Herbert Marcuse is slightly unfair, but interesting to note here is

one of Marcuse's own writings about consumer culture: "People recognize them-selves in their commodities; they find their souls in their automobiles, hi-fi sets, split level homes, kitchen equipment." Quoted in Stuart Jeffries, *Grand Hotel Abyss* (London: Verso, 2017), 307.

45. Evans, *The Education of Ronald Reagan*, 5; Ronnie Dugger, *On Ronald Reagan* (New York: McGraw-Hill, 1983), 119, 177, 181.

46. Andrew Busch, *Reagan's Victory* (Lawrence: University of Kansas Press, 2005), 144; Garry Wills, *John Wayne's America* (New York: Simon & Schuster, 1997); David Sirota, *Back to Our Future* (New York: Ballantine, 2011), 112; Dugger, *On Ronald Reagan*, 397.

47. Crass, "Tired," on *Stations of the Crass* (1979).

48. *The Birth of Tragedy and the Genealogy of Morals* (Garden City: Doubleday, 1956), 243.

49. Clippings about this show found in Mark Andersen Papers, Box 6; also *Capitol Crisis*, No. 3, 1981.

50. William Burroughs, *Naked Lunch* (1959; reissued New York: Grove, 2001), 137; Philip K. Dick, "A Scanner Darkly," in *Philip K. Dick: Five Novels of the 1960s and 1970s*, ed. Jonathan Lethem (New York: Library of America, 2008), 880, 1097 (see also Lawrence Sutin, *Divine Invasions* (New York: Da Capo, 2005), 201–203); *Creep Newsletter*, Vol. 1, No. 1, 1981: zine in Michael Stewart Foley's possession; Kim Gordon, *Is It My Body?* (Frankfurt: Sternberg, 2014), 104, (this essay was originally published in 1985).

51. *New Wave*, August 1977, 11; *NME*, December 17, 1977, 8.

52. David Markey and Jordan Schwartz, *We've Got Power!* (Brooklyn: Bazillion Points, 2012), 144; Lisa Birnbach, *The Official Preppy Handbook* (New York: Workman, 1980), 35, 105; see also the silly article, "Prep versus Punk," *Mademoiselle*, June 1980, 182.

53. *Capitol Crisis*, #3, February 1981, 17, 1; *Capitol Crisis*, March 1981; see also *Vintage Violence*, #1, for a story on the Slickee Boys (this was another early D.C. zine), and *The Infiltrator*, #5. The term "teeny punk" was also seen in Alan Keenan, "Angry Young Men," *Washington Tribune*, October 8–21, 1982, 12.

54. *Capitol Crisis*, #5, May 1981; for more on the trip west and the development of Straight Edge and X-ed hands, see Jeff Nelson to John Loder, found in Mark Andersen Papers, Box 6, Folder of "DC articles"; and Jack Boulware and Silke Toudor, *Gimme Something Better*, 48; MacKaye recounted the trip in *Ink Disease*, #11, 1985.

55. *Capitol Crisis*, March 1981; *Op*, Spring 1981; V. Vale, *Real Conversations No. 1* (San Francisco: Re/Search, 2011), 46.

56. *Op*, M issue, (1981?), 24; see Jello Biafra's comments in *Truly Needy*, Vol. 1, No. 3, 1982, 32.

57. Brendan Mullen and Don Bolles, *Lexicon Devil* (Port Townsend: Feral House, 2002); Barney Hoskyns, *Waiting for the Sun* (New York: Backbeat, 2009), 280.

58. Quoted in Arthur Rowse, *One Sweet Guy* (Washington, D.C.: Consumer News, 1981), 17.

59. *New York Times*, October 13, 1981, online: https://www.nytimes.com/1981/10/13/us/first-lady-tells-critics-i-am-just-being-myself.html; Haynes Johnson,

Sleepwalking through History (New York: Doubleday, 1992), 20; Nicolaus Mills, ed., *Culture in an Age of Money* (Chicago: I.R. Dee, 1990), 16.

60. Reagan's inaugural speech can be found here: https://www.presidency.ucsb.edu/documents/inaugural-address-11. On Treptow and reality, see Lou Cannon, *President Reagan* (New York: Public Affairs, 2000), 75–77.

61. Mary Harron, "Pop Art/Art Pop," originally published in *Melody Maker*, February 16, 1980, and then reprinted in *The Sound the Fury*, ed. Barney Hoskyns (New York: Bloomsbury, 2003), 354–377; *The Offense*, #13, 1981, 27. For more on Warhol's interview with Nancy Reagan, see Andy Warhol, *The Andy Warhol Diaries* (New York: Warner, 1989), 412–413. Here he explains how he didn't like Nancy Reagan, who seemed "boring" (she was chatting up her antidrug work, which probably made him uncomfortable). And when he thought about the meeting, he exclaimed, "She could have used the *good china!*"

62. *Outcry*, #2, 1981, 4.

63. *L.A. Times*, July 30, 1989, 49-E; Jack Grisham, *American Demon* (Toronto: ECW, 2011), 189; *Blur*, June 25, 1982; *Ripper*, #5, 1981, 34; for more on Proudhon's ideas about proprietorship, see George Woodcock, *Anarchism* (New York: New American, 1962), 115.

64. See Roberto Ohrt, ed. *Raymond Pettibon* (New York: D.A.P., 2000), *A New Wave of Violence* zine printed within.

65. *Noise*, #3, May–June 1981; Charles Shaar Murray, *Shots from the Hip* (London: Penguin, 1991), 96.

66. H. P. Lovecraft, "The Outsider," reprinted in *Tales of H.P. Lovecraft*, ed. Joyce Carol Oates (New York: Ecco, 1996), 1.

67. *Ripper*, #5, (1981?), 2; Lizabeth Cohen, *A Consumers' Republic* (New York: Knopf, 2003), 275.

68. *Damage*, September 1980, 31; the speech of Goldwater's can be found in Jeffrey Volle, *The Political Legacies of Barry Goldwater and George McGovern* (New York: Palgrave, 2010), 91.

69. *Ripper*, #3, 1980, 7–11.

70. *Ripper*, #4, 20; *Ripper*, #5, (1981?), 37; *Ripper*, #8, 1982; *Ripper*, #8, 5; *L.A. Weekly*, July 18–24, 1980, 4.

71. *L.A. Reader*, January 15, 1982, 3; *L.A. Reader*, August 13, 1982, 3.

72. *Noise*, July–August 1981; *Punk Lust*, #8, March 1982, 5; *The Attack*, #7, 24; *Ripper*, #7, May 1982, 16.

73. *Ripper*, #7, May 4, 1982, 17; *Night Voices*, #4, April–June 1981.

74. *MRR*, #2, 1982; Stephen Tow, *The Strangest Tribe* (Seattle: Sasquatch, 2011), 30; *Punk Lust*, March 1982, 1.

75. *Punk Lust*, September–October, 1982, 2; *Punk Lust*, January 1982, 3; *Punk Lust*, #7; *Punk Lust*, January 1982, 6; Lovecraft, "The Outsider," 1; *Punk Lust*, #8, March 1982, 2; *Punk Lust*, #2, 5; *Punk Lust*, #8, March 1982, 4.

76. *Punk Lust*, May–June 1982, 5; Oates, ed., *Tales of H.P. Lovecraft*, 58 (this collection includes both "The Shunned House" and "The Rats in the Walls"); MacKaye quoted in James Greene Jr., *This Music Leaves Stains: The Complete Story of the Misfits* (Lanham: Scarecrow, 2013), 47; Sigmund Freud, *The Uncanny* (1919; reprinted, New York: Penguin, 2003); *Subpop*, February 1982.

77. *The Attack*, #7, April 1982, 3.
78. *Patio X Table*, no date; *Desperate Times*, August 19, 1981, 5; by 1982, *Patio X Table* got recognition outside of Seattle: See *The Offense*, #15, 1982, 27.
79. *Desperate Times*, July 22, 1981, 1; *Desperate Times*, August 19, 1981, 10. Fortunately, this zine has been reissued in book form: See Maire M. Masco, *Desperate Times: The Summer of 1981* (Tacoma: Fluke Press, 2015).
80. *L.A. Weekly*, February 13–19, 1981; *L.A. Weekly*, March 20–26, 1981, 5; *The Decline of Western Civilization Collection* (this is a booklet that accompanied a re-issue of all three *Decline* movies in 2015), 1; *Discords*, September 1981, 6.
81. See the following article (Ann Friedman, "Penelope Spheeris: 'I sold out and took the money'") online: https://www.theguardian.com/film/2015/aug/23/penelope-spheeris-film-maker-the-decline-of-western-civilization; *L.A. Weekly*, March 20–26, 1981, 4–5.
82. *L.A. Weekly*, March 20–26, 1981, 5.
83. *East Village Eye*, Summer 1981, 24.
84. *L.A. Weekly*, August 8–14, 1980, 36; *Damage*, June 1981, 55; *The Offense*, #11, 1981, 60; *Wave Sector* (publication of KUSF, 90.3 radio station), June 1981, 2–3.
85. For Bessy on the Situationist International, see *Slash*, June 1979, 10. I also discuss this in more detail later. For an example of Bessy's assistance to a new zine, see the comment made in the *Offense*, #5, 1980, 32.
86. *Capitol Crisis*, March 1981, 27; *Capitol Crisis*, May 1981; *Desperate Times*, August 5, 1981, 12.
87. Quoted in *Ripper*, #5, (1981?): 25.
88. *No Mag*, 1981; Aimee Cooper, *Coloring outside the Lines* (no place: Rowdy's Press, 2002), 78.
89. *L.A. Weekly*, April 10–16, 1981, 28; Bob Batchelor and Scott Stoddart, *The 1980s* (Westport: Greenwood, 2007), 114; *Capitol Crisis*, May 1981; Al Clark, ed., *The Rock Yearbook, 1984* (New York: St. Martin's, 1983), 60; *Non LP B Side*, Holiday Issue.
90. *L.A. Weekly*, January 29–February 4, 1982, 11; *Sense of Purpose*, #1, December 1983; *Altered Statements*, #4; *Ripper*, #6, 1982: 2; *The Face*, April 1981; *Own the Whole World*, March 1983, 9.
91. Duran Duran quoted in George Gimarc, *Punk Diary* (San Francisco: Backbeat, 2005), 414; *I Wanna*, Fall/Winter 1982, 7; *Desperate Times*, July 22, 2; *Ripper*, #5, 11; *Cranial Crap*, Mid-November, 1981, front page; *Noise*, July 1981.
92. *Take It!*, 1981, 9; *Suburban Relapse*, #3, New Years 1982, 23.
93. *The Portable Karl Marx*, ed. Eugene Kamenka (New York: Penguin, 1983), 287.
94. *Scanlan's*, March 1970, 53; Barney Hoskyns, *Beneath the Diamond Sky* (New York: Simon & Schuster, 1997), 79; John Glatt, *Rage and Roll* (Secaucus: Carol, 1993), 180.
95. Bill Graham and Robert Greenfield, *Bill Graham Presents* (New York: Doubleday, 1992), 416–420; Glatt, *Rage and Roll*, 180–185.
96. Yohannan in Martin Sprouse, ed., *Threat by Example* (San Francisco: Pressure Drop, 1991), 47; Todd Gitlin, *The Sixties* (New York: Bantam, 1987), 355.
97. *Basement*, Vol. 1, No. 1, 1981 (zine in possession of Michael Stewart Foley); *Another Room*, Vol. 2, No. 5 (1980?); *Creep*, #1, 1979, 5; Belsito et al., eds., *Streetart*, 47.

98. *Ripper*, #5, 29.

99. *East Village Eye*, March 1981, 6.

100. Lester Bangs, "Jim Morrison: Bozo Dionysus a Decade Later," in *Mainlines, Blood Feasts, and Bad Taste*, ed. John Morthland (New York: Anchor, 2003), 214–215.

101. Bangs, *Mainlines*, 122–124; for the Muggeridge influence, see Jim DeRogatis, *Let It Blurt: The Life and Times of Lester Bangs, America's Greatest Rock Critic* (New York: Broadway, 2000), 211. Nor did Bangs consider that being simultaneously a "fascist" and a "nihilist" were not the same thing—fascists deified the state, while nihilists saw no higher meaning whatsoever.

102. Bangs, *Mainlines*, 33–34.

103. For more on the Detroit scene and Bangs's rethinking, see my "Leather Jackets for Flowers: The Death of Hippie and the Birth of Punk in the Long, Late 1960s," *The Sixties*, Vol. 12, No. 1 (2019): 1–44.

104. *Take It!*, # 5, "Star Issue," 1981, 14.

105. William Greider, "The Education of David Stockman," *The Atlantic*, November 1981, online: https://www.theatlantic.com/magazine/archive/1981/12/the-education-of-david-stockman/305760/.

106. Joseph McCartin, *Collision Course* (New York: Oxford University Press, 2011), 289, 331.

107. Greider, "The Education."

108. Greider, "The Education."

109. *New York Times*, September 9, 1981, A7; *Washington Post*, September 26, 1981, online: https://www.washingtonpost.com/archive/politics/1981/09/26/us-holds-the-ketchup-in-schools/9ffd029a-17f5-4e8c-ab91-1348a44773ee/?utm_term=.16b08168db2f.

110. *New York Times*, September 26, 1981, online: https://www.nytimes.com/1981/09/26/politics/reagan-abandons-proposal-to-pare-school-nutrition.html.

111. *Slash*, #10, 1978, 14.

112. Thomas Berger, *Neighbors* (New York: Delacorte, 1980), 4, 42, 53, 61, 217, 263, 275; see also David Madden, ed., *Critical Essays on Thomas Berger* (New York: G.K. Hall, 1995), 118–121.

113. For more on Belushi's biography, see Bob Woodward, *Wired* (New York: Simon & Schuster, 1984).

114. *Noise*, December 1981; *L.A. Weekly*, November 6–12, 1981, 20.

115. Tesco Vee and Dave Stimson, *Touch and Go: The Complete Hardcore Punk Zine, '79–'83*, ed. Steve Miller (Brooklyn: Bazillion Points, 2010), 357.

116. *Op*, M Issue; *Ink Disease*, #11.

117. Dennis Cooper, "Report Card," in *Idols*, 24.

118. *Washington Post*, December 6, 1981, online: https://www.washingtonpost.com/archive/politics/1981/12/06/california-suburb-sorts-out-fear-and-confusion-in-teen-slaying/85006272-e4e5-495f-9ab8-10ca0d2a46b9/?utm_term=.3cd5c4eb2126.

119. *New York Times*, February 22, 1987, online: https://www.nytimes.com/1987/02/22/us/youth-suicide-is-rising.html; see also Donna Gaines, *Teenage Wasteland* (New York: Pantheon, 1991), 7; David Elkind, *All Grown Up and*

No Place to Go (Reading: Addison-Wesley, 1984); Joel Garreau, *Edge City* (New York: Doubleday, 1991), 385.

120. Tom Wolfe, *In Our Time* (New York: FSG, 1980), 5; Theodore H. White, *America in Search of Itself* (New York: Warner, 1983), 353, 355; *New York Times*, July 6, 2011, online: https://www.nytimes.com/2011/07/10/magazine/the-divorce-delusion.html; Judith Wallerstein, *Surviving the Breakup* (New York: Basic Books, 1996), 6, 232; Elkind, *All Grown Up*, 116, and see also Natasha Zaretsky, *No Direction Home* (Chapel Hill: UNC, 2007), 11; Geoffrey Holtz, *Welcome to the Jungle* (New York: St. Martin's, 1995), 33, 56; Neil Postman, *The End of Childhood* (New York: Delacorte, 1982).

121. *R.I.P.*, #1; *Negative Print*, #5 (1983?); Craig Lee quoted in Mikal Gilmore, *Night Beat* (New York: Anchor, 1999), 190. For more on how shopping malls were transforming kids into passive consumers, see William Severini Kowinski, *The Malling of America* (New York: Morrow, 1985), 349–350.

122. L. Lev, ed., *Enter at Your Own Risk* (Madison: Fairleigh Dickinson, 2006), 243, 135, 69, 243, 246; *Little Caesar*, #10, 1980, found in Dennis Cooper Papers (NYU); Dennis Cooper, ed., *Coming Attractions* (Los Angeles: Little Caesar, 1980), 124, 128; David Trinidad, *Pavane* (Chatsworth, CA: Sherwood, 1981), 32–33.

123. *L.A. Weekly*, April 30–May 6, 1982, 17; *Creem*, September 1971: See "Fantasy Gave Me Fire," no pagination; Pettibon rewrite of "Howl" found in *Tripping Corpse*, 1981: found in Yale collections; the first statement comes from "Jag-arr of the Jungle," *Creem*, January 1973; the second from the play she wrote with Sam Shepard in 1971, *Cowboy Mouth*, reprinted in Sam Shepard, *"Fool for Love" and Other Plays* (New York: Bantam, 1984), 156; Patti Smith, *Early Work*, 1970–1979 (New York: Norton, 1994), 40.

124. Quoted in Daniel Kane, *Do You Have a Band?* (New York: Columbia University Press, 2017), 204; Cooper, *Idols*, 55, 29. "Sit on My Face" had been sung as a punk song a bit earlier, by the Rotters in Los Angeles and applied to Stevie Nicks of Fleetwood Mac.

125. *Little Caesar*, #2, 1977, no pagination; quote is from Hell's Journals, p. 46–47: found in Fales Library, Box One, Folder One. For more on language poetry see the collection, Ron Silliman, ed., *In the American Tree* (Orono: National Poetry Foundation, 1986), especially David Bromige, who writes, "The reader grows impatient irritated with my distancing style, coming at him in the rare book format" (216).

126. *L.A. Weekly*, April 30–May 6, 1982, 17; David Lehman, *The Last Avant-Garde* (New York: Anchor, 1999), 169.

127. Lev, ed., *Enter at Your Own Risk*, 246; Cooper, ed., *Coming Attractions*, 39. It's interesting to note that another punk band (a bit earlier) took on John Wayne Gacy: The Mentally Ill, "Gacy's Place."

128. Dennis Cooper, *The Tenderness of the Wolves* (Trumansburg: The Crossing Press, 1982), Section 2, 69–71; *L.A. Weekly*, April 30–May 6, 1982, 17.

129. *Outcry*, 1980, 8.

130. Edmund Morris, *Dutch* (New York: Random House, 1999), 482; Walter Lafeber, *Inevitable Revolutions* (New York: Norton, 1983), 296.

131. Lafeber, *Inevitable Revolutions*, 286; *Boredom*, #5, February 30, 1981, 5; *L.A. Weekly*, May 29–June 4, 1981, 18; *Night Voices*, December 1981–February 1982, 12.

132. *L.A. Times*, May 4, 1981, 7; see also *L.A. Reader*, July 10, 1981, 3, and *Modern Muzik*, May 1981.

133. *New York Times*, January 8, 1982: https://www.nytimes.com/1982/01/08/us/reagan-in-a-shift-plans-to-continue-sign-up-for-draft.html; Laurence Barrett, *Gambling with History* (Garden City: Doubleday, 1983), 203; see also *L.A. Reader*, August 13, 1982, 3, for numbers on nonregistrants and the crackdown; *L.A. Weekly*, June 20–26, 1980, 3.

134. Phyllis LaFarge, *The Strangelove Legacy* (New York: Harper & Row, 1987), 66–68; Robert Jay Lifton and Richard Falk, *Indefensible Weapons* (New York: Basic, 1982), 16–17; Ronald Reagan, *The Reagan Diaries*, ed. by Douglas Brinkley (New York HarperCollins, 2007), 52.

135. This is quoted in Robert Scheer, *With Enough Shovels* (New York: Random House, 1982), 18–24, Bush on p. 29; *The Attack*, July–August, 1982, 2.

136. Winston Smith, *Act Like Nothing's Wrong* (San Francisco: Last Gasp, 1994), 7; *Damage*, August–September 1979, 8; Alex Ogg, *Dead Kennedys* (Oakland: PM, 2014), 196. The Seattle zine *In the Ditch* (1980s sometime) has a large Smith feel to it. For instance, the zine makers have "Trident: Food for War" and a "luxury home and estates advertisement," where a man shows his family into a vault.

137. *Skank*, undated; Graham Thompson, *American Culture in the 1980s* (Edinburgh: Edinburgh University Press, 2007), 16.

138. *Bullet*, #1, November 1981. For more on "The Falwell Game," see Bob Black, "Mailing their Way into Anarchy," *Boston Review*, August 1986, online: http://bostonreview.net/archives/BR11.4/black.html; see also *RAD*, #34, 1986; *Antimedia*, #12, May 1986; *Daily Impulse*, October–November 1986; *MRR*, November 1985. Though these accounts suggest the rise of the anti-Falwell activities in 1985, they were already in operation by the early 1980s.

139. Slogan quoted in Kathleen McConnell, "The Handmade Tale," in Ian Peddie, ed., *The Resisting Muse: Popular Music and Social Protest* (Burlington: Ashgate, 2006), 163; *OOPS!*, no date; *Discords*, Summer 1981, 3; *Suburban Relapse*, #4, March 1982, 19; *Talk Talk*, March 1981, 13; Peter Titus in Clinton Heylin, ed., *The Penguin Book of Rock and Roll Writing* (London: Viking, 1992), 496–500.

140. *Independent America*, November 1982; see especially Thomas Bey William Bailey, *Unofficial Release* (No place: Belsona, 2012).

141. Ronald Reagan, "Remarks in Chicago, Illinois, at the Citizens for Thompson Fundraising Dinner for Governor James T. Thompson," July 7, 1981, posted at Reagan Presidential Library: https://www.reaganlibrary.gov/research/speeches/70781e; *Sluggo*, 1982; *Ripper*, #7, May 1982, 3.

142. *Truly Needy*, Vol. 1, No. 3, 32; Vee and Stimson, *Touch and Go*, 365; *Bad Meat*, no date.

143. Mark Andersen and Mark Jenkins, *Dance of Days* (New York: Akashic, 2003), 112; *Boston Rock*, #39; *Op*, M Issue (1981?), 24.

144. *MRR*, #1, 1982; *Forced Exposure*, #1; *BravEar*, #5, 1983: 16–19.

145. *Village Voice*, August 2, 1983, 61.

146. *Boston Rock,* #25, 10; *L.A. Reader,* October 16, 1981, Section 2, 3. A similar thing had happened to the MC5 back in 1969, when the band signed with Elektra. They were deemed "obscene" and a certain department store in Detroit (Hudson's) refused to carry the record. John Sinclair published an advertisement for the record, suggesting that people kick in the doors of Hudson's if they refused to sell a young person the album. Elektra immediately dropped the band.

147. *L.A. Reader,* November 27, 1981, 16–18; *Trouser Press,* June 1983, 23; *Village Voice,* December 30–January 5, 1982, 55.

148. *L.A. Weekly,* October 31–November 6, 1980, 3; see also *L.A. Weekly,* February 20–26 1981, 13; *L.A. Reader,* November 6, 1981, Section 2, 2. See also the documentary film, *Clockwork Orange County.* The assessment of the LAPD was accurate among punks. This was one of the most militarized police forces across America. It was headed up by Darryl Gates, who became chief in 1978, after serving as a cop some time before. The LAPD started spying and creating files via the Crime Intelligence Division and Public Disorder Intelligence Division (many punks from L.A. remember having their photo taken by a cop and told that they were going to create a file on them). See Joe Domanick, *To Protect and Serve* (New York: Pocket Books, 1994).

149. *Noise,* May–June 1981; *Skid,* #4; *Coolest Retard,* February–March, 1981.

150. Sten, *All Ages,* 213; Heylin, ed., *The Penguin Book of Rock and Roll Writing,* 131; *Trouser Press,* June 1983, 23; *Noise,* #3, May–June 1981.

151. *Capitol Crisis,* No. 5, May 1981; *Damage,* #11, 1981, 40; *Village Voice,* December 30–January 5, 1982, 55.

152. Russo, *We Were Going to Change the World.*

153. *Noise,* #3, May–June 1981; *I Wanna,* Fall Winter, 1982, 3; *Noise,* #5, July 22, 1981; *Noise,* December 1981.

CHAPTER 2

1. *MRR,* #1, 1982.

2. *MRR,* May–June 1983.

3. *Terminal,* #11 (1982?).

4. *Last Rites,* #8, 1984; *I Wanna,* Spring 1982, 8.

5. *Altered Statements,* #2, 1984; *MRR,* July 1984; *Sub Cin,* #6, 1984.

6. *MRR,* March–April, 1983; *Own the Whole World,* March 1983, 3 (see also *MRR,* March–April 1983); *MRR,* August 1984; *Negative Print,* #11 (1984?); *Negative Print,* #5, 1983.

7. *The Offense,* #5, (1980 ?), 41; *Boredom,* #4, no date, 2; *Boredom,* #9, 2 (see also the small collection of papers for the Progressive Student Alliance/Network held at Kent State University's Special Collections). Also, see the protest against a *Nightline* show that the Progressive Student Alliance worked on: discussed in *Boredom,* #10, 1983, 10; *Boredom,* February 1981; *Boredom,* #9, 6.

8. *The Offense,* #4, 1980; *Sub Pop,* February 1982; interview via email with Tim Anstaett, September 23, 2018.

9. *I Wanna,* Spring 1982, 4; *Blur,* November 1983; *Disposable Press,* May–June 1983; Bill Brown, *You Should've Heard Just What I Seen* (Cincinnati: Colossal, 2010), 264.

10. *MRR*, January–February 1983; *MRR*, January–February 1984; *Reagan Death* (1983?); *Underdog Fun Book*, 1984.
11. *Talk Talk*, May 1981: 15; *Bullet*, #2 (1982?), advert on inside cover; adverted also in *Blur*, #3, June 25, 1982; *Blur*, #8, June 1983; adverted in *Talk Talk*, Autumn 1981, 38; *Talk Talk*, January 1980, 9–10; *Talk Talk*, Autumn 1981, 24.
12. See Barry Miles, *Call Me Burroughs* (New York: Twelve, 2014), 566, 621; *Blur*, March 18, 1983; *Blur*, January 15, 1983; *BravEar*, #6, 25–27.
13. *MRR*, March–April 1983, May–June 1983, and September 1984; *Behind the Zion Curtain* (no date).
14. *Newsreal*, January 14–February 11, 1983, 2, 18; *MRR*, January–February 1983, October 1984, and October–November 1983; Dave Markey and Jordan Schwartz, *We Got Power* (Brooklyn: Bazillion Points, 2012), 239; *Matter*, September 1983; Joel Garreau, *Edge City* (New York: Doubleday, 1991), 184.
15. *MRR*, December 1983.
16. *Bad Newz*, no date, 28; *MRR*, September 1983; *Discords*, September 1981, 4; *Outcry*, #3, 1982, 20; *MRR*, December 1983; *Bullshit Detector*, #2, 1983, in Marie Kanger-Born, *Confessions of a Chicago Punk Bystander* (Morrisville: Lulu, 2010), 124; *Wild Dog*, Vol. 1, No. 1, 1979; two record reviews in *Blur*, June 25, 1982.
17. *Blur*, June 25, 1982; *MRR*, # 3, 1982; *MRR*, May–June 1983.
18. *Bad Meat*, no date; *Dry Heave*, Spring 1984; *MRR*, December 1983. See also the documentary about Tulsa's punk history: *Oil Capital Underground*.
19. *Suburban Relapse*, #2, October, 1981; *MRR*, August 1984; *Suburban Relapse*, October 1981, 17; *Suburban Relapse*, March 1982, 15; *Suburban Relapse*, January 1984, 3.
20. *Suburban Relapse*, February 1983, 22–23; Bob Suren, *Crate Digger* (Microcosm, 2015), 186; *MRR*, September 1983.
21. *MRR*, May–June 1983; *MRR*, October 1984.
22. *Ego*, #4, 28.
23. *L.A. Reader*, June 23, 1982, Section 2, 7; *Destroy L.A.*, #4; *L.A. Weekly*, May 14–20, 1982, 21; *MRR*, October–November 1983; *Suburban Relapse*, #8, February 1983, 24; *Flipside*, #34, 1982; *MRR*, October–November 1983; *MRR*, March 1984.
24. *Op*, M Issue, (1981?), 24; Mark Andersen and Mark Jenkins, *Dance of Days* (New York: Akashic, 2003), 97; *Thrillseeker*, #3, 31–32; *Truly Needy*, Vol. 1, No. 4, (1982–1983?), 8, 12; *Chow Chow Times*, #2; *Discords*, September 1981, 3.
25. *Suburban Relapse*, #8, February 1983, 34; *BravEar*, #2, 1982, 29; *I Wanna*, 1982, 7; *Rabies*, #1, 3; *MRR*, May/June 1983.
26. *Ripper*, #8, 18, 20; *L.A. Reader*, July 29, 1983, Section 2, 2; see also Gary Floyd, *Please Bee Nice* (Lexington: Left of the Dial, 2014), 20; *MRR*, May–June 1983.
27. *The Dispossessed* (New York: Avon, 1975), 127.
28. *Flipside*, #45, 17; *BravEar*, #5, 1983, 19; *Altered Statements*, #4, December 1984; *WDC Period*, December 1984, 13; *Truly Needy*, Vol. 1, No. 4, 7.
29. *Skin Effect*, July 1982; *MRR*, November/December 1982 (a list of people is provided here to contact if you wanted to perform in their locale); *Reagan Death*, no date; *Truly Needy*, Vol. 1, No. 3, 4–5; *Forced Exposure*, #2; *Zone V*, #1; Azzerad, *Our Band Could Be Your Life*, 74–75; Dewar MacLeod, *Kids of the Black Hole* (Norman: University of Oklahoma Press), 136.

30. *L.A. Weekly*, July 2–8, 1982, 10; *Suburban Relapse* praised Rough Trade and Constant Cause in #9, May 1983, 3; *MRR*, October–November 1983; Pete Dale, "It Was Easy, It Was Cheap, So What? Reconsidering the DIY Principle of Punk and Indie Music," *Popular Music History* 3 (2008), 174.

31. George Woodcock, *Anarchism* (New York: Meridian, 1962), 134; see Michael Crane and Mary Stofler, eds., *Correspondence Art* (San Francisco: Contemporary Arts, 1984); *Skid*, #3, 1982; *MRR*, November 1984; *Subpop*, February 1982.

32. "Radio Address to the Nation on Taxes, Tuition Tax Credit, and Interest Rates," April 24, 1982, posted at https://www.presidency.ucsb.edu/documents/radio-address-the-nation-taxes-the-tuition-tax-credit-and-interest-rates.

33. Government Issue, "Plain to See."

34. Fredric Wertham, *The World of Fanzines* (Carbondale: Southern Illinois University Pres, 1973), 133.

35. *TV Guide*, January 23–29, 1982, A-75; *Boredom*, #10, 7 (*Boredom* had the best treatment of the show).

36. *Chicago Tribune*, December 20, 1981, B1, B8; *Indianapolis Star*, April 25, 1982, 7H; *MRR*, #2.

37. Anthony Burgess, *A Clockwork Orange* (1962; reprint New York: Norton, 1963), 82–83; *Op*, January–February 1983, 45; *Your Flesh*, #5. On therapeutic politics, see also Christopher Lasch, *The Culture of Narcissism* (New York: Warner, 1979), 311–312.

38. *L.A. Times*, June 16, 1981, G1.

39. *Subpop*, February 1982.

40. Ronnie Dugger, *On Ronald Reagan* (New York: McGraw-Hill, 1983), 259; *Fallout*, no date. See also *New York Times*, May 18, 1982, online: https://www.nytimes.com/1982/05/18/us/reagan-proposes-school-prayer-amendment.html.

41. *Appeal to Reason*, Vol. 1, No. 5, 1982, 2; *L.A. Weekly*, August 27–September, 1982, 6; *The War Hawks*, 1983.

42. *New York Times*, February 2, 1982, online: https://www.nytimes.com/1982/02/02/world/us-disputes-report-of-926-killed-in-el-salvador.html; *L.A. Weekly*, December 5–11, 1980, 3; Edmund Morris, *Dutch* (New York: Random House, 1999), 482.

43. *New York Times*, July 13, 1981, online: https://www.nytimes.com/1981/07/13/us/reagan-s-military-strategists-plan-expanded-cruise-missile-program.html; Ted Kennedy and Mark Hatfield, *Freeze* (Toronto: Bantam, 1982), 85–89; *New York Times*, June 17, 1982, online: https://www.nytimes.com/1982/06/17/us/rough-hearing-for-reagan-crisis-relocation-plan.html.

44. William Martin, "Waiting for the End," *Atlantic*, June 1982, online: https://www.theatlantic.com/magazine/archive/1982/06/waiting-for-the-end/308707/; Robert Scheer, *With Enough Shovels* (New York: Random House, 1982), opening pages.

45. *L.A. Weekly*, June 18–24, 1982, 10–11; *L.A. Reader*, July 15, 1983, 3; Dugger, *On Ronald Reagan*, 269; *L.A. Weekly*, October 1–7, 1982, 3; *L.A. Weekly*, January 7–13, 1983, 3; *Reader's Digest*, October 1982, 206; *Negative Print*, #12, 1984.

46. Kennedy and Hatfield, *Freeze*, 2; Helen Caldicott, *Nuclear Madness* (New York: Bantam, 1980), 70, 81; *BravEar*, #3 (1982?), 3–5.

47. Mark Crispin Miller, ed., *Seeing through Movies* (New York: Pantheon, 1990), 135.

48. Tom Shone, *Blockbuster* (New York: Free Press, 2004), 133; Joel Glenn Brenner, *The Emperors of Chocolate* (New York: Random House, 1999), 275–278; Paul Slansky, *The Clothes Have No Emperor* (New York: Fireside, 1989), 45.

49. *Daily Impulse*, October–November 1987.

50. "Existentialism as a Humanism," in Walter Kaufmann, ed., *Existentialism* (New York: Meridian, 1975), 349.

51. *L.A. Reader*, August 13, 1982, 31; interview with Shawn Stern, via email, February 10, 2018.

52. Albert Camus, *The Stranger* (New York: Knopf, 1946), 154; George Cotkin, *Existential America* (Baltimore: Johns Hopkins University Press, 2003), 7; *Bang!*, #5, 1983, 5, 6.

53. *Forced Exposure*, #5; *L.A. Weekly*, February 5–11, 1982, 22, and December 11–17, 1981, 28.

54. *Let Them Know: The Story of Youth Brigade and BYO Records*: https://www.youtube.com/watch?v=5HIOLFZgXWE&t=14s; *L.A. Weekly*, May 7–13, 1982, 14.

55. *MRR*, February 1985; *L.A. Reader*, November 4, 1983, 16–17; Olivier Todd, *Albert Camus* (New York: Knopf, 1997), 143.

56. *MRR*, January–February 1983; *MRR*, May–June 1983.

57. Ben Nadler, *Punk in NYC's Lower East Side* (Portland: Microcosm, 2015), 8; *Damaged Goods*, October 1981, 2–3.

58. Nadler, *Punk In NYC's Lower East Side*, 6; *Flesh and Bones*, #1 (1982?); Woodcock, *Anarchism*, 205. There's an interesting parallel here to the early anarcho-surrealist writing of Alfred Jarry, especially his antiauthoritarian play *Ubu Roi*, which ridiculed an incompetent, vulgar, and imperialistic king. Jarry took much of his inspiration for the central character from a reactionary and absurd teacher he had as a student: See Alastair Brotchie, *Alfred Jarry: A Pataphysical Life* (Cambridge: MIT Press, 2011), 4. Also, in a reprinting of *Brave New World*, the author endorses a "Kropotkinesque cooperative" model of economic production as an alternative to his dystopian tale. Aldous Huxley, "Foreword" to *Brave New World* (New York: Harper & Row, 1946), ix.

59. *MRR*, November–December, 1982.

60. *Plan 9*, November 1982, 4–5.

61. *Ripper*, #8, 18; *Terminal*, #11 (1982?).

62. *MRR*, September 1983; *Ripper*, #8, 1982, 20; Dave Dictor, *MDC* (San Francisco: Manic, 2016), 59, 61; *Ego*, #3; *MRR*, #1, 1982; *Ripper*, #8, 18.

63. *Matter*, September 1983; Bill Brown, *You Should Have Heard Just What I Seen* (Cincinnati: Colossal, 2010), 267.

64. *Still Too Small*, no date; *Ripper*, #8, 1982, 25; *Ego* (1983?), #7, 5.

65. *Ripper*, #8, 1982, 25 (see also *Forget It!*, Spring 1982); *MRR*, January–February 1983. "Lie, Cheat, and Steal" was also the title of a song by Government Issue (D.C.) on the compilation album *Flex Your Head* (1982).

66. *Ego*, #1, June 1982, 42; *MRR*, January–February 1983; Ernest Callenbach, *Ecotopia* (Berkeley: Banyan Tree Books, 1975), 11; Ernest Callenbach, *Ecotopia Emerging* (Berkeley: Banyan Tree Books, 1981), 96; *MRR*, January–February 1983.

67. *Ripper*, #8, 1982, 25; *The Attack*, #7, September–October, 1982, 16.

68. *California Living Magazine*, March 4, 1984, 10, 13; Suren, *Crate Digger*, 174.

69. *Ripper*, #5, 17, 19; *MRR*, September 1983; Mykel Board, *I, a Meist* (San Francisco: AK, 2005), 96–98.

70. Bale in Martin Sprouse, ed., *Threat by Example* (San Francisco: Pressure Drop, 1991), 80; details come from an interview with Bale.

71. *Search and Destroy*, #10, 1978, 108; *Ripper*, #5; see Stuart Jeffries, *Grand Hotel Abyss* (London: Verso, 2015); *MRR*, January–February, 1984; *MRR*, October 1987; Sprouse, ed., *Threat by Example*, 86.

72. *Ripper*, #5, 14–15; *MRR*, May–June 1983; see how *MRR* originated "after Flipside decided to cease it's (*sic*) national scene coverage." *MRR*, March–April 1983.

73. *L.A. Reader*, December 16, 1983, 12; on the "police war": *L.A. Reader*, November 6, 1981, Section 2, 2. See also John Ortved, *The Simpsons* (New York: Faber and Faber, 2009), 12–22; see also Groening's own autobiographical sketch in *L.A. Reader*, August 5, 1983, Section 2, 2; and Jeff Lenburg, *Matt Groening* (New York: Chelsea House, 2011).

74. *L.A. Reader*, August 13, 1982, 19; *L.A. Reader*, October 21, 1983, Section 2, 7; *L.A. Reader*, December 16, 1983, 12. On the work of Kierkegaard, see Robert Bretall, ed., *A Kierkegaard Anthology* (New York: Modern Library 1946), especially 22.

75. *L.A. Weekly*, February 18–24, 1983, 4 (see also *L.A. Reader*, April 23, 1982, 18).

76. *L.A. Reader*, December 16, 1983, 12; *No Mag*, 1983; *Ripper*, #6, 1982, 2; *Point Drawn*, #1.

77. Dan Nadel, ed., *Gary Panter* (Brooklyn: PictureBox, 2008); 202, 316, 318, 320; it should also be pointed out that Panter and Groening collaborated together on a comic strip in 1982, calling themselves the Fuk Boys. See Hillary Chute's illuminating discussion in *Why Comics?* (New York: Harper, 2017), 213–214.

78. *Cheap Truth*, #3, 1983: found at http://fanac.org/fanzines/Cheap_Truth/.

79. See here especially George Slusser and Tom Shippey, eds., *Fiction 2000* (Athens: University of Georgia Press, 1992).

80. William Gibson, *Burning Chrome* (New York: Arbor, 1986), 196; Raymond Chandler, "Little Sister," in *Later Novels and Other Writings* (New York: Library of America, 1995), 292; Larry McCaffery, ed., *Storming the Reality Studio* (Durham: Duke University Press, 1991), 269; David Seed, ed., *A Companion to Science Fiction* (Malden: Blackwell, 2005), 225.

81. *Mississippi Review*, Vol. 16: No. 2–3 (special issue on cyberpunk), 1988, 236; Gibson, *Burning Chrome*, 178.

82. "Pac-Man," found at http://www.rudyrucker.com/transrealbooks/completestories/#_Toc15; see also Martin Amis, *Invasion of the Space Invaders* (London: Hutchinson, 1982).

83. *Cheap Truth*, #2, 1983; Gibson, *Burning Chrome*, 178, 184, 196.

84. Gibson, *Burning Chrome*, 184, 195–6; *Mississippi Review*, 56.

85. Bruce Sterling, *The Artificial Kid* (New York: Harper & Row, 1980), 6; Seed, ed., *A Companion to Science Fiction*, 222; *Cheap Truth*, #2, 1983. See John Shirley's gothic and horror novel, *Cellars* (New York: Avon, 1982).

86. Guy Debord, *Society of the Spectacle* (Detroit: Black and Red, 2002), Thesis 27.

87. *MRR*, #3, 1982.

88. Brown, *You Should Have Heard Just What I Seen*, 347; David Sirota, *Back to Our Future* (New York: Ballantine, 2011), 13.

89. *L.A. Weekly*, October 15–21, 1982, 56; *L.A. Reader*, August 19, 1983, Section 2, 14; Brown, *You Should've Heard Just What I Seen*, 347–348; Interview with Mark Lester, DVD version of film: Collector's Edition issued by Shout! Factory, 2015; *Reagan Death*, no date.

90. *East Village Eye*, August 1982, 28; *Forced Exposure*, #7/8, 5.

91. Tanooka in *MRR*, January–February 1983.

92. *No Mag*, Johana Went on cover, 1982; *L.A. Weekly*, January 7–13, 1983, 29.

93. *MRR*, March–April, 1983; *MRR*, no. 2, 1982. See also Sprouse, ed., *Threat by Example*, 83.

94. The Dicks, "I Hope You Get Drafted."

95. *Age Home*, no date.

96. Slanksy, *The Clothes Have No Emperor*, 54; the quote comes from the National Park Service's MX Missile site, online: https://www.nps.gov/articles/mx-peacekeeper-icbm.htm; *New York Times*, November 12, 1982, online: https://www.nytimes.com/1982/11/12/us/foreign-agents-linked-to-freeze-reagan-says.html; Helen Caldicott, *Missile Envy* (New York: Morrow, 1984), 31; Ronald Reagan, *The Reagan Diaries*, ed. Douglas Brinkley (New York HarperCollins, 2007), 117.

97. Reagan, *The Reagan Diaries*, 117; Ellison, "An Edge in My Voice," *L.A. Weekly*, January 3, 1982, online: http://harlanellison.com/iwrite/mayer.htm.

98. *L.A. Weekly*, December 3–9, 1982, 10; Ellison, "An Edge in My Voice"; *Fifth Estate*, Winter, 1982–1983, 1; *MRR*, January–February 1983.

99. Reagan quoted in Walter Lafeber, *Inevitable Revolutions* (New York: Norton, 1983), 276; Reagan, *The Reagan Diaries*, 118.

100. *New York Times*, January 22, 1983, online: https://www.nytimes.com/1983/01/22/us/us-issues-rules-denying-funds-to-students-not-signed-for-draft.html; *New York Times*, February 7, 1982, online: https://www.nytimes.com/1982/02/07/us/research-fares-well-but-aid-for-students-is-cut.html; see also Geoffrey Holtz, *Welcome to the Jungle* (New York: St. Martin's, 1995), 126; Theodore H. White, *America in Search of Itself* (New York: Warner, 1983), 421.

101. *Nuclear Times*, February 1983, 7; Roberto Ohrt, ed., *Raymond Pettibon* (New York: D.A.P., 2000), *A New Wave of Violence* zine printed within.

102. *New York Times*, January 27, 1983, online: https://www.targetsmartvan.com/Default.aspx?HasCommittee=1; see also James Hoopes, *Corporate Dreams* (New Brunswick: Rutgers University Press, 2011), 168.

103. *L.A. Weekly*, October 21–27, 1983, 18.

104. *MRR*, January–February 1983; *L.A. Weekly*, January 14–20, 1983, 24; Markey and Schwartz, *We Got Power*, 271; Jack Grisham, *American Demon* (Toronto: ECW, 2011), 242,

105. *BravEar*, #6, (1983?), 11.

106. *MRR*, March–April, 1983.

107. *L.A. Weekly*, February 18–23, 28; Markey and Schwartz, *We Got Power*, 271; *L.A. Reader*, March 4, 1983, Section 2, 5.

108. *MRR*, December 1983; the show has been posted to YouTube: https://www.youtube.com/watch?v=tuq75-8voiE.

109. *MRR*, March–April 1983.

110. William Burroughs, *The Adding Machine* (New York: Arcade, 1986), 77.

111. Details come from phone interview with Peter Belsito, February 28, 2018.

112. *Ego*, #4, 9; Kester in *Storms of Youth*, April 1982; Lasch, *The Culture of Narcissism*, 137.

113. *New York Times*, March 4, 1983, online: https://www.nytimes.com/1983/03/04/us/reagans-hosts-at-banquet-for-queen-at-glittering-museum-in-san-francisco.html.

114. *MRR*, May/June 1983; *Ego*, #7, 26–27.

115. The speech can be found at: https://www.reaganlibrary.gov/research/speeches/30883a; it can also be watched on YouTube; on Armed Forces recruiters as well as Reagan's speech, see Sirota, *Back to Our Future*, 155.

116. "Remarks at the Annual Convention of the National Association of Evangelicals in Orlando, Florida," March 8, 1983, online: https://www.reaganfoundation.org/library-museum/permanent-exhibitions/berlin-wall/from-the-archives/remarks-at-the-annual-convention-of-the-national-association-of-evangelicals-in-orlando-florida/; Whittaker Chambers, *Witness* (New York: Random House, 1952), 12; *New York Times*, March 10, 1983, online: https://www.nytimes.com/1983/03/10/opinion/abroad-at-home-onward-christian-soldiers.html.

117. Lawrence Wittner, *Toward Nuclear Abolition* (Stanford: Stanford University Press, 2003), 261, 190; Paul Boyer, *When Time Shall Be No More* (Cambridge: Harvard University Press, 1999), 145; *Nuclear Times*, August–September 1983, 25.

118. *Existential Rage*, no date; *Revealin Da Lies*, no date; *Reagan Death*, no date; *Negative Print*, October–November, 1983.

119. *New York Times*, April 1, 1983, online: https://www.nytimes.com/1983/04/01/world/reagan-calls-nuclear-freeze-dangerous.html

120. Peter Belsito and Bob Davis, *Hardcore California* (San Francisco: Last Gasp, 1983), no pagination.

121. *L.A. Weekly*, April 29–May 5, 1983, 3.

122. *L.A. Weekly*, April 29–May 5, 1983, 3; *MRR*, May–June 1983.

123. Lucy Lippard, "Real Estate and Real Art," *Seven Days*, April 1980, 32; for a good treatment of Colab within a wider historical framework, see Alan Moore, *Art Gangs* (Brooklyn: Autonomedia, 2011); Mark Jenkins, "What Do You Know about Punk? W.P.A.'s Uninventive Deception," *Washington Tribune*, June 3–17, 1978, 13 (found in John Holmstrom Papers, as is some correspondence between Denney and Holmstrom). See also http://www.98bowery.com/punk-years/punk-art-show.php.

124. *Washington Post*, April 2, 1983, online: https://www.washingtonpost.com/archive/lifestyle/1983/04/02/put-on-at-the-ritz/4b932571-5b3d-4136-a6f2-6daca267ee11/?utm_term=.22a5c2dcd5cb.

125. *Truly Needy*, Vol. 2, No. 2, 1983, 5.

126. *Overthrow*, April–May 1983, 7, and July–August, 1983, 16; Astrid Proll, ed., *Goodbye to London* (Ostfildern: Hatje Cantz, 2010), 24.

127. *Overthrow*, April–May 1983, 7.

128. *Overthrow*, April–May, 1983, 7; see also the zine *Squat for Life*.

129. *Creep*, #1, 1979,14; Peter Plate, *Black Wheel of Anger* (Edinburgh: Polygon, 1990), 177.
130. *Op*, September–October, 1983, 27.
131. *No Mag*, 1983; *BravEar*, #4, 1983, 14; Chris Burden, *Chris Burden: A Twenty Year Survey* (Newport Beach: Newport Harbor Art Museum, 1988), 35, 49, 38; George Cotkin, *Feast of Excess* (New York: Oxford, 2016), 325.
132. *BravEar*, #7, 1983, 8–11.
133. *MRR*, March–April 1983.
134. Charles M. Young, "Skank or Die," *Playboy*, June, 1984, 190 (from personal experience, this act of graffiti was being performed by 1983); graffiti pictured in *Sleeping Dogs* and *Cerebral Discourse*, 1984 (this is a quote from Bertrand de Jouvenel).
135. Neil Postman, *Amusing Ourselves to Death* (New York: Penguin, 1986), 111; Gil Troy, *Morning in America* (Princeton: Princeton University Press, 2005), 130; *Warning*, August 1983: 22; Luke Hauser, *Direct Action* (San Francisco: Groundwork, 2003), 490–491.
136. *Bound Together Newsletter*, #2, June 1983; *BravEar*, #3, 1982; *Ego*, #7, 18–19.
137. Norman Mailer, *The Faith of Graffiti* (New York: Praeger, 1974), no pagination; Jean Baudrillard, *Symbolic Exchange and Death* (London: Sage, 1993), 84; *Ripper*, #5, 18.
138. *Artforum*, November 1983, 72.
139. Bill Brown's review of the film can be found in his *You Should Have Heard Just What I Seen*, 352.
140. R. Serge Denisoff and William Romanowski, *Risky Business* (New Brunswick: Transaction, 2016), 347, 351–354; *Newsreal*, September 9–October 14, 1983, 7; *L.A. Weekly*, June 8–14, 1979, 27; Pat Aufderheide, "Music Videos," *Journal of Communication*, Winter 1986, 57; John Leland, *Hip: The History* (New York: Harper Perennial, 2004), 302; *L.A. Weekly*, March 18–24, 1983, 3.
141. Richard Meltzer, *A Whore Just Like the Rest* (New York: Da Capo, 2000), 384; *L.A. Weekly*, March 18–24, 1983, 3; Andrew Goodwin, *Dancing in the Distraction Factory* (Minneapolis: University of Minnesota Press, 1992), 33, 133; *Artforum*, November 1983, 72; Jim Farber, "MTV," in Anthony DeCurtis et al., eds., *The Rolling Stone Illustrated History of Rock n Roll* (London: Plexus, 1992), 647; *L.A. Times*, August 21, 1983, R66.
142. *The Rocket*, June 1984, 16. There's confusion about the movie's release date, with some suggesting it was released as late as 1984. The September 1983 issue of *MRR* makes it clear that kids were seeing the movie as early as the summer of 1983.
143. *The Rocket*, June 1984, 16.
144. *MRR*, September 1983.
145. *Creep*, #5; *L.A. Weekly*, February 11–17, 1983, 32; *Truly Needy*, #7, December 1983, 30.
146. *Fear and Loathing in Las Vegas* (New York: Warner, 1971), 156.
147. Haynes Johnson, *Sleepwalking through History* (New York: Doubleday, 1991), 168; Emanuel S. Savis, *Privatizing the Public Sector* (Chatham: Chatham House, 1982).
148. James Patterson, *Restless Giant* (New York: Oxford, 2005), 176; Ronnie Dugger, *On Ronald Reagan*, 277; William Martin, "Waiting for the End"; Mark Crispin Miller, *Boxed In* (Evanston: Northwestern University Press, 1988), 84.

149. Wayne Newton, *Once Before I Go* (New York: Morrow, 1989), 230–233; *The Rocket*, January 1984, 18; *Own the Whole World*, #4, Summer 1983, 10; *Washington Post*, April 7, 1983, online: https://www.washingtonpost.com/archive/politics/1983/04/07/watt-sets-off-uproar-with-music-ban/ddf51d7c-7161-46a9-a774-869fa71b6601/?utm_term=.76d0a88e4706.

150. *MRR*, May–June 1983.

151. *I Wanna*, Summer 1980, 15–17; *I Wanna*, Spring 1982, 3.

152. *If This Goes On*, #2; *MRR*, September 1983.

153. *MRR*, May–June, 1983; Arthur Rowse, *One Sweet Guy* (Washington, D.C.: Consumer News, 1981), 68; Dugger, *On Ronald Reagan*, 98; Reagan, *The Reagan, Diaries*, 131; Sean Wilentz, *The Age of Reagan* (New York: HarperCollins, 2008), 170.

154. *Suburban Outcast*, #2.

155. *Truly Needy*, #7, December 1983, 39; the concert is posted at: https://www.youtube.com/watch?v=qSHjUT4Dy1M

156. Reagan, *The Reagan Diaries*, 188.

157. *Damaged Goods*, October 1981, 2–3.

158. Denisoff and Romanowski, *Risky Business*, 387; Christopher Sterling, ed., *The Concise Encyclopedia of American Radio* (New York: Routledge, 2010), 153; Troy, *Morning in America*, 115.

159. Denisoff and Romanowski, *Risky Business*, 389, 391; Stephen Prince, ed., *American Cinema of the 1980s* (New Brunswick: Rutgers University Press, 2012), 103.

160. Jake Rossen, "How Jane Fonda's Workout Conquered the World," *Mental Floss*, June 29, 2015, online: http://mentalfloss.com/article/65314/how-jane-fondas-workout-conquered-world (see also Jerry Lembcke, *Hanoi Jane* [Amherst: University of Massachusetts Press, 2010]); *MRR*, June 1984; *All the Drugs You Can Eat*, #1, 4; Hendrik Hertzberg, "The Short Happy Life of the American Yuppie," in Nicolaus Mills, ed., *Culture in an Age of Money* (Chicago: Ivan R. Dee, 1990).

161. *East Village Eye*, January 1982, 21; Michael Gross, *My Generation* (New York: Cliff Street Books, 2000), 139; for debate about who actually crafted the idea of dropping money on Wall Street traders, see Jonah Raskin, *For the Hell of It: The Life and Times of Abbie Hoffman* (Berkeley: University of California Press, 1996), 112; much of Fouratt's biography can be gleaned from his own description in the *Village Voice*, October 23, 1984, 45.

162. *The Face*, October 1981, 11.

163. *Zone V*, #1, no date (1983?); *L.A. Weekly*, October 21–27, 1983, 20; Biafra in *I Wanna*, Fall/Winter 1982.

164. Kim Gordon, *Is It My Body?* (Frankfurt: Sternberg, 2014), 49, 86 (this book reprints Gordon's essay from 1983); Baudrillard in *The Anti-Aesthetic*, ed. by Hal Foster (Fort Townshend: Bay Press, 1983), 133.

165. *Kroptokin's Revolutionary Pamphlets*, ed. Roger Baldwin (New York: Dover, 1970), 272.

166. *L.A. Reader*, March 4, 1983, Section 2, 5; *MRR*, May/June 1983; *MRR*, January–February 1983; *MRR*, November 1983.

167. *Own the Whole World,* Summer 1983, 7; see here also the work that inspired Titus the most: Thomas Whiteside, *The Blockbuster Complex* (Middletown: Wesleyan University Press, 1981).

168. *The Disposable Press,* #3, September 1983, 6–7; *New York Times,* November 2, 1983, online: https://www.nytimes.com/1983/11/02/arts/the-pop-life-011530.html.

169. *Skid,* #4: 14; Dugger, *On Ronald Reagan,* 38; *MRR,* No. 2, 1982.

170. *The Attack,* July–August, 1982, 3, 5; *Boston Rock,* #39, 15; *Op,* January–February 1983, 44; *Noise,* #6, October–November 1981; *Forced Exposure,* #5.

171. *Bullshit Detector,* #1, 1982 and *Bullshit Detector,* #2, 1983, both reprinted in Kanger-Born, *Confessions of a Chicago Punk Bystander,* 132, 110; *BravEar,* #7, 1983, 14.

172. *Blur,* June 1983, 10; *MRR,* September 1983; *Bullshit Detector,* #2, 1983, in Kanger-Born, *Confessions of a Chicago Punk Bystander,* 129.

173. *MRR,* October–November 1983.

174. *The Noise,* November 1983, 9; *Riding the Blinds,* #4, 15 (1983–1984?); *MRR,* October–November 1983.

175. *Truly Needy,* #8, 33.

176. See the ad for *All The Drugs You Can Eat* in *Own the Whole World,* March 1983, 7.

177. *All the Drugs You Can Eat,* 1983, 3–13.

178. *Suburban Relapse,* #10, September 1983, 25.

179. *Bullshit Detector,* #2, 1983, reprinted in Kanger-Born, *Confessions of a Chicago Punk Bystander,* 130, 124, 125.

180. *MRR,* March–April 1983.

181. Newspaper article duplicated in Mark Sten, *All Ages* (Portland: Reptilicus, 2015), 57.

182. *MRR,* May–June 1983; *Suburban Relapse,* #6, August 1982, 27.

183. *Own the Whole World,* Summer 1983, 5; *Bullshit Detector,* #2, 1983, reprinted in Kanger-Born, *Confessions of a Chicago Punk Bystander,* 131; *MRR,* May–June and December 1983.

184. Colin Ward, *Anarchy in Action* (London: Allen and Unwin, 1973), 124.

185. *MRR,* May/June 1983; *MRR,* October/November 1983. For a citation of Ward, see *Vortex,* Fall 1981.

186. *Truly Needy,* Vol. 1, No. 4, 51–52; *Skank* (no date); *Playboy,* June 1984, 199; *Forced Exposure,* #4.

187. *Mutual Oblivion,* #6, 1984; quoted in Michael Azzerad, *Our Band Could Be Your Life,* 35; *Flipside,* #22; *Capitol Crisis,* #5, May 1981.

188. *BravEar,* #5, 1983.

189. The Proletariat, "Events Repeat."

190. *Washington Post,* April 8, 1984, C4–C5.

191. Speech posted online: https://www.reaganlibrary.gov/sites/default/files/archives/speeches/1983/102783b.htm.

192. Journalist quoted in Lou Cannon, *President Reagan* (New York: Public Affairs, 1991), 393; *Washington Post,* November 6, 1983, online: https://www.washingtonpost.com/archive/politics/1983/11/06/tidy-us-war-ends-we-blew-them-away/1dc47588-0f13-40c8-afbd-23528fb62759/?utm_term=.6a0eaf4bb2ed; Troy, *Morning in America,* 157; *MRR,* December 1983.

193. Cannon, *President Reagan*, 390; *Smash Apathy*, #9; "A Promise of Resistance," quoted in Christian Smith, *Resisting Reagan* (Chicago: University of Chicago Press, 1996), 79; *Negative Print*, #16, (1984?).
194. *New York Times*, November 1, 1983, online: https://www.nytimes.com/1983/11/01/us/senate-rejects-a-move-to-make-nucear-freeze-an-immediate-goal.html; Morris, *Dutch*, 503.
195. *MRR*, January–February 1984; *Skid*, 1983.
196. Morris, *Dutch*, 498; Reagan, *The Reagan Diaries*, 140; Edward Linenthal, *Symbolic Defense* (Urbana: University of Illinois Press, 1989), 15. For a fine treatment of "Star Wars" that illustrates its unrealistic side, see Marc Ambinder, *The Brink* (New York: Simon & Schuster, 2018), 127–129.
197. Speech posted online: https://www.reaganlibrary.gov/sites/default/files/archives/speeches/1983/121283b.htm.
198. Slansky, *The Clothes Have No Emperor*, 79; Cannon, *President Reagan*, 40; Lars-Erik Nelson, "Ron's War—and the Real War," *New York Daily News*, December 16, 1983.

CHAPTER 3

1. *Negative Print*, October 1983.
2. *Warning*, January–February 1984.
3. *Brouhaha*, no date (1985?); *Leading Edge*, #4, 1984; *MRR* March 1984; *Jersey Beat*, May–June 1984; *Flipside*, #39; *Playboy*, June 1984, 190; *Sense of Purpose*, #1, December 1983.
4. George Orwell, *1984* (New York: Signet, 1984), 32; Michael Shelden, *Orwell* (New York: HarperCollins, 1991), 432–433. For more on this, see Dorian Lynskey, *The Ministry of Truth* (New York: Doubleday, 2019).
5. *New York Times*, January 8, 1984, 8; *New York Times*, May 7, 1984, B9. Note that Fred Halliday would soon describe the Cold War under Reagan's and Thatcher's leadership as "Cold War II." Fred Halliday, *The Making of the Second Cold War* (London: Verso, 1986).
6. *MRR*, January–February 1984; *Fallout*, no date.
7. *MRR*, March 1984; Irving Howe, ed., *1984 Revisited* (New York: Harper & Row, 1983), 77, 80. There was also a conference of scholars trying to make sense of the book's importance, and the conference's proceedings can be found in Robert Mulvihill, ed., *Reflections on America, 1984* (Athens: University of Georgia Press, 1986).
8. Aldous Huxley, *Brave New World* (1932; New York: Perennial, 1998), 76–86; Aldous Huxley, *Brave New World Revisited* (New York: Harper, 1958), 8, 44.
9. *Bang!*, #4, 1983, 12.
10. *New York Times*, January 14, 1984, 11, online: https://www.nytimes.com/1984/01/14/arts/michael-jackson-at-25-a-musical-phenomenon.html; Lisa Campbell, *Michael Jackson* (Boston: Branden, 1993), 8, 78; R. Serge Denisoff and William Romanowski, *Risky Business* (New Brunswick: Transaction, 2016), 360; Monica Herrera, "Michael Jackson, Pepsi Made Marketing History,'" adweek.com, July

3, 2009, online: https://www.adweek.com/brand-marketing/michael-jackson-pepsi-made-marketing-history-99789/; Roger Enrico, *The Other Guy Blinked* (New York: Bantam, 1986), 11, 112.

11. Gareth Murphy, *Cowboys and Indies* (New York: Thomas Dunne, 2014), 294; *Time*, March 19, 1984, 54–60; *New York Times*, April 24, 1986, online: https://www.nytimes.com/1986/04/24/arts/critic-s-notebook-is-punk-rock-s-obituary-premature.html; *New York Times*, January 14, 1984, 11; Paul Slansky, *The Clothes Have No Emperor* (New York: Fireside, 1989), 87; *L.A. Reader*, September 14, 1984, 1; Enrico, *The Other Guy Blinked*, 11, 134; see here also Steve Knopper, *Appetite for Self-Destruction* (New York: Free Press, 2009), 10.

12. Stephen Price, *A New Pot of Gold* (New York: Scribner's 2000), 133.

13. Denisoff and Romanowski, *Risky Business*, 403; Susanna Gora, *You Couldn't Ignore Me If You Tried* (New York: Crown, 2010), 157–158.

14. Gora, *You Couldn't Ignore Me If You Tried*, 150, 317; for more on Capra, see Raymond Carney, *American Vision* (Cambridge: Cambridge University Press, 1986), 17.

15. Orwell, *1984*, 32.

16. Haynes Johnson, *Sleepwalking through History* (New York: Doubleday, 1991), 276.

17. Ronald Reagan, *The Reagan Diaries*, ed. Douglas Brinkley (New York HarperCollins, 2007), 220; Johnson, *Sleepwalking through History*, 277.

18. *Hard Times*, August 1984, 1, 11; *Silence*, #2, (1984?).

19. Alex Cox, *X Films* (Brooklyn: Soft Skull, 2008), 39; Chris Barber and Jack Sargeant, eds., *No Focus* (London: Headpress, 2006), 209; *East Village Eye*, October 1986, 18.

20. Alex Cox, *X Films*, 36, 74; see also the story posted at *Mental Floss*: http://mentalfloss.com/article/67675/15-atomic-truths-about-repo-man.

21. On the "Cinema of Transgression," see Jack Sargeant, *Deathtripping* (London: Creation, 1999).

22. *L.A. Reader*, May 11, 1984, 18–19; *The Attack*, December 1984, 15; *MRR*, February 1985.

23. *L.A. Reader*, March 9, 1984, 19.

24. Slansky, *The Clothes Have No Emperor*, 97; J. Randy Taraborrelli, *Michael Jackson* (New York: Grand Central, 2009), 309.

25. Campbell, *Michael Jackson*, 84; Reagan, *The Reagan Diaries*, 239.

26. *New York Times*, June 26, 2009, online: https://thecaucus.blogs.nytimes.com/2009/06/26/from-the-white-house-files-a-fight-over-michael-jackson/.

27. Jackson quoted in Angela McRobbie, ed., *Zoot Suits and Second Hand Dresses* (Boston: Unwin Hyman, 1988), 55; David Szatmary, *Rockin in Time* (Upper Saddle River: Prentice Hall, 1996), 251–252; Peggy Noonan, *What I Saw at the Revolution* (New York: Random House, 1990), 158; *Fallout,* no date; *Free Beer Press*, #6, 1984, online: https://archive.org/details/FreeBeerPress6.

28. *Own the Whole World*, #5, (1983 ?).

29. *Ink Disease*, #8 (1984?).

30. *Ink Disease*, #8 (1984?); *Tropical Depression*, (1984?).

31. *Flipside*, #46; *Truly Needy*, #9, 1985, 67; Ludwig Wittgenstein, *On Certainty* (New York: Harper & Row, 1972), 8c, 10c, 24c; most of what's here is indebted to the excellent book by Michael Fournier, *Double Nickels on the Dime* (New York: Continuum, 2007).

32. Fournier, *Double Nickels on the Dime*, 33.

33. *Village Voice*, November 6, 1984, 81; *MRR*, January–February 1984; *Truly Needy*, #10, 17.

34. *Thrillseeker*, #1, 28.

35. Bob Mould in *Mac Weekly*, March 5, 1982, found in the Husker Du Folder of the Cometbus Collection at Cornell University; lyrics also found in *Noise*, #7, December 1982. See also Michael Azzerad, *Our Band Could Be Your Life* (Boston: Little, Brown, 2001), 166; Andrew Earles, *Husker Du* (Minneapolis: Voyageur, 2010), 65. For more on the Minneapolis scene that Husker Du emerged from, see Cyn Collins, *Complicated Fun* (St. Paul: Minnesota Historical Society, 2017), especially chapters 16 and 17 as well as the book's epilogue.

36. *Ink Disease*, #5, 1984; *Destroy L.A.*, #4.

37. *The Rocket*, January 1985, 26; *Terminal*, #16/17, (1983?), 10; John Bunyan, *Pilgrim's Progress* (New York: Penguin, 1987), 51; *Altered Statements*, #2, 1984.

38. *Altered Statements*, #2, 1984; *Own the Whole World*, Fall 1984; *L.A. Reader*, August 7, 1984, 20. It should be noted here that in 1984 there were also important releases of records by Feederz, Heart Attack, Reagan Youth, and Tupelo Chain Sex, among others.

39. See the zine's issues reproduced in Dave Markey and Jordan Schwartz, *We Got Power* (Brooklyn: Bazillion Points, 2012).

40. *L.A. Reader*, July 20, 1984, Section 2, 2; *MRR*, August 1984.

41. William Gibson, *Neuromancer* (New York: Ace, 1984), 83, 45–6.

42. George Slusser and Tom Shippey, eds, *Fiction 2000* (Athens: University of Georgia Press, 1992), 237, 133, 172.

43. Tom Maddox, "Cobra, She Said," *Fantasy Review*, April 1986, 47.

44. Gibson, *Neuromancer*, 43, 15, 203, 101; Slusser and Shippey, eds, *Fiction 2000*, 246. Duly noted, there were two other novels related to punk, both written much earlier than their 1984 release (and not treated here): K. W. Jeter's *Dr. Adder* (written by the early 1970s) and Kathy Acker's *Blood and Guts in High School* (written in 1979). That both books were published in 1984 might suggest a window opening up for punk-infused literature.

45. *Cerebral Discourse*, 1984.

46. Alan Brinkley, *Liberalism and Its Discontents* (Cambridge: Harvard University Press, 1998), 262–263; *Washington Post*, May 16, 1984, online: https://www. washingtonpost.com/archive/lifestyle/1984/05/16/quaking-in-san-francisco/ 8104b074-1a01-457c-a399-e0a47e95d1d3/?utm_term=.f3fab6879ca9; Luke Hauser, *Direct Action* (San Francisco: Groundwork, 2003), 555.

47. *Village Voice*, August 7, 1984, 24; *Overthrow*, December 1984–January 1985, 10; *MRR*, August 1984; David Solnit's experience, posted online: http://www. foundsf.org/index.php?title=1984_War_Chest_Tours_II.

48. Hauser, *Direct Action*, 381 (there's also a fine statement regarding Solnit's activism found in the Cometbus Collection); *Protest and Survive*, July 1984; *MRR*, August 1984; Gary Roush, "Democratic Convention Crackdown: I Was There,"

originally in *It's About Times,* and reprinted at founds.org: http://www.foundsf. org/index.php?title=Democratic_Convention_Crackdown_1984; *Absolutely No Corporations,* (1984?).

49. *Squat for Life,* no date; *Bound Together,* #6, July 1984, 2; *Daily Battle,* no date.

50. Mike Davis and Michael Sprinker, eds., *Reshaping the U.S. Left* (New York: Verso, 1988), 81; *MRR,* June 1984; Jeffrey Goldthorpe, "Intoxicated Culture," *Socialist Review* 22 (1992): 50; *Nuclear Times,* July 1984, 15; *Direct Action,* September 1984; on Patrick Diehl's affiliation, see Barbara Epstein, *Political Protest and Cultural Revolution* (Berkeley: University of California, 1991), 141. For more on how the nuclear freeze movement was broadly conflicted, see Kyle Harvey, *American Anti-Nuclear Activism, 1975–1990* (New York: Palgrave, 2014), 36–39.

51. *Entertainment Venue,* 1984, 26.

52. *Village Voice,* August 7, 1984, 24; *MRR,* August 1984.

53. *Overthrow,* December 1984–January 1985, 10; *MRR,* October 1984.

54. For a nice treatment of the Butthole Surfers' experience with *P.E.A.C.E.,* see James Burns, *Let's Go to Hell* (No place: Cheap Drugs, 2015), 108–110.

55. *Bullshit Detector,* #2, 1983, reprinted in Marie Kanger-Born, *Confessions of a Chicago Punk Bystander* (Morrisville: Lulu, 2010), 131; the *P.E.A.C.E.* booklet can be found in the Cometbus Collection, Cornell University; Dave Dictor, *MDC* (San Francisco: Manic, 2016), 31.

56. *MRR,* March 1985.

57. *Leading Edge,* #5; *MRR,* December 1984.

58. Bunyan, *The Pilgrim's Progress,* 137.

59. *Op,* July–August, 1984, 4; Robin James, ed., *Cassette Mythos* (Brooklyn: Autonomedia, 1992), 131; *Negative Print,* #16, 1984.

60. *Op,* Spring 1980; *The Rocket,* August 1984, 28.

61. *Village Voice,* October 23, 1984, 44.

62. Mark Twain, *A Pen Warmed Up in Hell* (New York: Harper, 1972), 45.

63. Hua Hsu, "The Branding of the Olympics," *Grantland,* February 11, 2014, online: http://grantland.com/features/1984-olympics-los-angeles-branding/; Kenneth Reich, *Making It Happen* (Santa Barbara: Capra, 1986), 61; Christopher Hill, *Olympic Politics* (Manchester: Manchester University Press, 1992); Philip D'Agati, *The Cold War and the 1984 Olympic Games* (New York: Palgrave, 2013).

64. Michael Rogin, *Ronald Reagan, The Movie* (Berkeley: University of California Press, 1987), 15; Reich, *Making It Happen,* 139, 87; Hill, *Olympic Politics.*

65. *MRR,* September 1984; *RAD,* #23, 1984; Hill, *Olympic Politics.*

66. *Mutual Oblivion,* #6.

67. Arthur Miller, *Death of a Salesman* (New York: Penguin, 1985), 138.

68. *L.A. Times,* September 4, 1984, A5. On Orange County, see Lisa McGirr, *Suburban Warriors* (Princeton: Princeton University Press, 2002).

69. *L.A. Times,* September 4, 1984, A1 and A5, and September 16, 1984, A14; *MRR,* November 1984; Wally George, *Wally George: The Father of Combat TV* (Santa Ana: Seven Look Press, 1999), 111.

70. *New York Times,* September 19, 1984, online: https://www.nytimes.com/1984/ 09/19/us/college-students-heckle-mondale.html; quotes here from Mark Weinberg, *Movie Nights with the Reagans* (New York: Simon & Schuster, 2018),

131. *BravEar*'s 1984 issue also documented the Fritzbusters (Michael Miro sent me a digitized copy of this issue).

71. *The Rocket*, October 1984, 31; see also Kyle Smith, "How Reagan Used the Movies to His Advantage," *National Review*, March 27, 2018, online:: https://www.nationalreview.com/2018/03/how-reagan-used-the-movies-to-his-advantage/.

72. George Will, "Bruce Springsteen's USA," *Washington Post*, September 13, 1984, online: https://www.washingtonpost.com/archive/politics/1984/09/13/bruce-springsteens-usa/f6502baa-a8eb-48ad-ba85-7fa848d8833e/?utm_term=.0724a466a0c1; on CDs, see Greg Milner, *Perfecting Sound Forever* (New York: Faber and Faber, 2009), 190.

73. Marc Dolan, "How Ronald Reagan Changed Bruce Springsteen's Politics," *Politico*, June 4, 2014, online: https://www.politico.com/magazine/story/2014/06/bruce-springsteen-ronald-reagan-107448_full.html; Slansky, *The Clothes Have No Emperor*, 108.

74. Henry Rollins, *Get in the Van* (Los Angeles: 2.13.61, 1995), 146; Pettibon, *New Wavy Gravy 2*, 1985, Yale University.

75. "The Ecstasy of Communication," in Hal Foster, ed., *The Anti-Aesthetic* (Port Townsend: Bay Press, 1983), 130–131.

76. R. Serge Denisoff and William Romanowski, *Risky Business*, 399; *Own the Whole World*, Fall 1984; *The Rocket*, April 1985, 12; see also Annalee Newitz, "Madonna's Revenge," *Bad Subjects*, #9, November 1993, online: https://bad.eserver.org/issues/1993/09/newitz; and for Madonna's rise to celebrity, see J. Randy Taraborrelli, *Madonna: An Intimate Biography* (New York: Simon & Schuster, 2001).

77. *Jersey Beat*, October–November 1985; *Own the Whole World*, Fall 1984.

78. *End Times*, #3, 1984.

79. Thomas Pynchon, *Gravity's Rainbow* (1973; reprint New York: Penguin, 1995), 17.

80. Slansky, *The Clothes Have No Emperor*, 114.

81. John Patrick Diggins, *Ronald Reagan* (New York: Norton, 2007), 317–318.

82. Lou Cannon, *President Reagan* (New York: Public Affairs, 2000), 486.

83. The cartoon is reprinted in *The Best Comics of the Decade*, editors of the *Comics Journal* (Seattle: Fantagraphic Books, 1990), 111.

84. *New York Times*, October 11, 1984, online: https://www.nytimes.com/1984/10/11/us/brown-students-vote-on-atom-war-suicide-pills.html; see also Paull E. Hejinian, "Brown University Rejects Students' Suicide Pill Vote," *The Crimson*, October 24, 1984, online: https://www.thecrimson.com/article/1984/10/24/brown-university-rejects-students-suicide-pill; *MRR*, March 1985.

85. This is reported at Found SF Digital Archive: http://www.foundsf.org/index.php?title=The_Hotel_Owners_Laundry_Company_(HOLC)_Squat:_1984.

86. *Village Voice*, August 7, 1984, 41.

87. Peter Belsito, *Notes from the Pop Underground* (Berkeley: Last Gasp, 1985), 60; *L.A. Reader*, November 9, 1984, 14–15; Eva Buchmuller and Anna Koos, *Squat Theatre* (Arcana Press, 1996), 221; *Vacation*, Fall/Winter 1981, 13–15.

88. Juan Saurez, *Jim Jarmusch* (Urbana: University of Illinois Press, 2007), 4.

89. Belsito, *Notes from the Pop Underground*, 64; *L.A. Reader*, November 2, 1984, Section 2, 18; *L.A. Reader*, November 9, 1984, 15.

90. On the movie's financial success, see Saurez, *Jim Jarmusch*, 6. In many ways the success of this film was remarkably similar to the success in 1969 of *Easy Rider*, a movie that brought the images of the 1960s counterculture to a wide audience, and that cost very little to make while grossing a huge return.

91. *L.A. Weekly*, July 16–22, 1982, 25.

92. *MRR*, April–May, 1984.

93. *Slash*, #10, 1978, 14; *Rolling Stone*, October 20, 1977, 72; on Debord's politics, see Andrew Hussey, *Game of War* (London: Jonathan Cape, 2001), 114–115.

94. *Slash*, #8, February 1978, 14; *Slash*, May 1978, 3; *Slash*, June 1979, 10.

95. Jim DeRogatis, *Let It Blurt* (New York: Broadway, 2000), 214; Greil Marcus, *In the Fascist Bathroom* (London: Penguin, 1993), 183.

96. "Wreck This World," in Hussey, *The Game of War*, 112; *Village Voice* (Literary Supplement), May 1982, 14, 13.

97. Bill Brown, *Not Bored! Anthology* (Cincinnati: Colossal Books, 2011), 126 (reprinted from *MRR* November 1984). This was also recognized in an important 1982 essay by Frederic Jameson: See Jameson, "Postmodernism and Consumer Society," in Hal Foster, ed., *The Anti-Aesthetic* (Port Townsend: Bay Press, 1983).

98. *MRR*, October–November 1983.

99. *MRR*, October–November 1983; *MRR*, November 1984.

100. *Neuromancer*, 156.

101. *MRR*, August 1984.

102. *MRR*, August 1984; *RAD*, #25, 1984.

103. Cannon, *President Reagan*, 434; *Newsweek*, December 31, 1984, 31.

104. *Newsweek*, December 31, 1984, 30; *The Attack*, December 1984, 5.

105. *RAD*, #26 (1984–1985?).

106. The Fall, "In the Park," from the *Grotesque* Album (1980).

107. *MRR*, December 1984.

108. *Who Owns the World*, #9/10, Fall 1984; *The Rocket*, August 1985, 27; *Ink Disease*, #8.

109. *Radical America* 18 (1984): 615; *Flipside*, #48; Harley Flanagan, *Hard-Core* (Port Townsend: Feral House, 2016), 252.

110. Rollins, *Get in the Van*, 97, 98, 119; *Zone V*, (1983?).

111. *This Magazine*; *MRR*, September 1984; *MRR*, March 1984; *The Noise*, March 1984, 1.

112. Statement about Barile found in cut-out article in DC Public Library's Mark Andersen Papers, SS Decontrol Folder; *The Noise*, October 1984, 13; *MRR*, December 1984; *Truly Needy*, #9, 1985, 57; *Ink Disease*, #8 (1984?); *The Noise*, November 1984, 3.

113. Malin quoted in Tony Rettman, *NYHC* (Brooklyn: Bazillion Points, 2014), 230; *MRR*, March 1984; *MRR*, February 1985.

114. Stephen Tow, *The Strangest Tribe* (Seattle: Sasquatch, 2011), 94; Krist Novaselic, *Of Grunge and Government* (New York: RDV, 2004), 14–15; Greg Prato, *Grunge Is Dead* (Toronto: ECW, 2009), 101.

115. T. J. Leyden, *Skinhead Confessions* (Springville: Sweetwater, 2008), 26 (Leyden also states that he got his politics out of punk in part: "I particularly enjoyed the really hard-core metallic bands" [20]); *Zat*, no date, 34; on Marc Dagger, see the

long debate between him and Tim Yo in *MRR*, October 1984; on Clark Martell, see Christian Picciolini, *White American Youth* (New York: Hachette, 2017). It's unclear exactly when Clark Martell became active in forming Chicago skinhead culture, but this linked story from the *Chicago Reader* suggests 1984, which seems right. See Bill Wyman, "Skinheads," *Chicago Reader*, March 23, 1989, online: https://www.chicagoreader.com/chicago/skinheads/Content?oid=873583; on Nazi Jeff, see his own statement in *MRR*, August 1984; on Lefty, see Mark Andersen and Mark Jenkins, *Dance of Days* (New York: Akashic, 2003), 159–161. For an insightful study of skinheads, see Tiffini Travis and Perry Hardy, *Skinheads* (Santa Barbara: Greenwood, 2012), especially xxx.

116. *MRR*, December 1984; Solnit quoted in Goldthorpe, "Intoxicated Culture," 54.

117. Louis Auchincloss, *Diary of a Yuppie* (Boston: Houghton Mifflin, 1986), 94.

118. *Newsweek*, December 31, 1984, 19; (see also David Sirota, *Back to Our Future* [New York: Ballantine, 2011], 14); Jay McInerney, *Bright Lights, Big City* (New York: Vintage, 1984), 5, 4; William Buckley, *Overdrive* (Boston: Little, Brown, 1983), xxxv, 2, 158 (see also John Judis, *William F. Buckley, Jr.* [New York: Simon & Schuster, 1988], 431–432); Marissa Piesman, *The Yuppie Handbook* (New York: Pocket, 1984); Gil Troy, *Morning in America* (Princeton: Princeton University Press, 2005), 132; Daniel Bell's issue of "disjunction" is developed in *The Cultural Contradictions of Capitalism* (New York: Basic, 1976); see also *L.A. Reader*, November 30, 1984, 14.

119. *Newsweek*, December 31, 1984, 26, 24, 27; Neil Smith, "New City, New Frontier," in Michael Sorkin, ed., *Variations on a Theme Park* (New York: FSG, 1992), 81; *Art in America*, Summer 1984, 162–163.

120. *Newsweek*, December 31, 1984, 30, 31; Hendrik Hertzberg, "The Short Happy Life of the American Yuppie," in Nicolaus Mills, ed., *Culture in an Age of Money* (Chicago: I. R. Dee, 1990), 68.

CHAPTER 4

1. *Artforum*, April 1985, 77.

2. *New York Times*, January 21, 1985, online: https://www.nytimes.com/1985/01/21/us/reagan-sworn-for-2d-term-inaugural-parade-dropped-as-bitter-cold-hits-capital.html.

3. *Washington Post*, January 22, 1985, online: https://www.washingtonpost.com/archive/politics/1985/01/22/inaugural-parade-route-was-a-surreal-scene/7b799dd6-ba94-45a8-88d1-68187ae08b4e/?utm_term=.07eacd29e6b4.

4. Reagan's second inaugural address at: https://www.bartleby.com/124/pres62.html.

5. *New York Times*, January 20, 1985, online: https://www.nytimes.com/1985/01/20/us/for-visitors-fun-politics-and-protests.html.

6. These two paragraphs are based on the author's memory and a poster for the Inaugural Ball in his possession (it clearly shows that the roster of bands had changed, with the Poison Girls name on a sticker put over an original poster that listed the Canadian band DOA [who had once been considered headliners]).

7. *The Rocket*, April 1985, 12. The video tries to undercut the main story by having a wealthy director going to Madonna's dressing room, where he overhears her saying that she doesn't care for expensive gifts. He then pretends to be poorer than he is in order to win her over. Which creates a sort of "postmodern," shape-shifting feel to this anthemic song.

8. Faith No More, "We Care a Lot" (1985).

9. From the album, *Tacky Souvenirs of Prerevolutionary America* (1986), accessed at: https://www.youtube.com/results?search_query=culturcide+we+are+the+world.

10. David Breskin, *We Are the World* (New York: Perigee, 1985), no pagination.

11. Breskin, *We Are the World*; *L.A. Times*, February 13, 1985, online: http://articles.latimes.com/1985-02-13/entertainment/ca-4769_1_benefit-project; *New York Times*, May 4, 1985, online: https://www.nytimes.com/1985/05/04/movies/tv-how-the-hit-we-are-the-world-was-made.html.

12. Marcus in Angela McRobbie, ed., *Zoot Suits and Second Hand Dresses* (Boston: Unwin Hyman, 1988), 278. See also Lucy Robinson, "Putting the Charity into Charity Singles: Charity Singles in Britain 1984–1995," *Contemporary British History* 26 (2012): 420. Robinson states that charity songs "created and divided communities of the haves and the have-nots, framed around the 'common sense' logic of Thatcher's Authoritarian Populism."

13. Breskin, *We Are the World*.

14. Love quoted in Kevin Smokler, *Brat Pack America* (Los Angeles: Rare Bird, 2016), 69.

15. R. Serge Denisoff and William Romanowski, *Risky Business* (New Brunswick: Transaction, 2016), 489.

16. Evidence of the Minutemen doing well on college radio can be seen in the "Alternative Chart" in *Rockpool*, December 10, 1984.

17. Bruce Caen (really Bruce Kalberg), *Sub-Hollywood* (Los Angeles: Yes, 2005), 29.

18. *No Mag*, 1985. I originally accessed a run of this publication at CWRU, Rock Hall of Fame collections. As of this writing, digital copies can be found at: https://www.circulationzero.com/.

19. *People*, March 28, 1983, 96–97; see also *L.A. Weekly*, February 18–24, 1983, 4.

20. *People*, March 25, 1985, online: https://people.com/archive/a-finder-of-lost-looking-souls-turns-hollywood-street-punks-into-human-scenery-for-videos-and-films-vol-23-no-12/. It's interesting to note that the band Musical Suicide from Cincinnati, Ohio, talked in the summer of 1984 about "starting a rent a punk service—like pay us $25 to be rude and obnoxious. . . . Like, puke on their carpet, drink their beer and drink it up off the carpet—after we spill it." *Altered Statements*, #3, 1984. It should also be pointed out that the one movie that depicted "punk" during the summer of 1985 was *Return of the Living Dead*. It was a film about zombies who liked to eat brains, and there was absolutely no sense as to why "punk" looking kids were used in the filming, other than show.

21. *Short Teats, Bloody Milk*, March 1985, Yale University.

22. Author's recollection.

23. "A Call to Act," reprinted in *MRR*, March 1985.

24. *Going Under*, February–March 1986; Jello Biafra conveying Stephan's point in *MRR*, August 1985.
25. *Going Under*, January 1986. For more on the history of regulating speech in shopping malls, see Lizabeth Cohen, *A Consumers' Republic* (New York: Knopf, 2003), 275.
26. *RAD*, #23, 1984; *RAD*, #25, 1984.
27. See Michael Stewart Foley, *Front Porch Politics* (New York: Hill and Wang, 2013), 144–145.
28. *The Face*, May 1985, 33, 34.
29. See my *What the Heck Are You Up To Mr. President?* (New York: Bloomsbury, 2009), 199.
30. *People*, March 10, 1986, online: https://people.com/archive/the-arbiters-of-hip-vol-25-no-10/; Ann Fensterstock, *Art on the Block* (New York: Palgrave, 2013), 91.
31. Eric Fretz, *Jean-Michel Basquiat* (Santa Barbara: Greenwood, 2010), xiii, 5, 46, 44; Marvin Taylor, ed., *The Downtown Book* (Princeton: Princeton University Press, 2006), 35; Michael Musto, *Downtown* (New York: Vintage, 1986), 107; *Washington Post*, May 19, 1985, online: https://www.washingtonpost.com/archive/lifestyle/1985/05/19/every-night-fever/f889b9f2-3b32-42d9-906d-611173264301/?utm_term=.dc56c744b47f.
32. *October*, Winter, 1984, 99; *East Village Eye*, October 1985, 23.
33. *Vanity Fair*, August 1985, 71.
34. Michael Diamond and Adam Horowitz, *Beastie Boys Book* (New York: Spiegel and Grau, 2019), 152
35. Emily Listfield, *It Was Gonna Be Like Paris* (New York: Dial, 1984), 97.
36. David Blum, "Hollywood's Brat Pack," *New York*, June 10, 1985, online: http://nymag.com/movies/features/49902/; Jay McInerney, *Bright Lights, Big City* (New York: Vintage, 1984), 65.
37. Bret Easton Ellis, *Less Than Zero* (New York: Penguin, 1985), 93, 189.
38. Ellis, *Less Than Zero*, 9, 205; Elizabeth Young and Graham Caveney, *Shopping in Space* (New York: Serpent's Tail, 1992), 218; *East Village Eye*, September 1986, 17–19, 50.
39. Christopher Lasch, *The True and Only Heaven* (New York: Norton, 1991), 83.
40. Mark Andersen and Mark Jenkins, *Dance of Days* (New York: Akashic, 2009), 172.
41. *The Rocket*, June 1985, 36; Colleen O'Connor, "Good Punks, Tough Life," *Washington Weekly*, June 7, 1985, 9.
42. *WDC Period*, #12; see also the documentary: *More Than a Witness* (2014).
43. Gil Troy, *Morning in America* (Princeton: Princeton University Press, 2005), 192.
44. Sean Wilentz, *The Age of Reagan* (New York: HarperCollins, 2008), 214; Peggy Noonan, *What I Saw at the Revolution* (New York: Random House, 1990), 236; John Patrick Diggins, *Ronald Reagan* (New York: Norton, 2007), 297.
45. Ronald Reagan, *The Reagan Diaries*, ed. Douglas Brinkley (New York: HarperCollins, 2007), 308, 374–375; *MRR*, July 1985. I rely on Malcolm Byrne, *Iran-Contra* (Lawrence: University of Kansas Press, 2014).
46. Byron Coley, *Chuck Norris* (New York: St. Martin's 1986), 101, 119, 120, 121; Coley admitted in an interview that he did this book solely for money and had no love for Norris.

47. Bill Brown in his piece about the Situationist International for *MRR*. See the reprint in *NOT BORED! Anthology 1983-2010* (Cincinnati: Colossal, 2011), 125.

48. Robert Draper, *Rolling Stone Magazine* (New York: Doubleday, 1990), 125.

49. Joe Hagan, *Sticky Fingers* (New York: Knopf, 2017), 450, 425, 428; Draper, *Rolling Stone Magazine*, 344.

50. Hagan, *Sticky Fingers*, 367.

51. *Rolling Stone*, July 18–August 1, 1985, 28 (emphasis added by author).

52. *Spin*, July 1985, online: https://books.google.com/books?id=ImJFcBcCvUoC&r view=1&lr=; see also here Larry McCaffery, *Storming the Reality Studio* (Durham: Duke University Press, 1991), 341.

53. *Washington Post*, December 30, 1984, online: https://www.washingtonpost.com/ archive/entertainment/books/1984/12/30/science-fiction-in-the-eighties/ 526c3a06-f123-4668-9127-33e33f57e313/?utm_term=.aad39a1ca733.

54. Rudy Rucker, *Nested Scrolls* (New York: TOR, 2011), 207; Takayuki Tatsumi, "An Interview with Bruce Sterling," *Science Fiction Eye*, Vol. 1, No. 1, 1987, 30 (the interview was conducted on March 13, 1986). Much of what happened at this conference can be found at the website of Scott Edelman. See: http://www. scottedelman.com/2012/06/21/please-help-answer-a-question-about-the-1985-nasfic/; see also *Locus*, November 1985, 1, 29–35, 50.

55. Takayuki Tatsumi, "An Interview with Bruce Sterling," 40, 27; Bruce Sterling, *Schismatrix* (New York: Arbor, 1985), 273; *Cheap Truth*, #13, 1985, online: http:// fanac.org/fanzines/Cheap_Truth/Cheap_Truth13-02.html? To get a sense of the conservative nature of Pournelle, see the book he cowrote with Larry Niven, *Footfall* (1985). The book is full of pro-Reagan statements, for instance, "things looked better after Reagan was elected." The book describes systems where laser beams are used and space is colonized as the country is invaded by aliens with more powerful technology (here again, a sort of Reagan-like warning for preparedness). Larry Niven and Jerry Pournelle, *Footfall* (New York: Del Rey, 1985), 47.

56. Tatsumi, "An Interview with Bruce Sterling," 31; Sterling in *Mirrorshades* (New York: Arbor, 1986), ix, xii.

57. George Orwell, *A Collection of Essays* (New York: HBJ, 1981), 176.

58. The departure is announced by Tim Yo in *MRR*, November 1985.

59. All quotes come from the interview with Jeff Bale in *MRR*, October 1987.

60. *Leading Edge*, #5, 1985.

61. *Chicago Tribune*, October 3, 1985, online: http://articles.chicagotribune.com/1985-10-03/features/8503070308_1_nancy-reagan-drug-abuse-fund-antidrug-video.

62. *Washington Post*, October 9, 1985, online: https://www.washingtonpost.com/ar-chive/lifestyle/1985/10/09/white-house-starscape/2c60e9f1-5695-4384-ac5c-68663137e219/?utm_term=.3798bc78fae9.

63. Mark Weinberg, *Movie Nights with the Reagans* (New York: Simon & Schuster, 2018), 148–151.

64. Quoted in Weinberg, *Movie Nights with the Reagans*, 164.

65. James Agee and Walker Evans, *Let Us Now Praise Famous Men* (1939; New York: Ballantine, 1960), 5.

66. Jonathon Epstein, ed., *Adolescents and Their Music* (New York: Garland, 1994), 79; *Non LP B Side*, #14, May/June 1982.

67. *MRR*, March 1986.

68. On Tolkin, see *Rockpool*, November 28, 1983; on his use of "alternative," see Pat Blashill, *Noise from the Underground* (New York: Simon & Schuster, 1996), 51; *Big Takeover*, December 1985, 3; *Village Voice*, October 23, 1984, 44; *Rockpool*, January 10, 1983, 2. See also here *East Village Eye*, August 1982, 18.

69. Tony Rettman, *NYHC* (Brooklyn: Bazillion Points, 2014), 83; *Big Takeover*, December 1982, 9; *Big Takeover*, Vol. 5, No. 1 (1984?), 2; *Big Takeover*, August 1984, 3; *Big Takeover*, February 1985, 4; for Rabid's biography, I also consulted Jacob Kramer's thesis "Punk in New York, Jazz, and the Rural Radical Right," done at Columbia University and now in the John Holmstrom Papers, Box 54.

70. *Big Takeover*, July 1986, 2; *Big Takeover*, December 1987; *Big Takeover*, July 1986, 2.

71. *MRR*, February 1985; *MRR*, September 1984; *Matter*, September 1983.

72. *L.A. Weekly*, July 2–8, 1982, 10; *MRR*, July 1985.

73. Simon Frith and Howard Horne, *Art into Pop* (New York: Methuen, 1987), 153. The album *Frankenchrist* got the DKs into a good amount of trouble, landing Biafra in court for obscenity and for using a picture of Shriners on its cover. These cases nearly destroyed Alternative Tentacles.

74. Dylan Thomas, "A Refusal to Mourn the Death, by Fire, of a Child in London," online:https://www.poets.org/poetsorg/poem/refusal-mourn-death-fire-child-london.

75. Henry Rollins, *Get in the Van* (Los Angeles: 2.13.61, 1995), 212–213.

76. *Truly Needy*, #10, 1985.

77. *Spin*, May 1985, 33.

78. Andrew Earles, *Husker Du* (Minneapolis: Voyageur, 2010), 163.

79. *Bang*, #10, 1985, 20; *Truly Needy*, #10, 1985: 46.

80. *Uncle Fester*, 1985; *MMR*, November 1985; *Popular Reality*, February–March 1986, 11.

81. Earles, *Husker Du*, 176; *Op*, N Issue, (1982?).

82. Earles, *Husker Du*, 152; *The Rocket*, December 1985, 22; *Interview*, April 1986, 131; Bob Mould and Michael Azzerad, *See a Little Light* (New York: Little, Brown, 2011), 127–129.

83. *Spin*, December 1985, 22–25: https://books.google.com/books?id=CBAN_GTP9B4C&rview=1&lr=Posted at Google Books.

84. *Spin*, December 1985, 66.

EPILOGUE

1. *Forced Exposure*, #16, 24.

2. Pavitt quoted in Cyn Collins, *Complicated Fun* (St. Paul: Minnesota Historical Society Press, 2017), 342.

3. *Rolling Stone*, April 16, 1992, 97; Kevin Prested, *Punk USA* (Portland: Microcosm, 2014), 34; and Larry Livermore, *Spy Rock Memories* (New Brunswick: Don Giovanni Records, 2013), especially 198–206; Gina Arnold, *Kiss This* (New York: St. Martin's, 1997), x–xiii.

4. Neal Gabler, *Life: The Movie* (New York; Vintage, 2000), 110.

5. *Third Rail*, #23.
6. See Daniel Makagon, *Underground: The Subterranean Culture of DIY Punk Shows* (Portland: Microcosm, 2015).
7. On this point, see Anita Elberse, *Blockbusters: Why Big Hits and Big Risks Are the Future of the Entertainment Business* (New York: Henry Holt, 2013).

INDEX

Note: *For the benefit of digital users, indexed terms that span two pages (e.g., 52–53) may, on occasion, appear on only one of those pages.*

Sixteen Candles (film), 181–82

Skank (zine), 90–91

Skate Death (band), 174–75

Skelly, Jack, 66

Skid (zine), 95–96, 172

skinheads, 236–37, 258, 259–60, 279, 359–60n115

    start invading scenes around 1984, 236–37

    Tim Yo confronts, 237

    vigilante actions of, 237

slam dancing, ix, 11–14, 36, 63–64, 80–81, 96–97, 130–31, 258, 276–77

Slash (small magazine), 49, 50–51, 113–14, 117–18, 225–26, 247–48

Slash Records, 49

Slickee Boys (band), 35–36

Sluggo (band), 83–84

Sluggo (zine), 75–76

Smith, Patti, 1, 2, 3–4, 28, 29, 41, 67, 68, 107

Smith, Winston, 16, 73, 97–98, 99, 142–43, 160, 176, 177, 178, 287

Smithereens (film), 123

SOA (State of Alert) (band), 33, 91–92

Social Darwinism, 244–45

Social Distortion (band), 40–41, 78–79, 104–6

socialism, 112–13

    Bob Soltz (and others) seek out a libertarian version of, 166–67

    Jeff Bale develops idea of democratic and libertarian version of, 113–14

    Mike Watt has growing interest in, 20–21

Society Dog (band), 110

Software (novel), 119–20

Solnit, David, 203, 204–5, 206, 237

Soltz, Barry, 75, 89–90

Soltz, Bob, 166–67

Sonic Youth (band), 34, 157, 222–23, 276–77

Soviet Union (USSR), xiii, 8–134, 152, 171, 214–15

    decides to boycott the Olympics, 211

    makes statement about *1984* (novel), 176–77

    Reagan accuses of being an "evil empire," 135

    Reagan ties nuclear freeze movement to, 100–1, 135

Space Invaders, 119, 134, 288

Spandau Ballet, 52–53

Spheeris, Penelope, 48–51, 55–56, 147, 148, 266, 289

Spielberg, Steven, 101–3

Spike in Vain (band), 84

Spin (magazine), 266, 269–70, 280–81, 283–84, 286, 290

spray painting, x–xi, xii, 142, 143, 206, 214–15, 253

    See also graffiti

Springsteen, Bruce, xv–xvi, 215–16, 237, 239, 244, 254, 266

Sprouse, Martin, 270

Squatter, Jim, 140

squatting, 142–43, 167–68

    as act of preservation, 140

    depicted in *Suburbia*, 147

    how to do, 139

    MDC witnesses high levels of when in Europe, 139

SST, 78, 79–80, 94–95, 104–5, 194, 246, 265, 279–80, 282–83

St. Elmo's Fire, 256

Stallone, Sylvester, xv–xvi, 287–88

    comparison to Oliver North, 261

    helps write and stars in *Rambo: First Blood Part II*, 260–61

    as replacement for now-deceased John Wayne, 273

    tries to get Reagan to help publicize *Rocky IV*, 274

Star Wars (film), 102, 135, 172–73

Sten, Mark, 27

    embraces anarcho-syndicalism. 24–25

    organizes Portland's punk scene. 24

Sterling, Bruce, 267, 287

    compares William Gibson's writing to punk music, 120

    hosts panel on punk sci-fi, 118, 266–67

    publishes *Cheap Truth* (zine), 120–21

    tension between serious sci-fi serving as critique and desire for fame, 267–68

Stern, Shawn, 109–10, 115, 205, 208–9, 249–50

    faces challenges of DIY, 104–5